STUDIA POHL

DISSERTATIONES SCIENTIFICAE DE REBUS ORIENTIS ANTIQUI

14

E PONTIFICIO INSTITUTO BIBLICO

ROMAE

STEPHEN D. RICKS

LEXICON OF INSCRIPTIONAL QATABANIAN

EDITRICE PONTIFICIO ISTITUTO BIBLICO
ROMA 1989

The Pontifical Biblical Institute dedicates this series to the memory of P. Alfred Pohl, founder of its Faculty of Ancient Near Eastern Studies. *Studia Pohl* reproduces in offset studies on Ancient Near Eastern history and philology, and is intended particularly to benefit younger scholars who wish to present the results of their doctoral studies to a wider public.

The publication of this volume was made possible in part by a generous subvention from the College of Humanities, Brigham Young University, Provo, Utah.

ISBN 88-7653-570-5

Editrice Pontificia Università Gregoriana
Editrice Pontificio Istituto Biblico
Piazza della Pilotta 35 - 00187 Roma, Italia

TABLE OF CONTENTS

INTRODUCTION

During the past hundred years European and American explorers and scholars have recovered and researched a considerable body of epigraphic remains of the Semitic dialects used along the southern rim of the Arabian peninsula. The inscriptions in the Epigraphic South Arabian dialects of Sabaean, Minaean, Qatabanian, and Ḥaḍrami that have been edited and published now number in the thousands. The subjects of these epigraphic remains include simple graffiti, votive offerings, building inscriptions, lengthy historical annals, and regulations concerning the public order. Still, the Epigraphic South Arabian dialects remain among the least known of the Semitic languages. The study of these dialects has been rendered more difficult by the persistent scarcity of basic learning tools such as dictionaries, although this situation is being redressed, especially during the past two decades.

Study of the vocabulary of Old South Arabian by Western scholars extends back at least as far as the middle of the last century, when the Abbé Bargès published an article in the *Journal Asiatique* on "Termes himyariques rapportés par un écrivain arabe" (1849, 327-47). The glossary at the end of Fritz Hommel's *Südarabische Chrestomathie* (which, however, contains no Qatabanian inscriptions) is the first dictionary of Epigraphic South Arabian of which I am aware (1893, 121-36). Some four decades later, Conti Rossini published his *Chrestomathia arabica meridionalis epigraphica* , which included several Qatabanian selections and a long glossary (1931, 99-261). Walter Müller's Tübingen dissertation, *Die Wurzeln mediae und tertiae y/w im Altsüdarabischen—eine etymologische und lexikographische Studie* (1962), is arranged in alphabetical order but, as the title implies, only includes words with middle or final weak consonants. In the past decade further progress has been made in Epigraphic South Arabian with the publication of Alessandra Avanzini's *Glossaire des inscriptions de l'Arabie du Sud 1950-1973* (1977) and Joan Biella's *A Dictionary of Old South Arabic, Sabaean Dialect* (1982), and the appearance of the *Sabaic Dictionary/ Dictionnaire Sabéen* (1982) by A. F. L. Beeston, M. A. Ghul, W. W. Müller, and J. Ryckmans. To date no lexicons have been published that are devoted solely to the Qatabanian, Minaean, or Ḥaḍrami dialects.

A great advance was made in Epigraphic South Arabian onomastic studies with the publication of Monseigneur Gonzague Ryckmans' three-volume *Les noms propres sud-sémitiques* (1934-35). G. Lankester Harding's *An Index and Concordance of Pre-Islamic Arabian Names and Inscriptions* expanded the study to include other pre-Islamic dialects of the Arabian peninsula (1971). The latter part of Harding's large volume contains a concordance that provides cross-referencing to the various inscriptions. Harding's system of cross-referencing the inscriptions eliminates to a large extent the confusion caused because many inscriptions are identified according to several different systems of citation. Harding's work also contains a good representative bibliography of the Epigraphic South Arabian dialects. In 1977 the Academie des Inscriptions et Belles Lettres published a systematic bibliography of the Epigraphic South Arabian dialects as volume three of *Corpus des inscriptions et antiquités sud-arabes.* This admirable and very full bibliography, which contains references not only to the inscriptions themselves but also to the history and religions of South Arabia, updates and overshadows all previous efforts.

The first major effort at a collection of the Epigraphic South Arabian inscriptions, many of which had previously been edited in rather inaccessible publications, was the *Corpus Inscriptionum Himyariticarum.* This collection comprises Part Four of the *Corpus Inscriptionum Semiticarum.* Most of the nearly one thousand inscriptions treated there are Sabaean. The most important collection of Epigraphic South Arabian inscriptions, which also includes a substantial number of Qatabanian inscriptions, is the *Répertoire d'épigraphie sémitique* (volumes five through seven), edited by G. Ryckmans from 1929 to 1950. Until his death in 1969, Msgr. Ryckmans also continued to edit and publish inscriptions in his long-running series in *Le Muséon*, including many that are of Qatabanian provenance. Albert Jamme has also edited numerous Qatabanian inscriptions from various museum collections and from his own epigraphic researches. Besides the longer series of Ryckmans and Jamme there are several additional sources of Qatabanian inscriptions which have been published. The Foundation for the Study of Man organized an archaeological expedition to Qatabanian sites where a number of inscriptions were unearthed. Also of value is the collection made by Major M. D. Van Lessen of photographs and hand copies of inscriptions, which have subsequently been edited by, among others, A. F. L. Beeston, Mahmud Ali Ghul, Maria Höfner, Walter Müller, and Albert Jamme. Other individual Qatabanian inscriptions of varied provenance have been edited by Beeston, Ghul, Höfner, A. E. Honeyman, N. Rhodokanakis, and J. Walker. My debt to the patient, often brilliant, efforts of all of these individuals in the preparation of this lexicon is enormous and is evident on each page.

This lexicon of inscriptional Qatabanian is intended to be a contribution to Epigraphic South Arabian, as well as to general Semitic, lexicography. In order to make this lexicon more accessible to nonspecialists, I have made use, among other other means, of transliterations and morphemic renditions. I have made an effort to include as many relevant lexical items from the published corpus of Qatabanian inscriptions as possible, although I have not attempted to include all the occurrences of each form of every word. Still, because of the diffusion of these inscriptions through very disparate publications, some have doubtless been overlooked inadvertently. The definitions of many of the words, particularly the numerous technical terms found in the Qatabanian inscriptions, remain provisional pending further study. Further, certain words in Qatabanian have been analyzed both as proper nouns (not otherwise listed separately in this lexicon) as well as other parts of speech, so an additional tentativeness exists in some of the entries. The process of composing this work has given me some sense of the complexities and frustrations confronting the lexicographer.

I wish to thank my teachers, who have aided me in the preparation of this lexicon and guided me in the endlessly fascinating study of the Semitic languages: Ariel A. Bloch, William M. Brinner, and Martin Schwartz (University of California, Berkeley); William Fulco (formerly of the Jesuit School of Theology, Berkeley); Michael Guinan (Franciscan School of Theology, Berkeley); Jonas C. Greenfield and Chaim Rabin (Hebrew University, Jerusalem); and Joan C. Biella (William F. Albright Institute, Jerusalem, and Princeton University Library). I would also like to thank Charles D. Bush (Brigham Young University) who created the font that was used for this lexicon, and Werner Mayer (Pontifical Biblical Institute, Rome) who encouraged and advised me in the completion of the volume. I wish particularly to thank my wife, Shirley, who has spent countless hours in working out with me the details of the format of this lexicon and in other ways making suggestions for its improvement.

FORMAT

The entries in this lexicon will be listed according to root (normally triliteral, occasionally uni-, bi-, or quadriliteral). The order of the alphabet used is that of the Hebrew alphabet (with necessary additions)—with the exception of the sibilant series, which appears following r—and accords, in general, with the canons established in some previous dictionaries and concordances of Epigraphic South Arabian dialects (with minor variations):

ʾ b g d ḏ h w z ḥ ḫ ṭ ẓ y k l m n ʿ
ǵ f ṣ ḍ q r s^1 s^2 s^3 t ṯ

In accordance with one widely accepted procedure in the transliteration of the Epigraphic South Arabian dialects, I have transliterated the sibilant series in Qatabanian in the following manner (although I am persuaded of the correctness of A. F. L. Beeston's analysis—e.g., 1977, 50-57—of the sibilants in Epigraphic South Arabian):

𐩦 = s^1 𐩪 = s^2 𐩯 = s^3

Each entry contains a list of the passages where the word in its various forms occurs. Only a partial listing will be provided for words of frequent occurrence. When only a partial list is given a "+" will follow those passages which are cited. Except in rare instances, where the root is otherwise unattested and the resotration is certain, only forms with uneffaced root consonants will be cited in the lexicon (i.e., words containing restored root consonants will not be given).

In order to provide greater uniformity of citation I have given each inscription a Q (Qatabanian)-number. Appendix D at the end of this lexicon gives relevant cross-references to these Q-numbers. These cross-references include museum or collection numbers, citations of sources where the complete text of the inscription has been edited, as well as other places where it has been studied in part or *in toto*. In the interest of conserving space numerous abbreviations have been used in this appendix and are explained in the "List of Abbreviations" in Appendix C. (The abbreviations used in the body of the lexicon itself are explained in Appendix A, Appendix B, and part A of the Bibliography).

Under their respective roots, verbs precede substantives and adjectives. The forms of the verb appear in the following order: verb (= Qatabanian *fʿl*; this includes the orthographically indistinguishable Grundstamm, Doppelstamm, and Langstamm forms, if such existed in Qatabanian), s^1-prefix (which occasionally occurs as an h-prefix), t-prefix, t-infix, and s^1t-prefix. I have not attempted to indicate singular and plural in the finite forms of the verb. In general, verbal nouns are listed together with other verb forms, without being specifically identified as such. With occasional exceptions, participles indicating personal agents are listed separately from the verb forms under their respective roots as "subst./partcp."

Substantives with simpler forms will appear before those which are more complex (which add, e. g., a prefix *m-* or *t-* to the root morpheme) under their respective roots. Where only singular forms of a substantive occur, I have not indicated the forms as "singular," "dual," or "plural." If dual or plural forms are attested, they are designated as such, as are also singular forms, if they also occur. There is some tentativeness in certain of these designations, since they are sometimes based on contextual (rather than strictly morphological) considerations, and because the orthography does not always make apparent morphological distinctions.

In cases where homophonous roots occur, these roots are listed consecutively, followed by Roman numerals, e.g., BN I, BN II. Etymologies appear in parentheses immediately following the definition of the word. These etymologies are intended to be illustrative rather than exhaustive, and I have not attempted to adduce all relevant cognates.

Under each definition of a word I have given one or more contextual examples with an idiomatic translation. In some instances where the morphology or syntax (or both) of the example cited are particularly complex or unclear I have placed a morphemic rendition (which appears in parentheses) after the idiomatic translation. In these morphemic renditions, in the numerous instances where coordinate verbs are cited, I have treated the second and following verbs as verbal nouns, since, as Beeston (1984, 22) notes: "in any series of two or more closely coordinated verbs, it is normal for only the first to be a finite form, while the succeeding ones are infinitives."

LEXICON OF INSCRIPTIONAL QATABANIAN

Letter Order and Transliteration of the Qatabanian Alphabet

ʾ	𐩱	ṭ	𐩷	ṣ	𐩮
b	𐩨	ẓ	𐩼	ḍ	𐩳
g	𐩴	y	𐩺	q	𐩤
d	𐩵	k	𐩫	r	𐩧
ḏ	𐩹	l	𐩡	s1	𐩪
h	𐩠	m	𐩣	s2	𐩦
w	𐩥	n	𐩬	s3	𐩯
z	𐩸	ʿ	𐩲	t	𐩩
ḥ	𐩢	ǵ	𐩶	ṯ	𐩻
ḫ	𐩭	f	𐩰		

ʾ

ʾB

subst. *ʾbm* Q 528/2, *ʾbs^{1}* Q 83/9, Q 89.137/5, .159bis/5, Q 139/3, Q 183/4

FATHER, FOREFATHER [Sab *ʾab* "father, forefather," Ar *ʾab*, Heb *ʾāḇ* id.]

A) Q 89.137/5: *ḥg wqh ʾbs^{1} wdm bms^{1}ʾls^{1}*
"as his father WDM commanded in his oracle"
(according-as commanded his-father WDM in-his-oracle)

B) Q 183/4: *rṯd bs^{2}mm ʾḏns^{1} wmqms^{1} wʾbs^{1} whbʾl*
"[BRTʿ] entrusted his household, his property, and his father WHBʾL to BS^{2}MM"
(he-entrusted [to] BS^{2}MM his-goods and-his-property and-his-father WHBʾL)

ʾBL

subst. *ʾbls^{1}* Q 840/10; *ʾbls^{1}w* Q 171/2

MALE CAMEL [Sab *ʾbl* "camel," Ar *ʾibil* "camels," Akk *ibilu* id., Syr *heḇaltā* "group of camels"]

A) Q 840/9-10: *wwzʾ zydʾl rṯd mrʾs^{1} ḏs^{1}mwy ʾbls^{1} wdʿn*
"and ZYDʾL further entrusted his camel WDʿN to his lord Ḏū S^{1}amāwī"
(and-continued ZYDʾL the-entrusting [to] his-lord Ḏū-S^{1}amāwī his-camel WDʿN)

B) Q 171/2: *[ww]fy ʾbls^{1}w ʿys^{2}m*
"[and (for) the sa]fety of his camel ʿYS^{2}M"

subst. *ʾbltm* Q 900/3

FEMALE CAMEL [Sab *ʾblt*, Ḥar *ḥebyīt*, Meh *ḥebyīt*, Śḥ *yit* id.]

Q 900/1-2: *ḥmys^{2}m wrklm bnw s^{2}rḥwd bn ḫlbn ʿs^{1}yw ẓrbw qbrs^{1}my ẓrb bʾbltm*
"ḤMYS^{2}M and RKLM the two sons of S^{2}RḤWD of the clan ḪLBN acquired and secured the title to their tomb for a she-camel"
(ḤMYS^{2}M and-RKLM the-two-sons [of] S^{2}RḤWD member-of-the-clan ḪLBN they-took-possession they-secured their[dl.]-tomb a-securing for-a-female-camel)

ʾBN

subst. *ʾbnm* Q 40/21; *ʾbns¹* Q 769/2a; pl. (?) *ʾbnw* Q 80/6 (according to RÉS VI, 336, possibly a writing error)

STONE [Sab *ʾbn* "stone," Ug *ʾabn*, Heb *ʾeḇen*, Ph *ʾbn*, Syr *ʾaḇnā*, Eth *ʾebn*, Soq *ʾoben*, Śḥ *ḥobin*, Meh *ḥaubin*, Akk *abnu* id.]

Q 40/21: *wl yftḏ ḏn ftḥn wmḥrtn bʿḏm ʾw ʾbnm*

"and let this order and directive be inscribed in wood or stone"

(and-let be-inscribed this order and-directive in-wood or stone)

ʾGW

verb *ʾgw* Q 72/2

TO STRUGGLE [Cf. Heb *yiggēh* "to grieve, pain, afflict," Ar *wajiya* "to have pain in the hoof (of a horse)"; cf. also Akk *agāgu* "to be inflamed," Ar *wajaʾa* "to strike, beat," Eth *wagʾa*, Amh *waggā* id., Tña *wagʾe* "to beat, make war," and see Müller, 1962, 25.]

Q 72/2-3: *kḏm byfrwn wʾgw wʾhw wḥrṯ wqẓr wʿzz ws¹qḥ ws¹ʿhd s²ʿbm s²ʿbm*

"in order that they till, struggle, toil, plow, labor, work vigorously, make ready, and attend to (their task) tribe by tribe"

(in-order-that they-till and-struggling and-toiling and-plowing and-laboring and-working-vigorously and-making-ready and-attending-to tribe tribe)

ʾGY

s¹-prfx. *s¹ʾgy* Q 72/8 (according to Müller, 1962, 25, ʾGY is a byform of ʾGW)

TO REPRIMAND; TO VEX [Cf. the etymology given for ʾGW above]

Q 72/7-8: *wl ylṣq wqrw ws¹ʿḏb ws¹ʾgy wʿthd*

"and let [the lord of Timnaʿ] prosecute, accuse, punish, reprimand, and concern himself"

(and-let he-prosecute and-accusing and-punishing and-reprimanding and-concerning-himself)

ʾGL

subst. sing. *mʾgl* Q 678/3, Q 687/2; *mʾgln* Q 688/4, Q 690a/6; *mʾglk* Q 687/5; *mʾglhw* Q 679/8-9; *mʾglhmw* Q 678/3; dl. *mʾgly* Q 679/7; *mʾglyhmw* Q 678/2-3, Q 679/6

CISTERN, RESERVOIR, TANK [Sab *mʾgl* "tank, cistern"; cf. Ar *maʾjal* "pool, pond." See, however, Beeston, 1950a, 53-54, who denies the meaning "cistern, reservoir" in the case of the three occurrences—none of them Qatabanian—known at that time and suggests the sense "watchtower." See also M. A. Ghul, 1959, 428, who provides further details of the discussion, and Beeston, 1962c, 45-46, who concedes Ghul's point.]

Q 688/3-4: *wtqdm ʾrdʾhw bd̠n mʾgln bnʾ*

"and he directed his workers in (the construction of) this cistern BNʾ"

ʾGR

subst. *ʾgr* Q 482/2

SERVANT of a god (?) [See Jamme, 1952a, 177; cf. Ar *ʾajīr* "hireling," Min *ʾgr* "servant (of a god)," Śḥ *gor* "slave," Meh *ḥagōr*, Ḥar *ḥewgor* id; Akk *igru* "hire, rent, wages," Ug *ʾagr* "to hire."]

Q 482/2: *ʾgr s*^{2}*hr*

"[ʿMGS^{1}M son of YʿDRʾL] servant (of the god) (?) S^{2}HR"

ʾDB

subst *mʾdbs*^{1} Q 183/4

VASSAL [Cf. Sab *mʾdbt* "vassals"]

Q 183/4: *wmtʿ ʾbrtʿ mʾdbs*^{1}

"the support of ʾBRTʿ his vassal"

ʾDM

subst. (coll.) sing. *ʾdm* Q 73/5, Q 79/2; *ʾdms*^{1} Q 67/3, 6, 8, Q 68/2, 6, 7, Q 69/2, 4, 5, Q 70/1, 3(2x), Q 243/8; *ʾdms*^{1}*m* Q 243/2; pl. *ʾdwms*^{1}*m* Q 79/3; *ʾʾdmn* Q 840/1

1) MEN, PEOPLE [Ug *ʾadm* "people, humanity," Heb *ʾād̠ām* "man," Ph *ʾdm* id., Ar *ʾādamī* "human"]

Q 73/4-5: *wbrdʾ wʾh̠yl ʾdm bn qs*^{3}*mm*

"with the aid and support of the men of (the tribe) QS^{3}MM"

2) SUBJECTS, VASSALS of a king, etc. [Sab *ʾdm* "vassals, subjects"; cf. ModYem *ʾawādim* "domestics"]

A) Q 68/7: *wt̠fṭ s*^{2}*hr ʾdms*^{1} *ʾrby d̠lbh̠ ls*^{1}*ṭr wfth̠ d̠tn ʾs*^{1}*ṭrn*

"and S^{2}HR commanded his subjects, the *ʾrby* of D̠ū Labah̠, to write down and engrave these documents"

(and-commanded S^{2}HR his-subjects the-*ʾrby* [of] D̠ū-Labah̠ to-write-down and-engraving these documents)

B) Q 70/1: *s*^{2}*hr hll mlk qtbn s*^{1}*gdd lʾdms*^{1} *ʾrby ʿm d̠lbh̠*

"S^{2}HR HLL, king of Qataban, has renewed for his subjects, the *ʾrby* of ʿAmm D̠ū Labah̠"

(S^{2}HR HLL the-king [of] Qataban he-has-renewed for-his-subjects the-*ʾrby* [of] ʿAmm D̠ū-Labah̠)

ʾḎW

conj. *ʾḏw* Q 186A/14

THEN, THEREUPON [Ar *ʾiḏan* "then, in that case." On the final *-w* cf. Beeston, 1959, 7: "Qatabanian has a special fondness for forms ending in *-w*."]

Q 186A/13-14: *wmty yḫdr ḫdrm wʾḏw bys²tyṭ*

"and when he sets up a trading-stall he may then trade"

(and-when he-sets-up a-trading-stall and-then he-will-trade)

ʾḎN

verb *ʾḏn* Q 840/5

TO ALLOW, PERMIT [Ar *ʾaḏina* "to permit"]

Q 840/5: *wʾḏn ḏs¹mwy ʾlh ʾmrm ly*[..]

"and Ḏū S¹amāwī, god of the oracle, allowed Y[..]"

(and-allowed Ḏū-S¹amāwī god [of] the-oracle to-Y[..])

subst. sing. *ʾḏn* (esp. in the formula *bʾḏn* + name of a divinity) Q 14/3, Q 15, Q 16, Q 18/2-3, Q 19/3, Q 20/3, Q 24/2, Q 25/3, Q 26/3, Q 183/4, Q 542/3, Q 573, Q 574, Q 587/3, Q 652/2, Q 657/3, Q 666/3, Q 667/3-4, Q 671/2, Q 735/2, Q 797/2+; *ʾḏnk* Q 514; *ʾḏns¹* Q 1/6, Q 167/4, Q 254/5, Q 269/4, Q 492/1, Q 496/3-4, Q 906/6; Q 910/6 *ʾḏns¹m* Q 840/3; pl. *ʾʾḏn* Q 840/8; *ʾʾḏnhmw* Q 207/2; *ʾʾḏns¹my* Q 488/3, Q 840/7

1) AUTHORITY, POWER; PERMISSION [Sab *ʾḏn* "power, strength, authority," Ar *ʾiḏn* "permission," but see also Jamme, who renders *bʾḏn* at Q 565E/2 "*en sujétion*" and discusses the word at length in Jamme, 1952a, 210]

A) Q 14/1-3: *ʿmrtʿ ḏbynm bʾḏn ʿm*

"ʿAmmrataʿ of (the clan of) Bayyinum. By the authority of ʿAmm."

B) Q 565E/2: *bʾḏn ʿm ḏʿḏbtm*

"by the authority of ʿAmm of ʿAdbatum"

2) HOUSEHOLD, FAMILY [See Ghul, 1959, 6-7, for a discussion of *ʾḏn* in this sense, but see also the rendering of Jamme of this word as "*sens*," in Jamme, 1952a, 196.]

Q 496/3-4: *rṯd ʾnby ʾḏns¹ wwlds¹ wkl ʾqn(y)s¹m*

"he has entrusted to ʾAnbay his household, his children, and all his possessions"

ʾHW

verb *ʾhw* Q 72/2

TO TOIL, STRUGGLE [See W. Müller, 1962, 27, who compares Heb *ʾăhāh* "oh! alas!" and Ar *ʾāha, ʾawwaha, taʾawwaha* "to groan, sob"]

Q 72/2-3: *kḏm byfrwn wʾgw wʾhw wḥrṯ wqẓr wʿzz ws¹qḥ ws¹ʿhd s²ʿbm s²ʿbm*

"in order that they till, struggle, toil, plow, labor, work vigorously, make ready, and attend to (their task) tribe by tribe"

(in-order-that they-till and-struggling and-toiling and-plowing and-laboring and-working-vigorously and-making-ready and-attending-to tribe tribe)

ʾHL

subst. *ʾhl* Q 567/3

FAMILY, CLAN; COMMUNITY [Sab *ʾhl* "folk, people, community," Liḥ *ʾhl*, Saf *ʾl*, Tham *ʾl*, *ʾhl* "family," Ar *ʾahl* "family, clan"]

Q 567/1-3: *ẓlt wʾws¹ʾl [w]hwfʿṯt wbqs² ʾhl gzyn*

"ẒLT "and ʾWS¹ʾL (and) HWFʿṮT and BQS² of the clan of GZYN"

ʾW

conj. *ʾw* Q 40/15, 18, 21, Q 78/8, Q 89.140/8, Q 186A/14, 24, Q694/9, Q 695/7, 10, 11, 13

OR [Sab *ʾw* "or," Ar *ʾaw*, Heb *ʾô*, Syr *ʾō*, Akk *ū* id.]

A) Q 40/21: *wl yftḥ ḏn ftḥn wmḥrtn bʿḍm ʾw ʾbnm*

"and let this order and directive be inscribed in wood or stone"

(and-let be-inscribed this order and-directive in-wood or stone)

B) Q 186A/14-16: *wʾḏw bys²tyṭ ʾ w fṯr bʿm kl ḫdrm wms²ṭm*

"[when a trader sets up a stall] then he may trade or enter into a partnership with any possessor of a trading-stall and merchandise"

(and-then he-will-trade or entering-into-partnership with any possessor-[of]-a-trading-stall and-merchandise)

ʾWD

subst. sing. *ʾwd* Q 694/8; *ʾwdm* Q 694/9; pl. *ʾwwd* Q 694/11-12; *ʾwwds¹n* Q 694/10

(AREA HELD BY A) RETAINING WALL [Sab *ʾwd* "course of masonry." Pirenne, 1971, 127, in discussing this word, compares it with the Ar *ʾāda* (w), which has the root sense of supporting something which is heavy.]

(ʾWD)

Q 694/8: *mrḥbm bn nḫlm wḥrṯ ʾwd wbqlm bqlm wbny ḥrtm*
"this land shall be open to irrigation and free from palmgroves, the terracing of (the area held by) a retaining wall, the cultivation of plants, and the construction of an aqueduct"
(land-open-for-irrigation from palmgroves and-the-terracing [of] a-retaining-wall and-cultivating [of] plants and-the-building [of] an-aqueduct)

ʾḪ

subst. sing. *ʾḫs¹* Q 66/4, Q 78/4, Q 186A/25, Q 219/3, Q 245/1, Q 254/5, Q 263/6; *ʾḫs¹ww* Q 166/6; *ʾḫhw* Q 690a/1; *ʾḫhs¹m* Q 486/3; dl. *ʾḫyhw* Q 179/2, Q 679/1; *ʾḫys¹my* Q 551/2; pl. *ʾḫhs¹ww* Q 183/4, Q 254/9, Q 790/5, Q 904/5; *ʾḫhys¹my* Q 67/3-4; Q 69/2; *ʾḫhys¹m* Q 68/3, Q 166/7; *ʾḫwthw* Q 677/5

1) BROTHER [Sab *ʾḫ* "brother," Ar *ʾaḫ*, Heb *ʾāḥ*, Akk *aḫu* id.]

A) Q 551/2: *ws¹s³ḥr ʾḫys¹my nbṭʿm wlḥyʿm*
"and [WDʾL] made their two brothers, NBṬʿM and LḤYʿM, priests"
(and-he-made-priests their[dl.]-[i.e., the brothers of WDʾL and YS²RM]-two-brothers NBṬʿM and-LḤYʿM)

B) Q 183/4-5: *rṯd bs²mm … ʾbs¹ whbʾl wʾḫhs¹ww bnʾl wʾbʾns¹*
"he entrusted … his father WHBʾL and his brothers BNʾL and ʾBʾNS¹ to BS²MM"
(he-entrusted [to] BS²MM his-father WHBʾL and-his-brothers BNʾL and-ʾBʾNS¹)

2) FELLOW-TRADER; ANOTHER
Q 186A/24-25: *wzʾ ʾns¹m ʿly ʾḫs¹ bḫ[t]fr[m]*
"someone has consistently cheated his fellow-trader"
(he-continued someone against his-fellow-trader in-cheating)

ʾḪḎ

verb *ʾḫḏ* Q 695/3
TO TAKE, RECEIVE [Ar *ʾaḫaḏa* id.]
Q 695/3: *wʾḫḏ tbdd ʾrḍn*
"payment for the land has been received"

subst. *ʾḫḏ* Q 67/4, Q 68/4, Q 69/3
DETRACTION, TAKING, CONFISCATION [Sab *ʾḫḏ* "to take, seize," Heb *ʾāḥaz* "to grasp, take hold, take possession," Ar *ʾaḫaḏa* "to take, seize," Eth *ʾaḫaza* "to stop, seize," Ug *ʾḫd* "to seize, take hold of," Akk *aḫāzu* "to take, seize"]

Q 67/4-5: *bn s¹nṣfm ws¹kt wʾḥd̲ wgddm*
"without any falling short, ceasing, detraction, or termination"

ʾḪR

subst.[1] *ʾḫr* Q 40/11, Q 66/7, Q 694/13, Q 915/4
FUTURE (in the phrase *lʾḫr*): FOR THE FUTURE, HENCEFORTH [Sab *lʾḫr* "henceforth, for the future," Ar *ʾal-āḫir* "the hereafter," Heb *ʾaḥarīt* "end, future"]

Q 66/6-7: *bn s²hr wrḫn d̲tmnᶜ ḫrf mwhbm d̲drḥn ʾḫrn lʾḫr*
"from the new moon of the month D̲ū Timnaᶜ of the second eponymate (year) of MWHBM of the tribe D̲RḤN and henceforth"
(from the-new-moon [of] the-month D̲ū-Timnaᶜ [of] the-year [of] MWHBM D̲ū-D̲RḤN the-latter henceforth)

subst.[2] *tʾḫr* Q 687/7
DELAY

Q 687/7: *lys¹tq btʾḫr dnḫk zm ʾs¹rb wʾt̲wr*
"after a delay let this charge, the herd of sheep and cattle, be given water to drink"
(let-be-given-water-to-drink after-a-delay this-charge the-herd [of] sheep and-cattle)

adj. *ʾḫrn* Q 40/7, Q 66/7, Q 68/8-9, Q 69/6, Q 70/4, Q 202/6
SECOND, FOLLOWING; OTHER [Sab *ʾḫr* "other," Ar *ʾaḫar* "other," Śḥ *ʾaḫeri* "the second," Heb *ʾaḥēr* "following, second, other"; cf. further Cohen, 1970, 15.]

Q 68/8-9: *ḫrf s²hrm d̲ygr ʾḫrn*
"[in the month of D̲ū Timnaᶜ] in the second eponymate of S²HRM of (the tribe of) YGR"
(eponymate [of] S²HRM of-YGR the-second)

ʾYY

indef. rel. pro. *ʾy* Q 40/4, 4-5, 5, 7(2x), 8, 9, 11, 23, Q 72/4)
WHO-, WHAT(SO)EVER [Cf. Ar *ʾayyu* "whoever, whosoever"]

A) Q 72/4: *wʾy ʾy ʾs¹dm*
"whatever man"

B) Q 40/4-5: *wʾy ftḥ ws¹ḫr ʾftḥ wmḫrtm wʾt̲ft wḫwlltm ws¹ṭ s¹wt mqmn*
"whatever directives, orders, judgments, and decisions which [the Qatabanian lords and landowners] have directed and ordered in that meeting"

(ʾYY)

(and-whatever order and-directing directives and-orders and-judgments and-decisions in that meeting)

indef. pro. *ʾyhnmw* Q 40/17

WHERE(SO)EVER [Rhodokanakis, 1915a, 35, understands this as being composed of *ʾy* + *hn* + *mw*]

Q 40/17: *ʾyhnmw ʿkr*

"[let these decrees and directives be made known] wherever there may be opposition"

(wheresoever it-is-opposed)

indef. encl. -*ʾy* Q 40/4, 8, 9, Q 66/12, Q 67/11, Q 68/10, Q 69/7, Q 70/5, Q 72/10, Q 78/13, Q 79/7, Q 202/6 +

According to Beeston, 1962b, 66, *ʾy* seems originally to have been used for deixis but later lost this force and in the extant texts has no clear semantic function, but see also Jamme, 1972, 25, who states that "enclitics have no other value than that of emphasizing that very meaning of the words."

A) Q 40/8: *bʾy ws^{1}ṯ ʾḥrm byt ʿm*

"in ʾḤRM, the temple of ʿAmm"

B) Q 66/12: *wtʿlmʾy yd s^{2}hr*

"and S^{2}HR signed with his own hand"

(and-signed the-hand [of] S^{2}HR)

prep. + encl. *bʾy*

See entry under B.

ʾL I

subst. sing. *ʾls^1* Q 681/2, Q 857/2, Q 910/2; *ʾls^{1}m* Q 177/3, Q 840/2, Q 914/3; *ʾls^{1}my* Q 256/2; pl. *ʾlhn* Q 78/13; *ʾlhw* Q 177/3-4, Q 183/6, Q 203/2, 3, Q 218/2, Q 254/3; *ʾlhy* Q 11/6, Q 254/1, 5, Q 906/6 (according to Höfner, 1961, 455, in Q 254 *ʾlhw* is used for the nominative case, *ʾlhy* for the oblique.)

GOD [Sab *ʾl* "god," Heb *ʾēl* "god, God," Akk *ilu* "god"]

A) Q 177/3: *bn mṯbm ṯwbw lʾls^{1}m ʿm*

"from the offering which they made to their god ʿAmm"

B) Q 203/3-4: *ywm rdʾ ʿṯtr wʾlhw s^{1}qmtm s^{2}hrǵln mḫḍ ḥḍrmt wʾmrm*

"when ʿAṯtar and the gods of irrigation aided S^{2}HRǴLN in the defeat of ḤḌRMT and ʾMRM"

(when aided ʿAṯtar and-the-gods [of] irrigation S^{2}HRǴLN [in] the-defeat [of] ḤḌRMT and-ʾMRM)

ʾL II

neg. prt. *ʾl* Q 83/5, Q 186B/2, 18

NO, NOT [Sab *ʾl* "no, not," Śḥ *ol*, Har *ʾel*, Meh *ʾel*, Soq *ʾol*, Heb *ʾal*, BibAram *ʾal*, Akk *ʾul* id., Eth *ʾal-* (in *ʾalbo* "there is not")]

Q 186B/18-19: *wʾl bys²tyṭ kl s²yṭm kl ḏm byʿrb tmnʿ*

"anyone who pays the Timnaʿ [market-tax with the intention of doing business with a foreign tribe] may not do any business"

(and-not he-shall-trade any business anyone who he-pays [the tax of] Timnaʿ)

ʾLH

subst. *ʾlh* Q 71A, Q 840/2, 5; *ʾlhs¹m* Q 89.129/1

GOD [Sab *ʾlh* "god," Ar *ʾilāh* id., Heb *ʾelōah* "god, God"]

A) Q 71A: *ʿṣm ʿm ʾlh*

"he vowed to the god ʿAmm"

B) Q 840/5: *wʾḏn ḏs¹mwy ʾlh ʾmrm ly[..]*

"and Ḏū S¹amāwī, god of the oracle, allowed Y[..]"

(and-allowed Ḏū-S¹amāwī god [of] the-oracle to-Y[..])

ʾLF

card. num. pl. *ʾʾlfm* Q 73/3

THOUSAND [Sab *ʾlf* "thousand," Ar *ʾalf*, Heb *ʾelep̱*, Aram *ʾalap̱* id.]

Q 73/3: *ṯmnt ʾʾlfm bqlm*

"eight thousand plots of land"

ʾM

subst. sing. *ʾmt* Q 110, Q 167/1 Q 579/1-2; pl. *ʾmtys¹m* Q 79/3

MAIDSERVANT, FEMALE SLAVE [Sab *ʾmt* "maidservant, female slave," Ar *ʾama*, Eth *ʾamat*, Heb *ʾāmāh*, Akk *amtu* id.]

A) Q 110: *ʾmt ḏtlʿb*

"maidservant of (the clan of) TLʿB"

B) Q 167/1: *[..]s²m ḏt byt ḥys¹n ʾmt nb[…]*

"[..]S²M of the household of ḤYS¹N, maidservant of NB[…]"

ʾMM

verb *ʾmm* Q 78/3

TO BE AT THE HEAD, LEAD [Ar *ʾamma* "to march at the front, be at the head of," Tña *ammama* "to advance"]

Q 78/3: *wkl ʾs²ʿbn ymlk ydʿʾb bn mʾtmm wʾmm*

"and all the tribes, both the leading and the following, which YDʿʾB rules"

(ʾMM)

(and-all the-tribes [which] rules YDʿʾB from the-following and-leading)

t-infix *mʾtmm* Q 78/3

TO FOLLOW, BE LED [Sab *yʾtmmw* R 3945 "to be led"]

See entry above.

subst. *ʾmmm* Q 40/2

INSTRUCTION, COURSE OF CONDUCT [Cf. Ar *ʾimām* "exemplar, model"]

Q 40/2: *wʾmmm bs¹ʾlm s¹ʾl*

"as instruction for one inquiring"

(and-instruction for-the-one-asking a-question)

ʾMN

verb *s¹ʾmnn* Q 183/4, Q 909/3

TO PROTECT, SECURE [Cf. Sab *hʾmn* "to protect," Ar *ʾammana* "to assure," Ar *āmana* "to render secure," Heb *hĕʾemīn* "to believe," Eth *amna* "to be firm; to be true; to believe"]

Q 909/3: *[y]zʾn ṣdq ws¹ʾmn ʿqrbn bkl ʾʾrḫ tkrb*

"may [Wadd] [con]tinue to show favor and protection to ʿQRBN in all the affairs that he undertakes"

(may-[con]tinue favoring and-protecting ʿQRBN in-all affairs he-has-undertaken)

subst.[1] *ʾmnt* Q 67/12-13

PROTECTION (in phrase *ḏʾmnt*): PERSON UNDER THE PROTECTION of someone [Sab *ḏʾmnt* "person under protection *of someone*"]

Q 67/12-13: *nbṭʿm bn ʾls¹mʿ bn hybr ḏʾmnt ʿm ḏlbḫ wʾrbys¹*

"[the completion of this inscriptional record was carried out by] NBṬʿM the son of ʾLS¹Mʿ of the clan HYBR under the protection of ʿAmm of Labakh and his ʾRBY"

subst.[2] *s¹ʾmnts¹* Q 681/4

PLEDGE

Q 681/3-4: *ḥg ts²fts¹ ws¹ʾmnts¹*

"according to his promise and pledge"

subst.[3] *tʾmnm* Q 840/6

GRATITUDE, TRUST, FAITH [Sab *tʾmnt* "expression of gratitude, confidence"]

Q 840/6: *ws¹ṯbw lḏs¹mwy w[lʿm] tʾmnm*

"and they have witnessed their gratitude to Ḏū S¹amāwī and (to ʿAmm)" (and-they-have-testified to-Ḏū-S¹amāwī and[-to-ʿAmm] gratitude)

ʾMR

verb *ʾmrw* Q 37/3

TO COMMAND, PROCLAIM [Cf. Heb *ʾāmar* "to say," BibAram *ʾămar* id., Ar *ʾamara* "to command"]

Q 37/3: *ḥg ʾmrw bms¹ʾls¹m*

"as they [the deities ʿAṯtar and ʿAmm and S²MS¹] commanded through their oracle"

(according-as they-commanded through-their-oracle)

subst. *ʾmr* Q 35/2, Q 73/4, Q 80/3, 7, Q 91, Q 102/5, Q 176/6, Q 239/4, Q 769/1b; *ʾmrm* Q 840/2, 5

COMMAND of a god; ORACLE [Sab *ʾmr* "oracle; omen"]

A) Q 35/1-2: *s²hr hll … bn ydʿʾb mkrb qtbn bkr ʾnby wḥwkm ḏʾmr*

"S²HR HLL … the son of YDʿʾB, *mkrb* of Qataban, the firstborn of ʾAnbay and ḤWKM of the oracle"

B) Q 73/4: *bʾmr wmqdm ʿṯtr*

"[ǴLBM ( )YB did all this] at the command and direction of ʿAṯtar"

ʾNN

adv. *ʾn* Q 687/3

HERE [Thus Jamme, 1971, 87, who notes CIH 541/4 and compares Ar *ʾinna* not as a particle "*d'affirmation génerale … mais d'indication locale précise*"]

Q 687/2-3: *s¹wr bnʾ mʾgl ms¹qt gḏ wbrʾkh ʾn*

"[the dignitaries of S¹ʿDM YHS¹KR] built a wall around BNʾ, the irrigation cistern of GḎ, and its (supporting) cisterns here"

(built-a-wall-around BNʾ the-cistern [of] irrigation [of] GḎ and-its-cisterns here)

ʾNS¹

subst. *ʾns¹* Q 720/1; *ʾns¹m* Q 66/3, Q 186A/25, C/5; *ʾns¹n* Q 78/4, 7

1) PERSON; SOMEONE, ONE; EACH [Sab *ins¹* "man; male," Ar *ʾins, ʾunās* "man, people," Heb *ʾĕnôš* "men, mankind"]

A) Q 186A/24-25: *wzʾ ʾns¹m ʿly ʾḫs¹ bḫ[t]fr[m]*

"someone has consistently cheated his fellow-trader"

(he-continued someone against his-fellow-trader in-cheating)

B) Q 66/3: *td ns¹m*

"one, each man, every man"

(ʾNS¹)

2) FRIEND, COMPANION [Cf. Ar *anīs* "companion, friend," Ug *ʾnš* "to be a companion of, companionable"]

Q 720/1: *[...]t bn ṣdqʾl bn yhyṯʿ ʾns¹ ydʿʾb ḏbyn mlk qtbn*

"[...]T son of ṢDQʾL of the clan YHYṮʿ, companion of YDʿʾB Ḏū BYN, king of Qataban"

ʾNṮ

subst.[1] *ʾṯts¹* Q 901/4

WIFE [Sab *ʾnṯt*, *ʾṯt* "woman, wife," Arab *ʾunṯā*, Eth *ʾanest*, Heb *ʾiššāh*, Akk *aššatu* id.]

Q 901/4: *lʾṯts¹*

"for his wife"

subst.[2] *tʾnṯs¹m* Q 67/4, 6, 7, Q 68/3-4, 5, 6, Q 69/2, 4(2x), Q 70/1, 2, 3, Q 79/2

FEMALE RELATIVES

A) Q 68/3-4: *tʾnṯs¹m wʾwlds¹m*

"their female relatives and their children"

B) Q 69/4-5: *wṣry s²hr ʾdms¹ ʾrby ʿm ḏlbḫ wtʾnṯs¹m wbnys¹m*

"and S²HR instructed his subjects, the *ʾrby* of ʿAmm Ḏū Labaḫ, their female relatives, and their sons"

(and-instructed S²HR his-subjects the-*ʾrby* [of] ʿAmm Ḏū-Labaḫ and-their-female-relatives ... and-their-sons)

ʾṢL

subst. *ʾṣlmw* Q 695/11

FAMILY, LINEAGE [Thus Beeston, 1976, 421, who analyzes this form into *ʾṣl* and the enclitic *-mw*; cf. Ar *aṣl* "descent, lineage, stock." Jamme, 1972, 27, renders the word "statues" from *ṣlm*]

Q 695/11-12: *wʾṣlmw mlkm ʾw s²ʿbm bys³f ʾw byrbʿ ḍnt ḏt ʾrḍn*

"the family of the king or tribe which enlarges or decreases the extent of this land"

(and-the-family of-the-king or tribe which increase or decrease the-extent [of] this land)

ʾRḪ

verb *ʾrḫ* Q 183/2, Q 262/4, Q 840/5

TO INSTRUCT; TO ORDER, COMMAND [On the evolution from the concrete nominal sense "road, way" to the metaphorical sense of "order, prescription, command" see Rhodokanakis, 1936, 21.]

Q 840/5-6: *[wb]ḏtn ʾrḫ ls¹m*

"in respect to what [Ḏū S¹amāwī] instructed them"
(and-with-regard-to-which-thing he-instructed to-them)

subst. pl. *ʾʾrẖ* Q 909/3; *ʾʾrẖm* Q 40/10, Q 840/4

1) ORDERS, INSTRUCTIONS, COMMANDS
Q 840/4: *ʾʾrẖm qbl ʿlys¹m*
"(in fulfillment of) orders which he had enjoined upon them"
(the-commands he-enjoined on-them)

2) AFFAIR, MATTER [Sab *ʾrẖ* id.]
Q 909/3: *[y]zʾn ṣdq ws¹ʾmn ʿqrbn bkl ʾʾrẖ tkrb*
"may [Wadd] [con]tinue to show favor and protection to ʿQRBN in all the affairs that he undertakes"
(may-[con]tinue favoring and-protecting ʿQRBN in-all affairs he-has-undertaken)

ʾRM

verb *ʾrm* Q 186A/11-12

TO DO BUSINESS [See etymology on subst. *ʾrmm* below]
Q 186A/9-12: *wʾṯrm qtbn bms²ṭm wʾrmm wqnym byẖdr wʾrm ws¹s²ʾm bs²mr*
"one who goes to Qataban with merchandise, wares, and goods shall set up a trading-stall and conduct business and sell in S²MR"
(and-the-one-who-goes [to] Qataban with-merchandise and-wares and-goods he-will-set-up and-doing-business and-selling in-S²MR)

subst. *ʾrmm* Q 186A/10-11, 11-12

MERCHANDISE, WARES [Rabin 1983, 483-85. Other suggestions include "bale(s), perhaps related to Akk *erēmu* "covering, case, envelope," on which see Beeston, 1959, 6, or "small cattle," possibly related to Soq *ʾerehon* "sheep, goats," Ar *ʾirān* "male oryx," Syr *ʾarnā* "mountain ibex," Akk *arm* id., Śḥ *érún* "goats," Har *ḥewerūn*, Meh *ḥāráwn* id.]
See entry above.

ʾRḌ

subst. sing. *ʾrḍ* Q 74/6, Q 183/2-3, Q 244/10, Q 839/5; *ʾrḍm* Q 78/11, Q 695/1, Q 909/1; *ʾrḍn* Q 641/2, Q 695/3, 4, 10, 12; *ʾrḍs¹* Q 178/2, Q 700/3; *ʾrḍhw* Q 74/14; *ʾrḍs¹my* Q 182/2; *ʾrḍhmw*; Q 74/2; pl. *ʾrḍtm* Q 74/5; *ʾrḍtn* Q 74/13, Q694/10, 12; *ʾrḍty* Q 74/5

1) LAND [Sab *ʾrḍ* "land," Ar *ʾarḍ*, Heb *ʾereṣ* id., Akk *erṣetu* "earth"]
Q 74/13-14: *wrṯd yḏmrmlk ʿm wʾnby w[ʾlht] qtbn ws¹ẖl wṯwlm ws²ʿbn ḏbḥn … ʾrḍhw wqnyhw*

(ʾRḌ)

"and YḎMRMLK entrusted his land and possessions to ʿAmm, ʾAnbay, [the goddess] of Qataban, and S¹ḪL and ṮWLM the tribe of ḎBḤN"
(and-entrusted YḎMRMLK [to] ʿAmm and-ʾAnbay and-the-[goddess-of] Qataban and-S¹ḪL and-ṮWLM and-the-tribe [of] ḎBḤN … his-land and-his-possessions)

2) PROPERTIES, LANDS
Q 74/5-6: *wḏn ʾbyt wʾrḍtm qny wʿs¹y ws²ʾm yḏmrmlk*
"and these are the houses and lands which YḎMRMLK acquired, obtained, and purchased"
(and-these the-houses and-lands he-acquired and-obtaining and-purchasing YḎMRMLK)

ʾS¹

subst. *ʾs¹m* Q 40/23(2x); *ʾs¹s¹* Q 186C/6 (but see Beeston, 1959, 10-11)
MAN; SOMEONE, ONE [Cf. ʾNS¹; cf. also Sab *ʾs¹* "man," Heb *ʾîš*, Moab *ʾš* id.]
Q 40/23: *wʿtlyw ʾs¹dm ʿlmw bḏn ftḥn ʾs¹m ʾs¹m bhṯ ḏmrs¹*
"those who have signed this decree have each seen to the promulgation of its correct reading"
(and-they-supervised who signed in-this decree man man the-announcement [of] its-correct-reading)

ʾS¹D

subst. *ʾs¹dm* Q 67/10, Q 72/4, Q 202/2
MAN; PERSON [Sab *ʾs¹d* "men; soldiers, warriors"; cf. Ar *ʾasad* "lion." Semantic development "lion"> "warrior">"man"? Beeston, 1951a, 30-31, sees a possible Heb cognate in *ʾšdt* "brave, courageous man," Deut. 33:2 (*qerē* "*ʾēš dāṯ*," probably also a collective).]

A) Q 72/4-5: *wʾy ʾy ʾs¹dm bydr ws¹ḫdʿ bn wfr wʿs²q*
"and whatever man refuses and balks at plowing and tilling"
(and-whatever whatever man he-refuses and-balking at plowing and-tilling)

B) Q 202/2: *wḏtw tḥrgn ʾs¹dm ys³mk bn t[…*
"and (according to) this directive a man will undertake from T[…"

rel. pro. *ʾs¹dm* Q 40/23
WHO, WHICH
See entry under ʾS¹.

ʾS¹Y

verb *ʾs¹y* Q 695/1

TO GRANT; TO ESTABLISH [Beeston, 1976, 422, and 1981a, 57, translates *ʾs¹y* "to grant"; Robin and Ryckmans, 1978, 54, and Drewes, 1979, 103, render it "to establish, while Jamme, 1972, 27, 28, gives it the sense "to order." W. Müller, 1980, 71, while agreeing with Beeston's interpretation, sees the form *ʾs¹y* as a dual of the root ʾWS¹, with which he compares Ar *ʾāsa* (w) "to give as a gift," hence rendering *ʾs¹y* in this context "*lastenfrei schenken.*"]

Q 695/1: *ḏn qf ʾrḍm ʾs¹y wnḥl ws¹ʿqb wqyḍ hwfʿm yhnʿm*

"this marks land which HWFʿM YHNʿM [and YDʿʾB YGL] have granted, leased, transferred, and assigned"

ʾS¹N

prep. *ʾs¹n* Q 36/3

BETWEEN [This word is otherwise unknown in ESA. Its meaning is conjectured on the basis of the context; cf. Sab *s¹wn* "towards," and see RÉS VI, 203, which translates this word as "entire"; cf. Höfner, 1943, 153, who understands it in the sense "(*in der Richtung*) *nach*," and Jamme, 1972, 57-58, who, in a lengthy discussion of the word, prefers to see it as a pl. of Qat *s¹n* "road" (cf. Ar *sanan* "roads"), thus "the road of Barum and Ḥarîb."]

Q 36/3-4: *ʾs¹n brm wḥrb*

"between BRM and ḤRB"

ʾTW

subst. sing. *mʾtws¹m* Q 73/2; dl. *mʾtws¹yw* Q 700

CHANNEL (FOR WATER) [Sab *mʾt* "inlet/outlet channel," Ar *ʾatī* id.]

Q 73/2: *wkl ʾbʾrs¹m wṯqwls¹m wmʾtws¹m wbnys¹m*

"and all their wells and their accoutrements, channels, and buildings"

(and-all their-wells and-their-hanging-paraphernalia and-their-channels and-their-buildings)

ʾTM

verb *ʾtm* Q 40/3

TO AGREE, MAKE AN AGREEMENT [Sab *ʾtm* "to bring together, reconcile," Ar *ʾatama* "unite, join"]

Q 40/3: *qwmw wʾtm wʾttm*

"they assembled and agreed and adhered to the agreement"

t-infix. *ʾttm* Q 40/3; *ʾttmm* Q 40/7

(ʾTM)

TO ADHERE TO AN AGREEMENT

See entry above.

subst.[1] dl. *ʾtmtnyhn* Q 40/13; pl. *ʾtmtm* Q 40/7, 10

1) AGREEMENT, SETTLEMENT

Q 40/10: *bkl ʾʾrḫm wʾftḥm wmḥrtm wʾṯftm wʾtmtm*

"by all the orders, directives, decisions, judgments, and agreements"

2) ASSEMBLY, MEETING

Q 40/7: *ṯnym mqmm wʾtmtm wḥd bnblm*

"for a second time in their meeting and assembly jointly through a delegation"

(a-second-time meeting and-assembly jointly through-a-delegation)

subst.[2] *mʾtmn* Q 40/5

ASSEMBLY [Cf. Ar *maʾtam* "funeral assembly"]

Q 40/5: *ws¹ṭ s¹wt mqmn wmʾtmn*

"in this meeting and assembly"

ʾṮR

subst./partcp. *ʾṯrm* Q 186A/10, C/12

1) ONE WHO GOES, MAKES HIS WAY TOWARD [Cf. Soq *ʾihor* "to follow," Heb *ʾāšar* "to walk straight," Ug *ʾaṯr* "to march"]

Q 186A/9-10: *wʾṯrm qtbn bms²tm*

"one who goes to Qataban with merchandise [shall set up a trading-stall]"

(and-the-one-who-goes [to] Qataban with-merchandise)

2) ONE WHO SUPERVISES, SUPERVISOR [For discussion on this semantic range of *ʾṯr*, see Beeston, 1959, 11]

Q 186C/10-14: *wmlkmw qtbn ʾṯrm bkl s²[y]ṭm wqnym btmẓʾ bḍʿs¹*

"the king of Qataban has supervisory jurisdiction over every piece of merchandise and goods which enters his territory"

(and-the-king [of] Qataban is-supervor over-every piece-of-merchandise and-goods it-enters his-territory)

B

B

prep. *b* Q 14, Q 15, Q 16, Q 18, Q 19+

IN, ON, BY MEANS OF, THROUGH [Sab *b* "in, at, with, by," Ar *bi* "in, by," Eth *ba* "in," Heb *bə* "in, on, with." See Beeston, 1962b, 53-54, for a discussion of the semantic range of *b* in ESA, and 1984, 54.]

local:

A) Q 504: *mʿmr rṯdʾl ḏt hrn brṣfm*
"statue of RṮDʾL of (the clan of) HRN in RṢFM"

B) Q 186A/3-4: *mlk qt[bn wq]tbn btmnʿ*
"the king of Qata[ban and the Qata]banians in Timnaʿ"

C) Q 74/10: *bhgrn ḫdṣm*
"in the town of ḪDṢM"

temporal:

Q 72/3: *bʿs¹tnm ḏfrʿm*
"on the first of Ḏū FRʿM"

instrumental:

Q 37/3: *ḥg ʾmrw bms¹ʾls¹m*
"as they [the deities ʿAṯtar and ʿAmm and S²MS¹] commanded through their oracle"
(according-as they-commanded through-their-oracle)

in invocatory contexts (with the name or epithet of a god, usually in the closing formula of an inscription):

Q 36/6: *bʿṯtr wb ʿm wb ʾnby wb ḥwkm wbḏt ṣntm wbḏt ẓhrn wbḏt rḥbn*
"by ʿAṯtar and by ʿAmm and by ʾAnbay and by ḤWKM and by Ḏāt ṢNTM and by Ḏāt ẒHRN and by Ḏāt RḤBN"

accordance:

Q 73/4: *bʾmr wmqdm ʿṯtr*
"[ǴLBM ( )YB did all this] at the command and direction of ʿAṯtar"

price:

Q 72/6: *bʿs²r ʿs²r ḫbṣtm*
"for (the price of) ten *ḫbṣt* (monetary unit) each"

prep. + encl. *bʾy* Q 8, 9

This combination of the prep. *b* plus the encl. -*ʾy* (q.v.) has a sense which is not substantially different from the prep. alone.

(B)

A) Q 40/7: *bʾy wrḫn ḏbrm*
"in the month of Ḏū BRM"

B) Q 40/8: *bʾy ws¹ṭ ʾḥrm*
"in ʾḤRM"
(in the-midst [of] ʾḤRM)

prep. + pro. *bḏt* Q 172/4, Q 183/2; *bḏtm* Q 89.86/3, Q 254/3-4, Q 256/5, Q 398/3, Q 481/2, Q 496/2-3, Q 806/2, Q 844/6; *bḏtn* Q 840/6, Q 694/10, Q 916/3

1) BECAUSE [comp. of the prep. *b* and the pro. *ḏt* with suffixal material *-m* and *-n*]

Q 898/2-4: *ṣḥwm bn yʾzl ḏkrs¹ s¹qny ʿm ḏdymtm bḥt mrtn bḏtm s¹wfy ʿm ʿbds¹ ṣḥwm*
"ṢḤWM, the son of YʾZL of (the clan of) KRS¹, dedicated to ʿAmm Ḏū DYMTM this limestone votive object because ʿAmm protected his servant ṢḤWM."
(ṢḤWM the-son [of] YʾZL Ḏū-KRS¹ he-has-dedicated [to] ʿAmm Ḏū-DYMTM the-piece [of] limestone because protected ʿAmm his-servant ṢḤWM)

2) IN RESPECT OF [See Beeston, 1981, 26]

Q 840/6 (Cf. Q 481/2, Q 496/2-3, Q 844/6-7): *bḏtn tkrbs¹*
"in respect of that which he has undertaken for him"

comp. prep. *bws¹ṭ* Q 183/2

IN, IN THE MIDST OF [comp. of the prep. *b* and *ws¹ṭ*]

Q 183/2: *bws¹ṭ hgrn ṯbyr*
"in the middle of the town of ṮBYR"

prep. + prep. *bḥg* Q 82/4, Q 89.141/3, Q 99/5, Q 100/4, Q 101/2, Q 102/4, Q 182/2, Q 186B/24, Q 265/4, Q 266/4, Q 268/2, Q 478/2, Q 490A/3, B/3, Q 556/2, Q 790/3, Q 874/4, Q 899/3, Q 900/3, Q 903/3

IN ACCORDANCE WITH, IN AGREEMENT WITH [comp. of the prep. *b* and the prep. *ḥg*. Cf. Ghul, 1959, 422, for further discussion of the word.]

A) Q 899/3: *bḥg ʾnby wʾl tʿly*
"[ʾWS¹ʾL built a burial-place] in agreement with ʾAnbay and ʾL TʿLY"

B) Q 101/1-3: *ʾyhr wṯwbʾl ḏrḥn brʾw byts¹my gs²mm wʾḫṭbs¹ bḥg ʾnby*
"ʾYHR and ṮWBʾL ḎRḤN have built their house GS²MM and its lower stories in agreement with ʾAnbay"
(ʾYHR and-ṮWBʾL ḎRḤN they-built their[dl.]-house GS²MM and-its-lower-stories in-agreement-with ʾAnbay)

prep. + prep. *bʿl* Q 694/2

CONCERNING [comp. of the prep. *b* and *ʿl*; cf. Sab RÉS 3945/3]
Q 694/1, 2-3: *kn wqh ʾnby wrbq brm ... bʿl s²bʿt wmtntm wḍḥyn wfryḍ*
"Anbay and the administrator of BRM have decreed thus ... concerning S²BʿT and MTNTM and ḌḤYN and FRYḌ"

prep. + prep. *bʿlw* Q 67/6, 10, Q 68/5, Q 69/4, Q 74/4, Q 186B/4, Q 901/3

1) ACCORDING TO [comp. of the prep. *b* and *ʿlw*]
Q 68/5-6: *bʿlw ḏt mḥrtn wṣrytn*
"according to this law and directive"

2) AGAINST
Q 74/3-4: *bḍrm tns²ʾ ydʿʾl byn ... bʿlw ydʿʾb wqtbn*
"during the war which YDʿʾL BYN ... undertook against YDʿʾB and Qataban"
(in-the-war undertook YDʿʾL BYN ... against YDʿʾB and-Qataban)

3) ON, FOR
Q 186B/2-5: *ʾl byʿdwn nʿmt bz[w]rtm bʿlw ms²ṭm bys²tyṭwn ws²tʾm qtbn*
"they shall not calculate 'seed privileges' on merchandise which the Qatabanians may trade and buy"
(not they-will-calculate benefits [of] seeds on merchandise they-trade and-buying the-Qatabanians)

4) OVER, IN COMMAND OF
Q 901/3: *bms¹ʾls¹ kn kwn bʿlw ḏtw ḍ(m)[rn]*
"in his oracle when he was over the clan of Ḍ(M)[RN]"

prep. + prep. *bʿly* Q 679/8
OVER, ABOVE [comp. of the prep. *b* and *ʿly*]
Q 679/8: *ḏbʿly s¹rhmw s²rgn*
"[the two reservoirs] which are above their valley ŚRGN"

prep. + prep. *bʿm* Q 1/3, Q 35/6, Q 66/2, 5, Q 72/6, Q 80/5, Q 186A/15, 18, B/22

1) WITH, ALONG WITH, AMONG [comp. of the prep. *b* and *ʿm*]
A) Q 186A/14-16: *wʾḏw bys²tyṭ ʾw ftḥr bʿm kl ḫdrm wms²ṭm*
"[when a trader sets up a stall] then he may trade or enter into a partnership with any possessor of a trading-stall and merchandise"
(and-then he-may-trade or entering-into-partnership with any possessor-[of]-a-trading-stall and-merchandise)
B) Q 66/2: *bs²ʿbn kḥd ḏdtnt bʿm kbrm bykbr wḥrg s²ʿbn kḥd*
"with regard to the tribe KḤD of DTNT along with the *kabīr* who directs and administers the tribe KḤD"

(B)

(with-regard-to-the-tribe [of] KḤD of-DTNT with the-*kabīr* he-directs and-administering the-tribe KḤD)

2) FROM

Q 80/4-5: *bʿl ẓrbt ltk bḏ[bḥtm w]bʿm ʾḍfrm*

"lord of the fields of LTK by BḤTM from ʾḌFRM"

prep. + prep. *bqdmw* Q 183/2, Q 840/3-4

BEFORE [comp. of the prep. *b* and *qdmw*. The prep. *qdm(w)* is otherwise unattested in Qat. On *qdmw* cf. the Sab prep. *qdm* "before" used in both spatial and temporal senses.]

Q 183/2: *bqdmw ywmn*

"before this day (today—i.e., in the past)"

comp. prep. *bs²hd* Q 177/2

BEFORE, IN FRONT OF [comp. of the prep. *b* and *s²hd*; cf. Ar *šahdan* "before, in front of," Sab *s²hd* "testimony"]

Q 177/2: *bs²hd gnʾ hgrs¹m hrbt*

"before the wall of their town HRBT"

BʾR

subst. sing. *bʾr* Q 270/1; *bʾrm* Q 694/13; *bʾrs¹* Q 239/3, Q 240/5; dl.(?) *bʾrn* Q 679/8(2x); pl. *ʾbʾrs¹* Q 700/5; *ʾbʾrs¹m* Q 73/2

WELL [Sab *bʾr* "well, cistern," Ar *biʾr* "well,"Heb *bəʾēr* "well, pit," Akk *būru* "pit"]

Q 73/2: *wkl ʾbʾrs¹m wṯqwls¹m wmʾtws¹m wbnys¹m*

"and all their wells and their accoutrements, channels, and buildings"

(and-all their-wells and-their-hanging-paraphernalia and-their-channels and-their-buildings)

BʾS¹

subst. *bʾs¹tm* Q 166/5

HARM, DAMAGE, MISFORTUNE [Sab *bʾs¹* "harm, damage, misfortune," Ar *baʾs* "harm, evil, injury"]

Q 166/5: *kl bʾs¹tm wtlf[ ]m*

"every damage and lo[s]s"

BDD

subst.[1] *bd* Q 72/4, Q 83/5

SERIES, CHANGE, FLUCTUATION [Cf. Ar verb *badda* "to separate," Heb *bāḏaḏ* "to be separate," Ph *bdd* id. Pirenne, however, in commenting on *bd*, Q 83/5 in CIAS 2:159-61, translates it as "*chapelle*," comparing it with Ar *budd* "idol, the house of an idol."]

Q 72/3-4: *bwrḫm wrḫm bʿbrs¹ bd ʾwrḫn wḫrwfn*
"month by month on his terraced field in the succession of months and years"
(by-month month on-his-terraced-field series [of] months and-years)

subst.² *tbdd* Q 695/3
PAYMENT [See Beeston, 1976, 420. It may also be understood in the sense "division," with which cf. Ar *badda* "to divide, separate."]
Q 695/3: *wʾḫḏ tbdd ʾrḍn*
"payment for the land has been received"

BḎL
verb *bḏl* Q 79/5, Q 202/5
TO ENTRUST, DELIVER [Cf. Ar *baḏala* "to give, deliver," Sab *bḏlm* "concessionary *document*"]
Q 202/5-6: *wbḏl wflṭ nfs¹s¹ wqnys¹ lydʿʾb*
"he entrusted and delivered himself and his possessions to YDʿʾB"

BḎR
subst. *bḏr* Q 687/8
FIELD, ARABLE LAND [Cf. Ar *baḏara* "to sow"]
Q 687/8-9: *ʿlbḏr ʾḫyr s³md hwyḫr*
"near the field of the elite of the dignitaries of HWYḪR"
(near-the-field [of] the-elite [of] the-dignitaries [of] HWYḪR)

BHṮ
subst. *bhṯ* Q 40/23
ANNOUNCEMENT [RÉS VI, 233, compares the Ar verb *baṯṯa* "to promulgate, to proclaim"; the *h* is seen as being intrusive, a phenomenon which occurs in Min.]
Q 40/23: *wʿtlyw ʾs¹dm ʿlmw bḏn fthn ʾs¹m ʾs¹m bhṯ ḏmrs¹*
"those who have signed this decree have each seen to the promulgation of its correct reading"
(and-they-supervised who signed in-this decree man man the-announcement [of] its-correct-reading)

BWḤ
subst. *bḥtn* Q 656/3
PLACE, SPOT [Cf. Ar *bāḥa* "open court, space between the walls of a house"]
Q 656/1-4: *ʾs¹lbm ḏʾbʿly tḥḏr bḏt bḥtn*

(BWḤ)

"ʾS¹LBM Ḏū ʾBʿLY was present in this place"

BZR

subst. pl. *bzrtm* Q 186B/3 (Beeston, 1959, 8, posits the form *bzwrtm* on the basis of the pl. form *fʿwlt*)

SEED [Cf. Ar *bizra* "seed"]

Q 186B/2-4: *ʾl byʿdwn nʿmt bz[w]rtm bʿlw ms²ṭm*

"they will not calculate 'seed privileges' on merchandise"

(not they-will-calculate benefits [of] seeds on merchandise)

BḤT

subst. sing. *bḥt* Q 1/5, Q 898/3; *bḥtm* Q 168/2; *bḥtn* Q 8/4, Q 89.142, Q 90/3; dl. *bḥty* Q 167/2-3

(PHALLUS?) VOTIVE OBJECT [Sab *bḥt* "votive object (phallus ?)." See the discussion of this word by Ghul, 1959, 17-19, who renders *bḥt* "phallus." RÉS VIII, 174, notes that the fundamental sense of *bḥt* is "pure, unmixed," which may be compared with Ar *baḥt* which means "pure, unmixed," approximating the Heb *ṭahōr* "pure," which also has the meaning "pure offering" and "pure vessel." The term *bḥt* may have undergone the same semantic development from "pure">"pure offering" (i.e., offering made of pure material).]

A) Q 90/1-3: *ʿqrbm grbyn ʿbd ʾbʾns¹ bn ʿsbm s¹qny ʿm ryʿn bḥtn*

"ʿQRBM GRBYN servant of ʾBʾNS¹ son of ʿS³BM dedicated this votive object to ʿAmm RYʿN"

(ʿQRBM GRBYN servant [of] ʾBʾNS¹ son [of] ʿS³BM dedicated [to] ʿAmm RYʿN the-votive-object)

B) Q 167/2-3: *wbḥty blqm*

"and two votive objects of limestone"

BYN I

verb *ybnwn* Q 186C/9-10

TO KEEP APART [Sab *ybnnn* "to intervene, separate *boundary*," Ar *bāna* "to be separated," Eth *bayyana* "to consider, discern, distinguish," Heb *bîn* "to discern"]

Q 186C/6-10: *wklḏw bys²ṭ kl ms²ṭm bs²mr blyl ybnwn lyṣbḥ*

"and everyone who sells any merchandise in S²MR at night shall keep his distance until morning"

(and-all-who sell any merchandise in-S²MR at-night they-shall-keep-apart until-it-dawns)

BYN II

prep. *byn* Q 183/3; *bynhtys^{1}m* Q 40/6

BETWEEN [Sab *byn* "between, among," Ar *bayna*, Heb *bên*, Akk *ina bīri, ina bīrīt* id.]

Q 183/3: *bywm kwn ḍr byn s^{2}mr ḏrydn wby[n] ʾbʾns^1*

"on the day that there was war between S^{2}MR Ḏū Raydan and between ʾBʾNS^1"

(on-the-day was war between S^{2}MR Ḏū-Raydan and-betwe[en] ʾBʾNS^1)

BYT

subst. sing. *byt* Q 35/6, Q 36/4, Q 66/11, Q 68/8, Q 80/5, Q 173/1-2, Q 269/1, Q 500/1, Q 856/3+; *bytn* Q 112/2, Q 177/4, Q 203/2, 4, Q 254/1, 3, 5, Q 265/3, Q 569/3, Q 838/2; *byts^1* Q 82/2-3, Q 99/3, Q 167/3, Q 186B/12, Q 264/3, Q 266/2, Q 844/5-6, Q 878/2, 909/1; *bythw* Q 265/2; *byts^{1}my* Q 101/1-2, Q 860/2; *bythmy* Q 790/2; *byts^{1}m* Q 100/3; dl. *bytw* Q 74/6 (2x); pl. *ʾbyt* Q 40/12, Q 74/5 (2x), 8(2x), 9(2x); *ʾbytn* Q 243/3, 5, 8, Q 679/5; *ʾbyts^{1}m* Q 40/20, Q 489/3; *ʾbythmw* Q 611/4

1) HOUSE; ESTATE [Sab *byt* "house, estate," Ar *bayt* "house, building," Heb *bayiṯ* "house, home, family," *bītu* "house"]

A) Q 74/6: *rbᶜ bytw ḏdkrn*

"a fourth of the two houses of the clan of ḎKRN"

B) Q 101/1-2: *ʾyhr wṯwbʾl ḏrḥn brʾw byts^{1}my gs^{2}mm*

"ʾYHR and ṮWBʾL ḎRḤN have built their[dl.] house GS^{2}MM"

2) HOUSEHOLD

Q 167/1: *[ ]s^{2}m ḏt byt ḥys^{1}n ʾmt nb[…*

"[..]S^{2}M of the household of ḤYS^{1}N, maidservant of NB[…]"

3) TEMPLE [Cf. Heb *bēṯ YHWH* for the temple in Jerusalem, Ar *bayt ʾAllāh* for the "Kaᶜba"]

A) Q 856/3: *wkl mhlk wḥdṯn byt wdm*

"and the whole reconstruction and renovation of the temple of WDM"

(and-all the-reconstruction and-the-renovation [of] the-temple [of] WDM)

B) Q 36/4: *wbny ws^{1}ḥdṯ byt wdm*

"and he built and newly constructed the temple of WDM"

BKL

subst. *bkl* Q 899/1; *bkls^{1}m* Q 183/5, Q 254/4, 6

(BKL)

DEPENDENT, SUBJECT, RESIDENT [Cf. Sab *bkl* "settlers, colonists, inhabitants." See J. Ryckman's discussion on the position and character of the *bkl* (1967, 271).]

Q 183/4-5: *rṯd bs²mm ʾḏns¹ … [w]kl bkls¹m*

"and he entrusted to BS²MM his household … [and] all his dependents"

BKR

subst. *bkr* Q 35/2, Q 80/2, Q 769/1a

FIRSTBORN [Sab *bkr* "firstborn," Ar *bikr*, Heb *bəḵôr*, Eth *bakʷr*, Syr *būḵrā*, Akk *bukru*, Soq *békir* id.]

Q 35/1-2: *s²hr hll […] bn ydʿʾb mkrb qtbn bkr ʾnby*

"S²HR HLL […] son of YDʿʾB *mkrb* of Qataban the firstborn of ʾAnbay"

BLQ

subst. *blq* Q 80/6; *blqm* Q 167/3; *blqn* Q 1/5, Q 916/3; *blqs¹* Q 769/2a

LIMESTONE, MARBLE [Sab *blq* "limestone"; cf. Ar *balaq* "speckled marble," Eth *balaq* "marble," ModYem *balag* "the white or yellowish sandstone used for most ESA inscriptions"; see also Rossi, 1940, 301.]

Q 1/5: *bḥt blqn*

"a votive object of limestone"

BLT I

adj. *bltn* Q 40/4, 6, 9

AGREEABLE, FAITHFUL to a directive [Cf. Ar *baluta* "to be courageous, stout-hearted"]

Q 40/4: *ḫlṣmʾy ws³nḥm wbltn*

"in sincerity, with goodwill, and agreeably"

BLT II

prep. *blty* Q 186A/16

WITHOUT [Cf. Heb *biltî* "not, except," Ph *blt* "only," Soq *bal*, *bilā* "without," Ar *bilā* "without," Eth *ʾenbala* "without, except for, excepting." For a discussion of words having the sense "without" which are associated with the root BLW, see D. Cohen, 1970, 70.]

Q 186A/16: *blty ʿhr s²mr*

"without (the interference of) the overseer of S²MR"

BN I

prep. *bn* Q 1/3(2x), Q 35/8, Q 66/6, Q 67/1, 2, 13, Q 89.129/2, Q 177/3, Q 490A/3, Q 495/5, Q 497/4(2x), Q 899/2+

FROM, OUT OF, FROM AMONG [Beeston, 1962b, 57, does not believe that *bn* is etymologically related to the Ar *min*; rather he views it as an enlargement of the prep. *b* with the encl. suf. *n*.]

local:

Q 899/2: *bn s²rs¹n ʿd frʿm*

"from the foundation to the top"

temporal:

Q 66/6: *bn s²hr wrḫn ḏtmnʿ*

"from the new moon of the month Ḏū Timnaʿ"

exclusive or prohibitive:

A) Q 495/5: *rṯdw ʾṣlms¹m bn mnkrm*

"they have entrusted [to ʾAnbay] their statues to protect them from whoever would alter them"

(they-have-entrusted their-statues from one-who alters)

B) Q 497/3-4: *rṯdt ṣlmts¹ bn ms¹nkrm bn brṯs¹*

"she has entrusted her statue [to ʾAnbay] from whoever would remove it from its place"

(she-entrusted her-female-statue from one-who-removes from its-place)

origin:

Q 67/1-2: *ṣry ws¹fḥ bn ḥṭbm mḥrm ʿm*

"[S²HR HLL] decided and made public from (i.e., at the instigation of) ḤṬBM, the sanctuary of ʿAmm"

(he-decided and-making-public from ḤṬBM the-sanctuary [of] ʿAmm)

partitive:

Q 490A/3-4: *wkwn lʾs²hrm bn ḏt qbrn wms³wds¹ wnfs¹hs¹yw s²lṯt ʾḫms¹m wl s²krm ws²ʿbm ṯnw ḫms¹myw*

"three-fifths of this tomb and its outer chamber and interior belong to ʾS²HRM and two-fifths to S²KRM and S²ʿBM"

(and-was to-ʾS²HRM from this tomb and-its-outer-chamber and-its-inner-chambers three fifths and-to S²KRM and-S²ʿBM two fifths)

privative:

Q 67/4-5: *bn s¹nṣfm ws¹kt wʾḫḏ wgddm*

"without any falling short, ceasing, detraction, or termination"

prep. + prep. *bnḥg* Q 79/5

ACCORDING TO [comp. of the prep. *bn* and the prep. *ḥg*]

Q 79/5: *bnḥg ḏn ḥgrn wḥrmnn*

(BN I)

"according to this directive and inviolable law"

conj. *bnkm* Q 66/3

SINCE (in temporal sense) [comp. of the prep. *bn* and *km*]

Q 66/3-4: *bnkm bynft ʿdkm bys¹fd ḫr[f]myw*

"since he was proclaimed until he completes two years"

(since he-is-proclaimed until he-finishes two-years)

adv. *bnkn* Q 40/11, 16

(in the expression *bnkn lʾḫr*): HENCEFORTH [comp. of the prep. *bn* and adv. *kn*]

Q 40/11: *bnkn lʾḫr*

"henceforth"

(from-thus to-after)

prep. + prep. *bnʿlw* Q 40/12, 19-20, 20, Q 844/7-8; *bn ʿlw* 695/8

ON, UPON [comp. of the prep. *bn* and *ʿlw*]

Q 40/19-20: *bnʿlw mqmhs¹m wbnʿlw ʾbyts¹m wbnʿlw bns¹m wbnts¹m*

"on their property and on their houses and on their son and daughter"

[on their-property and-on their-houses and-on their-son and-their-daughter]

prep. + prep. *bn ʿm* Q 74/5, 6, Q 186A/21, B/21

WITH [comp. of the prep. *bn* and *ʿm*]

Q 186A/20-21: *wl ys²tyṭwn qtbn bn ʿm ʾs²ʿbm*

"the Qatabanians may trade with the tribes"

(and-let trade the-Qatabanians with the-tribes)

prep. + prep. *bn tḥt* Q 40/2, Q 66/9, Q 67/2, Q 68/2, Q 69/2

FROM [comp. of the prep. *bn* and *tḥt*; Q 40/2 is emended in RÉS VII, 220]

Q 67/2: *wbn tḥt s²ms¹*

"from (i.e., at the behest of) S²MS¹"

BN II

subst.[1] sing./dl./pl. *bn* Q 37/1+; *bns¹* Q 231/1, Q 239/1, Q 483/4, Q 771/3, Q 860/1, Q 898/5, 6, Q 906/6; *bns¹ww* Q 100/1, Q 261/3, Q 489/2, Q 898/10; *bnhw* Q 1/8, Q 112/3, Q 178/4, Q 688/1, Q 839/3; *bns¹my* Q 102/2, Q 244/1, Q 246/1, Q 487/3, Q 840/7; *bns¹m* Q 40/20, Q 69/4, Q 70/1, 2, Q 183/5, Q 243/3, Q 245/2, Q 840/1; dl. *bnw* Q 102/8, Q 254/9, Q 551/1(2x) , Q 677/6, Q 806/1, Q 839/3, Q 858/1, Q 900/1, Q 903/1; *bny* Q 551/5, Q 676/2, Q 678/1; *bnwy* Q 68/2, 3; *bnyhw* Q 551/4; *bnys¹my* Q 806/3; pl. *bnw* Q 65, Q 74/7(2x), 8, 9(2x), Q 89.147, Q 100/2, Q 102/2, Q 679/2(2x), Q 839/3; *bny* Q 688/5-6, Q 690a/6;

bnwhw Q 690a/5; *bnyhw* Q 551/3; *bnys¹m* Q 68/5, 6, Q 69/4-5, Q 70/3, Q 79/2; *bnyhmw* Q 200/2

1) SON [Sab *bn* "son," Ar *ibn*, Heb *bēn*, Akk *bin* id.]

A) Q 177/4-5: *wrwʾl ǵyln yhnʿm bn s²hr ygl yhrgb*
"WRWʾL ǴYLN YHNʿM the son of S²HR YGL YHRGB"

B) Q 856/1: *ydʿᵒb ḏbyn bn s²hr*
"YDʿᵒB ḎŪ BYN, son of S²HR"

2) MEMBER OF A FAMILY, CLAN, or TRIBE [Sab *bn* "member of a societal group, clan, or tribe."; cf. Ar *banū* as a marker of clan affiliation. According to Jamme, 1952a, 18-24, where there are two consecutive occurrences of *bn*, e.g., Q 551/2: *wdʾl wys¹rm bnw ʾbʾns¹ bnw mghmm* "WDʾL and YS¹RM, sons of ʾBʾNS¹ of (the family of) MGHMM," the first *bn* introduces the father, the second, the family.]

A) Q 74/7: *wrbʿ byt bnw nhrbt*
"and a fourth of the house of the Banū NHRBT"

B) Q 66/13: *wnbṭʿm bn ʾls¹mʿ bn hybr*
"and NBṬʿM the son of ʾLS¹Mʿ of the clan of HYBR"

subst.² sing. *bnt* Q 89.74, .78, .82, .89, .127, Q 106, Q 249/1, Q 556bis/1, Q 559/1, 3, Q 560/1; *bt* Q 543m/3; *btm* Q 913/1 *bnts¹* Q 492/1; *bnts¹m* Q 40/20; dl. *bnty* Q 249/2, Q 556bis/2, Q 557/2, Q 560/3; pl. *bntys¹m* Q 68/5

DAUGHTER [Sab *bnt* "daughter," Ar *bint* id., but see W. Müller, 1974a, 145, 147-48, for a discussion of Q 556bis-560, who prefers the sense "Gabe"]

A) Q 89.74: *ʾfḍty bnt klbm ḏʾbydʿ*
"ʾFḌTY daughter of KLBM of (the clan of) ʾBYDʿ"

B) Q 68/5: *wtʾnṯs¹m wbnys¹m wbntys¹m*
"and their female relatives and their sons and their daughters"

BNY

verb *bny* Q 36/4, Q 80/5, Q 203/1, Q 265/1, Q 556/1, Q 694/8, Q 696/2, Q 700/2, 4, 5, Q 769/1b, Q 915/1; *bnyw* Q 486/4, Q 490A/2, B/2, Q 874/2-3, Q 899/2

TO BUILD, CONTRUCT; TO REBUILD, RECONSTRUCT [Sab *bny* "to build, construct," *banā* (y), Heb *bānāh* id., Akk *banū* "to build, create, bring forth"]

A) Q 769/1b-2a: *bny ws¹ḥdṯ kl mbny wmhlk [ḫ]lfn ḏs³dw*
"[(S²)HR ǴYLN] built and newly constructed the whole construction and building of the gate of S³DW"

B) Q 899/2: *bnyw wʿly ws¹ḥdṯ qbrhmw*
"[ʾWS¹ʾL and MʿN] built, raised, and newly constructed their burial-place"

(BNY)

subst.[1] *bn*ʾ Q 720/2

BUILDING [Jamme, 1972, 36, compares Ḥaḍ *hbn*ʾ in RÉS 2687/2; cf. Ar *binā*ʾ id.

Q 720/2: *kl bn*ʾ *wmḥfd wḫlf*

"every building and tower and gate"

subst.[2] *mbny* Q 39/2, Q 76/1, Q 80/6, Q 112/2, Q 131/2, Q 769/1b, Q 770/3, Q 899/5: *mbnys¹m* Q 73/2

(ACT OF) BUILDING, CONSTRUCTION; (ACT OF) REBUILDING, RECONSTRUCTION [Sab *mbny* "*act of* building, construction"]

Q 899/5: *tqdmw mhlk wmbny qbrn*

"[ʾS¹LMM and ḎYMM and ʾWS¹N] directed the construction and the building of this burial-place"

BNN

verb *ybnnn* Q 839/3

TO SET, ESTABLISH [Cf. Ar *banna* "to stop, halt"]

Q 839/3: *ʾwṯn ybnnn bynht*

"limits which are set in YNHT"

(limits they-are-established in-YNHT)

BNT

subst. *bntm* Q 67/5, Q 68/4, Q 69/3, Q 70/2

AFFILIATION, FRIENDSHIP [Beeston, 1971b, 9, posits a relationship between this vocable and BN II.]

Q 67/5: *lʿṣm wdm wbntm ws²ftm lʿm wʾṯrt*

"[S²HR YGL has promulgated the formation of] a patronage-tie of friendship, affiliation, and protection to ʿAmm and ʾAṯirat"

BʿW

verb *bʿ[w]* Q 172/4 (according to Höfner, 1935, 32, the restoration of final *w* is certain)

TO ATTACK a fortified place [Sab *bʿw* "to overcome *an enemy*, to assault *an enemy position*"; cf. Ar *baʿā* (w) "to commit a crime, behave unjustly"]

Q 172/4-5: *wbḏt mtʿs¹ ʿm bʾywm bʿ[w] wdmr ʾbʿm bn mʿhr hgrn*

"and since ʿAmm saved him in the days when ʾBʿM the son of MʿHR attacked and destroyed the town"

(and-since saved-him ʿAmm in-the-days attacked and-destroying ʾBʿM the-son [of] MʿHR the-town)

BˁL

subst.[1] sing. *bˁl* Q 35/5, 8, Q 80/4, Q 254/8, Q 681/2, 4, Q 904/2, Q 905/1, 6, Q 906/5, Q 910/2, Q 915/2; pl. *ʾbˁl* Q 72/2, 6, Q 218/2, Q 611/3, Q 679/5, Q 902

(DIVINE) LORD; OWNER [Sab *bˁl* "*divine* lord, owner, " Heb *baˁal*, Akk *bēlu* id., Ar *baˁl* "lord, husband"]

A) Q 35/7-8: *ʾnby bˁl ḥgn*

"ʾAnbay, lord of the pilgrimage"

B) Q 72/1-2: *s²ˁbn qtbn wḏˁls³n wmˁnn wḏˁṯtm ʾbˁl ẓrwb ˁdw s³dw*

"[S²HR HLL proclaimed a law to] the tribe of Qataban, Maˁin, Ḏū ˁLS³N, and Ḏū ˁṮTM, owners of the fields in S³DW"

subst.[2] *bˁlt* Q 239/6

LADY, MISTRESS

Q 239/6: *[ws²m]s¹s¹my bˁlt [...]*

"and their[dl.] sun deity the mistress of [...]"

BḌˁ

subst. sing. *bḍˁ* Q 74/11(3x), 13, Q 611/2, Q 694/10, Q 909/2; *bḍˁs¹* Q 186C /14; pl. *ʾbḍˁhmw* Q 74/2

(TRIBUTARY) TERRITORY [Sab *bḍˁ* "tributary territory *of a town*." Pirenne, 1971, 128, however, sees Q 694/10 as a verb, which she renders "to be clear, plain," with which she compares Ar *baḍḍaˁa* "to make one clearly understand a word or speech."]

A) Q 74/1-2: *whgrhmw wmnḫlhmw wʾrḍhmw wʾbḍˁhmw*

"their town and their palmgroves and their land and their tributary territories"

B) Q 74/11: *wʾrbˁ ʾnḫlm bbḍˁ hgrn*

"and four palmgroves in the territory of the town"

BQL

verb *bql* Q 73/1, 2-3, Q 611/1; *bqlw* Q 679/7

TO PLANT, CULTIVATE [Sab *bql* "to plant," Ar *baqala* "to sprout," ModYem *baggal* "to plant seedlings at a distance from each other for better development" (cf. Rossi, 1940, 301), Eth *baqʷala* "to sprout, grow"]

Q 73/2-3: *wgrb wbql wrʾb bs¹rs¹ ḏrbḍt*

"and he constructed terraces and planted and harvested in his valley Ḏū RBḌT"

(and-he-constructed-terraces and-planting and-harvesting in-his-valley Ḏū-RBḌT)

subst.[1] *bqlm* Q 73/3, Q 694/8, 11, 695/5, 7; *bqlk* Q 687/5;

(BQL)

1) PLANTING

Q 695/5-7: *wl yḥrm ʾẖr wbrm bn ws³f bʿlw bn tqbln kl ḥrṯm ʾw tbqlm*

"it is forbidden that ʾẖR and BRM be enlarged beyond these dimensions by any cultivation or planting"

(and-let be-forbidden ʾẖR and-BRM from enlargement over from this-dimension any cultivation or planting)

2) FIELD, PLOT OF LAND

Q 687/5: *bqlk nʿmn*

"this field NʿMN"

3) *BQL*, unit of measure [See Beeston, 1976, 420-21]

Q 695/4-5: *wkwn tqbl kl ʾrḍn kwḥd mṯmn wmfẓr ws²lṯy bqlm ws¹bʿt wʿs²ry ʾqblm*

"the size of the whole land together in value and extent is thirty *bql* and twenty-seven *qbl*"

(and-is the-dimension [of] all the-land together value and-extent both-thirty *bql* and-seven and-twenty *qbl*)

subst.² *tbqlm* Q 695/7; *tbqlhmw* Q 690a/8

FIELD

Q 690a/8: *wtbqlhmw nqrn*

"and their field NQRN"

BQR

verb *bqr* Q 73/1, Q 181/2, Q 700/3

1) TO PLOW [Cf. Sab *bqr* "to dig up, level fields," Ar *baqara* "to open wide, to split" MSA *baqara* "to dig up, level *fields*"]

Q 73/1: *ǵlbm [ ]yb bn dws¹m bn qs³mm ṣyr wbqr wgrb wbql ws¹qḥ kl ʾs¹rrs¹ wgrwbs¹*

"ǴLBM [ ]YB the son of DWS¹M of the clan QS³M M embanked, plowed, terraced, cultivated, and set all his valleys and terraces in order"

(ǴLBM [ ]YB the-son [of] DWS¹M [of] the-clan [of] QS³MM embanked and-plowing and-terracing and-cultivating and-setting-in-order all his-valleys and-his-terraces)

2) TO WIDEN

Q 700/3: *wbqr mʾtws¹yw ǵyln wys¹rn*

"he widened its two channels ǴYLN and YS¹RN"

BRʾ

verb *brʾ* Q 99/2, Q 100/2, Q 179/1, Q 268/1, Q 857/1; *brʾw* Q 101/1, Q 102/2, Q 177/2, Q 678/2, Q 679/6, Q 790/1, Q 860/2, Q 914/1-2

TO BUILD, CONSTRUCT [Sab *brʾ* id.; cf. also Ar *barā* (y) "to form, fashion," and Heb *bārāʾ* "to shape, create"]

Q 101/1-2: *ʾyhr wṯwbʾl ḏrḥn brʾw byts¹my gs²mm*

"ʾYHR and ṮWBʾL ḎRḤN have built their[dl.] house GS²MM"

subst. *brʾn* Q 688/3

CONSTRUCTION

Q 688/2-3: *kbr nhmn wbrʾn wmgyrtn*

"[HWFᶜM ʾWLṬ] directed the dressing of the stone and the construction and the plastering"

(he-directed the-dressing-of-the-stone and-the-construction and-the-plastering)

BRK

subst. pl. *brʾkh* Q 687/3

CISTERN [Sab *brkt* "cistern," Ar *birka* "cistern, pond," Heb *bərēḵāh* "pond," Ug *brky* "puddle, pool"]

Q 687/2-3: *s¹wr bnʾ mʾgl ms¹qt gḏ wbrʾkh ʾn*

"[the dignitaries of S¹ᶜDM YHS¹KR] built a wall around BNʾ, the irrigation cistern of GḎ, and its (supporting) cisterns here"

(built-a-wall-around BNʾ the-cistern [of] irrigation [of] GḎ and-its-cisterns here)

BRR

verb *brr* Q 36/3, Q 176/5

TO DIG [Cf. Eth *barara* "to penetrate, perforate"]

Q 36/3-4: *mḫḍ wbrr wwzl wṣll mnqln mblqt ʾs¹n brm wḥrb*

"[YDᶜB Dū BYN] hewed out, dug up, smoothed, and paved the mountain pass road MBLQT between BRM and ḤRB"

(he-hewed-out and-digging-up and-smoothing and-paving the-mountain-pass-road MBLQT between BRM and-ḤRB)

subst. *br* Q 40/8, Q 135/1

PLAIN [Sab *br* "open country, plain," Ar *barr* "country, field." See Beeston, 1954, 320, who argues that *brm* in Q 186A/4 may be understood "as a quasi-proper name applying to the open parts of the lower Wādī Baiḥān."]

Q 135/1: *br nḫlšm*

"the plain of their palmgrove"

BRṮ

subst. sing. *brṯm* Q 78/6(2x); *brṯn* Q 67/12, Q 83/4; *brṯs¹* ; Q 9/2, Q 77/4, Q 83/6-7, Q 89.140/6, Q 183/6, Q 201/3, Q 244/15, Q 245/3, Q 254/7, Q

(BRṮ)

256/8-9, Q 497/4, Q 681/6, Q 905/7; pl. *ʾbrṯs¹m* Q 73/6; *ʾbrṯs¹n* Q 244/14, Q 246/13

PLACE [Sab *brṯ* "place, location, site"; cf. also Jamme, 1952a, 199, who compares the Ar *barṯ* "soft earth." Beeston, 1981, 67, notes a possible semantic development in this word "place">"proper place/function" and compares the English word "place" which can have both senses, although he says with regard to J. Ryckmans' interpretation of *brṯ* in Q 83/6-7 as "role, function" that it "is acceptable as an alternative to simple 'place, locality' though there does not seem to me to be any cogent reason for regarding it as positively preferable." See also Beeston, 1976, 408, and Pirenne, CIAS 1:153-54, who gives the meaning "progéniture" for Q 244/14.]

Q 497/3-4: *rṯdt ṣlmts¹ bn ms¹nkrm bn brṯs¹*

"she has entrusted her statue [to ʾAnbay] from whoever would remove it from its place"

(she-entrusted her-female-statue from one-who-removes from its-place)

BTL

subst. *btln* Q 40/1, 2, 10, 13, 14, 15, Q 78/2

BTL, class or social group [According to Rhodokanakis, 1924, 37-38, the *btl*, as well as the *fqḍ*, belong to the *ṭbn* or "the people" as opposed to the *ms³wd* or "lords"]

Q 40/14-15: *kl ʾfṯḥm wmḥrtm wʾṯftm wẖwlltm fṯḥw ws¹ḥr wṯfṭ ws¹ṯb ws¹ẖl qtbn ms³wdn wfqḍtn wbtln*

"all orders, directives, decisions, and regulations which the Qatabanian lords-in-council and the *fqḍ* and the *btl* have ordered, directed, decided, determined, and regulated"

(all orders and-directives and-decisions and-regulations [which] they-ordered and-directing and-deciding and-determining and-regulating the-Qatabanians the-lords-in-council and-the-*fqḍ* and-the-*btl*)

G

GBʾ

verb *ygbʾ* Q 74/4-5

TO RETURN [Sab *gbʾ*, Eth *gabʾa* id.]

Q 74/4-5: *wygbʾ wh[t]b yḏmrmlk ʾbyt wʾrḍty wʾqny qtbn bn ʿm ḏbḥn*

"and YḎMRMLK will return and gi[ve] over the houses and lands and possessions of Qataban from ḎBḤN"

(and-will-return and-give-over YḎMRMLK the-houses and-the-lands and-the-possessions [of] Qataban from with ḎBḤN)

GBḎ

verb *ygbḏ* Q 694/10

TO DESTROY [Sab *gbḏ* "to ravage"]

Q 694/10: *lygbḏ wwḍʾ ḥrts¹n wʾwwds¹n*

"[it is forbidden] that one destroy and damage their irrigation canals or their retaining walls"

(that-one-destroys and-damaging their-irrigation-canals or-their-retaining-walls)

GBL

subst. *gblt* Q 839/4

TERRITORY, REGION [Sab *gblt* "cultivated land," Heb *gəḇūl* "territory, boundary," Ph *gbl* "territory, boundary"

Q 839/4: *wb[ʾ]rḍ wgblt [...]*

"and in the [l]and and territory of [...]"

GDD

s¹-prfx. *s¹gdd* Q 70/1(2x), 2

TO RENEW; TO VALIDATE [Cf. Ar jaddada "to renew," and the discussion of this root in the ESA dialects by Lundin, 1987, 51-53, who compares the custom of renewing edicts and decrees in the ancient world. For the other possible sense of the root, "to validate," cf. Sab *hgdd* "to enforce, validate."]

Q 70/1-2: *s²hr hll mlk qtbn s¹gdd lʾdms¹ ʾrby ʿm ḏlbḥ wl bns¹m wtʾnṯs¹m ḥg ṣrytm wgdytm wmḥrtm ṣry w[s¹]ḥr ws¹[g]dd ls¹m wl bns¹m wtʾnṯs¹m ʾmlk qtbn*

(GDD)

"S²HR HLL the king of Qataban has renewed for his subjects the *ʾrby* of ʿAmm Ḏū Labaḫ and for their sons and female relatives according to the decree and decision and directive which the former kings of Qataban decreed, [or]dered, and [de]cided for them and their sons and female relatives"
(S²HR HLL the-king [of] Qataban he-has-renewed for-his-subjects the-*ʾrby* [of] ʿAmm Ḏū-Labaḫ and-for their-sons and-their-female-relatives according-to the-decree and-the-decision and-the-directive [which] they-decreed and-[or]dering and-[de]ciding for-them and-for their-son and-their-female-relatives the-kings [of] Qataban)

subst. *gddm* Q 67/5, Q 68/4, Q 69/3

TERMINATION [Cf. Ar *jadda* "to cut off, Heb *gāḏaḏ* id., Akk *gadādu* "to separate." The root GDD in this sense has perhaps undergone the semantic development "cutting off, separation">"termination."]

Q 67/4-5: *bn s¹nṣfm ws¹kt wʾḫḏ wgddm*
"without any falling short, ceasing, detraction, or termination"

GDY

subst. *gdytm* Q 70/1, 2; *gdytn* Q 243/1, 6, 8, 10

RENEWAL [Lundin, 1987, 52, gives the meaning "renewal" for *gdyt* which, according to him, may be seen as "a special noun form ending in *-yt* from geminated verbs." According to W. Müller, 1962, 38: "*die Wurzel* gdy *ist eine Nebenform zu* gdd *mit der gleichen Bedeutung.*" Höfner, 1987, 41, understands the word as "*Verleihung* (*von Landbesitz*)," with which cf. Sab *gdyt* "grant *of property.*"]

Q 70/1-2: *ḥg ṣrytm wgdytm wmḥrtm ṣry w[s¹]hr ws¹[g]dd ls¹m*
"according to the decree, renewal, and directive which they decreed, [re]newed, and [de]cided for them"
(according-to the-decree and-the-renewal and-the-directive [which] they-decreed and-[re]newing and-[de]ciding for-them)

GWY

subst. *gw* Q 40/1, 13

BODY, GROUP [Sab *gwm* "community, group," Heb *gôy* "troop, crowd, people," Ph *gw* "community, body, group"]

Q 40/13: *wys¹ṯb s²hr wqtbn ms³wdn gw qhlm wfqḍtn wbtln*
"and (which) S²HR and the Qatabanian lords-in-council as a body and the *fqḍ* and *btl* will decree"
(and-will-decree S²HR and-the-Qatabanians the-lords-in-council [as] body [of] assembly and-the-*fqḍ* and-the-*btl*)

GWL

subst.^{1} *glm* Q 99/6, Q 100/4, Q 265/4 Q 266/3, Q 268/2, Q 478/2, Q 556/2, Q 700/3, Q 770/5, Q 790/3, Q 860/4, Q 874/3, Q 899/3, Q 903/3; *gls^1* Q 82/6; *gls^{1}m* Q 82/5-6

ENTIRETY; (used adverbially): ENTIRELY, IN ITS ENTIRETY [Cf. Sab *gl* "entirety" and Ar verb *jāla*(w) "to go around, enclose." It could also, however, be understood as semantically equivalent to Sab *glm*, *gwlm*, which is used in an adverbial sense, "with full ownership rights"; cf. also Ar *jawl* "enclosed property," Eth *g^{w}elt* "estate or other object transferred for use and enjoyment." J. Ryckmans, 1965, 273, compares Heb *gāʾal* "redeem free from obligation," and translates Sab *gwl* as "property so redeemed and held."]

Q 99/2-4, 5-6: *brm s^{2}ʾm wqny wbrʾ wẓrb byts^1 mrdʿm wʾḫṭbs^1 ... kls^{1}m glm*

"[... (son of) FLS^{1}ʾB] purchased, acquired, and constructed, and took possession of his house MRDʿM and its lower stories ... all of them in their entirety"

(BRM he-purchased and-acquiring and-building and-taking-possession-of his-house MRDʿM and-its-lower-stories ... all-of-them entirely)

subst.^{2} dl. *gwly* Q 687/6

PROPERTY, PLAIN, FIELD [Cf. discussion under *gwl* above, and cf. also Ar *jūla, majāl* "plain."]

Q 687/6: *bknf gwly ḥṣdnn*

"at the edge of the two fields of ḤṢDNN"

GZM

verb *gzm* Q 40/5; *gzmw* Q 40/13

TO REGULATE, DECIDE [Sab *gzm* "to swear *an oath;* to conclude a *pact.*" Cf. Eth *gazama* "to cut down (a tree); to fell" and Ar *jazama* "to cut, split." There may be here a semantic development of "to cut">"to decide; to allot"]

Q 40/5-6: *wʾy gzm wgtzm bḏtw gzwm bynhtys^{1}m*

"and whatever they decide and determine among themselves with regard to these regulations"

(and-whatever decide and-determining on-these regulations among-themselves

s^1-prfx. *s^{1}gzmw* Q 40/13

TO CAUSE TO DECIDE

Q 40/12-13: *kl ˣḏb wdyn wtwṭf gzwmm gzmw ws^{1}gzmw bs^{1}myt mqmnyhn wʾtmtnyhn*

(GZM)

"all punishments, judgments, and the carrying out of decisions which they have made and caused to make in those two meetings and assemblies"

(all punishments and-judgments and-the-carrying-out [of] the-decisions they-have-made and-they-have-caused-to-make in-those two-meetings and-two-assemblies)

t-infix *gtzm* Q 40/6

TO CONSIDER, DETERMINE

See entry under verb *gzm*.

subst. pl. *gzwm* Q 40/6; *gzwmm* Q 40/13

REGULATION, DECISION

See entry under verb *gzm*.

GZF

verb *bygzf* Q 186C/1-2

TO TRADE WHOLESALE [Sab *gzf* "to effect a *gzf* transaction with someone," Ar *jazafa* "to buy or sell something en bloc without weighing or measuring"]

Q 186C/1-2: *w[k]ld̲w b[y]gzf ms²ṭm b[y]s²t̲*

"everyone who deals wholesale in merchandise"

GYR

subst. *mgyrtn* Q 688/3

PLASTERING [Sab *gyr* "plaster," Ar *jayr* "plaster, lime," Heb *gīr* "lime, plaster," Aram *gīrā* "birdlime, plaster"; cf. Eth *gayara* "to whitewash"]

Q 688/2-3: *kbr nhmn wbrʾn wmgyrtn*

"[HWFʿM ʾWLṬ] directed the dressing of the stone and the construction and the plastering"

(he-directed the-dressing-of-the-stone and-the-construction and-the-plastering)

GLB

subst. *glbm* (corrected from the attested form *ggbm*) Q 35/8-9

ADVERSITY (?); HUNGER (?) [Cf. Ar *julba*, "bad year; adversity; attack," Ar *jalaba* "to attack," and see Jamme, 1972, 63]

Q 35/1, 7-9: *s¹qny ʾnby bʿl ḥgn qnyhw bn glbm*

"[S²HR HLL] dedicated this property to ʾAnbay, lord of the festival, from adversity (?)"

GML

adj. *gmwln* Q 839/3

JOINED, UNITED; (adverbially): TOGETHER [Cf. Ar *jamal* "totality"]

Q 839/2-3: *wbnhw bnw ʿrgn gmwln*

"and his son(s), the Banū ʿRGN together"

GNʾ

subst. *gnʾ* Q 177/2

WALL [Sab *gnʾ* "wall." Perhaps related to Com. Sem. root GNN "to protect, defend."]

Q 177/3: *bs²hd gnʾ hgrs¹m hrbt*

"before the wall of their town HRBT"

GNN

verb *gnw* Q 679/9

TO CULTIVATE, GARDEN [Cf. Sab *gtnn* "to gather crops, harvest," and Ar *janā* (y) id.]

Q 679/9-10: *wʿḏbw ḥrt wynhmw ys²gb wgnw klhw*

"they repaired the aqueduct of their vineyard YS²GB and cultivated all of it"

(and-they-repaired the-aqueduct [of] their-vineyard YS²GB and-they-cultivated all-of-it)

subst. *gnn* Q 915/2

GARDEN [Cf. Ar *janna*, Heb *gān*, Ug *gn*, Akk *ganna* id.]

Q 915/1-2: *bny ws¹ḥdṯ tḥmy gnn s³dw lʿm ḏdwnm*

"[S²HR HLL YHNʿM] built and newly constructed the wall of the garden of S³DW for ʿAmm Ḏū DWNM"

(he-built and-newly-constructing the-wall [of] the-garden [of] S³DW for-ʿAmm Ḏū-DWNM)

GṢṢ

subst. pl. *mgṣt* Q 687/9

FLOCK [Jamme, 1971, 88, compares Ar *jaṣṣa* "to be tightly bound by fetters (said of livestock, cattle)"]

Q 687/9: *wmgṣt wʾzmt*

"flocks and herds"

GRB

verb *grb* Q 73/1, 2, Q 700/4

TO TERRACE [Sab *grb* "to lay out *fields* in terraces," ModḤaḍ *garb* "any field, cultivated or not, surrounded by a wall against torrents," Ar *jirba* "field prepared for sowing, or land cleared for sowing and planting," *jarīb* "cultivated land." Irvine, 1962, 161-62, gives a further discussion of this root.]

Q 73/1: *ǵlbm [ ]yb bn dws¹m bn qs³mm ṣyr wbqr wgrb wbql ws¹qḥ kl ʾs¹rrs¹ wgrwbs¹*

"ǴLBM [ ]YB the son of DWS¹M of the clan of QS³MM embanked, plowed, terraced, and cultivated, and set all his valleys and terraces in order"

(ǴLBM [ ]YB the-son [of] DWS¹M [of] the-clan [of] QS³MM embanked and-plowing and-terracing and-cultivating and-setting-in-order all his-valleys and-his-terraces)

subst.[1] pl. *grwbs¹* Q 73/1

TERRACE, TERRACED FIELD [See etymology above.]

See entry above.

subst.[2] *grbtn* Q 688/3

STEPPED INTERIOR FACING [In regard to Q 688/3, Ghul, 1959, 427, notes "the reference here is to the internal appearance of the tank or reservoir which resembles a flight of stairs"; cf. Höfner, 1943, 103, who translates *grbtn* "*Feldterrasse*," and Jamme, 1971, 88, "*terrassements*"]

Q 688/2-3: *kbr nhmn wbrʾn wmgyrtn wgrbtn*

"[HWFʿM ʾWLṬ] directed the dressing of the stone and the construction, plastering, and facing of the stepped interior"

(he-directed the-dressing-of-the-stone and-the-construction and-the-plastering and-the-facing-of-the-stepped-interior)

D

DWD

subst. *dd* Q 266/7

PATERNAL UNCLE [Heb *dôḏ* "uncle," Syr *dāḏā*, id., Akk *dādu* "beloved," Ḥar *ḥedēd, ḥedōd* "uncle," Meh *ḥedēd, ḥedōd* id., Śḥ *díd, edíd* id., Soq *dédoh* id.]

Q 266/7: *wb frʿkrb ḏḏrḥn dd wẖwl s²hr*

"and by FRᶜKRB, of the clan of ḎRḤN, paternal uncle and regent of S²HR"

DWR

verb *bydr* Q 72/4, 7

TO REFUSE [Cf. Ar *ʾadāra ᶜan* "to turn from." Further, see Rhodokanakis, 1922, 24.]

Q 72/4-6: *wʾy ʾy ʾs¹dm bydr ws¹ḫdᶜ bn wfr wᶜs²q … wl yhb ws¹twfy dwrn wms¹ḫdᶜn*

"and whatever man refuses and balks at plowing and tilling … shall give over and pay"

(and-whatever whatever man he-refuses and-balking at plowing and-tilling and-let he-gives-over and-paying the-refuser and-the-balker)

subst. *dwrn* Q 72/5-6

ONE WHO REFUSES

See entry above.

DYN

subst. *dyn* Q 40/12, 20

JUDGMENT, PUNISHMENT [Cf. Ar *dāna* (y) "to judge," Heb *dān*, Ug *dn*, Aram *dīn*, Akk *dānu*, Eth *dayyana* id. However, the meaning of the word might also be understood as "debt, obligation" and compared with Min *dyn* "to impose an obligation," Ar *dāna*(y) "to be indebted."]

Q 40/12-13: *kl ʾᶜḏb wdyn wtwṭf gzwmm*

"all punishments, judgments, and the carrying out of decisions"

(all punishments and-judgments and-the-carrying-out [of] the-decisions)

DMR

verb *dmr* Q 172/5

TO DESTROY [Cf. Ar *dammara* "to destroy (people)," Ḥar and Meh *demōr* id., ModYem *dāmir* "that which is destroyed"]

Q 172/4-5: *wbḏt mtᶜs¹ ᶜm bʾywm bᶜ[w] wdmr ʾbᶜm bn mᶜhr hgrn*

"and since ᶜAmm saved him in the days when ʾBᶜM the son of MᶜHR attacked and destroyed the town"

(and-since saved-him ᶜAmm in-the-days attacked and-destroying ʾBᶜM the-son [of] MᶜHR the-town)

DNẖ

subst. *dnẖk* Q 687/7

CHARGE (?), RESPONSIBILITY (?) [Cf. perhaps Ar *danaẖa* "to march slowly under the weight of a load"]

Q 687/7: *lys^{1}tq btʾẖr dnẖk zm ʾs^{1}rb wʾṯwr*

"after a delay let this charge (?), the herd of sheep and cattle, be given water to drink"

(let-be-given-water-to-drink after-a-delay this-charge the-herd [of] sheep and-cattle)

DRF

verb *drf* Q 898/8

TO SELECT [Ghul, 1959, 5, compares Ar *tarrafa* "to choose."]

Q 898/7-9: *wʾmrʾs^1 rs^{2}ww ywm drf wntṣf … ʾrb[ʿ]t wẖms^{1}y ẖrwf s^{1}tlwt*

"and his lords were paid their dues when he selected and paid out … fifty-four sheep for their bearing responsibility for (his) safety"

(and-his-lords they-were-paid when he-selected and-he-paid … four and-fifty sheep bearing-responsibility-for-safety)

Ḏ

Ḏ- I

rel. pro. sing. (also used for pl.) *ḏ-* Q 1/1 + *ḏm* Q 9/2 + *ḏt* Q 1/7 + *ḏtm* Q 40/16 + *ḏw* Q 19/1; dl. *ḏw* Q 487/1 + *ḏy* Q 690a/2; pl. *ʾl* Q 40/11; *ʾlht* Q 688/2; *ʾwlw* Q 186B/6; *ḏtw* Q 266/1 + *ʾlḏw* Q 186C/1; *ʾlḏy* Q 67/10

WHICH, WHO, THAT; HE (SHE) WHO, THAT WHICH; OF; OF THE FAMILY/CLAN OF [Sab *ḏ-* id. For a discussion of the morphology and syntax of the relative, see Beeston, 1962b, 48-50, and 1984, 66. According to Höfner, 1943, 51, the forms *ʾlḏw* and *ʾlḏy* are relatives, a combination of *ʾl* and *ḏ-*. However, Beeston, 1962b, 49, believes both forms are suspect.]

with expressed antecedent:

Q 40/21-22: *wl ys^{1}kn mnkṯs^1 ḥg ẓrʾs^1 ʾs^{1}mʿm ḏm ʿtlm bftḥn*

"and let the witnesses who have signed this order punish its violation according to his proclamation"

(and-let punish its-violation according-to his-proclamation the-witnesses who signed this-order)

with unexpressed antecedent:

A) Q 66/4-5: *wl yqny wṯʿd ḏm byḥrg ḏn ṣḥfn ... ʿs²r kl hnʾm wmwblm*

"let the one who administers this agreement acquire and enjoy ... a tenth of all crops watered by irrigation and by rain"

(and-let acquire and-enjoying he-who administers this agreement ... a-tenth [of] every irrigated-crop and-rain-watered-crop)

B) Q 265/5: *bḏt ṣntm wbḏt ẓhrn*

"by Ḏāt ṢNTM and by Ḏāt ẒHRN"

indicating clan or familial affiliation:

Q 677/1-2: *mwhbʾln ʾḥs²r ḏḥrmn nḥl ʾfrs¹n*

"MWHBʾLN ʾḤS²R of the clan of ḤRMN, commander of the cavalry"

in epithets of gods:

Q 67/2: *ʿm ḏdwnm*

"ʿAmm of DWNM"

prep. + pro. *bḏt, bḏtm, bḏtn*

See under B.

prep. + pro. *lḏt, lḏtm*

See under L.

Ḏ- II

dem. adj. *ḏn* Q 40/9 + *ḏt* Q 67/7 + dl. *ḏwy* Q 267; pl. *ḏtw* Q 40/21 + *ḏtn* Q 67/8 +

THIS; THESE [Sab *ḏ-*, id. See Beeston, 1962b, 47-48, and 1984, 66, for a discussion of these forms of "demonstratives of nearer deixis."]

Q 265/3: *ms²rqytm bnḏn bytn*

"east from this house"

ḎʾG

subst. *ḏʾgn* Q 677/7(2x)

CISTERN [Cf. Ar *ḏaʾaja* "to drink, swallow"]

Q 677/4-5, 7-8: *tqdmw whqs²bn lmrʾhmw ... ḏʾgn bylgb wḏʾgn ḏtḥthw yhlgb*

"they directed and built for their lord ... the cistern at YLGB and the cistern which is under it, YHLGB"

(they-directed and-building for-their-lord ... the-cistern at-YLGB and-the-cistern that-which-under-it YHLGB)

ḎBḤ

subst. *ḏbḥtm* Q 35/6

SACRIFICIAL ANIMAL [Sab *ḏbḥ* "sacrificial animal," Ar *ḏābiḥa* "any animal that is allowable to slaughter"]

Q 35/5-6: *bʿl ẓrbt ltk bḏbḥtm*

"owner of the field LTK for sacrificial animals"

ḎHB I

subst. *ḏhbm* Q 495/3 + *ḏhbn* Q 6/8, Q 89.86/3, .137/4, Q 494/3-4 +

BRONZE [Sab *ḏhbm* "gold; bronze"; cf. Ar *ḏahab*, Heb *zāhāḇ* "gold." Beeston, in CIAS 2:206, and Jamme, 1957, 3-4, give the translation "bronze"—despite the meaning "gold" in the cognates of other Semitic languages—since it is used to describe pieces of bronze.]

Q 495/2-3: *ṯlṯt ʾṣlmm ḏhbm*

"three statues of bronze"

ḎHB II

subst. dl. *ḏhbw* Q 186A/5

ALLUVIAL VALLEY, ALLUVIAL PLAIN [Sab *ḏhbn* id; cf. Sab *mḏhbt* "alluvial land below dam," ModYem *zahb* "field," and Beeston, 1959, 4-5]

Q 186A/4-5: *dḏhbw ḥwkm*

"(the region) of the two alluvial plains of ḤWKM"

ḎMR

subst. *ḏmrs*^{1} Q 40/23

CORRECT READING; SOLEMN PRONOUNCEMENT [Sab *ḏmr* "to give judgment," Eth *ʾazmara* "to declare solemnly," and see the discussion of this word in Beeston, 1950b, 265-66]

Q 40/23: *wʿtlyw ʾs*^{1}*dm ʿlmw bḏn ftḥn ʾs*^{1}*m ʾs*^{1}*m bhṯ ḏmrs*^{1}

"those who have signed this decree have each seen to the promulgation of its correct reading"

(and-they-supervised who signed in-this decree man man the-announcement [of] its-correct-reading)

H

HGR

subst. sing. *hgr* Q 78/11; *hgrn* Q 74/8, 9, 10, 11, Q 78/10, Q 136/3, Q 172/5, Q 177/1, Q 183/2, Q 244/5, Q 611/2, Q 857/1, Q 909/2, Q 914/1; *hgrs¹* Q 240/4; *hgrs¹m* Q 177/3; *hgrhmw* Q 74/1

TOWN [Sab *hgr* id. In Hamdānī, 1884, *Ṣifat al-Jazīra* 86:3 *al-hajor* = *al-qarya.* ModYem *hajar* "ruins of an ancient city"; cf. further the discussion of Beeston, 1971a, 26-28.]

A) Q 177/1: *s²ᶜbn ḏhrbt ḥwr hgrn s³wm*
"the tribe Ḏū HRBT, resident in the town of S³WM"

B) Q 74/9-10: *wrbᶜ byt bn ᶜglm bhgrn ḫdṣm*
"and a fourth of the house of the clan of ᶜGLM in the town of ḪDṢM"

HLB

verb *hlb* Q 551/7

TO ADMINISTER (?) [Conjectural. See Jamme, 1955c, 97-98, who renders *hlb* "to clear"]

Q 551/7: *wrs²w rbs² ḏnhlb wdʾl wṣbḥm*
"and *rs²w* of (the temple) RBS² which WDʾL and ṢBḤM administered (?)"
(and-*rs²w* [of] RBS² which-administered WDʾL and-ṢBḤM)

HLK

verb *yhlkwn* Q 68/9

TO COMPLY, CONFORM [G. Ryckmans, 1947, 164, compares the Sab inscription Nami 27/4-5 and the Heb *halāḵ* "to go, to direct oneself"]

Q 68/9: *wl yhlkwn wṣtdq ʾrby ᶜm ḏlbḫ ḥgḏt mḥrtn wṣrytn*
"and let the *ʾrby* of ᶜAmm Ḏū Labaḫ comply and receive their due according to this directive and announcement"
(and-let comply and-receiving-just-rights the-*ʾrby* [of] ᶜAmm Ḏū-Labaḫ according-to this directive and-announcement)

s¹-prfx. *s¹hlk* Q 38/2, Q 39/2, Q 803/3, Q 856/2

TO COMPLETE; TO EFFECT, BRING ABOUT [Rhodokanakis, 1924, 46-47, compares *s¹hlk* with Ar *ʾamḍā* "to finish, complete"]

Q 39/2: *tqdm wḥrg ws¹hlk ᶜs²q wmbny mḥfdn brm*
"[LHYᶜM] directed and supervised and completed and carried out the construction and building of the tower BRM"

(HLK)

subst.[1] *mhlk* Q 769/1b, Q 770/3, Q 855/1, Q 856/3, Q 899/5

CONSTRUCTION; RECONSTRUCTION; UNDERTAKING, PROJECT

A) Q 856/3: *wkl mhlk wḥdṯn byt wdm*

"and the whole reconstruction and renovation of the temple of WDM"

(and-all the-reconstruction and-the-renovation [of] the-temple [of] WDM)

B) Q 899/5: *tqdmw mhlk wmbny qbrn*

"[ʾS¹LMM and ḎYMM and ʾWS¹N] directed the construction and building of this burial place."

subst.[2] pl. *hlks¹* Q 906/7

DEPENDENT [Ar *hālik, hullak* "poor, indigent"]

Q 906/6-7: *[kl] bns¹ [w]hlks¹*

"[all] his children [and] his dependents"

HM

conj. *hmw* Q 72/8

IF [comp. of the conj. *hm* plus the encl. *-mw*. According to Conti Rossini, 1931, 132, it is uncertain whether this is *hm* plus *-mw* or *hn* plus *-mw*. Cf. Sab *hm* and *hn* (in texts from Haram) "if," Heb *ʾim*, Ar *ʾin*, Meh *hen* id.]

Q 72/8-9: *whmw ys¹s¹lb kbrn bn lṣq wqrw*

"and if the *kabīr* refuses to prosecute and accuse"

(and-if refuses the-*kabīr* from prosecuting and-accusing)

HMD

verb *hmd* Q 186B/6

TO ASSESS TAX [Cf. Ar *hamīd* "tribute, tax listed in the register"]

Q 186B/5-7: *wʾwlw hmd ʿqr s²mr*

"those whom the overseer of S²MR has assessed a market tax"

(those-who assessed-a-tax the-overseer [of] S²MR)

HNʾ

subst. *hnʾm* Q 66/5

CROPS WATERED BY IRRIGATION; PROFIT [Cf. Sab *hnʾt* "prosperity," Syr *henyānā* "advantage, profit," JewAram *hnʾ* "to be pleasant, be of use," Ar *haniʾa* "to take pleasure in." According to Beeston, 1971b, 14, *hnʾm* is here substantivized in the sense of "crops," and is perhaps here specifically "artificially irrigated crops," in contrast to the "naturally watered crops" implied in *mwblm*.]

Q 66/5: *ʿs²r kl hnʾm wmwblm wtqntm wtrṯm*
"a tenth of all crops watered by irrigation and by rain and (and a tenth of all) acquisitions and inheritances"
(a-tenth [of] every irrigated-crop and-rain-watered-crop and-acquisitions and-inheritance)

HRG

verb *byhrg* Q 78/11, 12

TO KILL, MURDER [Sab *hrg* "to kill, slaughter, massacre" Heb *hārag*, OAram *hrg*, Moab *hrg*, Aram *hărag* id.; cf. Ar *haraja* "to fall into war, slaughter, or bloodshed," Ar *harj* "bloodshed, murder"]

Q 78/11-12: *wḏm byhrg … bn mts¹km bʾrḍm bs¹ byhrg nḥql*
"if the murderer is not apprehended in the particular land in which he committed the killing"
[and-the-one-who kills … from arrest in-the-land in-it he-kills in-particular]

subst. *hrgn* Q 78/4

MURDERER

Q 78/4: *wl yḥrm s¹w ʾns¹n hrgn*
"let this murderer be punished"

W

W I

conj. *w-* passim

AND [Sab *w* "and," Ar *wa*, Eth *w-*, Heb *w-*, Akk *u-* id. See Beeston, 1962, 60-62, for a discussion of the semantic fields of *w-*.]

A) Coordinating conjunction: *w-* functions as a simple coordinating conjunction linking words, phrases, or clauses.

Q 38/5: *bʿṯtr wb ʿm wb ʾnby*
"by ʿAṯtar and by ʿAmm and by ʾAnbay"

B) When *w-* links verbs in a sequence, the first verb in the sequence is usually finite while those which follow are infinitives.

Q 72/7-8: *wl ylṣq wqrw ws¹ʿḏb*
"let [the lord of Timnaʿ] prosecute, accuse, and punish"
(and-let he-prosecute and-accusing and-punishing)

W II

subst. *w* Q 186B/7

GOLD PIECES [abbrv. for *wrq*. See Irvine, 1964, 34, and Beeston, 1959, 8-9.]

Q 186B/7: *n w*

"*n* pieces of gold" (*n* refers presumably to a numerical unit)

WBL

subst. *mwblm* Q 66/5

CROPS WATERED BY HEAVY RAIN [Ar *wabl*, *wābil* "heavy rain," Heb *yāḇāl* "heavy rain; water ditch"]

Q 66/5: *ʿs²r kl hnʾm wmwblm*

"a tenth of all crops watered by irrigation and by rain"

(a-tenth [of] every irrigated-crop and-rain-watered-crop)

WGL

subst. *mwgln* Q 241/3

ALABASTER [Sab *mwgl* id. However, Pirenne, in CIAS 1:128, explains *mwgl* as a plural of *mʾgl* "cistern, tank, reservoir" on the basis of the plural of the Ar *maʾjal*, *mawājil* "pool, pond"]

Q 241/3: *s²mry mwgln*

"this alabaster votive object (?)"

WDD

subst. *wdm* Q 67/5, Q 68/4, Q 69/3, Q 70/2

FRIENDSHIP [Cf. Heb *yāḏîḏ* "friend, beloved," *yəḏîḏûṯ* "friendship," Ug *ydd* "friend, beloved," Syr *yaddeḏ* "to love," Arab *wadda* id.]

Q 67/5: *lʿṣm wdm wbntm ws²ftm lʿm wʾṯrt*

"[S²HR YGL has promulgated the formation of] a patronage-tie of friendship, affiliation, and protection to ʿAmm and ʾAṯirat"

WDY

subst. *mwdyn* Q 696/2

RESERVOIR, CISTERN [Cf. Sab *wdyn* "wadi," Ar *wādī* "watercourse," and Ar *madīy* "reservoir without masonry"]

Q 696/1-3: *ydʿʾb ḏbyn bn s²hr mkrb qtbn bny mwdyn byḥn bn s²rs¹m ʿd frʿm*

"YDʿʾB Ḏū BYN son of S²HR, *mkrb* of Qataban, built the cistern Bayḥān from the foundation to the top"

WHB

verb *whb* Q 66/1, Q 839/5, Q 911/1; *yhb* Q 72/5

TO GIVE, GRANT [Sab *whb* "to give, grant, hand over, transfer," Ar *wahaba*, Eth *wahaba*, Aram *yəhab̲*, Heb *yāhab̲* id.]

Q 66/1: *s²hr ǵyln bn ʾbs²bm mlk qtbn whb ws¹qny lʿm d̲lbh̲ wʾrbys¹ ṣfḥ thrg s²ʿbn kḥd*

"S²HR ǴYLN the son of ʾBS²BM king of Qataban has granted and dedicated to ʿAmm D̲ū Labah̲ and his *rby* a document for the administration of the tribe KḤD"

(S²HR ǴYLN the-son [of] ʾBS²BM king [of] Qataban he-gave and-dedicating to-ʿAmm D̲ū-Labah̲ and-his-*rby* a-document [of] the-administration [of] the-tribe KḤD)

WZʾ

verb *wzʾ* Q 186A/24-25, Q 695/10, 13, Q 840/9, Q911/1; *yzʾ* Q 244/10-11, Q 246/9; *wzʾw* Q 40/7

TO CONTINUE, DO AGAIN; TO ADD [Sab *wzʾ* "to do again." According to Beeston, 1962b, 25, and 1975a, 191-92, *wzʾ* may be followed by an infinitive or, less frequently, a finite verb in the ESA dialects.]

Q 186A/24-25: *wzʾ ʾns¹m ʿly ʾh̲s¹ bh̲[t]fr[m]*

"someone has consistently cheated his fellow-trader"

(he-continued someone against his-fellow-trader in-cheating)

WZL

verb *wzl* Q 36/3, Q 176/5, Q 856/2

TO SMOOTH, LEVEL a road [Sense from context; cf. Jamme, 1955f, 511]

Q 36/3-4: *mh̲ḍ wbrr wwzl wṣll mnqln mblqt ʾs¹n brm wḥrb*

"[YDʿB D̲ū BYN] hewed out, dug up, smoothed, and paved the mountain pass road MBLQT between BRM and ḤRB"

(he-hewed-out and-digging-up and-smoothing and-paving the-mountain-pass-road MBLQT between BRM and-ḤRB)

subst. *wzl* Q 176/10

SMOOTHING, LEVELING a road

Q 176/9-11: *ʾws¹ʿm bn yṣrʿm bn mdhm tqdm wḥrg kl ʿs²q wwzl wṣll mnqln ẓrm btḥrg mrʾs¹ ydʿb*

"ʾWS¹ʿM the son of YṢRʿM of the clan of MDHM directed and supervised all the digging up, smoothing, and paving of the mountain pass ẒRM under the direction of his lord YDʿB"

(WZL)

(ʾWS¹ʿM the-son [of] YṢRʿM [of] the-clan [of] MDHM directed and-supervising the-whole digging-up and-smoothing and-paving the-mountain-pass ẒRM under-the-direction [of] his-lord YDʿʾB)

WḤD

subst. *mḥds¹m* Q 67/9, Q 68/7, Q 69/6

ASSEMBLY PLACE [According to Beeston, 1971b, 11, this means "the place which brings them all together," just as the Ar *jāmiʿ* is the place which brings all Muslims together. Note also Deut. 33:5 *yaḥad* "assembly."]

Q 67/9: *wb mḥds¹m bbyt ʿm ḏlbḫ*

"and in their assembly place in the temple of ʿAmm Ḏū Labaḫ"

adv. *wḥd* Q 40/7, Q 687/8

JOINTLY, TOGETHER [Cf Sab *kwḥd* "together," Ar *waḥid* "one"]

Q 40/7: *ṯnym mqmm wʾtmtm wḥd bnblm*

"for a second time in their meeting and assembly jointly through a delegation"

(a-second-time meeting and-assembly jointly through-a-delegation)

WḤS¹

s¹-prfx. *s¹wḥs³s¹* Q 83/6

TO REMOVE, DISPLACE [Cf Ar *waḥḥaša* "to throw away one's clothes or weapons." However, J. Ryckmans, 1953, 343-69, in a long article on this inscription, suggests the meaning "to usurp" for this verb.]

Q 83/5-7: *wʾl s³n s¹wḥs³s¹ bn brṯs¹*

"and it is not permitted to remove it from its place"

(and-not permitted its-removal from its-place)

WṬF

subst. *twṭf* Q 40/12

EXECUTION, CARRYING OUT [Cf. Ar *waṭf* "carrying out of a judicial action"]

Q 40/12-13: *kl ʾxḏb wdyn wtwṭf gzwmm gzmw ws¹gzmw bs¹myt mqmnyhn wʾtmtnyhn*

"all punishments, judgments, and the carrying out of decisions which they have made and caused to make in those two meetings and assemblies" (all punishments and-judgments and-the-carrying-out [of] the-decisions they-have-made and-they-have-caused-to-make in-those two-meetings and-two-assemblies)

WYN

subst. *wynhw* Q 611/1-2; *wynhmw* Q 679/9, 10(2x)

VINEYARD [Sab *wyn* id., Eth *wayn* "grape; wine," Ar *wayn* "black grapes," Heb *yayin* "wine," Ug *yn*, Akk *īnu* id.]

Q 611/1-2: *[h]w[f]ʿm ḏʿrgn hqḥ wbql wynhw*

"[H]W[F]ʿM Ḏū ʿRGN prepared and planted his vineyard"

WLD

verb *byld* Q 79/4

TO BE BORN, BE GIVEN BIRTH TO [Sab *wld* "to bear; to beget; to be born," Ar *walada* "to bear; to beget," Heb *yālaḏ* id.]

Q 79/4: *kl ʾwldm wmrʾtm byld btmnʿ wʾmwrs¹*

"all the men and women born in Timnaʿ and its confines)"

(all male-children and-women born in-Timnaʿ and-its-confines)

s¹-prfx. *s¹wld* Q 172/3

TO BEGET

Q 172/3: *ḏs¹wld bn fḫḏs¹ mrʾm*

"(a child) whom he sired from his clan, a male"

(whom-he-begot from his-tribe a-male)

subst. sing./pl. *wld* Q 36/2, Q 55, Q 61, Q 74/4, Q 176/2-3, Q 186A/5, 6, Q 540/1, Q 695/12-13+; *wlds¹* Q 1/6, Q 10/5, Q 51/2, Q 73/3, Q 77/2, Q 82/2, Q167/4, Q 213/2, Q 254/5-6, Q 494/5, Q 496/4, Q 695/14; *wldhw* Q 74/14, Q 178/3; pl. *ʾwldm* Q 79/4; *ʾwlds¹* (in each case form appears as *ʾlwds¹*) Q 495/3-4, Q 909/1; *ʾwldhw* (form appears as *ʾlwdhw*) Q 689/5; *ʾwlds¹my* Q 806/4; *ʾwlds¹m* Q 68/4, Q 69/3, Q 247/3

1) CHILD; SON; DESCENDENT

A) Q 176/2-3: *mkrb qtbn wkl wld ʿm*

"*mkrb* of Qataban and all the children of ʿAmm"

B) Q 82/1-3: *hʿs¹mm bn lbtm wlqtm wwlds¹ qny wẓrb byts¹*

"HʿS¹MM the son of LBTM and LQṬM and his son acquired and dedicated his house."

2) MALE

See entry above under verb *wld*.

WMY

subst. *wmys¹m* Q 79/3

DEPENDENT [Cf. Syr *yīmī* "to swear, to take an oath," to which RÉS VI, 335, compares semantically Ar *ḥilf* "an ally" and suggests the underlying notion of intimate social and economic relations]

Q 79/3: *wʾmtys¹m wʾdwms¹m wǵbrs¹m wwmys¹m*

"and their maidservants, vassals, common people, and dependents"

(and-their-female-servants and-their-subjects and-their-common-people and-their-dependents)

WʿL

subst. dl. *wʿly* Q 183/1; *wʿlys¹m* Q 183/5

IBEX, MOUNTAIN GOAT [Sab *wʿl* "mountain goat, ibex," Ar *waʿl*, Eth *wāʿl*, Heb *yāʿēl* id.]

Q 183/1-2: *ʿd mḥrms¹ nʿlm wʿly d̲hbn*

"[BRTʿ D̲ū ḤDN ʾLS¹R dedicated to the god BS²MM] in his temple NʿLM two ibexes in bronze."

WFY

verb *wfy* Q 40/19

TO PROTECT, SAFEGAURD [Sab *wfy* "safety, well-being"; cf. Eth *tawafaya* "to be whole"]

Q 40/19: *wkd̲m lynfs¹wn wḥtll wwfy qtbn ms³wdn wqtbn ṭbnn*

"and in order that the Qatabanian lords and landowners may find alleviation, relief, and safety"

(and-in-order-that they-may-find-alleviation and-finding-relief and-being-safe the-Qatabanians the-lords and-the-Qatabanians the-landowners)

s¹-prfx. *s¹wfy* Q 89.129/1, Q 898/4; *s¹wfys¹m* Q 70/3; *hwfy* Q 128/4, Q 910/3

1) TO PROTECT [Sab *hwfy* "to save, protect"]

Q 89.129/1: *[bd̲]tm s¹wfy ʿt̲tr wʾnby wʿm wʾlhs¹m [bn] s²nʾm*

"because ʿAt̲tar and ʾAnbay and ʿAmm and their god preserved (him from) the enemy"

(because preserved ʿAt̲tar and ʾAnbay and-ʿAmm and-their-god from the-enemy)

2) TO PAY SOMEONE HIS DUE; TO GRANT, SATISFY [Sab *hwfy* "to grant, bestow, satisfy"; cf. Eth *awaffaya* "give into someone's power; give back"]

Q 70/2-3: *wṣry s²hr ʾdms¹ ʾrby ʿm d̲lbḥ wbnys¹m wtʾnṯs¹m bṣdqs¹m ws¹wfys¹m ḥgd̲t gdytn*

"and S²HR directed his subjects the *ʾrby* of ʿAmm Ḏū Labaḫ and their sons and their female kin in their due and satisfied them according to this renewal"
(and directed S²HR his-subjects the-*ʾrby* [of] ʿAmm Ḏū-Labaḫ and-their sons and-their-female-kindred in-their-due and-he-satisfied-them according-to-this renewal)

s¹t-prfx. *s¹twfy* Q 72/5

TO PAY a fine [Sab *wfyw* "to pay a debt"]

Q 72/5-6: *wl yhb ws¹twfy dwrn wms¹ḫdʿn*

"and let whoever refuses and balks at (plowing the fields) give over and pay"
(and-let he-gives-over and-paying the-refuser and-the-balker)

subst. *wfy* Q 8/4, Q 244/7, 12, 13, Q 246/6, 11, 13, Q 261/2-3, Q 269/3-4, Q 489/3, Q 905/3; *wfys¹* Q 269/3; *wfys¹m* Q 489/3, Q 495/3; *wfys¹n* Q 244/13

SAFETY, WELL-BEING [Sab *wfy* "safety; success; well-being"; cf. Ar *wafāʾ* "fulfillment of a promise; payment of a debt"]

Q 8/1, 3-4: *rdʾ lʾṯrt ts¹ʿn bḥtn lwfy [...*

"[(ʿ)BDʾL MʿDN] vowed to ʾAṯirat nine votive-objects for the safety of [..."

WFQ

s¹-prfx. *ys¹twfq* Q 695/9-10

TO REFRAIN [Beeston, 1976, 421 compares Sab *ʾfq* "to keep under control."]

Q 695/9-10: *nl ys¹twfq bn wzʾ ʾw nky ḏt ʾrḍn*

"let them refrain from adding to or diminishing this land"
(let refrain from the-adding-to or the-diminishing [of] this land)

WFR

verb *wfr* (verbal noun) Q 72/4; *byfrwn* Q 72/2; *yfrwn* Q 173/3

1) TO PLOW, PLANT, CULTIVATE (FIELDS) [Daṯ *wafara* "to be saturated with water">"to be fertile, produce crops"; cf. also perhaps Eth *wafara* "to go out into the country," Heb *pārāh* "to bear fruit," Eth *parya* id., and see Lundin, 1987, 55-56, for a discussion of this root in the ESA dialects]

Q 72/4-5: *wʾy ʾy ʾs¹dm bydr ws¹ḫdʿ bn wfr wʿs²q*

"and whatever man refuses and balks at plowing and tilling"
(and-whatever whatever man he-refuses and-balking at plowing and-tilling)

2) TO BE ABUNDANT [Ar *wafara* "to abound, be ample, abundant]

Q 173/3: *wl yfrwn ṣbḥt ṣfn[ ]*

(WFR)

"may the taxes be abundant which have been gathered"

(and-let be-abundant the-taxes [which] have-been-gathered)

WṢL

subst. *wṣln* Q 901/4; pl.*ʾwṣl* Q 901/2

OFFERING [Sab *ṣlt* "gift." Brown and Beeston, 1954, 54-55, compare this word with the Sab verb *hwṣl* in Fakhry 3/8 and note further: "The fact that it is there associated with *hyʿ* (a verb which commonly means "consecrate") suggests that it may also have had a sacral connotation."]

Q 901/4: *kl mwḍʾ s¹wt wṣln lʾṯts¹*

"all the dedication of this offering for his wife"

WṢR

subst. *wṣrs¹m* Q 174/2

LAND ALLOTMENT [Possibly connected with Ar *wiṣr* "treaty, contract"]

Q 174/2: *s¹ʿs²q wṣrs¹m*

"[ʾLS¹ʿD ḎʾB...] cultivated their land allotment"

WḌʾ

verb *yḍʾ* Q 694/9, 10; *yḍʾwn* Q 40/18

TO REMOVE, DESTROY, DAMAGE [Cf. Sab *hwḍʾ* "to destroy"]

Q 694/9: *lyḍʾ wḥrts¹ wbqlm kwn bḏtn ʾrḍtn*

"[it is forbidden] that one destroy its aqueduct and the crops which are in these lands"

(that-one-destroy its-aqueduct and-the-crops [which] are in-these lands)

subst.[1] *mwḍʾ* Q 901/4

OFFERING [The specialized sense here is of something separated (i.e., "going out") from other things by being dedicated to a deity; cf. Sab *mwḍʾ* "expenses, outgoings"]

Q 901/4: *kl mwḍʾ s¹wt wṣln lʾṯts¹*

"all the dedication of this offering for his wife"

subst.[2] *twḍʾ* Q 40/20

DRIVING OUT, EXPULSION [Cf. Sab *hwḍʾ* "to drive out," Eth *ʾawḍeʾa* "to expel"]

Q 40/20-21: *bnkl dyn wʿḏb wtlf wtwḍʾ wtwṭf s¹mt ḏtw gzwmm*

"(that they may find safety) from every judgment, punishment, injury, expulsion, and the carrying out of these decisions"

WḌḤ

subst. *ḍḥtn* Q 695/11

ANNOUNCEMENT, PROCLAMATION [Cf. Ar *waḍḍaḥa*, *ʾawḍaḥa* "to explain, clarify"]

Q 695/10-11: *ʾs^{1}ṭr ḏt ḍḥtn*

"the text of this announcement"

WQH

verb *wqh* Q 83/9, Q 89.137/5, Q 139/3, Q 186B/30, Q 694/1; *wqhhw* Q 688/4

TO COMMAND, ORDER [Sab *wqh* id., Heb *yiqhāh* "obedience," Ar *waqiha* "to be obedient"]

Q 89.137/5: *ḥg wqh ʾbs^1 wdm bms^{1}ʾls^1*

"as his father WDM commanded in his oracle"

(according-as commanded his-father WDM in-his-oracle)

subst. *qhtn* Q 694/14

COMMAND; ORDINANCE

Q 694/13-14: *wkwnt ḏt qhtn ywmyt s^{2}lṯm ḏfqḥw ḏbs^{2}mm*

"this ordinance was given on the third of Ḏu FQḤW (of the month) Ḏū BS^{2}MM"

(and-took-place this command date [of] the-third [of] Ḏu-FQḤW [of] Ḏu-BS^{2}MM)

WRḪ

subst. sing. *wrḫm* Q 72/3, 4(2x); *wrḫn* Q 40/7, 9, 22, Q 66/6, Q 694/13; *wrḫs^1* Q 66/12, Q 67/9, Q 68/8, Q 69/6, Q 70/4, Q 72/10, Q 79/6(2x); *wrḫhw* Q 690a/9; pl. *ʾwrḫn* Q 72/4

MONTH [Sab *wrḫ* "month," Eth *warḫ* "moon, month," Heb *yeraḥ* "month," Heb *yārēaḥ* "moon"]

Q 67/9: *wrḫs^1 ḏbs^{2}mm*

"in the month Ḏū BS^{2}MM"

(its-month Ḏū-BS^{2}MM)

WRF

subst. *wrfw* Q 102/5, Q 239/4, Q 246/3-4, 9, Q 263/4

WRF, function or capacity of a deity [See Beeston, 1962c, 47-48, where he also notes the discussion of this word by Rhodokanakis, 1931, 41, who understands it as the defining power of ʿAmm's oracle, as well as the function of defining the boundaries of irrigated land; cf. also Jamme in Van Beek, 1969b, 340-41]

Q 239/3-5: *bws^{2}ʿn ʿṯtr s^{2}rqn wʿ[ṯtr ḏdw]nm wʾnby s^{2}ymn wwrfw ʾmr ʿm[m]*

(WRF)

"through the favor of ʿAṯtar S^2RQN and ʿA[ṯtar of DWNM] and ʾAnbay the patron and *wrf* of ʿAm[m]"

WRQ

subst. *wrqm* Q 186A/26

(PIECE OF) GOLD [Sab *wrq* "gold," Eth *warq* "name of a standard gold coin in Ethiopia"; cf. also Heb *yāraq* "to be yellow," Akk *arāqu* "to grow pale" and *arqu* "yellow"]

Q 186A/26-27: *lyh̲rṯ h̲ms¹y wrqm lmlk qtbn*

"let him pay a fine of fifty pieces of gold to the king of Qataban"

WRṮ

subst. *trṯm* Q 66/5

INHERITANCE [Ar *wirṯ* "inheritance, legacy"]

Q 66/5: *ʿs²r kl hnʾm wmwblm wtqntm wtrṯm*

"a tenth of all crops watered by irrigation and by rain and acquisitions and inheritances"

(a-tenth [of] every irrigated-crop and-rain-watered-crop and-acquisitions and-inheritance)

WS¹Ṭ

prep. *ws¹ṭ* Q 40/4, 5, 8, Q 242/5;

IN, IN THE MIDDLE OF [Sab *ws¹t* "middle, midst" Ar *wasṭa* id.]

Q 40/8: *bʾy ws¹ṭ ʾḥrm byt ʿm*

"in ʾḤRM, the temple of ʿAmm"

comp. prep. *bws¹ṭ*

See entry under *B*.

WS¹M

verb *ws¹m* Q 694/6

TO BE MARKED, INSCRIBED [Cf. Sab *s¹mt* "line, mark, sign," Ar *wasama* "to make a mark with a hot iron." Acording to Pirenne, 1971, 127, this refers to the *wasm* to the right of the inscription.]

Q 694/6: *ʿd s¹mtm wʾs¹ṯrn ḏtm ws¹m ws¹ṯr bh̲lbṣm llʿl*

"to the mark and inscription which have been made on H̲LBṢM above"

(to the-mark and-the-inscription [which] have-been-marked and-inscribing on-H̲LBṢM above)

subst. *s¹mtm* Q 694/6
MARK, INSCRIBED SYMBOL
See entry above.

WS²B

subst. *ws²wb* Q 67/11
PRODUCE [Cf. Ar *wisb* "plants, herbs." Beeston, 1971b, 11, translates *ws²wb* at 67/11 "mixed farming land"]
Q 67/11: *ws²wb wṯmr ʿm*
"produce and crops of ʿAmm"

WS²ʿ

subst. *ws²ʿn* Q 239/3
HELP, AID; FAVOR [Cf. Sab *hws²ʿ* "to grant a favor," Ar *wusʿ* "ability, capacity"]
Q 239/3: *bws²ʿn ʿṯtr s²rqn*
"with the favor of ʿAṯtar S²RQN"

WS³ʿ

t-infx. *byts³ʿ* Q 186B/31
TO BE WIDE, EXTENSIVE [Ar *ittasaʿa* "to expand, widen, grow, increase"]
Q 186B/31-32: *wḏm byts³ʿ ʾw ʿdw ms²t qtbn*
"whatever is more extensive or goes beyond the trade of Qataban"

WS³F

verb *ws³f* Q 695/6, Q 911/1; *bys³f* Q 695/11
1) TO INCREASE [Cf. Sab *wsf* "to increase; add members (*specifically, children*) to *a social group*," Heb. *yāsap* "to add, increase"]
Q 911/1: *wḏm wzʾt whb wws³f*
"and that she continue to give and increase"
2) TO ENLARGE
Q 695/5-7: *wl yḥrm ʾḫr wbrm bn ws³f bʿlw bn tqbln kl ḥrṯm ʾw tbqlm*
"it is forbidden that ʾḪR and BRM be enlarged beyond these dimensions by any cultivation or planting"
(and-let be-forbidden ʾḪR and-BRM from enlargement over from this-dimension any cultivation or planting)

WṮB

subst. *mwṯb* Q 1/4

SANCTUM, SEAT, SHRINE of a god [Sab *mwṯb* id.]

Q 1/4: *mwṯb mkntn*

"the sanctum of the inner shrine"

WṮN

verb *twṯnw* Q 839/2

TO SET, ESTABLISH LIMITS [Sab *wṯn*, *twṯn* "to delimit, set bounds"; cf. Eth *wassana* "delimit, determine"]

Q 839/2: *ʾwṯn twṯnw s²ʿbn yqhmlk wbn br[ṣm]*

"bounds which the tribe of YQHMLK and BN BR[ṢM] set"

(bounds set the-tribe of YQHMLK and BN BR[ṢM])

subst. *wṯnn* Q 839/1; dl. *wṯny* Q 839/1; pl. *ʾwṯn* Q 839/2, 3

LIMITS, BOUNDS

Q 839/1: *ln ḏn wṯnn*

"from this boundary"

WṮR

s¹(h)-prfx. *s¹wṯr* Q 70/3, Q 100/3, Q 102/2-3, Q 177/2, Q 179/1, Q 183/1, Q 239/2, Q 240/4, Q 268/2, Q 857/1; *hwṯrn* Q 678/2

TO LAY THE FOUNDATION [Sab *hwṯr* "to lay foundations, groundwork"]

Q 857/1: *rbn ḥ[w]r hgrn ḍfr brʾ ws¹wṯr ws¹s²qr [...*

"RBN, res[i]dent of the town ḌFR, built, laid the foundation of, and completed [..."

subst. *mwṯr* Q 179/1

FOUNDATION

Q 179/1: *lḥyʿt bn ṣwbn yʿb brʾ ws¹wṯr ws¹qḥ mrsʿt wmwṯr byt[s¹]*

"LḤYʿT the son of ṢWBN YʿB constructed, laid the foundation, and set in order the upper story and foundation of his house"

(LḤYʿT the-son [of] ṢWBN YʿB he-constructed and-laying-the-foundation and-setting-in-order the-upper-story and-the-foundation [of] his-house)

Z

ZBR

subst. *zbr* Q 687/8

BUILDING, STRUCTURE [Cf. Sab *zbr* "to erect a structure, build," ModYem *zābūr* "mud wall," *zawbar* "to construct a mud wall"; further, see W. Müller in Wissmann, 1968, 81; Rossi, 1940, 304.]

Q 687/8-9: *wzbr ywnbr dnm ʿlbḏr ʾḫyr s³md hwyḫr*

"the building which DNM is erecting near the field of the elite of the dignitaries of HWYḪR"

(and-the-structure erects DNM near-the-field [of] the-elite [of] the-dignitaries [of] HWYḪR)

ZWR

s¹t-prfx. *s¹tzr* Q 186A/22

TO ASK TO VISIT [According to Beeston, 1959, 7, this has a desiderative meaning and is cognate with the Ar *zāra* (w) "to visit," *istazāra* "to ask to visit."]

Q 186A/21-23: *wmn lyks³ʾwn ʿhr s²mr kḏm s¹tzr bn qtbn bms²ṭm*

"and whoever informs the overseer of S²MR that any foreigner has attempted to visit any part of Qataban with merchandise"

(and-he-who informs the-overseer [of] S²MR that he-asked-to-visit from Qataban with-merchandise)

ZYM

subst. sing. *zm* Q 687/7; pl. *ʾzmt* Q 687/9

HERD [Ar *zīma* "herd, band of camels"]

Q 687/7: *zm ʾs¹rb wʾṯwr*

"(a) herd of sheep and cattle"

Ḥ

ḤBL

subst. *ḥbls¹* Q 89.129/2

TROOP [Cf. Heb *ḥeḇel* "troop, band" (1 Sam 10:5, 10), Ug *ḥbl* "company, group"]

Q 89.129/2: *wḏm ḥbls¹*

"[before the enemy] and its troops"

ḤBS²

subst. dl. *ḥbs²y* Q 772/2

OFFICIAL [Sab *ḥbs²y* "title of royal official or adherent"; cf. Ar *ḥabaša* "to collect." Based on the Arabic cognate, it would be tempting to translate this "tax collector" or something similar (cf. Jamme, 1972, 45-46, who translates this word as "collectors"), but our present knowledge hardly allows so specific a conjecture.]

Q 772/1-3: *ʾls²wʿ rmln wnhbn ḥbs²y ydᵓb mlk qtbn*

"ʾLS²Wʿ of the family RMLN and NHBN officials of YDᵓB, king of Qataban"

ḤGG

subst. *ḥgn* Q 35/8

FESTIVAL, PILGRIMAGE [Cf. Ar *ḥajj* "festival, pilgrimage," Sab *ḥgtn* "pilgrimage," Heb *ḥāḡ* "procession, dance, feast"]

Q 35/1, 7-9: *s¹qny ʾnby bʿl ḥgn qnyhw bn glbm*

"[S²HR HLL] dedicated this property to ʾAnbay, lord of the festival, from adversity (?)"

ḤGR

verb *ḥgr* Q 79/1, Q 173/1, Q 202/1, Q 909/2

TO DIRECT, COMMAND [Cf. Ar *ḥajara* "forbid (access)." Perhaps there is a semantic development in this root of "command">"command against, restrict, forbid."]

Q 173/1: *hg ḥgr ws¹ḥr s²hr hll*

"thus commanded and directed S²HR HLL"

subst. *ḥgrn* Q 79/5, Q 173/5, 6

DIRECTIVE, ORDER

Q 173/6: *bḏn ḏḥgrn wmḥrn*

"through this directive and ordinance"

ḤDṮ

s[1]-prfx. *s¹ḥdṯ* Q 36/4, Q 131/2, Q 248/2, Q 265/2, Q 486/4, Q 769/1b, Q 899/2, Q 915/1

TO NEWLY CONSTRUCT, MAKE NEW, INAUGURATE; TO RENEW, RESTORE [Sab *hḥdṯ* "to build, found, establish; initiate; inaugurate," Ar *ḥadaṯa* "to make new," Eth *ḥadasa*, Heb *ḥiddeš* id. Both senses—"to make new, newly construct (i.e, to bring into existence for the first time)" and "rebuild, renew, renovate"—are possible, the context usually not allowing us to determine which is more appropriate. For discussion of this term see Beeston, 1972b, 541, and J. Ryckmans, 1974, 138. See also Jamme, 1972, 43-67, who prefers to render *s¹ḥdṯ* at Q 769/1b and Q 899/2 as "to erect."]

Q 36/4: *wbny ws¹ḥdṯ byt wdm*

"and he built and newly constructed the temple of WDM"

subst. *ḥdṯn* Q 856/3

RENOVATION, RESTORATION; MAKING NEW, NEW CONSTRUCTION

Q 856/3: *wkl mhlk wḥdṯn byt wdm wʾṯrt*

"and the whole reconstruction and renovation of the temple of WDM and ʾAṯirat"

(and-all the-reconstruction and-the-renovation [of] the-temple [of] WDM and-ʾAṯirat)

ḤḎK

subst. *ḥḏk* Q 155, Q 530bis, Q 530ter, Q 538

PUNGENT INCENSE (?) [Sab *ḥḏk* id.; cf. Ar *ḥaḏaqa* "to sting, bite, burn the mouth," and see K. Nielsen, 1986, 18]

Q 530ter: *md ḏrw ḥḏk ldn*

"nard (?), balsam, (pungent) incense (?), ladanum"

ḤWF

subst. *ḥwf* Q 687/5

EDGE, BORDER [Cf. Ar *ḥāfa*(w) "edge, border; bank of a river"]

Q 687/5: *ḥwf mʾglk ʾṣfr*

"the edge of the reservoir ʾṢFR"

ḤWR

verb *ḥwr* Q 78/13; *yḥr* Q 83/4, Q 203/4

1) TO ORDER, DECREE [Sab *ḥwr* "to be ordained, be issued (*command, decree*)"]

Q 78/13: *ʿdkm byṣrš mlkn knm byʿbr wḥwr*

"until the king decrees it, as he arranges and orders"

(ḤWR)

(until decrees-it the-king as he-arranges and-ordering)

2) TO ESTABLISH; TO REMAIN

Q 83/3-4: *wl yḥr bdn brṯn*

"and may it be established in this place"

s¹-prfx. *s¹ḥr* Q 40/1, 5, 9, 15, 16, Q 69/6, Q 70/2, Q 72/1, Q 78/1, 5, Q 89.148/2, Q 173/1, Q 186A/1; *s¹hrs¹m* Q 70/5, Q 186B/24; *bys¹ḥrs¹* Q 78/6

TO DECREE, ORDER

Q 72/1: *ḥgkm s¹ḥr wḥrg s²hr hll bn ḏrʾkrb*

"thus S²HR HLL the son of ḎRʾKRB decreed and established (a law)"

(thus decreed and-establishing S²HR HLL the-son [of] ḎRʾKRB)

t-prfx. *tḥwr* Q 809/2

TO CAUSE TO RETURN [Cf. Ar *ḥawwara* "to cause to return"]

Q 809/1-3: *mlḥwṣ tḥwr hln yḥm bʾḏn ʿm*

"MLḤWṢ caused HLN YḤM to return. By permission of ʿAmm"

subst.¹ *ḥwr* Q 177/2, Q 186B/11-12, Q 914/1

RESIDENT, INHABITANT [Sab *ḥwr* "inhabitant, settler *of a town*," Eth *ḥora* "go," Daṯ *ḥārat* "village" (although this word is listed by Landberg, 1920, 535, under the root *ḥyr*), Ar *ḥāra* "quarter of a city"; cf. Beeston, 1971b, 3-4—who also gives the sense "immigrant"—for a further discussion of this root]

Q 177/1-2: *s²ʿbn ḏhrbt ḥwr hgrn s³wm brʾw ws¹wṯr ws¹s²qr ḏn m[ḥ]fdn yḥḏr*

"the tribe Ḏū HRBT, resident in the town of S³WM, built, laid the foundation, and completed this [to]wer YḤḎR"

(the-tribe Ḏū-HRBT resident [in] the-town [of] S³WM they-built and-laying-the-foundation and-completing this [to]wer YḤḎR)

subst.² *mḥrn* Q 72/5, 7, 8, 9, 10, Q 173/5, 6, C/16; *mḥrtm* Q 40/5, 10, 14, 17, Q 70/1; *mḥrtn* Q 40/16, 18, 21, Q 67/6, 7, Q 68/5, 6, 9, Q 69/4, 5

DIRECTIVE, ORDER [According to Müller, 1962, 44, this meaning is to be compared with Eth *ḥora* "to go, to direct oneself."]

Q 72/5: *hgḏn ḏmḥrn*

"in accordance with this directive"

ḤLL

verb *ḥll* Q 40/11-12; *ḥlt* Q 78/7; *byḥllwn* Q 40/12

1) TO CANCEL, RELIEVE, END [Cf. Ar *ḥalla* "to dissolve, melt; unloose, untie"]

Q 40/11-12: *wʾy ḥll byḥllwn wnfs¹ wmtᶜ ws¹ẖlᶜ bnᶜlw mqmh[w] wʾbyt wʾqny qtbn ms³wdn wqtbn ṭbnn*

"whatever they cancel, reduce, defer, and waive on the proper[ty], houses, and possessions of the lords and landowners of Qataban"

(and-whatever cancelling they-cancel and-reducing and-deferring and-waiving on-the-proper[ty] and-the-houses and-the-possessions [of] the-Qatabanians the-lords and-the-Qatabanians the-landowners)

2) TO LOSE, FORFEIT

Q 78/7: *y]mt s¹w ʾns¹n ms¹tᶜdwn knm byks³ʾ wḥlt nfs¹s¹*

"let that wrongdoer [d]ie as (the king) commands, and his life is forfeit"

t-infix *ḥtll* Q 40/19

TO FIND RELIEF, BE RELIEVED

Q 40/19: *wkḏm lynfs¹wn wḥtll wwfy qtbn ms³wdn wqtbn ṭbnn*

"and in order that the Qatabanian lords and landowners may find alleviation, relief, and safety"

(and-in-order-that they-may-find-alleviation and-finding-relief and-being-safe the-Qatabanians the-lords and-the-Qatabanians the landowners)

subst. pl. *mḥllts¹m* Q 135/3

SLUICE GATE [RÉS VII, 138, compares Ar *ḥalla* "to open"]

Q 135/3: *[…] wmḥllts¹m […*

"[…] and their sluice gates […"

ḤMY

verb *yḥmy* Q 555/4

TO PROTECT, DEFEND [Cf. Sab *yḥmyn* "to protect *from flooding*" Ar *ḥamā* (y) "to defend, " Heb *ḥāmāh* "to protect, defend"]

Q 555/1-5: *s²rḥm ḏbrlm yᶜẓm yḥmy bʾḏn ḏt ḥ[…*

"S²RḤM of the family of BRLM honors and defends. By permission of Ḏāt Ḥ[…"

subst. *tḥmy* Q 915/1-2

WALL [Cf. Heb *ḥômāh* "wall (of a city)," Ug *ḥmt* "wall," Ph pl. *ḥmyt* "walls"]

Q 915/1-2: *bny ws¹ḥdṯ tḥmy gnn s³dw lᶜm ḏdwnm*

(ḤMY)

"[S²HR HLL YHNᶜM] built and newly constructed the wall of the garden of S³DW for ᶜAmm D̲ū DWNM"
(he-built and-newly-constructing the-wall [of] the-garden [of] S³DW for-ᶜAmm D̲ū-DWNM)

ḤNG I

prep. *ḥg* Q 40/21, Q 66/10, Q 67/7, Q 68/6, 9, Q 69/5, Q 70/1, 2, 3, Q 244/6, Q 246/5, Q 257B, Q 681/3

ACCORDING TO [Sab *ḥg* "as, because, according to, because of." Beeston, 1972, 353B, sees this as a nonassimilated form of the common conj. *ḥg* and compares the Him *ḥinj* = Ar *mit̲l* "like, as" cited by Nashwan. Pirenne, in CIAS 1:151-52, sees *ḥg* in the sense of "witness" at Q 244/6, with which she compares Ar *ḥujja* "proof, evidence, witnesss."]

Q 67/6-7: *wṣry s²hr ᵓdmsˡ ᵓrby ᶜm d̲lbḫ wtᵓnt̲sˡm bṣdqsˡm ḥg d̲t mḥrtn*

"and S²HR made a promulgation to his subjects the *ᵓrby* of ᶜAmm D̲ū Labaḫ and their womenfolk with their goodwill in accordance with this ordinance"
(and-promulgated S²HR [to] his-subjects the-*ᵓrby* [of] ᶜAmm D̲ū-Labaḫ and-their-womenfolk with-their-goodwill in-accordance-with this ordinance)

conj. *ḥg* Q 6/4, Q 37/3, Q 83/9, Q 89.137/5, Q.139/3, Q 173/1, Q 183/2, Q 254/2, Q 495/3, Q 909/2, Q 910/3; *ḥgn* Q 269/3, Q 494/4, Q 840/3, Q 904/3; *ḥngn* Q 688/4-5

AS, ACCORDING AS [Pirenne, in CIAS 1:132, understands *ḥgn* at Q 269/3 as "witness," with which she compares Ar *ḥujja* "proof, evidence, witness"]

Q 37/3: *ḥg ᵓmrw bmsˡᵓlsˡm*

"as they [the deities ᶜAt̲tar and ᶜAmm and S²MS¹] commanded through their oracle"
(according-as they-commanded through-their-oracle)

conj. *ḥgkm* Q 70/4-5, Q 72/1, Q 771/2

AS, JUST AS[comp. of the conj. *ḥg* and *km*]

Q 70/4-5: *wl yṣtdqwn ḥgkm sˡḥrsˡm ᵓmlk qtbn*

"may they receive their due as the kings of Qataban have ordered for them"
(may-they-receive-their-due according-as ordered-for-them the-kings [of] Qataban)

adv. *ḥgkm* Q 72/1

THUS, SO

Q 72/1: *ḥgkm s¹ḥr wḥrg s²hr hll bn ḏrʾkrb*
"thus S²HR HLL the son of ḎRʾKRB decreed and established (a law)"
(thus decreed and-establishing S²HR HLL the-son [of] ḎRʾKRB)

prep. + prep. *bḥg*
See entry under B.

prep. + prep. *bnḥg*
See entry under BN I.

ḤFD

subst. *mḥfd* Q 720/2; *mḥfdn* Q 38/3, Q 39/2, Q 177/2; *mḥfds¹my* Q 182/1-2; *mḥfds¹m* Q 914/2

TOWER, FORTIFICATION [Sab *mḥfd* "tower, projecting element of wall," Eth *māḫfad* id.]

Q 177/1-2: *brʾw ws¹wṯr ws¹s²qr ḏn mḥfdn yḥḍr*
"[the tribe Ḏū HRBT] constructed, laid the foundation, and completed this tower YḤḌR"
(they-constructed and-laying-the-foundation and-completing this tower YḤḌR)

ḤFR

verb *ḥfr* Q 785e/2

TO BURY [Sab *ḥfr* "to dig," Arab *ḥafara*, Heb *ḥāp̱ar*, Aram *ḥăp̱ar*, Akk *ḫapāru* id.; see also Jamme, 1972, 50, who cites the same verb in the Ḥaḍ inscription J 885/1 with the meaning "to hollow."]

Q 785e/2: *myfʿm ḏmḥrṯm ḥfr ḥwdn ḥbny*
"MYFʿM Ḏū MḤRṮM has buried ḤWDN of the clan ḤBNY"

ḤḌR

t-prfx. *tḥḍr* Q 656/3

TO BE PRESENT in a place; TO BE [Cf. Ar *taḥaḍḍara* "to be, to be present"]

Q 656/1-4: *ʾs¹lbm ḏʾbʿly tḥḍr bḏt bḥtn*
"ʾS¹LBM Ḏū ʾBʿLY was present in this place"

ḤQL

subst. *ḥql* Q 694/4, 7

PLAIN, FIELD; COUNTRY [Sab *ḥql* "fields, countryside," Ar *ḥaql* "field, domain"]

Q 694/4: *ḥql ʿynm*
"the field of ʿYNM"

(ḤQL)

adv. *nḥql* Q 67/11, Q 73/3, Q 78/12, Q 695/10

PARTICULARLY, IN PARTICULAR [Sab *nḥql* "specially"; cf. Heb *ḥeleq* "part, portion, share, lot" and the most recent discussion of this word in Beeston, 1976, 414-22, but see also Jamme, 1972, 30, 77, who translates it as "share, part, portion"]

Q 67/10-11: *wḏn ʾs¹dn ʾrby ḏlbḫ ʾlḏy bʿlw mlkn nḥql ḏbn ṣḥf dtnt*

"these persons, the *ʾrby* of Ḏū Labaḫ, are the ones in possession of the property, and in particular that which is (specified) in the agreement of Datinat"

(and-these persons the-*ʾrby* [of] Ḏū-Labaḫ [are] those-who they-have-taken-possession-of the-property particularly that-which-from the-document [of] Datinat)

ḤRG

verb *ḥrg* Q 38/2, Q 39/2, Q 40/2, Q 66/2(2x), 6, 8, Q 72/1, Q 74/3, Q 78/11, Q 113/1, Q 176/9, Q 202/4, Q 254/2; *ḥrgs¹* Q 898/1, Q 904/3, Q 905/3; *byḥrg* Q 40/21, Q 66/5

1) TO DIRECT, SUPERVISE, ADMINISTER; TO PUT INTO EFFECT, ESTABLISH; TO COMMAND [Sab *ḥrg* "to wield authority"; cf. perhaps Ar *ḥarraja* "to forbid"]

Q 66/6: *wl yṣḥf wḥrg ʿṣmn bn s²hr wrḫn ḏtmnʿ*

"and let this patronage-tie be written and administered from the new moon of the month Ḏū Timnaʿ"

(and-let be-written and-administering this-patronage-tie from the-new-moon [of] the-month Ḏū-Timnaʿ)

2) TO PROTECT

Q 898/1: *ywm ḥrgs¹ mrʾs¹ ydʿb ḏbyn*

"on the occasion when his lord YDʿB Ḏū BYN protected him"

subst.[1] *tḥrg* Q 66/1-2, Q 74/3, Q 79/6, Q 176/10, Q 177/4, Q 856/4, Q 898/4, Q 914/4; *tḥrgm* Q 770/6; *tḥrgn* Q 66/4, Q 202/2; *tḥrgs¹* Q 244/12, Q 246/11

1) ORDER, COMMAND; DIRECTION

Q 856/4: *btḥrg mrʾs¹ ydʿb*

"(he finished the whole project) at the command of his lord YDʿB"

2) PROTECTION

Q 898/4: *s¹wfy ʿm ʿbds¹ ṣḥwm btḥrg ʾmrʾs¹ s²hr ygl wbns¹*

"ʿAmm kept his servant ṢḤWM safe under the protection of his lords S²HR YGL and his son" (and-kept-safe ʿAmm his-servant ṢḤWM under-the-protection [of] his-lords S²HR YGL and-his-son)

3) OFFICE, ADMINISTRATION

Q 66/4: *wṯwb ʾhs¹ lḏn tḥrgn*

"[when he completes two years] and another succeeds to this administration"

subst.² pl. *mḥrgw* Q 679/5

ADMINISTRATOR, COMMANDER [Cf. Sab *mḥrg* "person in authority"]

Q 679/5-6: *ʾqwl wmḥrgw ʾs²ʿbn mḏḥym wdtnt ws¹frm*

"the governors and administrators of the tribes MḎḤYM and Datinat and S¹FRM"

ḤRM

verb *ḥrmw* Q 694/13; *yḥrm* Q 78/4, Q 694/11, Q 695/5-6; *byḥrm* Q 40/21

1) TO BE FORBIDDEN [Cf. Sab *ḥrm, hḥrm* "to be sacred, taboo, incur interdict," Ar *ḥarama* "to forbid, prohibit"]

Q 694/13: *ḥrmw bn qwr bs¹m kl bʾrm bn ḏn wrḫn lʾḫr*

"it is forbidden to dig any well in them (i.e., in these lands) from this month on"

(they-have-forbidden from the-digging in-them any well from this month on)

2) TO BE PUNISHED; TO INCUR INTERDICTION

Q 78/4: *wl yḥrm s¹w ʾns¹n*

"let this man be punished"

3) TO ORDER, COMMAND [Perhaps there is a semantic development "forbid">"command, order"]

Q 40/21: *wl yftḫ ḏn ftḥn wmḥrtn bʿḍm ʾw ʾbnm knm byḥrm mlkn*

"let this order and directive be inscribed in wood or stone as the king commands"

(and-let be-inscribed this order and-directive in-wood or stone as commands the-king)

s¹-prfx. *s¹ḥrm* Q 79/1, Q 186A/2, Q 202/1; *s¹ḥrms¹m* Q 186 B/24

ENACT, DECLARE IRREVOCABLY

Q 79/1: *s²hr [y]gl bn ydʿʾb mlk qtbn hgr ws¹ḥrm ḥrmn ʿṣm*

"S²HR [Y]GL the son of YDʿʾB king of Qataban declared and enacted this taxation law"

(S²HR [Y]GL the-son [of] YDʿʾB king [of] Qataban he-declared and-he-enacted the-law [of] taxing)

subst.¹ *ḥrmn* Q 79/1, Q 202/1; *ḥrmnn* Q 79/5

(IRREVOCABLE) LAW, DIRECTIVE [Cf. Sab *ḥrmn* "interdict, ban"]

Q 79/5: *bnḥg ḏn hgrn wḥrmnn*

(ḤRM)

"according to this directive and law"

subst.[2] *mḥrm* Q 40/4, Q 67/2(2x), Q 68/1(2x); Q 69/1(2x); *mḥrmn* Q 40/6; *mḥrms¹* Q 4/5, Q 89.137/4, .139/4, Q 183/1, Q 246/4, Q 905/5, Q 906/6, Q 908/3-4

SANCTUARY, ENCLOSURE [Cf. Sab *ḥrmt* "enclosure," *mḥrm* "sanctuary"]

Q 67/1-2: *bn ḥṭbm mḥrm ʿm*

"from ḤṬBM the sanctuary of ʿAmm"

subst.[3] *mḥrm* Q 186B/24

SANCTION

Q 186B/23-25: *lyṣtdqwn qtbn hg mḥrm s¹ḥrms¹m ʾmlk qtbn*

"in order that the Qatabanians may have their due in accordance with the sanction which the kings of Qataban have ordered for them"

(in-order-that-have-their-due the-Qatabanians according-to the-sanction [which] ordered-them kings [of] Qataban)

ḤRḌ

subst. *mḥrḍw* Q 73/5

JUDGE; LAWGIVER [Cf. Heb *ḥāraṣ* "to cut; to decide, determine, fix," and see Beeston, 1950b, 267]

Q 73/5: *kl s²ʿbn ḏmḥrḍw wms²rqytn*

"every tribe of 'the lawgiver' and 'the rising sun'"

ḤRR I

subst.[1] *ḥrt* Q 679/9, 10; *ḥrtm* Q 694/8, 11; *ḥrts¹* Q 694/9 *ḥrts¹n* Q 694/10

AQUEDUCT with embanked sides, PRIMARY CANAL [Cf. Sab *ḥrt* "irrigation canal," ModYem *ḥarra* "stone wall or embankment" which was, acording to Irvine, 1962, 31, "intended to support fields on hillsides against the impetus of the pluvial run-off."]

Q 694/8: *mrḥbm bn nḫlm wḫrṯ ʾwd wbqlm bqlm wbny ḥrtm*

"this land shall be open to irrigation and free from palmgroves, the terracing of (the area held by) a retaining wall, the cultivation of plants, and the construction of an aqueduct"

(land-open-for-irrigation from palmgrove and-the-terracing [of] a-retaining-wall and-cultivating [of] plants and-the-building [of] an-aqueduct)

subst.[2] *mḥrr* Q 687/6

ROCKY TERRAIN, STONY LAND [Cf. Ar *ḥarra* "land full of stones"]

Q 687/6: *ṯwbk ʾrḥb bmḥrr ṯwyʿn*
"this abode ʾRḤB in the (stony) land ṮWYʿN"

ḤRR II

subst. *ḥr* Q 647/1

FREEMAN, FREE-BORN MAN [Sab *ḥr*, Ar *ḥurr* "free; freedom"]

Q 647/1-2: *ʾbs¹rk ḥr s¹bʿ[ ] b[ʾḏn] ʿm ḏbhl*
"ʾBS¹RK, freeman of S¹Bʿ. By permission of ʿAmm Ḏū BHL"

ḤRṮ

verb *ḥrṯ* Q 72/2, Q 694/8, 9

TO CULTIVATE, TERRACE, PLOW [Cf. Sab *mḥrṯt* "ploughland,", Ar *ḥaraṯa*, Heb *ḥārаš*, Aram *ḥrš*, Akk *erēšū* "to plow"]

Q 72/2-3: *kḏm byfrwn wʾgw wʾhw wḥrṯ wqẓr wʿzz ws¹qḥ ws¹ʿhd s²ʿbm s²ʿbm*
"in order that they till, struggle, toil, plow, labor, work vigorously, make ready, and attend to (their task) tribe by tribe"
(in-order-that they-till and-struggling and-toiling and-plowing and-laboring and-working-vigorously and-making-ready and-attending-to tribe tribe)

subst. *ḥrṯm* Q 695/6

CULTIVATION

Q 695/5-7: *wl yḥrm ʾḫr wbrm bn ws³f bʿlw bn tqbln kl ḥrṯm ʾw tqblm*
"it is forbidden that ʾḪR and BRM be enlarged beyond these dimensions by any cultivation or planting"
(and-let be-forbidden ʾḪR and-BRM from enlargement over from this-dimension any cultivation or planting)

ḤS¹Y

subst. *ḥs¹y* Q 9/1

SILENCE [Cf. Heb *ḥāšāh* "to be silent," Aram *ḥăšāh*, *ḥās¹ī* id., and see the discussion on this word and the inscription in which it is found in Beeston, 1953, 111-12.]

Q 9/1-2: *s¹hlm ḏrʾn wḥs¹y wns¹ym lḏm byns²ʾ mʿmrn bn brṯs¹*
"S¹HLM ḎRʾN. Silence and oblivion to whoever removes this memorial monument from its place"

Ḫ

ḪBL

subst./partcp. *ḫblm* Q 73/6

ONE WHO DEFACES, DAMAGES [Sab *ḫbl* "ruin."; cf. Ar *ḫabala* "to corrupt or render unsound (in mind, a limb)," Eth *taḫabbala* "to be arrogant, audacious," Heb *ḥāḇal* "act corruptly," Akk *ḫabālu* "to injure"]

Q 73/5-6: *wrṯd ǵlbm ḏtn ʾs¹ṭrn ʿṯtr s²rqn wʿm wns¹wr wʾl fḫr bnkl ḫs³s³m wḫblm*

"ǴLBM entrusted these inscriptions to ʿAṯtar S²RQN and to ʿAmm and NS¹WR and ʾL FḪR to prevent any damage and defacement"

(and-entrusted ǴLBM these inscriptions [to] ʿAṯtar S²RQN and-ʿAmm and-NS¹WR and-ʾL FḪR from-any one-who-damages and-defaces)

ḪBṢ

subst. *ḫbṣtm* Q 72/6

ḪBṢT, coin of little value [Irvine, 1964, 30, suggests the basic sense of "mix," citing Ar *ḫabaṣa* "he turned over and mixed and made *ḫabiṣ* (i.e. a kind of food made of crushed dates and clarified butter)," and proposes that this may point to base silver, bullion coinage.]

Q 72/6-7: *bʿs²r ʿs²r ḫbṣtm mṣʿm lṯt ṯt ywmm*

"for the price of ten *ḫbṣt* of full value for each day"

(for-the-price-of-ten ten *ḫbṣt* of-full-value for-one one day)

ḪDʿ

s¹-prfx. *s¹ḫdʿ* Q 72/4, 7;

BALK AT, AVOID [Cf. Ar *ḫadaʿa* "circumvent, deceive"]

Q 72/4: *wʾy ʾy ʾs¹dm bydr ws¹ḫdʿ bn wfr*

"and whatever man refuses and balks at plowing"

(and-whatever whatever man he-refuses and-balking-at plowing

subst. *ms¹ḫdʿn* Q 72/5-6

ONE WHO BALKS AT, AVOIDS something

See entry above.

ḪDR

verb *ḫdr* Q 186A/9, 15, 19, B/13; *yḫdr* Q 186A/13; *byḫdr* Q 186A/11

TO SET UP a trading-stall [Beeston, 1959, 5, views this verbal root as a denominative deriving from a noun parallel to the Ar *ḫidr* "chamber, house, tent" and Heb *ḥeḏer* "room, chamber," and meaning here a stall where a merchant may set up his wares.]

Q 186A/13-14: *wmty yḫdr ḫdrm wʾḏw bys²tyṭ*

"when he sets up a trading-stall he may then trade"

(and-when he-sets-up a-trading-stall and-then he-may-trade)

subst. sing. *ḫdrm* Q 186A/13-14, B/13; pl. *ḫdwr* Q 186B/28

PLACE OF BUSINESS; TRADING STALL [Beeston, 1971b, 3, gives the meaning "place of business"; Jamme, 1972, 65, translates it "warehouse"]

See entry above.

ḪW

subst. *ḫw* Q 72/10

DOOR, GATE [Cf. reduplicated form in Ar *ḫawḫa* id. Eth *ḫōḫt* "aperture in the wall"]

Q 72/10: *bḫw ḫlfn ḏs³dw*

"at the gateway of Ḏū S³DW"

ḪWL

verb *ḫwl* Q 74/3

TO DIRECT, ADMINISTER [Ar *ḫāla* (w) "to administer, direct the affairs (of)"]

Q 74/2-3: *ywm ḫwl wḥrg yḏmrmlk … btḥrg wḫlt ydᶜᵒb bḍrm*

"at that time YḎMRMLK administered and directed them … under the management and direction of YDᶜᵒB during the war"

(when administered and-directed YḎMRMLK … under-the-management and-direction [of] YDᶜᵒB during-the-war)

subst.[1] *ḫlt* Q 74/3

DIRECTION, MANAGEMENT, ADMINISTRATION

See entry above.

subst.[2] *ḫwl* Q 266/7

REGENT, ADMINISTRATOR

Q 266/7: *wb frᶜkrb ḏḏrḥn dd wḫwl s²hr*

"and by FRᶜKRB of the clan of ḎRḤN, paternal uncle and regent of S²HR"

ḪṬʾ

subst. *ḫṭʾtn* Q 72/9

CRIME, TRANSGRESSION [Sab *ḫṭʾ*(m) "sin, offense," Heb *ḥaṭṭāʾṯ* "sin, sin-offering," Ar *ḫaṭʾ* "error, offense, fault," Eth *ḫaṭiʾat* "sin"]

(ḪṬʾ)

Q 72/9: *fl yʿtny mlkn bḫṭʾtn*

"let the king take the responsibility (for punishing) this offense"

(then-let take-responsibility the-king for-this-offense)

ḪṬB

subst. sing. *ḫṭb* Q 904/2; *ḫṭbs¹* Q 74/8, Q 100/3, Q 203/2, 4, Q 268/2; *ḫṭbs¹my* Q 74/6; pl. *ʾḫṭbs¹* Q 51/3, Q 82/3, Q 99/3-4, Q 101/2, Q 266/2, Q 790/2; *ʾḫṭbs¹m* Q 243/4, 5; *ʾḫṭbhw* Q 265/2

LOWER STORY [Sab *ʾḫṭb* id. See also Jamme, 1958a, 184, where he defines the word as "workroom, workshop," and compares it with the Ar *ḥaṭaba* "to gather firewood" and Heb *ḥāṭaḇ* "to cut or gather wood."]

Q 266/2: *s²ʾm wẓrb byts¹ yfs² wkl ʾḫṭbs¹ wṣrḥts¹ww wnfs¹hs¹ww wms¹qfts¹*

"[ṮWYBM, son of YS²RHʿM] purchased and took possession of his house YFS² and all its lower stories and its upper-rooms and its roof terraces and its arcades"

(he-purchased and-he-took-possession-of his-house YFS² and-all its-lower-stories and-its-upper-rooms and-its-roof-terraces and-its-arcades)

ḪṬM

subst. *ḫṭm* Q 178/1; *ḫṭmn* Q 855/2

TOP, SUMMIT [Cf. Ar *ḫuṭma* "peak, summit"]

Q 855/2: *hwfʾl s²ḥz tqdm kl mhlk ḫṭmn*

"HWFʾL S²ḤZ directed the whole project at the top (of the inscription)"

(HWFʾL S²ḤZ he-directed all the-project [of] the-top)

ḪYL

subst. *ʾḫyl* Q 36/5, Q 73/4-5

RESOURCES, MEANS, AID [Sab *ḫyl* "*material* resources," Eth *ḫayl* "strength; army," Heb *ḥayl* "strength, power"]

Q 73/4-5: *wbrdʾ wʾḫyl ʾdm bn qs³mm*

"with the resources and support of the men of (the tribe) QS³MM"

ḪYR

subst. pl. *ʾḫyr* Q 687/8

ELITE [Sab *ʾḫyr* "noblemen,", Ar *ḫayr* "good, superior"]

Q 687/8-9: *ʿlbḏr ʾḫyr s³md hwyḫr*
"near the field of the elite of the dignitaries of HWYḪR"
(near-the-field [of] the-elite [of] the-dignitaries [of] HWYḪR)

ḪLL

s¹-prfx. *s¹ḫl* Q 40/15

TO ARRANGE, ORDER [Cf. perhaps Ar *ḫāla* (w) "supervise, manage, administer"]

Q 40/14-15: *kl ʾftḥm wmḥrtm wʾṯftm wḫwlltm ftḥw ws¹ḥr wṯfṭ ws¹ṯb ws¹ḫl*

"all orders, directives, decisions, and regulations which they ordered, directed, decided, determined, and regulated"

(all orders and-directives and-decisions and-regulations [which] they-ordered and-directing and-deciding and-determining and-regulating)

subst. *ḫwlltm* Q 40/5, 14; *ḫwlltn* Q 40/16

REGULATION, ARRANGEMENT, ORDER

See entry above.

ḪLʿ

s¹-prfx. *s¹ḫlʿ* Q 40/12

TO WAIVE [Cf. Ar *ḫalaʿa* "to remove, take off"]

Q 40/11-12: *wʾy ḥll byḥllwn wnfs¹ wmtʿ ws¹ḫlʿ bnʿlw mqmh[w] wʾbyt wʾqny qtbn ms³wdn wqtbn ṭbnn*

"whatever they cancel, reduce, defer, and waive on the proper[ty], houses, and possessions of the lords and landowners of Qataban"

(and-whatever cancelling they-cancel and-reducing and-deferring and-waiving on the-proper[ty] and-the-houses and-the-possessions [of] the-Qatabanians the-lords and-the-Qatabanians the-landowners)

subst. pl. *ḫlwʿ* Q 40/18

ABROGATION, WAIVER

Q 40/18: *nl yḍʾwn wkwn s¹m ʾftḥn ʾw [w]mḥrtn wmnkṯs¹m sḫwl wʿṣwb wnfwq wḫlwʿ wlkwʿ*

"let these ordinances or directives and the penalty for their violation be published and be a duty, obligation, requirement, and an abrogation of previous laws and a confirmation of current statutes"

(let go-forth and-being these ordinances or directives and-their-violation duties and obligations and-requirements and-abrogations and-confirmations)

ḪLF

subst. *ḫlf* Q 720/2, Q 770/3-4; *ḫlfn* Q 68/8, Q 70/4, Q 72/10

GATE [Sab *ḫlf* "gate," cf. MSA *ḫalfa* "window"]

Q 68/8: *wb ḫlfn ḏs³dw*

"and at the gate of Ḏū S³DW"

ḪLṢ

adj. *ḫlṣmʾy* Q 40/4; *ḫlṣnʾy* Q 40/6, 9

SINCERE [Cf. Ar *ḫālaṣa* "act sincerely toward someone"]

Q 40/4: *ḫlṣmʾy ws³nḥm wbltn*

"in sincerity, with goodwill, and agreeably"

ḪMY

subst. dl. *ḫmyw* Q 694/4

PRESERVE, RESTRICTED LAND, PROPERTY [Jamme, 1972, 23, adduces Ar *ḫiman* from the root ḪMY "reserved territory, place to which access is forbidden." Pirenne, 1971, 126, 129, restores the form to *ḫmywl* and suggets the meaning "arable lands" on the basis of the Arabic cognate *ḫamīla*, pl. *ḫamāyil* "land suitable for agriculture"]

Q 694/4-5: *bn ḫmyw byḥn wḏʿdnm*

"from the two preserves of Bayḥān and Ḏū ʿDNM"

ḪMS¹

card. num. *ḫms¹t* Q 690a/10

FIVE [Sab *ḫms¹*, Ar *ḫams* id.]

Q 690a/9-12: *wrḫhw ḏʿddn ḏlḫms¹t wʾrbʿy wṯlṯ mʾtm ḫrftm*

"in the month ʿDDN of the year 345"

[its-month Ḏū-ʿDDN which-to-five and-forty and-three hundred years]

card. num. *ḫms¹y* Q 186A/26, Q 897/9

FIFTY [Ar *ḫamsūna* "fifty", Heb *ḥămîšîm*, Akk *ḫamššāti* id.]

Q 186A/26: *ḫms¹y wrqm*

"fifty pieces of gold"

subst. dl. *ḫms¹myw* Q 490A/4, B/4; pl. *ʾḫms¹m* Q 490A/4, B/4

FIFTH (fraction) [Sab *ḫms¹* "fifth," Ar *ḫums* id.]

Q 490A/3-4: *wkwn lʾs²hrm bn ḏt qbrn wms³wds¹ wnfs¹hs¹yw s²lṯt ʾḫms¹m wl s²krm ws²ʿbm ṯnw ḫms¹myw*

"three-fifths of this tomb and its entrance chamber and interior belong to ʾS²HRM and two-fifths to S²KRM and S²ʿBM"

(and-was to-ʾS²HRM from this tomb and-its-entrance-chamber and-its-inner-chambers three fifths and-to S²KRM and-S²ʿBM two fifths)

ḪFR

t-infix (?) *ḫ[t]fr[m]* Q 186A/25

TO CHEAT, CIRCUMVENT [Beeston, 1959, 8, compares Ar *ʾaḫfarahu* "he acted perfidiously towards him."]

Q 186A/24-25: *wzʾ ʾns¹m ʿly ʾḫs¹ bḫ[t]fr[m]*

"someone has consistently cheated his fellow-trader"

(he-continued someone against his-fellow-trader in-cheating)

ḪRḤ

subst. pl. *mḫrḥw* Q 74/13

CANALS [Sense from context; cf. perhaps Syr *ḥārītā* "canal, ditch"]

Q 74/13: *wmḫrḥw ḏtn ʾrḍtn*

"and canals of these domains"

ḪRF I

subst. sing. *ḫrf* Q 40/7, 22, Q 66/6, 12, Q 67/9-10, Q 68/8, Q 69/6, Q 70/4, Q 72/10, Q 78/9, Q 202/6, Q 694/14; *ḫrfm* Q 844/8; dl. *ḫrfmyw* Q 66/3; pl. *ḫrwf* Q 695/8; *ḫrwfn* Q 72/4; *ḫryfm* Q 96bis/14; *ḫryftm* Q 570/3; *ḫrftm* Q 690a/12

1) AUTUMN, AUTUMN HARVEST [Sab *ḫrf* "autumn," Ar *ḫarīf* "freshly gathered autumn fruit; rain of autumn or the beginning of the winter," Heb *ḥōrep* "harvesttime, autumn," Akk *ḫarpu* "(early) autumn," Soq *ḥorf* "fruit, harvest, autumn," Sḥ *ḫorf* "autumn," Meh *ḫarf* "flower," Har *ḫoref* "autumn"]

Q 844/6-8: *bḏtn tkrbs¹ bnʿlw ḫrfm*

"[HWFʾL gave to ʿAmm an offering] from the autumn harvest of that which he had dedicated to him"

(in-that-which he-dedicated-to-him from the-autumn-harvest)

2) YEAR [The basic sense of *ḫrf*, "autumn," is used here by synecdoche for the whole year; cf. Eth *ḫarif* "the current year"; for dating in general, see Beeston, 1956.]

A) Q 66/3: *ṣ̌mm byʿṣm ʿm ḏlbḫ ṭd ʾns¹m ḫrfmyw*

"a patronage tie which binds each man to ʿAmm Ḏū Labaḫ for two years"

(patronage-tie [which] ties-to ʿAmm Ḏū-Labaḫ one man two-years)

B) Q 72/4: *bd ʾwrḫn wḫrwfn*

"in the succession of months and years"

3) EPONYMATE [used in dating documents]

A) Q 40/7: *bʾy wrḫn ḏbrm ḫrf ʿs³bm ḏḥḍrn*

"in the month of Ḏū BRM in the eponymate of ʿS³BM Ḏū ḤḌRN"

(Ḫ̱RF I)

B) Q 72/10: *wrḫ̱s¹ ḏʿm ḫ̱rf ʾbʿly bn s²ḥz qdmn*
"in the month Ḏū ʿAmm in the first eponymate of ʾBʿLY of the clan of S²ḤZ"
(its-month Ḏū-ʿAmm the-eponymate [of] ʾBʿLY clan [of] S²ḤZ the-former)

ḪRF II

subst. pl. *ḫ̱rwf* Q 898/9

SHEEP [Ar *ḫ̱arūf* "lamb, male young of the sheep"]

Q 898/8-9: *ʾrb[ʿ]t wḫ̱ms¹y ḫ̱rwf*
"[and his lords were paid] fifty-fo[ur] sheep"

ḪRṮ

verb *yḫ̱rṯ* Q 186A/26

TO PAY A FINE [See Beeston 1971b, 2.]

Q 186A/26-27: *lyḫ̱rṯ ḫ̱ms¹y wrqm lmlk*
"let him pay a fine of fifty pieces of gold to the king"

ḪS³S³

subst./partcp. *ḫ̱s³s³m* Q 73/6

ONE WHO DAMAGES [Cf. Sab *ḫ̱s³s³* "injury," Ḥar *ḫ̱ass* "worse," Soq *ḫ̱as* "weakness, feebleness"]

Q 73/5-6: *wrṯd ǵlbm ḏtn ʾs¹ṭrn ʿṯtr s²rqn wʿm wns¹wr wʾl fḫ̱r bnkl ḫ̱s³s³m wḫ̱blm*
"ǴLBM entrusted these inscriptions to ʿAṯtar S²RQN and to ʿAmm and NS¹WR and ʾL FḪ̱R to prevent any damage and defacement"
(and-entrusted ǴLBM these inscriptions [to] ʿAṯtar S²RQN and-ʿAmm and-NS¹WR and-ʾL FḪ̱R from-any one-who-damages and-defaces)

ḪTM

verb *ḫ̱tmw* Q 40/35

TO AFFIX ONE'S SEAL [Ar and Eth *ḫ̱atama* "to sign, affix a seal," Heb *ḥāṯam* id. This appears to be a loanword from Eg; see Lambdin, 1953, 151.]

Q 40/35: *wḫ̱tmw*
"and they have affixed their seal" (added after a long list of witnesses and concluding the inscription)

ḪTN

susbt. *mḫtn* Q 36/4, Q 856/3-4; *mḫtns¹* Q 186B/13

HOUSE, RESIDENCE [See Rabin 1983, 492, Jamme, 1972, 65, and Beeston, 1971b, 2-3, for a discussion of this word; cf. also Sab *mḫtn* "house, residence; family," Akk *ḫatānu* "protect, shelter"]

Q 856/3-4: *byt wdm wʾṯrt wmḫtn mlkn*

"the temple of WDM and of ʾAṯirat and the residence of the king"

Ṭ

ṬBN

subst. *ṭbnn* Q 40/4, 5, 6, 8, 11, 12, 19

LANDOWNER [Sab *ṭbnt* "landlord"; cf. perhaps Min (R 2791/6) *ʾhl ṭbn bms¹qy* "to be in charge of irrigation." Conti Rossini, 1931, 159, cites MSA *ṭabyīn* "patron of farmers."]

Q 40/19: *qtbn ms³wdn wqtbn ṭbnn*

"the Qatabanian lords and landowners"

ṬD

card. num. *ṭd* Q 66/3, Q 74/10; fem. *ṭt* Q 72/6(2x)

ONE [Cf. Meh *ṭād*, fem *ṭeyt*, *ṭit* "one," Soq masc. *ṭad*, fem. *ṭey*, Śḥ masc. *ṭad*, fem *ṭit* id.]

Q 72/6-7: *bʿs²r ʿs²r ḫbṣtm mṣʿm lṭt ṭt ywmm*

"for the price of ten *ḫbṣt* of full value for each day"

(for-the-price-of-ten ten *ḫbṣt* of-full-value for-one one day)

ṬWD

s¹-prfx. *s¹ṭd* Q 1/2

SACRIFICE (?) [See W. Müller, who compares Ar *ṭāda* "to take root," *inṭāda* "to rise in the air," and cf. also RÉS I, 261]

Q 1/2: *šṭd ṭly*

"[TBʿKRB Ḏū ḎRḤ] sacrificed (?) a lamb"

ṬYB

subst. *ṭyb* Q 260

INCENSE [Sab *ṭyb* "incense (?)"; cf. Ar *ṭayyib* "giving forth a pleasant odor" and K. Nielsen, 1986, 18, according to whom "*ṭyb* seems to be a general term for aroma" in ESA]

(ṬYB)

Q 260: *ṭyb mʿm[r]*

"incense as a votive off[ering]"

ṬLY

subst. *ṭly* Q1/2

KID, LAMB [Sab *ṭlyn*, Ar *ṭalā* id.]

Q 1/2: *s¹ṭd ṭly bṣryn ʿm wḥwkm*

"he sacrificed (?) a lamb because of the protection of ʿAmm and ḤWKM"

Ẓ

ẒWR

verb *hẓr* Q 105

TO FORTIFY, ESTABLISH [Cf. Sab *ẓwr* "invest, besiege," Nab *ṭwr* "wall," Ar *ẓiʾr* "buttress," Soq *ṣwr* "to bear, carry," Eth *ṣōra* id.]

Q 105: *ʾls²rḥ ḏḏrḥʾl hẓr*

"ʾIls²araḥ of the clan of Ḏaraḥʾil has fortified"

ẒYH

s¹-prfx. *s¹ẓyh* Q 186A/28

TO ORDER [Cf. Heb *ṣiwwāh* "to order, command"]

Q 186A/26-27: *lyhrṯ ḫms¹y wrqm lmlk qtbn wʿhr s²mr ys¹mẓʾwn ws¹ẓyh*

"let him pay a fine of fifty pieces of gold to the king of Qataban and the overseer of S²MR, who will carry it out and order (its observance)"

(let-pay-a-fine fifty gold-pieces to-the-king [of] Qataban and-the-overseer [of] S²MR will-carry-out and-will-order)

ẒLL

s¹(h)-prfx. *hẓl* Q 688/6

TO COMPLETE, FINISH [Jamme 1972, 88, notes the Ar *ẓalla* "*exister, être*," and suggests the causative meaning "*donner l'existence*," and from there "*realiser*" in this case.]

Q 688/6: *whẓl fʿln*

"and he completed the work"

ẒLM

subst. *ẓlmt* Q 6/3

STATUE [Sab *ẓlm* "image, statue *of man,*" var. of *ṣlm*]

Q 6/3: *ẓlmt ḏhbn*

"a bronze statue"

ẒLʿ

verb *ẓlʿ* Q 173/4

TO PAY A FINE, PENALTY [Sab *ẓlʿ* "to be fined, pay a fine"]

Q 173/4: *wẓlʿ ḏʾyd ẓlʿ ṯwr[m]*

"Ḏū ʾYD paid the penalty of a ste[er]"

subst. *ẓlʿ* Q 173/4

PENALTY

See entry above.

ẒMʾ

adj. *mẓmʾtm* Q 74/11

UNIRRIGATED, DRY [Sab *ẓmʾ* "to suffer thirst," Ar *ẓamiʾa* "unirrigated, dry," Ar *maẓmaʾīy* "field watered by rain rather than by irrigation," Heb *ṣāmēʾ* "unirrigated, dry," Eth *ṣamʾa, ṣamāʾu* "to be thirsty"]

Q 74/10-11: *wṭd ʿs2r ʾnḫlm mẓmʾtm*

"and eleven unirrigated palmgroves"

ẒRʾ

subst. *ẓrʾs1* Q 40/21-22

PROCLAMATION (?) [Rhodokanakis, 1915, 49, compares Ar *ṣaraʾa* = *ṣaraḫa* "call out loudly," but in 1924, 32, writes, "*Bedeutung und Etymologie von* ẓrʾ *ist mir unbekannt.*" In any event, the context is difficult and there are no fully satisfying cognates.]

Q 40/21-22: *wl ys1kn mnkṯs1 ḥg ẓrʾs1 ʾs1mʿm ḏm ʿtlm bftḥn*

"and let the witnesses who have signed this order punish its violation according to his proclamation (?)"

(and-let punish its-violation according-to his-proclamation the-witnesses who signed this-order)

ẒRB

verb *ẓrb* Q 82/2, Q 99/3, Q 265/1, Q 266/2, Q 478/1, Q 790/2, Q 900/2; *ẓrbw* Q 100/2, Q 490A/2, B/2, Q 556/1, Q 874/2, Q 900/2, Q 903/3

1) TO SECURE TITLE TO [Sab *ẓrb* "to hand over, transfer *property,*" cf. Ar *ẓariba* "to adhere, cling to," and see Jamme, 1958a, 184-85, who translates "to assure definitively"]

(ẒRB)

Q 900/1-3: *ḥmys²m wrklm bnw s²rḥwd bn ḫlbn ˤs¹yw ẓrbw qbrs¹my ẓrb bʾbltm*

"ḤMYS²M and RKLM the two sons of S²RḤWD of the clan ḪLBN acquired and secured the title to their tomb for a female camel"

(ḤMYS²M and-RKLM the-two-sons [of] S²RḤWD member-of-the-clan ḪLBN they-took-possession they-secured their[dl.]-tomb a-securing for-a-female-camel)

2) TO DEDICATE, CONSECRATE

Q 82/1-3, 4-5: *hˤs¹mm bn lbtm wlqṭm wwlds¹ qny wẓrb byts¹ … bḥg ʿnby wʾl tˤly*

"HˤS¹MM the son of LBTM and LQṬM and his son purchased and dedicated his house ... to ˤAnbay and ʾLTˤLY."

subst.¹ *ẓrbt* Q 35/5, Q 80/4; *ẓrbtn* Q 72/6; *ẓrbts¹* Q 72/3, 5, 7; *ẓrwb* Q 72/2

FIELD, LAND, PROPERTY [Cf. Sab *ẓrb* "propietary right"]

Q 35/5-6: *bˤl ẓrbt ltk bḏbḥtm*

"owner of the field LTK for sacrificial animals"

subst.² *tẓrbn* Q 243/6, 8

LAND GRANT, CONCESSION

Q 243/8: *bnḥl ḏn ḏtẓrbn wgdytn*

"(this decree also applies) in the event of any lease (subsequent) to this land grant and renewal"

(in-granting-the-lease [of] that-which [is] of-a-land-grant and-renewal)

adj. *ẓrbm* Q 98/3

SECURE

Q 98/3: *mqbrm ẓrbm ls¹m*

"(as) a secure grave site for themselves"

(a-grave-site a-secure-location for-themselves)

Y

YD

subst. sing. *yd* Q 66/12, Q 67/11, Q 68/10, Q 69/7, Q 70/5, Q 72/10, Q 78/13-14, Q 79/8; *ydm* Q 681/2; pl. *ʾydw* Q 40/23-24, Q 78/14, Q 89.144A/3

HAND [Sab *yd* "hand," Ar *yad*, Eth *ʾed*, Heb *yāḏ* id., Akk *ittu* "side"]

Q 66/12: *wtˤlmʾy yd s²hr*

"S²HR signed with his own hand"
(and-signed the-hand [of] S²HR)

YDᶜ

verb *ydᶜ* Q 40/2

TO INQUIRE, FIND OUT [Cf. Sab *hydᶜ* "to make known to, inform someone," Heb *yādaᶜ* "to know," Syr *yidaᶜ*, Ug *ydᶜ*, Soq *ʾedaᶜ*, OAram *ydᶜ*, ImpAram *ydᶜ*, JewAram *ydᶜ*, Akk *edū* id.]

Q 40/2: *wʾmmm bs¹ʾlm s¹ʾl wydᶜ ḏm ḥrg mlkn*

"as instruction for one inquiring and finding out what the king has directed"

(and-instruction for-the-inquirer [who] inquiring and-finding-out that-which directed the-king)

YWM

subst.¹ sing. *ywm* Q 183/3, Q 244/8-9, Q 246/7; *ywmm* Q 72/7; *ywmn* Q 183/2, Q 840/4, 5, Q 913/4; dl. *ywmmyw* Q 72/3(2x); dl. (?) *ywmy[ ]* Q 173/2; pl. *ʾywm* Q 172/4; *ywmtyn* Q 78/12

DAY [Sab ywm "day," Arab *yawm*, Heb *yôm*, Akk *ūmu* id.]

A) Q 183/3: *bywm kwn ḍr byn s²mr ḏrydn wby[n] ʾbʾns¹*

"on the day that there was war between S²MR Ḏū Raydan and ʾBʾNS¹"

(on-the-day was war between S²MR Ḏū-Raydan and-betwe[en] ʾBʾNS¹)

B) Q 72/6-7: *bᶜs²r ᶜs²r ḫbṣtm mṣᶜm lṭt ṭt ywmm*

"for the price of ten *ḫbṣt* of full value for each day"

(for-the-price-of-ten ten *ḫbṣt* of-full-value for-one one day)

subst.² sing. *ywmyt* Q 40/22, Q 694/14

DATE [See the discussion of Beeston, 1962b, 28, 37, who describes *ywmyt* in Q 40/22 as a "secondary abstract formation meaning 'date'" and notes that it may be a fem. *nisba* form. See further Jamme, 1972, 26.]

Q 40/22-23: *wftḥ ftḥn ywmyt ts¹ᶜm ḏʾgbyw wrḫn ḏtmnᶜ ḫrf ᶜmᶜly ḏrs²m wbn qfʾn qdmn*

"this directive was given on the date of the ninth of Ḏū ʾGBYW in the month Ḏū Timnaᶜ in the first eponymate of ᶜMᶜLY Ḏū RS²M and clan of QFʾN"

(and-was-directed this-directive the-date [of] the-ninth [of] Ḏū-ʾGBYW the-month Ḏū-Timnaᶜ the-eponymate [of] ᶜMᶜLY Ḏū-RS²M and-descendent [of] QFʾN the-former)

conj. *ywm* Q 74/2, Q 1/2-3, Q 203/3, Q 241/4, Q 248/3, Q 898/1, 7-8, Q 915/2

(YWM)

WHEN [Sab *ywm* "(on the day) when," Ar *yawma* "when"]

Q 203/3-4: *ywm rdʾ ʿṯtr wʾlhw s¹qmtm s²hrǵln mḫḍ ḥḍrmt wʾmrm*

"when ʿAṯtar and the gods of irrigation aided S²HRǴLN in the defeat of ḤḌRMT and ʾMRM"

(when aided ʿAṯtar and-the-gods [of] irrigation S²HRǴLN [in] the-defeat [of] ḤḌRMT and-ʾMRM)

YMN

adj. *ʾymnn* Q 176/4

SOUTH; OF THE SOUTH [Sab *ymnt* "south," Arab *yamīn* "south; right, right hand," Heb *yāmîn* "right hand, right side; south"

Q 176/1-5: *ydʿʾb ḏbyn bn s²hr mkrb qtbn wkl wld ʿm wʾws¹n wkḥd wdhs¹m wtbnw wyrfʾ ʾymnn wʾs²ʾmn*

"YDʿʾB Ḏū BYN the son of S²HR *mkrb* of Qataban and all the children of ʿAmm and ʾWS¹N and KḤD and DHS¹M and TBNW and YRFʾ, those of the south and the north"

YFʿ

verb *yfʿ* Q 844/8; *yyfʿwn* Q 40/17

1) TO PROCLAIM, ANNOUNCE [Sab *yfʿ* "to announce, make known"]

Q 40/16-17: Q 40/16-17: *s¹mt ʾftḥn wmḥrtn wʾṯftn wḫwlltn wmnkṯs¹m wtʿlms¹m wʾnfṣs¹m ʾyhnmw ʿkr lyyfʿwn*

"let them proclaim these orders, directives, decisions, regulations, and their violation, documentation, and distribution wherever there is opposition"

(these orders and-directives and-decisions and-regulations and-their-violation and-their-documentation and-their-distribution wherever it-is-opposed let-them-announce)

2) TO TAKE AWAY, TAKE OFF, DEDUCT [Sab *yfʿ* "to rise up, oppose"; cf. Ar *yafaʿa* "to grow up, grow tall"]

Q 844/8-9: *yfʿ bṣdrs¹*

"he deducted the best part of it (as an offering)"

YS¹M

verb *ys¹m* Q 571z

TO BE LOVELY FACED, ATTRACTIVE, HANDSOME [Cf. Ar *wasuma* id.]

Q 571/2: *ḍmy ys¹m*

"ḌMY is lovely faced"

K

K

prep. k(ʾy) Q 40/2 (the *ʾy* following *k* is enclitic)

LIKE, AS [Sab *k*- "like, as," Ar *ka*-, Heb *k*-, Ug *k*-, OAram *k*- id.]

Q 40/2: *kʾyḏm[r]m*

"as a solemn pronoun[ce]ment"

conj. *kḏm* Q 40/9,14, 19, Q 72/2, Q 186A/7, 17, 22, B/14

THAT [comp. of *k* + *ḏm*]

A) Q 186A/16-18: *wmty lyksʾʾ ʿhr s²mr kḏm bys¹tḍf qtbn bʿm ʾs²ʿbm*

"and when the overseer of S²MR announces that he wishes the Qatabanians to make trading journeys among the tribes" (and-when announces the-overseer [of] S²MR that wishes-that-trade the-Qatabanians among the-tribes)

B) Q 72/1-2: *s¹ḥr wḥrg … kḏm byfrwn*

"ordained and commanded that they should work in the fields" (ordained and-commanding that they-work-in-the-fields)

adv. *kwḥd* Q 695/4

TOGETHER, AS A UNIT [Comp. of *k* + card. num. *wḥd*]

Q 695/4-5: *wkwn tqbl kl ʾrḍn kwḥd mṯmn wmfẓr ws²lṯy bqlm ws¹bʿt wʿs²ry ʾqblm*

"the size of the whole land together in value and extent is thirty *bql* and twenty-seven *qbl*"

(and-is the-dimension [of] all the-land together value and-extent both-thirty *bql* and-seven and-twenty *qbl*)

KBR

verb *kbr* Q 688/2; *ykbr* Q 66/6; *bykbr* Q 66/2

TO DIRECT [Sab *kbr* "to control, supervise," perhaps a denominative development from Qat *kbr* "*kabīr*, magistrate"]

A) Q 688/2: *kbr nhmm*

"directed the dressing of the stone"

B) Q 66/2: *bʿm kbrm bykbr wḥrg s²ʿbn kḥd*

"along with the *kabīr* who directs and administers the tribe KḤD"

(with the-*kabīr* he-directs and-administering the-tribe KḤD)

subst. *kbr* Q17, Q 72/6, 8, Q 209/1, Q 238/2, Q 899/1; *kbrm* Q 66/2, 6; *kbrn* Q 18; *kbr[n]* Q 28

(KBR)

MAGISTRATE, *KABĪR* [Sab *kbr* "magistrate," Ar *kabīr* "chief, important (person)"]

A) Q 17: *ʿḏḏ kbr*
"ʿḎḎ the *kabīr*

B) Q 72/6: *kbr tmnʿ*
"the *kabīr* of Timnaʿ"

KWM

adv. *kwmw* Q 66/8

SO, THUS [Cf. Eth *kama* "thus, so"]

Q 66/8: *wkwmw lyṣḥf wḥrg wʿtqb wṯtwb ḏn ṣḥfn ʾrbym byrby ʿm ḏlbḫ*
"and thus let (all) whom ʿAmm Ḏū Labaḫ chooses as *ʾrby* write down, administer, implement, and adhere to this agreement"
(and-thus let-him-write-down and-administering and-implementing and-adhering [to] this agreement the-*ʾrby* he-makes-*ʾrby* ʿAmm Ḏū-Labaḫ)

KWN

verb *kwn* Q 40/3, 8, 10, 18, Q 66/7, Q 183/3, Q 262/3, Q 490A/3, B/3, Q 694/10, Q 695/4, 7, 8, Q 901/3, Q 902/3; *kwnt* Q 694/13; *kwnw* Q 803/3; *ykn* Q 186B/25, Q 695/14; *bykn* Q 243/5

TO BE, EXIST [Sab *kwn* "to be," Ar *kāna* id., Ph *kn* "to be, exist"]

A) Q 490A/3-4: *wkwn lʾs²hrm bn ḏt qbrn wms³wds¹ wnfs¹hs¹yw s²lṯt ʾḫms¹m wl s²krm ws²ʿbm ṯnw ḫms¹myw*
"three-fifths of this tomb and its outer chamber and interior belong to ʾS²HRM and two-fifths to S²KRM and S²ʿBM"
(and-was to-ʾS²HRM from this tomb and-its-outer-chamber and its-inner-chambers three fifths and-to S²KRM and-S²ʿBM two fifths)

B) Q 183/3: *bywm kwn ḍr byn s²mr ḏrydn wby[n] ʾbʾns¹*
"on the day that there was war between S²MR Ḏū Raydan and ʾBʾNS¹"
(on-the-day was war between S²MR Ḏū-Raydan and-between ʾBʾNS¹)

s¹-prfx. *s¹knw* Q 40/14; *ys¹kn* Q 40/21; *bys¹knwn* Q 40/14, 18-19

TO IMPOSE PUNISHMENT, PUNISH [Sab *hkn* "to bring to pass; determine, arrange, fix"]

Q 40/21-22: *wl ys¹kn mnkṯs¹ ḥg ẓrʾs¹ ʾs¹mʿm ḏm ʿlm bftḥn*

"and let the witnesses who have signed this order punish its violation according to his proclamation (?)"
(and-let punish its-violation according-to-his-proclamation the-witnesses who signed this-order)

subst.[1] *kwns¹m* Q 40/3, 8
STATUS, STATION
Q 40/3: *ḏm kwn kwns¹m bn ʾs²bʿm*
"those among the tribes who are equal in status"
(those-who is their-status from the-tribes)

subst.[2] *mkntn* Q 1/4
INNER SHRINE, CELLA, CHAPEL of a temple [Sab *mknt* "inner shrine *of a temple*"; cf. Ar *makān* "place," Ḥaḍ *makān* "small chamber"; cf. Heb use of *maqōm* "place" for "shrine" or "temple." Some compare ESA *mknt* with Ar *kanna* "to hide, conceal."]
Q 1/4: *mwṯb mkntn*
"the sanctum of the inner shrine"

KLL I

verb *kl* Q679/9
TO ENHANCE, COMPLETE [Jamme, 1971, 85, compares the Sab *kl* in J 842/3]
Q 679/9: *ḏkl tnʿthw*
"which enhances its excellence"

pro. *kl* Q 38/2, Q 131/2, Q 186A/12, 15, Q 488/4, Q 855/1+; *kls¹* Q 268/2; *klhw* Q 679/10; *kls¹m* Q 82/4, Q 99/5-6, Q 100/4, Q 266/3, Q 790/3; *klhmw* Q 265/4
ALL, EVERY, ANY [Sab *kl* "all, every, any," Arab *kull*, Heb *kōl* id., Akk *kullatu* "the whole of"]

A) Q 186A/14-16: *wʾḏw bys²tyṭ ʾw fṯhr bʿm kl ḫdrm wms²ṭm*
"[when a trader sets up a stall] then he may trade or enter into a partnership with any possessor of a trading-stall and merchandise"
(and-then he-may-trade or entering-into-partnership with any possessor-[of]-a-trading-stall and-merchandise)

B) Q 488/4: *wkl ʾwlds¹my wʾqnys¹my*
"and all their children and possessions"
(and-all their[dl.]-children and-their[dl.]-possessions)

KLL II

subst. *kll* Q 745
SERVANT, SLAVE of a god [Cf. Ar *kall* "domestic"]
Q 745: *mwhbm bn s²mr zwrn kll ʿm*

(KLL II)

"MWHBM son of S²MR of the clan ZWRN, servant of ʿAmm"

KN

conj.[1] *kn* Q 78/5; *knm* Q 40/21, Q 78/5, 7, 13, Q 89.140/7, Q 694/1

AS, JUST AS [Cf. Sab *kn* "thus," Hēb *kēn* "thus, therefore," JewAram *kēn* id., Syr *ken* "and so, and then"]

Q 40/21: *wl yftẖ ḏn ftḥn wmḥrtn bʿḍm ʾw ʾbnm knm byḥrm mlkn*

"let this order and directive be inscribed in wood or stone as the king commands"

(let be-inscribed this order and-directive in-wood or stone as commands the-king)

conj.[2] *kn* Q 901/3, *knm* Q 78/13

WHEN [Sab *kn* "when"]

Q 901/3: *kn kwn bʿlw ḏtw ḍ(m)[rn]*

"when he was over the clan of Ḍ(M)[RN]"

KNF

subst. *knf* Q 687/6

EDGE, BORDER, SIDE [Sab *knf* "border, side, direction"; cf. Ar *kanafa* "fence in," Ar *kanaf* "wing," Heb *kānāp̱* "wing, extremity"]

Q 687/6-7: *bknf gwly ḥṣdnn wys²gb*

"at the edge of the two fields of ḤṢDNN and YS²GB"

KRB I

t-prfx. *tkrbs¹* Q 183/2, Q 481/2, Q 487/2-3, Q 494/4, Q 496/3, Q 771/3, Q 806/2, Q 840/3, 6, Q 844/7, Q 858/3, Q 904/3, Q 916/3; *tkrbs¹m* Q 1/5; *tkrbts¹* Q 269/3

1) TO DEDICATE, SET APART [Sab *hkrbn* "to dedicate," Akk *karābu* "to render homage"]

Q 840/3-4: *ḥgn tkrbs¹ s²rḥ[ʾl wzy]dʾl bqdmw ḏn ywmn*

"[S²RḤʾL and ZYDʾL gave Ḏū S¹amāwī an offering of bronze] as S²RḤ[ʾL and ZY]Dʾl had dedicated to him in the past"

(according-as dedicated-to-him S²RḤ[ʾL and-ZY]Dʾl in-the-former [of] this day)

2) TO UNDERTAKE, ENGAGE IN [See Beeston, 1981, 26, for a disscussion of this verb in the sense "to undertake"]

Q 909/3: *[y]zʾn ṣdq ws¹ʾmn ʿqrbn bkl ʾʾrḫ tkrb*

"may [Wadd] [con]tinue to show favor and protection to ʿQRBN in all the affairs that he undertakes" (may-[con]tinue favoring and-protecting ʿQRBN in-all affairs he-has-engaged)

t-infix *byktrbwn* Q 244/11, *byktrbw[n]* Q 246/10

TO BE GRANTED

Q 244/10-12: *wʿm lyzʾ ṣdqs*^{1}*n bkl mngw byktrbwn ʿmn tḥrgs*^{1}

"as for ʿAmm, may he continue to give them their due by all the good fortune which will be granted by his order"

(and-ʿAmm may-he-continue granting-them-their-due through-all the-good-fortune [which] will-be-granted by his-order)

subst. *mkrb* Q 35/1, Q 36/1, Q 54, Q 56, Q 57, Q 58, Q 80/1, Q 176/2, Q 696/1-2, Q 697/1, Q 915/2

MKRB, RULER, OVERLORD [According to Beeston, 1972, 264-66, the *mkrb* is not a priest-ruler, as Hommel concluded on the basis of an Akk etymology, but the head of a commonwealth of *s*^{2}*ʿb* groups.]

A) Q 35/1-2: *s*^{2}*hr hll [...] bn ydʿʾb mkrb qtbn bkr ʾnby*

"S^{2}HR HLL [...] son of YDʿʾB *mkrb* of Qataban the firstborn of ʾAnbay"

B) Q 36/1: *ydʿʾb ḏbyn bn s*^{2}*hr mkrb qtbn*

"YDʿʾB Ḏū BYN the son of S^{2}HR, *mkrb* of Qataban"

KRB II

subst. *mkrbt* Q 218/3

FEMALE DEITY WHO BESTOWS BLESSINGS [Sab *krbt* "blessing, favor." See Beeston, in CIAS 2:165 who comments that Q 218 "further yields a new type of description of a deity as *mkrb* "bestower of blessing." However, it may also be understood as "place of assembly, sanctuary," cf. Sab *mkrbn* "temple, sanctuary," Eth *mek*^{w}*rāb* "temple (esp. temple in Jerusalem, or Jewish synagogue)"]

Q 218/3: *[mk]rbm wmkrbt*

"[MʿDʾL King of Aws^{1}an has committed his tomb to the protection of ... every] male or female deity who bestows blessings"

KS^{3}ʾ

verb *ks*^{3}*ʾ* Q 172/5-6; *yks*^{3}*ʾ* Q 186A/17, Q 243/5 *yks*^{3}*ʾwn* Q 186A/21-22; *byks*^{3}*ʾ* Q 78/7

1) TO COMMAND [Ḥaḍ *kṯʾ* (R 2693/4) "to command (said of a god)"]

Q 78/7: *knm byks*^{3}*ʾ*

"as (the king) commands"

(KS^{3}ʾ)

2) TO ANNOUNCE [With regard to the semantic distinction "to command" and "to announce" of *ks^{3}ʾ*, Beeston, 1959, 7, writes: "The connection between 'making a declaratory utterance = announce' and 'making a mandatory utterance = command' is of course very close, and both senses are found in the common Semitic *ʾmr* and Eng 'tell'."

Q 186A/16-18: *wmty lyksʾ ʿhr s^{2}mr kḏm bys^{1}tḍf qtbn bʿm ʾs^{2}ʿbm*
"and when the overseer of S^{2}MR announces that he wishes the Qatabanians to make trading journeys among the tribes"
(and-when announces the-overseer [of] S^{2}MR that wishes-that-trade the-Qatabanians among the-tribes)

3) TO BE RESIDENT; TO BE, BE PRESENT [Höfner, 1987, 43, cites Meh *kesū* "to find," Śḥ *ksé*, subjunctive *yĕkséʾ* id.]

Q 243/5: *bykn wks^{3}ʾ ws^{1}ṭ ḏtn ʾbytn*
"[WRWʾL ǴYLN YHNʿM decreed and announced to his subjects] who live and are resident in these houses"

KS^{3}W

subst. dl. *ks^{3}wtnyhn* Q 912/2-3

GARMENT [Sab *ʾks^{3}wt* "garments," Ar *kiswa* "clothing, clothes, apparel"]

Q 912/1-3: *w s^{1}qnyt ʿm ks^{3}wtnyhn*
"she has dedicated to ʿAmm these two garments"

L

L I

prep. *l-* Q 40/11, Q 72/6, Q 83/7, Q 172/6, Q 178/2(2x), Q 186A/27, Q 486/4, Q 489/3, Q 490A/3, Q 840/6+; *ls^1* Q 73/3, Q 855/2; *lhw* Q 74/14, Q 178/1, Q 611/3; *ls^{1}m* Q 68/8-10, Q 98/3, Q 840/5-6

TO, TOWARD, FOR, ABOUT, CONCERNING [Sab *l-* "to, toward; for;" Ar *li-*, Heb *l-*, id. See Beeston, 1962b, 55, for a discussion of the various uses of *l-* in the ESA dialects.]

in spatial or temporal sense:

Q 40/11: *bnkn lʾẖr*
"henceforth"
(from-thus to-after)

dative sense:

A) Q 186A/26-27: *lyẖrṯ ẖms^{1}y wrqm lmlk*

"let him pay a fine of fifty pieces of gold to the king"

B) Q 840/6: *ws^{1}ṯbw lḏs^{1}mwy w[lʿm] tʾmnn*

"and they have witnessed their gratitude to Ḏū S^{1}amāwī and (to ʿAmm)"

(and-they-have-testified to-Ḏū-S^{1}amāwī and[-to-ʿAmm] gratitude)

in sense of purpose:

Q 489/3: *lwfys^{1}m wwfy ʾbyts^{1}m*

"[MʿDM dedicated these two statues for his sons] for their protection and the protection of their houses"

dativus commodi :

A) Q 178/1-2: *mḫḍ nqzn bḫṭm ʿrn ḏmwẓm lʾrḍs^1*

"[NBṬʿM] dug the well for his land on the summit of the fortress hill Ḏū MWẒM"

(he-dug the-well on-the-summit [of] Ḏū-MWẒM for-his-land)

B) Q 486/4-5: *bnyw ws^{1}ḥdṯ lʾnby hdtn*

"[YṢRʿM and ʾLḎRʾ] built and newly constructed for ʾAnbay HDTN"

in sense of "about, concerning":

Q 172/5-6: *fks^{3}ʾ s^{1}bʾm lqrḥn wʿqls^1 bms^{1}ʾls^1*

"he announced to S^{1}BʾM through his oracle concerning the wound and its compensation"

(so-he-announced [to] S^{1}BʾM concerning-the-wound and-its-compensation-money in-his-oracle)

marking possession:

Q 490A/3-4: *wkwn lʾs^{2}hrm bn ḏt qbrn wms^{3}wds^1 wnfs^{1}hs^{1}yw s^{2}lṯt ʾḫms^{1}m wl s^{2}krm ws^{2}ʿbm ṯnw ḫms^{1}myw*

"three-fifths of this tomb and its entrance chamber and interior belong to ʾS^{2}HRM and two-fifths to S^{2}KRM and S^{2}ʿBM"

(and-was to-ʾS^{2}HRM from this tomb and-its-entrance-chamber and-its-inner-chambers three fifths and-to S^{2}KRM and-S^{2}ʿBM two-fifths)

prep. + pro. *lḏt* Q 910/3; *lḏtm* Q 487/2

BECAUSE OF, IN ACCORDANCE WITH, AS [comp. of prep. *l-* plus pro. *ḏt* plus suf. *-m*. On the similarity in usage between *lḏtm* and *bḏtm*, see Jamme, 1952a, 182.]

Q 487/1-3: *yṣrʿm wgwṯʾl ḏwʿhlm s^{1}qnyw ʾnby s^{2}ymn ʿd rṣfm ṣlmn lḏtm tkrbs^1*

"YṢRʿM and GWṮʾL of the clan of ʿHLM dedicated this statue to ʾAnbay S^{2}YMN in RṢFM as he had vowed to him"

(YṢRʿM and-GWṮʾL they[dl.]-of-ʿHLM dedicated-to ʾAnbay S^{2}YMN in RṢFM this-statue as he-vowed-to-him)

(L I)

prep. + pro. *lˁlw* Q 700/6

OVER [combination of *l* + *ˁl(w)*]

Q 700/5-6: *wbny qrḏn yrtᶜ ḏflgn ḏs¹ybn lˁlw mhyws¹r lgrbtn*

"he built the dam YRTᶜ Ḏū FLGN Ḏū S¹YBN over MHYWS¹R to GRBTN"

adv. *llˁl* Q 694/5, 6, 11, 12

UPWARD, ABOVE [May be analyzed as *l* + (*l* + *ˁl*). The form *lˁl* is attested in Min RÉS 2774/5 and 3459/3 in essentially the same sense]

Q 694/12: *lms²rq wllˁl*

"eastward and upward (from this point)"

L II

conj. *l-* Q 186C/10

UNTIL

Q 186C/6-10: *wklḏw bys²t kl ms²ṭm bs²mr blyl ybnwn lyṣbḥ*

"and everyone who sells any merchandise in S²MR at night shall keep his distance until morning"

(and-all-who sell any merchandise in-S²MR at-night they-shall-keep-apart until-it-dawns)

L III

prt. *l-* Q 40/21, Q 66/2, 4, 6, Q 68/9, Q 70/4, Q 72/5, 7, 8, 9, 11, Q 78/4, 11, Q 83/3, Q 90/4, Q 173/3, Q 186B/9, 23, Q 203/4, Q 256/4, Q 840/8 +

1) LET, MAY (introducing jussive sentences with prfx. form without *b-*)

A) Q 66/2-3: *wl yṣḥf wḥrg ḏn ṣḥfn*

"let this document be written and administered"

(and-let be-written and-administering this document)

B) Q 72/7-8: *wl ylṣq*

"let him prosecute"

C) Q 78/4: *wl yḥrm s¹w ʾns¹n hrgn*

"let this murderer be punished"

2) IN ORDER THAT, SO THAT (with prfx. form without *b-*)

Q 186B/23-24: *lyṣtdqwn qtbn*

"in order that the Qatabanians may have their due"

3) pleonastic use after a conjunction of a relative with prfx. form without *b-* [see Beeston, 1962b, 53]

Q 186B/9-14: *wmn lys¹ˁrb bn qtbn wbn mˁnm wbn ḥwr tmnᶜ byts¹ wmḫtns¹ ḫdrm byˁrb tmnᶜ*

"any Qatabanian, Minaean, or resident of Timnaᶜ who uses his house or residence as a place of business shall pay (the) Timnaᶜ (market tax)"
(and-he-who uses from-among the-Qatabanians and-from-among the-Minaeans and-from-among the-residents [of] Timnaᶜ his-house and-his-residence [as] a-place-of-business he-shall-pay Timnaᶜ)

LBN
subst. *lbny* Q 161
STORAX [Sab *lbny*, Heb *ləḇônāh*, Ar *lubnā* id. W. Müller, who has written two articles on frankincense and other spices of South Arabia (1974, 53-59 and 1976, 124-36), notes that *lbny* is properly translated "storax" and not "frankincense." Cf. also the comments of K. Nielsen, 1986, 18, 60-61]
Q 161: *rnd ḍrw lbny qs¹ṭ*
"nard (?), balsam, storax, costus"

LGʾ
subst. *mlgʾs¹* Q 73/3
TENANT FARMLAND [Ar *lajaʾa* "to seek refuge," Ar *ʾaljaʾa* "*céder la propriété (d'une terre) et en devenir fermier,*" G. Ryckmans, 1935, 321]
Q 73/2-4: *wgrb wbql wrʾb bs¹rs¹ ḏrbḍt wmlgʾs¹ nḥql ṯmnt ʾʾlfm bqlm ls¹ wl wlds¹ wḏᶜdrs¹*
"and he constructed terraces and planted and harvested in his valley Ḏū RBḌT, and in its tenant farmland in particular, eight thousand plots for himself and his children and dependents"
(and-he-constructed-terraces and-planting and-harvesting in-his-valley Ḏū-RBḌT and-its-tenant-farmland in-particular eight thousand plots for-himself and-for his-children and-his-dependents)

LDN
subst. *ldn* Q 530ter
LADANUM, a kind of aromatic resin used as incense [Sab *ldn*, Ar *ladan*, Eth *lōzān* id.; cf. K. Nielsen, 1986, 18, 63-64, and Crone, 1987, 56-57]
Q 530ter: *rnd ḍrw ḥḏk ldn*
"nard (?), balsam, (pungent) incense (?), ladanum"

LZM
s¹-prfx. *s¹lzmkm* Q 902

(LZM)

TO ENJOIN, REQUIRE [Cf. Ar ʾ*azlama* "to enjoin obligations upon someone"]

Q 902: *s¹lzmkm ʾbʿl qbrn s²ymn bn s¹qbrbs¹ kl ms²kmym*

"the owners of the grave S²YMN have enjoined you not to bury anyone of base birth in it"

(have-enjoined-you the-owners [of] the-grave S²YMN from burying-in-it any base-born)

LYL

subst. *lyl* Q 186C/9

NIGHT [Sab *lly* "night," Ar *layl*, *layla*, Eth *lēlīt*, Heb *laylāh* id., Akk *līlātu* "evening"]

Q 186C/6-10: *wklḏw bys²ṭ kl ms²ṭm bs²mr blyl ybnwn lyṣbḥ*

"and everyone who sells any merchandise in S²MR at night shall keep his distance until morning"

(and-all-who sell any merchandise in-S²MR at-night they-shall-keep-apart until-it-dawns)

LKʿ

subst. pl. *lkwʿ* Q 40/18

CONFIRMATION [Cf. Ar *lakaʿa* "to cling, adhere, persist"]

Q 40/18: *nl yḏʾwn wkwn s¹m ʾftḥn ʾw [w]mḥrtn wmnkṯs¹m s³ẖwl wʿṣwb wnfwq wẖlwʿ wlkwʿ*

"let these ordinances or directives and the penalty for their violation be published and be a duty, obligation, requirement, and an abrogation of previous laws and a confirmation of current statutes"

(let go-forth and-being these ordinances or directives and-their-violation duties and obligations and-requirements and-abrogations and-confirmations)

LMḤ

verb *lmḥ* Q 571w

TO SPY, LOOK AT SECRETLY [Ar *lamaḥa* "to view furtively"]

Q 571w: *wgmʿm lmḥ ḍrḥm*

"and GMʿM looked at ḌRḤM secretly"

LN

prep. *ln* Q 839/1

FROM [Sab *ln* "from"; cf. Ug *l-* "from" extended by the suf. *-n* and see Beeston, 1962, 57.]

Q 839/1: *ln d̲n wt̲nn ʿ[d] wt̲ny lmʿbrh[n]*
"from this boundary t[o] the borders on two of its sid[es]"

LFY

verb *bylfy* Q 66/5-6

TO GET, OBTAIN, MAKE [Sab *lfy* "to get *something*"]

Q 66/5-6: *wkl lfym wylfy kbr kḥd d̲dtnt*
"and every gain that the *kabīr* of KHD of Datinat realizes"

subst. *lfym* Q 66/5

EXACTION, PROFIT [Semantic development "something obtained" > "exaction, profit"; cf. Beeston, 1971, 14 (who, however, reads the word as *gfy*), and Jamme, 1972, 60]

See example above.

LṢQ

verb *lṣq* Q 72/8-9; *ylṣq* Q 72/7-8

TO PROSECUTE, PUNISH [Sab *lṣq* "to hunt down"; cf. Ar *laṣiqa* "to cling to, hang on to, stick to," Eth *laṣaqa* "to stick to, fasten to"]

Q 72/7-8: *wl ylṣq wqrw ws¹ʿd̲b ws¹ʾgy wʿthd ḥgd̲n d̲mḥrn kbr tmnʿ*
"and let the lord of Timnaʿ prosecute, accuse, punish, reprimand, and concern himself according to this directive"
(and-let he-prosecute and-accusing and-punishing and-reprimanding and-concerning-himself according-to-this this-directive the-lord [of] Timnaʿ)

LS²S²

verb *ls²* Q 623

TO REMOVE [Cf. Ar *lašša* "remove, push away"]

Q 623: *ʿmd̲rm ls² myṣ bn d̲qm*
"MD̲RM removed MYṢ the son of D̲QM"

M

Mʾ

card. num *mʾt* Q 570/3; *mʾtm* Q 690a/11

ONE HUNDRED [Sab *mʾt* "one hundred," Ar *miʾa*, Eth *meʾet*, Heb *mēʾāh*, Akk (construct state) *meʾet* id.]

Q 570/2-3: *lʿln d̲mʾt h̲ryftm*
"to ʿLN the hundred-year-old"
(to-ʿLN he-of one-hundred years)

MDD

verb *bymd* Q 243/6, Q 695/12

1) TO PRESUME, BE PRESUMPTUOUS [See Beeston, 1976, 421, who compares Ar *madda ʾl-yad* "stretch out the hand" = "presume, take liberties"]

Q 695/13-14: *wmn ḏm bymd ... lwzʾ ʾw nky bʾqtnt ʾs¹ṭr ḏt ṣḥftn*

"(let) whoever presumes ... to add to or diminish the details of the text of this document (be consigned to oblivion)"

2) TO ADD, INCREASE [See Höfner, 1987, 44, who understands *bymd* in 243/6 as "*ausdehnen, hinzufügen,*" and compares Ar *madda* "to extend, grow," and *māda* (y) "to increase, grow," Tig *mdd* "to extend, stretch," Heb *middeḏ* "to stretch out, extend " and Soq *med* "to extend"]

Q 243/6-8: *lyʿtbr klḏm bymd wnkr ʾḥrm wḏrʾm wʾḥdb ws¹ʿdm wḏʿdrs¹m wḏtn ʾbytn bnḥl ḏn ḏtẓrbn wgdytn*

"(this decree) applies to whatever ʾḤRM and ḎRʾM and ʾḤDB and S¹ʿDM and their dependents and these houses add and change through any lease (subsequent) to this land grant and renewal"

(let-apply everything-which add and-changing ʾḤRM and-ḎRʾM and-ʾḤDB and-S¹ʿDM and-their-dependents and-these-houses in-granting-the-lease [of] that-which [is] of-a-land-grant and-renewal)

MHR

subst. *mhrts¹* Q 905/4

POSSESSIONS, WEALTH [Sab *mhrt* "possessions, wealth"; cf. Ar *mahr* "price, stake"]

Q 905/4: [...] *mhrts¹ rṯd ṯwbn* [...]"

"his possessions ṮWBN entrusted "

MW

indef. encl. *-mw* Q 40/11+

(Enclitic particle) [*-mw* is an enclitic participle which may attach itself to various parts of speech in Qatabanian. It has no clear semantic function in the extant texts. Cf. Sab enclitic particles *-m*, *-mw*, *-my*]

Q 40/11: *wbkl ʾftḥm bs¹m ftḥw qtbnmw ms³wdn wqtbn ṭbnn*

"by all the orders on the basis of which the Qatabanian lords and landowners have given orders"

(and-by-all orders on-them have-ordered Qatabanians lords and-Qatabanians landowners)

MWR

subst.[1] *ʾmwrs¹* Q 79/4

BORDER, CONFINES [Cf. Sab *mwrt* "access way," Ar *māra* (w) "go around," Daṯ *māra* "border"]

Q 79/4: *kl ʾwldm wmrʾtm byld btmnᶜ wʾmwrs¹*

"all the men and women born in Timnaᶜ and its confines"

(all male-children and-women born in-Timnaᶜ and-its-confines)

subst.[2] *mwrt* Q 239/2; *mwrtn* Q 239/2

FORTIFICATION, TOWER [Cf. Conti Rossini, 1931, 176, and Beeston, 1962c, 47, and see Jamme in Van Beek, 1969b, 338-39, who rejects Beeston's interpretation of the word at Q 239/2 as "fortification," and proposes instead the meaning "road," comparing Ar *mawr* "road, trodden and even road"]

Q 239/1-2: *yhnᶜm bn s²hr hll wbns¹ mrṯdm mlkw q[tbn b]rʾw ws¹wṯr ws¹s²qr mwrtn yfᶜn*

"YHNᶜM the son of S²HR HLL and his son MRṮDM the two kings of Qa[taban con]structed, laid the foundations of, and completed the fortification YFᶜN"

MWT

subst. *mwt* Q 78/8

DEATH [Cf. Sab *mwt* "death," Ar *mawt*, Eth *mot*, Heb *maweṯ*, Syr *mawta*, Ug *mt* id.; cf. also Eg *mt* "to die"]

Q 78/8: *mwt ʾw mᶜbr bnfs¹ ms¹tᶜdwn*

"(whoever kills the culprit need not fear) death or compensation for the life of that wrongdoer"

MḪḌ

verb *mḫḍ* Q 34B, Q 36/3, Q 178/1

TO DIG, HEW OUT [Cf. Sab *mḫḍ* "to hew out *from rock*," Ug *mḫṣ*, Akk *maḫāṣu*, id., Heb *māḥaṣ* "to beat, break to pieces"]

Q 178/1-2: *mḫḍ nqzn bḫṭm ᶜn ḏmwẓm lʾrḍs¹*

"[NBṬᶜM] dug a well for his land on the summit of the fortress hill Ḏū MWẒM"

(he-dug the-well on-the-summit [of] the-fortress-hill Ḏū-MWẒM for-his-land)

subst. *mḫḍ* Q 203/4

DEFEAT [Cf. Sab verb *mḫḍ* "to smite, defeat"]

Q 203/3-4: *ywm rdʾ ᶜṯtr wʾlhw s¹qmtm s²hrǵln mḫḍ ḥḍrmt wʾmrm*

"when ᶜAṯtar and the gods of irrigation aided S²HRǴLN in the defeat of ḤḌRMT and ʾMRM"

(MḎḌ)

(when aided ʿAṯtar and-the-gods [of] irrigation S²HRǴLN [in] the-defeat [of] ḤḌRMT and-ʾMRM)

MẒʾ

verb *bymẓʾ* Q 83/7; *btmẓʾ* Q 186C/14

1) TO ENTER, GO THROUGH [Cf. Sab *mẓʾ* "to reach, arrive, come to," Eth *maṣʾa* "to come," cf. perhaps Ar *maḍā* (y) "to go away," and Ug *mǵy* "to arrive, come to"]

Q186C/10-14: *wmlkmw qtbn ʾṯrm bkl s²[y]ṯm wqnym btmẓʾ bḍʿs¹*

"the king of Qataban has supervisory jurisdiction over every pie[ce] of merchandise and goods which enters his territory"

(and-the-king [of] Qataban is-supervising every pie[ce]-of-merchandise and-goods it-enters his-territory)

2) TO REPLACE, DO AWAY WITH [See Beeston, in CIAS 2:158; cf. Ar *ʾatā ʿalā* "to annihilate, wipe out, sweep away with"]

Q 83/5-8: *wʾl sn s¹wḥs³s¹ bn brṯs¹ lmʿmrm bymẓʾ ʿls¹ww*

"it is not permitted to remove it from its place for a memorial that replaces it"

(and-not-permitted removing-it from its-place for-a-memorial replaces it)

s¹-prfx. *ys¹mẓʾwn* Q 186A/28

TO CARRY OUT

Q 186A/26-27: *lyḫrṯ ḫms¹y wrqm lmlk qtbn wʿhr s²mr ys¹mẓʾwn ws¹ẓyh*

"let him pay a fine of fifty pieces of gold to the king of Qataban and the overseer of S²MR, who will carry it out and order (its observance)"

MLʾ

subst. *mlʾt* Q 66/7, Q 83/5, Q 183/4

PERIOD, DURATION [Sab *mlʾ* "duration of time, period"; cf. Beeston, 1981a, 84]

Q 66/7: *lḏt bd mlʾt*

"for all time to come"

(to-possessor [of] space-of-time [of] duration)

MLK

verb *ymlk* Q 78/3

TO RULE, REIGN [Ar *malaka* "to rule, reign"; cf. Sab *mlk* "to become king," Heb *mālak̠* "to become king, be king, reign"]

Q 78/3: *wkl ˀs²ˁbm ymlk ydˁᵓb*
"and all the tribes which YDᵓB rules"

subst.[1] sing. *mlk* Q 34A, Q 37/2, Q 39/6, Q 40/1, Q 50/1+; *mlkm* Q 695/11; *mlkn* Q 36/5, Q 40/2, 11, 15, 17-18, 21, Q 72/6, 9, Q 78/5, 6-7, 11, Q 79/2, Q 89.194, Q 856/4; *mlkhmw* Q 74/2; dl. *mlkw* Q 112/3, Q 178/5, Q 239/1, Q 695/2; pl. *ˀmlk* Q 40/19, 70/2, 5, Q 74/4(2x), Q 83/8, Q 183/3, Q 186B/25, Q 243/2

KING [Sab *mlk* "king," Ar *malik*, Heb *meleḵ* id., Akk *maliku*, *malku* "prince"]

A) Q 177/4-5: *wrwˀl ǵyln yhnˁm bn s²hr ygl yhrgb mlk qtbn*
"WRWˀL ǴYLN YHNˁM the son of S²HR YGL YHRGB, king of Qataban"

B) Q 34A: *s²hr ygl yhrgb bn hwfˁm yhnˁm mlk qtbn*
"SHR YGL YHRGB the son of HWFˁM YHNˁM king of Qataban"

subst.[2] *mlkn* Q 67/11-12

PROPERTY [Sab *mlk* "property," Ar *mulk* "right of possession"]

Q 67/10-11: *wḏn ˀs¹dn ˀrby ḏlbḫ ˀlḏy bˁlw mlkn nḥql ḏbn ṣḥf dtnt*
"these persons, the *ˀrby* of Ḏū Labaḫ, are the ones in possession of the property, and in particular that which is (specified) in the agreement of Datinat"
(and-these persons the-*ˀrby* of-Labaḫ [are] those-who they-have-taken-possession-of the-property particularly that-which-from the-document [of] Datinat)

MN

pro. *mn* Q 186B/9, A/7, 21, Q 695/12

HE WHO, WHOEVER [Sab *mn* "who, whoever," Ar *man* "who, whoever," Aram *man* "whoever," Akk *mannu(ša)* "whoever"]

Q 186B/9-14: *wmn lys¹ˁrb bn qtbn wbn mˁnm wbn ḥwr tmnˁ byts¹ wmḫtns¹ ḫdrm byˁrb tmnˁ*
"any Qatabanian, Minaean, or resident of Timnaˁ who uses his house or residence as a place of business shall pay (the) Timnaˁ (market tax)"
(and-he-who uses from-among the-Qatabanians and-from-among the-Minaeans and-from-among the-residents [of] Timnaˁ his-house and-his-residence [as] a-place-of-business he-shall-pay Timnaˁ)

pro. + pro. *mnḏm* Q 202/4

WHATEVERY, WHOEVER [comp. of pro. *mn* and *ḏm*]

Q 202/4: *m]nḏm byṯfṭ wḥrg ydᵓb wmnḏm […]*
wh]atever YDᵓB decides and commands and whatever […]

MNN

t-infix *mtnn* Q 695/9

TO AGREE, CONSENT [Cf. Ar *imtanna bi* "to concede graciously, consent"]

Q 695/9: *bs¹n mtnn ydᶜᵓb wqtbn*

"YDᶜᵓB and the Qatabanians have consented to them (the laws and statutes)"

MṢᶜ

adj. *mṣᶜ* Q 72/6

OF FULL VALUE, OF LEGAL STANDARD [Sab *mṣᶜm* "freshly-minted"; cf. Ar *naṣaᶜa* "to be pure = up to standard," and see Irvine, 1964, 20, 25-26]

Q 72/6: *bᶜs²r ᶜs²r ḫbṣtm mṣᶜm*

"for (the price of) ten *ḫbṣt* of full value each"

MQṬ

verb *mmqṭm* Q 177/3; *mmqṭytm* Q 694/5

1) TO COLLAPSE [Cf. Ar *maqaṭa* "to break," Akk *maqāṭu* "to collapse"]

Q 177/1-2: *brᵓw ws¹wṯr ws¹s²qr ḏn mḥfdn yḥḍr ḏm bs²hd gnᵓ hgrs¹m hrbt mmqṭm*

"[the tribe Ḏū HRBT] constructed, laid the foundation, and completed this tower YḤḌR which stood before the wall of their town HRBT when it collapsed"

(they-constructed and-laying-the-foundation and-completing this tower YḤḌR which before the-wall [of] their-town HRBT collapsing)

2) TO INCLINE, MOVE [Sab *mqṭt* "setting of the sun"]

Q 694/5: *bn ᶜḍd byḥn mmqṭytm lms²r[q]*

"from the border of Bayḥān eastward"

(from the-border [of] Bayḥān inclining to-the-east)

MRᵓ

subst. sing. *mrᵓs¹* Q 89.137/1-2, Q 99/8, Q 118/2, Q 176/10, Q 241/4, Q 254/1, Q 266/5, Q 268/4, Q 681/2, Q 683b, Q 720/1, Q 840/9, Q 844/3, Q 855/2, Q 856/4, Q 898/1, Q 905/1, Q 908/2, Q 910/2, Q 916/4; *mrᵓhw* Q 38/4, 7, Q 265/5, Q 479/3; *mrᵓs¹my* Q 39/3, 6, Q 112/3, Q 182/4, Q 838/4; *mrᵓs¹m* Q 40/4, 6, 9, Q 177/4, Q 254/7, Q 790/5, Q 840/2, Q 914/4; *mrᵓs¹n* Q 244/12, Q 246/3, 6, 11; *mrᵓhmw* Q 677/4-5; pl. *ᵓmrᵓs¹* Q

254/8, 9, Q 898/5, 7; *ʾmrʾhw* Q 688/5; *ʾmrʾs¹m* Q 102/6-7; *ʾmrʾhmw* Q 690a/3-4

1) MAN, PERSON; LORD [Sab *mrʾ* id., BibAram *mārē* "lord"]

A) Q 177/4-5: *wb rdʾ wtḥrg mrʾs¹m wrwʾl ǵyln yhnʿm*
"with the help and direction of their lord WRWʾL ǴYLN YHNʿM"

B) Q 840/9-10: *wwzʾ zydʾl ṯd mrʾs¹ ḏs¹mwy ʾbls¹ wdʿn*
"and ZYDʾL further entrusted his camel WDʿN to his lord Ḏū S¹amāwī"
(and-continued ZYDʾL entrusting-to his-lord Ḏū-S¹amāwī his-camel WDʿN)

2) MALE CHILD
Q 172/3: *ḏs¹wld bn fḫḏs¹ mrʾm*
"(a child) whom he sired from his clan, a male child"
(whom-he-begot from his-tribe a-male)

subst. *mrʾtm* Q 79/4; *mrʾtn* Q 128/2

(FREE)WOMAN [Sab *mrʾt* "woman, girl; lady," Ar *imraʾa* "woman, girl"]

Q 79/4: *kl ʾwldm wmrʾtm byld btmnʿ wʾmwrs¹*
"all the men and women born in Timnaʿ and its confines"
(all male-children and-women born in-Timnaʿ and-its-confines)

MRT

subst. *mrt* Q 80/6; *mrtn* Q 898/3; *mrt*[ ] Q 769/2a

LIMESTONE, GYPSUM [Ghul, 1959, 4, cites possible cognates in Ar *malāṭ* "gypsum," and in ModYem *mrṭ* "plaster"; cf. however, Sab *mrtn* "limestone (?)," Eth *marēt* "dirt, dust"]

Q 898/3: *bḥt mrtn*
"a limestone votive object"

MS¹K

t-infx. *mts¹km* Q 78/12

TO ARREST, SEIZE [Cf. Ar *imtasaka* "to lay hand on, to seize"; Ḥaḍ *mts¹k* "to be trapped"]

Q 78/11-12: *wḏm byhrg … bn mts¹km bʾrḍm bs¹ byhrg nḥql*
"if the murderer is not apprehended in the particular land in which he committed the killing"
[and-the-one-who kills … from arrest in-the-land in-it he-kills in-particular]

MS²R

subst. pl. *ʾms²r* Q 687/5 (Pirenne, 1971, 126, emends *ms²r* at Q 694/5 to *ms²rq*, although Jamme, 1972, 25, views it as coming from this root)

PLANTS, SPROUTS [Cf. Ar *mas¹ra* "sprouts, vegetation"]

Q 687/5: *bqlk nʿmn bʾms²r*

"this field NʿMN (provided) with plants"

MTY

conj. *mty* Q 186A/13, 16

WHEN [Cf. Heb *māṯay* "when?," Akk *mati*, *immati*, JewAram *ʾemaṯ*, Ar *matā*, Syr *ʾemaṯ* id., and see Beeston, 1962b, 73,]

Q 186A/16-18: *wmty lyks³ʾ ʿhr s²mr kḏm bys¹tḏf qtbn bʿm ʾs²ʿbm*

"and when the overseer of S²MR announces that he wishes the Qatabanians to make trading journeys among the tribes"

(and-when announces the-overseer [of] S²MR that wishes-that-trade the-Qatabanians among the-tribes)

MTʿ

verb *mtʿ* Q 40/12; *mtʿs¹* Q 172/4; *bymtʿ* Q 186C/15

SUPPORT, PROTECT; SAVE [Sab *mtʿ* "to save, deliver," Ar *ʾamtaʿa* "to grant enjoyment (said of God); have the use, usufruct of something"]

Q 186C/14-17: *wnl bymtʿ ḏn mḥrn klmklm*

"and let every king support this decree"

subst.¹ *mtʿ* Q 183/4

SUPPORT, SAVING

Q 183/4: *wmtʿ ʾbrtʿ mʾdbs¹*

"the support of ʾBRTʿ his vassal"

subst.² pl. *ʾmtʿs¹* Q 860/4; *ʾmtʿs¹m*; Q 99/4-5, Q 790/2

GUEST CHAMBER [Cf. Daṯ *matīʿ* "guest"; see Jamme, 1972, 52]

Q 790/2: *rydʾl wys²fʾl nʿmwd ḏtw ḏrḥn s²ʾmw wbrʾ wẓrb bythmy grl wʾḫtbs¹ wṣrḥts¹ww wʾmtʿs¹m*

"RYDʾL and YS²FʾL of the NʿMWD of the clan ḎRḤN have purchased, built, and secured title to their home GRL and its lower stories, its upper rooms, and its guest chambers"

(RYDʾL and-YS²FʾL [of] the-NʿMWD [of] ḎRḤN they-have-purchased and-building and-securing-title-to their-home GRL and-its-lower-stories and-its-upper-rooms and-its-guest-chambers)

N

N I

prt. *nlk* Q 186C/3-4; *nl* Q 40/18, Q 67/5, Q 68/5, Q 69/3, Q 78/12, Q 186C/3-4, 15

SO [Beeston, 1962, 53, presumes that *nl* is "a deictic *n*- reinforcing the jussive (deictic) *l* and introducing a non-subordinate jussive clause." Beeston, 1959, 10, calls the form *nlk* "a strengthened form of the jussive particle *l*."]

Q 68/5: *nl ys¹tfḥwn*

"so let them be governed"

N II

card. num. *n* Q 186B/7

Symbol probably having a numerical value based on its position in the alphabet [Irvine, 1964, 34, and Beeston, 1959, 8-9.]

Q 186B/7: *n w*

"*n* pieces of gold"

N III

prt. *nʾy* Q 40/9(2x)

CONCERNING [Cf. perhaps Eth *na* "behold," Eg *nw* "to look at, to see." Beeston, 1962, 53, suggests that this may be a combination of a deictic prt. *n*- plus *ʾy* but says of Q 40/9, "the syntax of that passage is obscure."]

Q 40/9-10: *nʾy kḏm ftḥ byfṯḥwn ws¹ḫr s²hr wqtbn ms³wdn wfqḏtn wbtln*

"whatever S²HR and the Qatabanian lords and *fqḏ* and *btl* order and direct"

NB

prep. *nb* Q 186B/21

INSTEAD OF [Cf. Ar *nāba* (w) "to represent, take the place of"]

Q 186B/21-23: *[b]n ʿm nkr s²ʿbm nb bʿm qtbn wb ʿm s³fln*

"with another tribe instead of with Qataban and the tableland"

NBṬ

s[1]-prfx. *s¹nbṭ* Q 240/5, Q 700/5

TO DIG DOWN TO WATER in making a well [Sab *hnbṭ* id.; cf. Ar *nabbaṭa* "to reach water by digging a pit"]

Q 700/5: *ws¹nbṭ ʾbʾrs¹ wbny qrḍn yrtʿ*

"he has dug its wells and he has built the dam YRTʿ"

NBL

subst. *nblm* Q 40/3, 7

MESSENGER, DELEGATE [Cf. Sab *tnblt* "diplomatic mission, delegation, envoys, Sab *nbl* "to send messengers, an embassy, send on a mission," Eth *tanbal* "ambassador," Eth *tanbala* "to be sent"]

Q 40/3: *fʾy qwmw wʾtm wʾttm wngs² wntgs² bnblm*

"whereto they assembled and agreed and adhered to the agreement and imposed taxes and submitted to taxes through a delegation"

(and-they-have-assembled and-agreeing and-adhering-to-the-agreement and-imposing-taxes and-submitting-to-taxes through-a-delegation)

NBR

verb *ywnbr* Q 687/8 (Jamme, 1971, 87, describes the *w* as a *mater lectionis*)

TO BUILD, ERECT [Ar *nabara* "to raise, elevate, erect"]

Q 687/8-9: *wzbr ywnbr dnm ʿlbḏr ʾḫyr s³md hwyḫr*

"the building which DNM is erecting near the field of the elite of the dignitaries of HWYḪR"

(and-the-structure erects DNM near-the-field [of] the-elite [of] the dignitaries [of] HWYḪR)

NGW

subst. *mngw* Q 244/11; *mngwm* Q 246/10

RESULT, OUTCOME; LUCK, FORTUNE [Sab *mngwn* id., cf. Ar *najā* (w) "to save one's self, come out." See discussion by Beeston, in CIAS 1:84, and Pirenne, in CIAS 1:153.]

Q 244/10-12: *wʿm lyzʾ ṣdqs¹n bkl mngw byktrbwn ʿmn tḥrgs¹*

"as for ʿAmm, may he continue to give them their due by all the good fortune which will be granted by his order"

(and-ʿAmm may-he-continue granting-them-their-due through-all the-good-fortune [which] will-be-granted by his-order)

NGS[2]

verb *ngs*[2] Q 40/3

TO DEMAND, IMPOSE TRIBUTE, TAXES [Cf. Heb nôḡēś "ruler, exactor of tribute," Eth *nagsa* "to reign"]

Q 40/3: *fʾy qwmw wʾtm wʾttm wngs*[2] *wntgs*[2] *bnblm*

"whereto they have assembled and agreed and adhered to the agreement and imposed taxes and paid taxes through a delegation"

(and-they-have-assembled and-agreeing and-adhering-to-the-agreement and-imposing-taxes and-paying-taxes through-a-delegation)

t-infix *ntgs*[2] Q 40/3

TO PAY TRIBUTE, TAXES

See entry above.

NHM

subst. *nhmn* Q 688/2

STONE DRESSING [Sab *nhmt* "polishing, smooth dressing of stone"; cf. MSA *ḥajar manhum* "bright whitish building stone," Daṯ *nahama* "to strike vigorously"]

Q 688/1-2: *hwfʿm ʾwlṭ nḥln wbnhw hlʿw wḥṭbm ʾlht qyln kbr nhmn*

"HWFʿM ʾWLṬ the commander and his sons HLʿW and ḤṬBM, those of the tribal leader, directed the dressing of the stone"

NWḤ

t-infix *yntwḥ* Q 78/12

TO MOURN PUBLICLY [Ar *nawḥ* "(public) mourning." See discussion in Beeston 1976, 416-17.]

Q 78/11-12: *bn ʾrbʿ ywmytm nl yntwḥ ʿd [m]ḥrm ʾlhn ḏtw mʿbrn*

"let there be a public mourning within four days at the [san]ctuary of the gods of vengeance"

(within four days let it-be-mourned-publicly at the-[san]ctuary [of] the-gods those-of vengeance)

NḤL I

verb *nḥl* Q 243/8, Q 695/1

TO GRANT LEASE; TO GIVE A PART OF, SHARE, DISTRIBUTE [Sab *nḥl* "to grant lease"; cf. Ar *naḥala* "to give someone a part of something," Heb *nāḥal* "to take possession of; to divide as a possession," Ug *nḥl* "to inherit"]

(NḤL I)

Q 243/8: *bnḥl ḏn ḏtẓrbn wgdytn*

"(this decree also applies) in the event of any lease (subsequent) to this land grant and renewal"

(in-granting-the-lease [of] that-which [is] of-a-land-grant and-renewal)

subst. *nḥl* Q 677/2, Q 689/1-2; *nḥln* Q 688/1

COMMANDER, OFFICER [Sab *nḥl* "mercenary captain"; see a discussion of the word in Beeston, 1973, 452-53]

Q 677/1-2: *mwhbʾln ʾḥs²r ḏḥrmn nḥl ʾfrs¹n*

"MWHBʾLN ʾḤS²R of the clan of ḤRMN, commander of the cavalry"

NḤL II

subst. *mnḥlm* Q 248/3

BEE SHED, APIARY [Cf. Ar *naḥl* "bees," *naḥla* "a bee." See discussion of this word and of beekeeping practices by Pirenne, in CIAS 1:242-43.]

Q 248/1-3: *ʾlʾz bn ḍbʾm bn mrn s¹ḥḏṯ lʾṯrt ws²ms¹ ywm s²ʿb mnḥlm*

"ʾLʾZ son of ḌBʾM of the clan MRN when he moved the bee shed"

NḪY

prep. *mnḫy* Q 76/2

IN THE DIRECTION OF [Cf. Heb *nāḥāh* "to lead," Ar *naḥā* "to go toward someone, toward a place," Ar *naḥwa* "in the direction of, toward," Ar *manḥā* "goal"]

Q 76/1-2: *rbḥm bn ʾbln qdm mbny rydn mnḫy ḥdnm*

"RBḤM son of ʾBLN has undertaken the construction of RYDN in the direction of ḤDNM."

(RBḤM the-son [of] ʾBLN he-has-undertaken the-construction [of] RYDN in-the-direction-of ḤDNM)

NḪL

subst. sing. *nḫl* Q 74/12(3x), Q 839/7; *nḫlm* Q 74/12, Q 694/12; *nḫln* Q 839/5; *nḫls¹* Q 34B; *nḫls¹m* Q 135/1; *nḫlhmw* Q 74/2; dl. (?) *nḫlmyw* Q 74/10; pl. *ʾnḫlm* Q 74/10(2x), 10-11, 11(3x)

PALMGROVE [Sab *nḫl* "palmgrove," Ar *naḫl* (coll.) "palm trees"]

Q 74/11: *ws¹dṯt ʿs²r ʾ nḫlm bbḍʿ ḫdṣm*

"sixteen palmgroves in the area of ḪDṢM"

(and-six ten palmgroves in-the-area [of] ḪDṢM)

NṬᶜ

subst. *nṭᶜn* Q 74/7

GROUNDS [Cf. Heb *nāṭaᶜ* id.]

Q 74/7: *wrbᶜ byt ḏrdᶜ wṣrḥts¹ bḥmrr bnṭᶜn*

"[YḌMRMLK acquired] a fourth of the house of Ḏū RDᶜ and its upper story in ḤMRR in the grounds"

NKW

subst. *nkwn* Q 186B/9

COINAGE [Beeston, 1959, 9, sees this as a noun-formation of the pattern *fᶜln* from a root NKW to be compared with Heb *hikkāh* "to strike, smite"; cf. also Syr *nǝḵā* "to strike, injure," Eth *nakaya* "to strike, injure," Tña *nakʾe* "to touch," Tig *nakʾa* "hit on the wound," Amh *nakka* "to touch" Ar *nakā* (y), *nakaʾa* "injure"]

Q 186B/9: *nkwn qtbn*

"in Qatabanian coinage"

(coinage [of] Qataban)

NKY

verb *nky* Q 695/10, 13

TO INJURE, DIMINISH [See etymologies cited above under NKW.]

Q 695/9-10: *nl ys¹twfq bn wzʾ ʾw nky ḏtn ʾrḍn*

"let them refrain from adding to or diminishing this land"

(let refrain from the-adding-to or the-diminishing [of] this land)

NKR

verb *nkr* Q 243/6

1) TO CHANGE [Thus Höfner, 1987, 42, 44; cf. Sab *nkr* "stranger, alien, metic," and Heb *nikkar* "to make oneself unrecognizable"]

Q 243/6-8: *lyᶜtbr klḏm bymd wnkr ʾḥrm wḏrʾm wʾḥdb ws¹ᶜdm wḏᶜdrs¹m wḏtn ʾbytn bnḥl ḏn ḏtẓrbn wgdytn*

"(this decree) applies to whatever ʾḤRM and ḎRʾM and ʾḤDB and S¹ᶜDM and their dependents and these houses add and change through any lease (subsequent) to this land grant and renewal"

(let-apply everything-which add and-changing ʾḤRM and-ḎRʾM and-ʾḤDB and-S¹ᶜDM and-their-dependents and-these-houses in-granting-the-lease [of] that-which [is] of-a-land-grant and-renewal)

(NKR)

2) TO WEAR OUT, DAMAGE [See Jamme, 1971, 87, who compares Ar *nakkara* "to wear out, change, make unrecognizable," but cf. also W. Müller in von Wissmann, 1968, 81, who gives the form as *tnkr* "to be damaged"]

Q 687/2-3: *s¹wr bnʾ mʾgl ms¹qt gḏ wbrʾkh ʾn ḏtnkr ṯws²qr*

"[the dignitaries of S¹ʿDM YHS¹KR] built a wall around BNʾ, the irrigation cistern of GḎ, and its (supporting) cisterns here, which has damaged ṮWS²QR"

(built-a-wall-around BNʾ the-cistern [of] irrigation [of] GḎ and-its-cisterns here which-has-damaged ṮWS²QR)

subst./partcp. *mnkrm* Q 495/5

ONE WHO ALTERS, CHANGES [Cf. Sab *hnkr* "to deface, damage *monument*," Ar *nakkara* "to alter, change"]

Q 495/5: *rṯdw ʾṣlms¹m bn mnkrm*

"they have entrusted [to ʾAnbay] their statues to protect them from whoever would alter them"

(they-have-entrusted their-statues from one-who-alters)

subst./partcp. *ms¹nkrm* Q 73/6, Q 201/3, Q 244/15, Q 245/3, Q 246/14-15, Q 254/6, Q 256/8, Q 497/4, Q 681/6, Q 904/6

ONE WHO REMOVES

Q 497/3-4: *rṯdṯ ṣlmts¹ bn ms¹nkrm bn brṯs¹*

"she has entrusted her statue [to ʾAnbay] from whoever would remove it from its place"

(she-entrusted her-female-statue from one-who-removes from its-place)

subst. *nkr* Q 186A/24, B/21

FOREIGNER [Cf. Ar *nakira* "not to know, be ignorant; to deny," Heb *nēḵār* "that which is foreign, foreignness," Heb *ben hannēḵār* "foreigner," Syr *nūḵrāya* "strange, foreign; anothers," Eth *nakīr* "strange, alien, foreign," Akk *nakru* "alien, enemy"]

Q 186A/24: *bn nkr s²ʿbm*

"son of (=member of) a foreign tribe"

NKṮ

subst./partcp. *mnkṯs¹* Q 40/21; *mnkṯs¹m* Q 40/17, 18

ONE WHO VIOLATES; VIOLATION [Ar *nakaṯa* "to violate, break a covenant or treaty,"; it is also possible to understand the meaning as "to remove," cf. Sab *nkṯ* "to remove something from its place"]

Q 40/21-22: *wl ys¹kn mnkṯs¹ hg ẓrʾs¹ ʾs¹mʿm ḏm ʿlm bfṯḥn*

"and let the witnesses who have signed this order punish its violation according to his proclamation"
(and-let punish its-violation according-to his-proclamation the-witnesses who signed in-this-order)

subst./partcp *ms¹nkṯ[m]* Q 183/6
ONE WHO REMOVES
Q 183/5-6: *bn ms¹fʾlm wms¹nkṯ[m b]n brṯs¹*
"[ʾBRTᶜ Ḏū ḤDN ʾLS²R has placed his household and his property] against any ill-wisher or one who remove[s it fr]om its place"

NMR

subst. pl. (?) *nmrs¹ww* Q 769/2a, Q 770/4
WALL WITH INTERSTICES [Cf. Sab *nmr* "control wall, *part of dam structure*," Ar *namira* "to be spotted, marked with points"]
Q 769/1b-2a: *bny ws¹ḥdṯ kl mbny wmhlk [ḫ]lfn ḏs³dw wnmrs¹ww ḥmrr*
"[(S²)HR ǴYLN] built and newly constructed the whole building and construction on the gate of Ḏū S³DW and its intersticed wall ḤMRR"
(they-built and-newly-constructing all-the-building and-construction [of] gate [of] Ḏū-S³DW and-its-intersticed-wall ḤMRR)

NᶜM

verb *nᶜm* Q 183/5; *nᶜmt* Q 254/4; *tnᶜm* Q 254/4
TO BE FAVORABLE, AUSPICIOUS [Sab *nᶜm* "to please, be pleasant," Ar *naᶜama* "to live in prosperity, be happy," Heb *nāᶜam* "to be pleasant, agreeable"]
Q 254/3-4: *lyrdʾwn ᶜbds¹m s²ᶜrm bdtm nᶜmt wb tnᶜm*
"may they aid their servant, S²ᶜRM, in what was and will be auspicious"

subst. *nᶜmt* Q 186B/3; *nᶜmtm* Q 90/4, Q 256/5
PROSPERITY, FAVOR; ADVANTAGE, BENEFIT [Sab *nᶜmt* "prosperity, success," Ar *niᶜma* "blessing; wealth"]
A) Q 90/4: *wl yrdʾs¹ bnᶜmtm*
"and may he [ᶜAmm RYᶜN] favor him with prosperity"
B) Q 186B/2-5: *ʾl byᶜdwn nᶜmt bz[w]rtm bᶜlw ms²ṭm bys²tyṭwn ws²tʾm qtbn*
"they will not calculate 'seed privileges' on merchandise which the Qatabanians may trade and buy"

(not they-will-calculate benefits [of] seeds on merchandise they-trade and-buying the-Qatabanians)

NᶜT

subst. *tnᶜthw* Q 679/9

EXCELLENCE [Cf. Ar *naᶜt* "excellence"]

Q 679/9: *dkl tnᶜthw*

"which enhances its excellence"

NFṢ

subst. pl. *ʾnfṣšm* Q 40/17

DISTRIBUTION [Cf. Eth *nafṣa*, "to disperse, be scattered," Heb *nāp̄aṣ* id., Sab *nfṣ* "to march, march off"]

Q 40/16-17: *s¹mt ʾftḥn wmḥrtn wʾṯftn wḫwlltn wmnkṯs¹m wtᶜlms¹m wʾnfṣs¹m ʾyhnmw ᶜkr lyyfᶜwn*

"let these orders, directives, decisions, regulations, and their violation, documentation, and distribution be announced wherever there is opposition"

(these orders and-directives and-decisions and-regulations and-their-violation and-their-documentation and-their-distribution wherever it-is-opposed let-be-announced)

NFQ

subst. pl. *nfwq* Q 40/18

REQUIREMENT, OBLIGATION [Cf. Sab *mnfq* "binding document," Ar *nafaqa* "to go out," parallel to *yāṣāʾ* "to go out; be promulgated (laws, judicial decisions)"]

Q 40/18: *nl yḏʾwn wkwn s¹m ʾftḥn ʾw [w]mḥrtn wmnkṯs¹m s³ḫwl wᶜṣwb wnfwq wḫlwᶜ wlkwᶜ*

"let these ordinances or directives and the penalty for their violation be published and be a duty, obligation, requirement, and an abrogation of previous laws and a confirmation of current statutes"

(let go-forth and-being these ordinances or directives and-their-violation duties and obligations and-requirements and-abrogations and-confirmations)

NFS¹

verb *nfs¹* Q 40/12; *ynfs¹wn* Q 40/19

TO REDUCE [Cf. perhaps Heb *nōp̄eš*, "rest, repose," Heb *wayyinnap̄ēš* (Ex. 31:17) "to take breath, refresh oneself," Daṯ *naffis li* "to make room for me," Daṯ *tanaffasa* "to take one's ease," Soq *néfoš* "to revive, come to life again"]

Q 40/11-12: *wʾy ḥll byḥllwn wnfs^1 wmtʿ ws^{1}ẖlʿ bnʿlw mqmh[w] wʾbyt wʾqny qtbn ms^{3}wdn wqtbn ṭbnn*

"whatever they cancel, reduce, defer, and waive on the property, houses, and possessions of the lords and landowners of Qataban"

(and-whatever cancelling they-cancel and-reducing and-deferring and-waiving on the-property and-the-houses and-the-possessions [of] the-Qatabanians the-lords and-the-Qatabanians the-landowners)

subst.^{1} sing. *nfs^1* 78/8; *nfs^{1}m* Q 78/8; *nfs^{1}s^1* Q 1/5, Q 11/3, Q 78/7, Q 186B/18, Q 202/5, Q 247/2, Q 249/2, Q 263/3, Q 492, Q 844/10; pl. *ʾnfs^{1}s^{1}my* Q 806/3; *ʾnfs^{1}s^{1}m* Q 484/1, Q 877/2

SOUL, SELF, LIFE [Sab *nfs^1* id., Ar *nafs* id.]

Q 78/8: *mwt ʾw mʿbr bnfs^1 ms^{1}tʿdwn*

"(whoever kills the culprit need not fear) death or compensation for the life of that wrongdoer"

subst.^{2} sing. *nfs^1* Q 89.134/1; *nfs^{1}m* Q 902; pl. *nfs^{1}hs^{1}yw* Q 490A/2-3, 4, B/2, 3-4, Q 491/2, Q 556/2, Q 900/2, Q 903/3; *nfs^1[ ]yw* Q 556/2

1) FUNERARY MONUMENT, STELA [Sab *nfs^1*, Eth *nafes*, Ph *nfš*, Ug *nfš* id.]

Q 89.134/1-2: *nfs^1 zydʾl bn ḥbn*

"funerary monument of ZYDʾL the son of ḤBN"

2) (INNER) CHAMBER in a funerary monument; INTERIOR

Q 900/2-3: *ʿs^{1}yw ẓrbw qbrs^{1}my … wnfs^{1}hys^{1}yw*

"[HMYS^{2}M and RKLM] acquired and secured title to their[dl.]-tomb … and its inner chambers"

subst.^{3} pl. *nfs^{1}hs^{1}ww* Q 266/3; *nfs^{1}hys^{1}m* Q 99/5, Q 265/3, Q 790/3

ROOF TERRACE

Q 99/2-5: *brm s^{2}ʾm wqny wbrʾ wẓrb byts^1 mrdʿm wʾẖṭbs^1 wṣrḥts^{1}ww wʾmtʿs^{1}m wnfs^{1}hys^{1}m wms^{2}qṣs^{1}m*

"[… (son of) FLS^{1}ʾB] purchased, acquired, built, and dedicated his house MRDʿM and its lower stories and its upper story and their guest chambers, roof terraces, and rooms"

(he-purchased and-acquiring and-building and-taking-possession-of his-house MRDʿM and-its-lower-stories and-its-upper-story and-their-guest-chambers and-their-roof terraces and-their-rooms)

NFṮ

verb *bynfṯ* Q 66/3; *byfṯ* (with assimilation of n?) Q 66/4

(NFṮ)

TO APPOINT [Ar *nafaṯa* "to blow on something." According to Beeston, 1971b, 14, this usage of the verb derives "from the antique past when authority was conveyed by a literal spitting or blowing on the person to be invested."]

Q 66/3-4: *bnkm bynfṯ ʿdkm bys^{1}fd ḫr[f]myw*

"since he was-appointed until he completes two years"

(since he-is-appointed until he-finishes two-years)

NṢF

s^1-prfx. *s^1nṣfm* Q 67/4, Q 68/4, Q 69/3

TO FALL SHORT [Cf. Ar *ʾanṣafa* "fall short." Further see Beeston, 1965, 105-07, and cf. Jamme, 1955f, 511, who understands this as the "owed part," the "part to be given by the colonists to the state after the estimate of the harvest made by the fiscal service."]

Q 67/4-5: *bn s^{1}nṣfm ws^{1}kt wʾḫḏ wgddm*

"without any falling short, ceasing, detraction, or termination"

t-infix *ntṣf* Q 898/8

TO PAY, PAY OUT [Cf. Ar *intaṣafa* "to be paid by someone that which he owes"]

Q 898/7-9: *wʾmrʾs^1 rs^{2}ww ywm drf wntṣf … ʾrb[ʿ]t wḫms^{1}y ḫrwf s^{1}ṯlwt*

"and his lords were paid their dues when he selected and paid out … fifty-f[ou]r sheep for their bearing responsibility for (his) safety"

(and-his-lords they-were-paid when he-selected and-he-paid … f[ou]r and-fifty sheep bearing-responsibility-for-safety)

subst. *nṣf* Q 856/1

SLAVE, SERVANT [Cf. Sab *mnṣf(m)* "servant, servitor," Ar *naṣafa* "to serve"]

Q 856/1: *ʾws^{1}ʿm bn yṣrʿm bn [m]dhm nṣf ydʿʾb ḏbyn*

"ʾWS^{1}ʿM son of YṢRʿM of the clan of [M]DHM servant of YDʿʾB Ḏū BYN"

NḌḤ

subst. sing. *mnḍḥ* Q 611/4; *mnḍḥs^{1}m* Q 913/7; *mnḍḥs^1[m]* Q 102/5; dl. *mnḍḥw* Q 244/18

TUTELARY DEITY [SAB *mnḍḥ* id.; cf. Ar *ʾanḍaḥa* "to defend, protect someone," Ar *munḍiḥ* "protector, defender"]

Q 244/15-18: *bʿṯtr s^{2}qrn wʿm ḏdwnm wʾnby s^{2}ymn wns^{2}bt wʿzyn mnḍḥw ḥrb* "by ʿAṯtar S²QRN and ʿAmm Ḏū DWNM and ʾAnbay the patron and NS²BT and ʿZYN the tutelary deities of ḤRB"

NQB

verb *nqb* Q 687/4

TO BORE A HOLE, PIERCE [Sab *nqb* "to cut, excavate," Ar *naqaba* "to bore, pierce," Heb *nāqab̲*, Syr *nəqab̲* id.]

Q 687/4: *wnqb hs¹gf bmṯbr ṯwyfm*

"he bored a hole (for runoff water) and built a roof over the ruin ṮWYFM"

subst. sing. *nqbn* Q 34B

CHANNEL [Sab *nqb* id, cf. MSA *neqāba* "cisterns; chambers excavated in the clay subsoil"]

Q 34B: *mẖḍ whnql kl ʿs²[…]fl nqbn ys¹rm lnẖls¹*

"[S²HR YGL YHRGB] dug out and channelled the whole […] the channel YS¹RM for his palmgrove"

(he-dug-out and-channelling all […] the-channel YS¹RM for-his-palmgrove)

NQZ

subst. *nqz* 176/5; *nqzn* Q 178/1

WELL [Cf. Sab *nqz* "to excavate, dig out," Ar *nuqz* "well," ModYem *mangaz* "small well"]

Q 178/1-2: *mẖḍ nqzn bẖṯm ʿrn ḏmwẓm lʾrḍs¹*

"[NBṬʿM] dug a well for his land on the summit of the fortress hill Ḏū MWẒM"

(he-dug the-well on-the-summit [of] the-fortress-hill Ḏū-MWẒM for-his-land)

NQL

s¹(h)-prfx. *hnql* Q 34B

TO EXCAVATE, DIG OUT [Sab *nql* "to quarry stone (?)," *hql* "to excavate"]

Q 34B: *mẖḍ whnql kl ʿs²[…]fl nqbn ys¹rm lnẖls¹*

"[S²HR YGL YHRGB] dug out and channelled the whole […] the channel YS¹RM for his palmgrove"

(he-dug-out and-channelling all […] the-channel YS¹RM for-his-palmgrove)

subst. *mnql* Q 176/10; *mnqln* Q 36/3, Q 176/6, 10, Q 856/3

MOUNTAIN ROAD, PASS [Sab *mnql* "path cut on mountain side," Ar *naqīl* "mountain pass," ModḤaḍ *manqal* "road through mountains"]

(NQL)

Q 176/9-11: *ʾws¹ʿm bn yṣrʿm bn mdhm tqdm wḥrg kl ʿs²q wwzl wṣll mnqln ẓrm btḥrg mrʾs¹ ydʿʾb*

"ʾWS¹ʿM the son of YṢRʿM of the clan of MDHM directed and supervised all the digging up, smoothing, and paving of the mountain pass ẒRM under the direction of his lord YDʿʾB" (ʾWS¹ʿM the-son [of] YṢRʿM [of] the-clan [of] MDHM directed and-supervising the-whole digging-up and-smoothing and-paving the-mountain-pass ẒRM under-the-direction [of] his-lord YDʿʾB)

NS¹Y

subst. *ns¹ym* Q 9/1-2, Q 695/14

OBLIVION [Cf. Ar *nasiya* "to forget," and see Beeston, 1953, 111-12]

Q 9/1-2: *s¹hlm ḏrʾn wḥs¹y wns¹ym lḏm byns²ʾ mʿmrn bn brṯs¹*

"S¹HLM ḎRʾN. Silence and oblivion to whoever removes this memorial monument from its place"

NS²ʾ

verb *byns²ʾ* Q 9/2

TO TAKE AWAY, REMOVE [Sab *ns²ʾ* "to take, take away," Eth *nas¹ʾa* "to remove"]

Q 9/1-2: *s¹hlm ḏrʾn wḥs¹y wns¹ym lḏm byns²ʾ mʿmrn bn brṯs¹*

"S¹HLM ḎRʾN. Silence and oblivion to whoever removes this memorial monument from its place"

t-prfx. *tns²ʾ* Q 74/3

TO CARRY ON, UNDERTAKE a military action [Sab *tns²ʾ* "to initiate hostilities, wage *war*," Ar *našaʾa* "to raise (forces)"]

Q 74/3: *bḏrm tns²ʾ ydʿʾl byn ws¹mhʿly ynf*

"during the war which YDʿʾL BYN and S¹MHʿLY YNF undertook"

subst. *mns²ʾ* Q 36/5, Q 80/8, Q 769/2b

TRIBAL LEVIES [Cf. sense of Qat *tns²ʾ* "to carry on, undertake a *military action*," Sab *mns²ʾ* "tribal levies">"military expedition, campaign," and Jamme, 1972, 44, who translates *mns² ʾ* "bringing"]

"Q 769/2a-b: *ws²ẖb ʾbns¹ wblqs¹ wʿḍs¹ wmrt[s¹ …] bmns²ʾ qtbn*

"[(S²)HR ǴYLN] provided its stone, its marble, its wood, and [its] limestone […] with the tribal levies of Qataban"

"(he-provided its-stone, and-its-marble, and-its-wood, and-[its]-limestone […] with-the-tribal-levies [of] Qataban"

ʿ

ʿBD

subst. *ʿbd* Q 89.94, Q 90/1; *ʿbdk* Q 514, Q 772/1; *ʿbds¹* Q 898/4 *ʿbds¹m* Q 254/3

SLAVE, SERVANT [Sab *ʿbd* "slave, servant," Ar *ʿabd*, Heb *ʿeḇeḏ* id., Akk *abdu* "slave"]

Q 89.94: *mqf lḥyʿm ʿbd mlkn*

"votive object of LḤYʿM, servant of the king"

ʿBR

verb *byʿbr* Q 78/13

TO ARRANGE [Sab *ʿbr* "to be put into effect (?)"]

Q 78/13: *ʿdkm byṣrs¹ mlkn knm byʿbr wḥwr*

"until the king decrees it, as he arranges and orders"

(until decrees-it the-king, as he-arranges and-ordering)

s¹-prfx. *s¹ʿbr* Q 78/5, 6

TO COMMAND, ORDER [Cf. Sab *mʿbrn* "judicial examination (?)"; cf. also Ar *ʿabara* "to examine (coins) to determine their weight and value." Irvine, 1967, 280, compares the MSA *bišʿa* or "trial by ordeal."]

Q 78/5: *knm byṯfṭs¹ ws¹ḥr ws¹ʿbr wṣry mlkn*

"as the king decides, directs, orders, and announces"

t-infix *yʿtbr* Q 243/6

TO INCLUDE [Cf. Ar *ʿabara* "to pass over," Heb. *hĕʿeḇîr* "to transfer"]

Q 243/6-8: *lyʿtbr klḏm bymd wnkr ʾḥrm wḏrʾm wʾḥdb ws¹ʿdm wḏʿḏrs¹m wḏtn ʾbytn bnḥl ḏn ḏtzrbn wgdytn*

"(this decree) applies to whatever ʾḤRM and ḎRʾM and ʾḤDB and S¹ʿDM and their dependents and these houses add and change through any lease (subsequent) to this land grant and renewal"

(let-apply everything-which add and-changing ʾḤRM and-ḎRʾM and-ʾḤDB and-S¹ʿDM and-their-dependents and-these-houses in-granting-the-lease [of] that-which [is] of-a-land-grant and-renewal)

subst.[1] *ʿbrs¹* Q 72/4

TERRACED FIELD [Sab *ʿbr*, *ʿbrt* "wadi-side cultivation; terraced field"]

Q 72/3-4: *bwrḫm wrḫm bʿbrs¹ bd ʾwrḫn wḫrwfn*

"month by month on his terraced field in the succession of months and years"

(ʿBR)

(by-month month on-his-terraced field series [of] months and-years)

subst.[2] *mʿbr* Q 78/8; *mʿbrm* Q 78/6; *mʿbrn* Q 78/13, Q 89.144A/2

PUNISHMENT, COMPENSATION; VENGEANCE

Q 78/8: *mwt ʾw mʿbr bnfs¹ ms¹tʿdwn*

"(whoever kills the culprit need not fear) death or compensation for the life of that wrongdoer"

subst.[3] *mʿbrh[n]* Q 839/1 (See Beeston, 1962b, 33, for a discussion of this form)

SIDE [Cf. Sab *tʿbr* "delimitation, fixing (of boundaries)," Heb *ʿēḇer* "side," Akk *abartu* "far bank of a river," Soq *ʿaber* "bank of a river"]

Q 839/1: *ln ḏn wṯnn ʿ[d] wṯny lmʿbrh[n]*

"from this boundary to the borders on its two sides"

prep. *ʿbr* Q 244/9, Q 246/8; *ʿbrn* Q 839/6, 7

TO, TOWARD [Sab *ʿbr* id.]

Q 244/9-10: *ʿbr mlk s¹bʾ wʾrḍ ḥmyrm*

"to the king of Sabaʾ and the land of Ḥimyar"

ʿGLM

subst. *ʿglmts¹* Q 700/2

WATER CONDUIT [Sab *ʿglmt* "diversion mole"; cf. ModYem *ʿijlama*, pl *ʿajālim* "small stone wall used to divert the waters of a torrent, provide with an opening to allow the water to flow on to the cultivated field" and see further Rossi, 1940, 308.]

Q 700/2: *bny qrḏn ylbʾ wʿglmts¹ wrʾs¹s¹*

"[S²HR YGL] built the dam YLBʾ and its conduit and its spout"

ʿD

prep. *ʿd* Q 4/4-5, Q 38/4, Q 39/3, Q 102/3 + *ʿdw* Q 72/2

1) UP TO, AS FAR AS [Sab *ʿd* id., Heb *ʿaḏ* "until, while, even," Ug *ʿd* "until," Akk *ʾadi* id.]

Q 102/3-4: *bn s²rs¹m ʿd frʿm*

"from the bottom to the top"

2) IN

Q 72/2: *ʾbʿl ẓrwb ʿdw s³dw*

"[S²HR HLL issued an edict to] the owners of properties in S³DW"

conj. *ʿdkm* Q 66/3, Q 78/13

UNTIL [comp. of the prep. *ʿd* and *km*]

Q 66/3-4: *bnkm bynfṯ ʿdkm bys¹fd ḫr[f]myw*

"since he was appointed until he completes two yea[r]s"
(since he-is-appointed until he-finishes two-yea[r]s)

ʿDD

verb *byʿd* Q 186B/17; *byʿdwn* Q 186B/2-3

TO CALCULATE, RECKON [Cf. Sab *ʿdd* "period *of time*," Ar *ʿadda* "to reckon, compute, calculate"]

Q186B/1-5: *mlk qtbn wʿhr s²mr ʾl byʿdwn nʿmt bz[w]rtm bʿlw ms²ṭm bys²tyṭwn ws²tʾm qtbn*

"the king of Qataban and the overseer of S²MR shall not calculate 'seed privileges' on merchandise which the Qatabanians may trade and buy"
(king [of] Qataban and-overseer [of] S²MR not they-will-calculate benefits [of] seeds on merchandise they-trade and-buying the-Qatabanians)

ʿDW

verb *ʿdw* Q 186B/32; *byʿd* Q 186B/17

TO GO BEYOND, EXCEED [Ar *ʿadā* (w) "to go beyond," Sab *ʿdw* "to move, march, go," Eth *ʿadawa* "to go through, pass beyond," Heb *ʿāḏāh* "to pass on, advance"]

Q186B/16-18: *wḏm byʿd mrṯdn bḏl nfs¹s¹*

"or if it surpasses his goods, then by his own means"
(and-that-which surpasses the-goods by-that-which-to himself)

s¹t-prfx. *ys¹tʿdw* Q 79/5; *ms¹tʿdwn* Q 78/7, 8

TO BE GUILTY OF WRONGDOING [Cf. Sab *ʿdw* "to commit a hostile action *against someone*"]

Q 78/8: *mwt ʾw mʿbr bnfs¹ ms¹tʿdwn*

"(whoever kills the culprit need not fear) death or compensation for the life of that wrongdoer"

ʿḎB

verb *ʿḏbw* Q 679/9, 10

TO REPAIR [Sab *ʿḏb* id., Heb *ʿāzaḇ* "to help, assist," Ug *ʿdb* "to prepare," Daṯ *ʿaḏḏab* "cut and hew to give something the desired shape"]

Q 679/9: *wʿḏbw ḫrt wynhmw*

"they repaired the aqueduct of their vineyard"

s¹-prfx. *s¹ʿḏb* Q 72/8; *s¹ʿḏbm* Q 72/9

TO PUNISH [Cf. Sab *ʿḏb* "to demand a penalty *from someone*," Ar *ʿaḏḏaba* "to punish"]

Q 72/7-8: *wl ylṣq wqrw ws¹ʿḏb*

(ʿḎB)

"let [the lord of Timnaʿ] prosecute, accuse, and punish"
(and-let he-prosecute and-accusing and-punishing)

subst. sing. *ʿḏb* Q 40/20; pl. *ʾʿḏb* Q 40/12

PUNISHMENT

Q 40/12-13: *kl ʾʿḏb wdyn wtwṯf gzwmm gzmw*

"all punishments, judgments, and the carrying out of decisions which they have made"
(all punishments and-judgments and-the-carrying-out [of] the-decisions they-have-made)

ʿḎR

subst. (used only in combination with *ḏ*) *ʿḏrs¹* Q 73/3, Q 206/2; *ʿḏrhw* Q 74/14, Q 178/3, Q 611/3; pl. *ʾʿḏrs¹m* Q 243/3, 7

(used in combination with *ḏ*): PROTEGÉ, DEPENDENT [Sab *ḏʿḏr* id.; cf. Ar *ʿaḏara* "to excuse or clear someone," Heb *ʿāzar* "to help," Ug *ʿḏr* "to rescue" OAram *ʿzr* "to help," Syr *ʿăḏar* id]

Q 178/3: *lhw wl wldhw wḏʿḏrhw*

"for himself and his children and his dependents"

ʿHD

s¹-prfx. *s¹ʿhd* Q 72/2; *s¹ʿhdm* Q 72/5, 7

TO ATTEND TO, TAKE CARE OF [Cf. Ar *taʿahhada* id.]

Q 72/2-3: *kḏm byfrwn wʾgw wʾhw wḥrṯ wqẓr wʿzz ws¹qḥ ws¹ʿhd s²ʿbm s²ʿbm*

"in order that they till, struggle, toil, plow, labor, work vigorously, make ready, and attend to (their task) tribe by tribe"
(in-order-that they-till and-struggling and-toiling and-plowing and-laboring and-working-vigorously and-making-ready and-attending-to tribe tribe)

t-infix *ʿthd* Q 72/8; *ʿthdm* Q 72/9

TO CONCERN ONESELF, TAKE CARE OF [Cf. Sab *ʿthd* "to take *someone* under protection," Ar *iʿtahada* "to have charge of something, take care of it"]

Q 72/7-8: *wl ylṣq wqrw ws¹ʿḏb ws¹ʾgy wʿthd*

"let [the lord of Timnaʿ] prosecute, accuse, punish, reprimand, and concern himself"
(and-let he-prosecute and-accusing and-punishing and-reprimanding and-concerning himself)

subst. dl. *mʿhdy* Q 543n/2; pl. *mʿhd* Q 803/4

TEMPLE FUNCTIONARY [Sab *mʿhd* "temple functionary"; cf. Ar *muʿāhid* "ally, confederate," and perhaps Ar *ʿahida* "to delegate, authorize"]

Q 543n/1-2: *ʿmynm d̲ʿmʿly mʿhdy ʿm*

"ʿMYNM D̲ū ʿMʿLY, the two temple functionaries of ʿAmm"

ʿHR

subst. *ʿhr* Q 186A/16, 17, 22, 27, B/1-2, 6, 28

OVERSEER, SUPERINTENDENT, LORD [Sab *ʿhrw* "nobles"; cf. perhaps Ar *ʿāhil* "sovereign, prince"]

Q 186A/16-18: *wmty lyks³ʾ ʿhr s²mr kd̲m bys¹tḏf qtbn bʿm ʾs²ʿbm*

"and when the overseer of S²MR announces that he wishes the Qatabanians to make trading journey among the tribes (then they may trade on their own account)"

(and-when announces the-overseer [of] S²MR that wishes-that-trade the-Qatabanians among the-tribes)

ʿWM

subst. *ʿmm* Q 1/1, Q 35/3, Q 80/3 (2x), Q 240/2, Q 769/1b, Q 915/2

YEAR [Cf. Sab *ʿwm* "year (?)", Ar *ʿām* "year." See the discussion in Bron, 1987, 24-25, of *ʿmm* in the meaning "year"]

Q 35/3-4: *qẓr qyn rs²w ʿmm ṯntm*

"administrator of the money offerings, attendant, and *rs²w* for the second year"

ʿWT

verb *ʿwt* Q 80/6

TO CARRY OUT (?) [Rhodokanakis, 1924, 47, translates "*durchführen; anordnen*" according to the context; cf. perhaps Tig *ʿawtē* "victory"]

Q 80/6-7: *wʿwt mʿs²q ms²mn bʾmr ʿm d̲dwnm*

"[D̲ū BYN YHNʿM] carried out (?) the cultivation of the field at the behest of ʿAmm D̲ū DWNM"

(and-he-carried-out the-cultivation [of] the-field at-the-command [of] ʿAmm D̲ū-DWNM)

ʿZZ

verb *ʿzz* Q 72/2

TO WORK VIGOROUSLY [Cf. Sab *hʿzz* "to uphold, respect *law*," Ar *ʿazza* "to be strong, powerful," Eth *ʿazzaza*, Heb *ʿāzaz* id.]

Q 72/2-3: *kd̲m byfrwn wʾgw wʾhw wḥrṯ wqẓr wʿzz ws¹qḥ ws¹ʿhd s²ʿbm s²ʿbm*

(ʿZZ)

"in order that they till, struggle, toil, plow, labor, work vigorously, make ready, and attend to (their task) tribe by tribe"

(in-order-that they-till and-struggling and-toiling and-plowing and-laboring and-working-vigorously and-making-ready and-attending-to tribe tribe)

ʿẒM

verb *yʿẓm* Q 555/3

TO HONOR, RESPECT [Cf. Ar *ʿaẓẓama* "to honor, respect, venerate"]

Q 555/1-5: *s²rḥm ḏbrlm yʿẓm yḥmy bʿḏn ḏtḥ[ ]*

"S²RḤM of the family of BRLM honors and defends, by permission of Ḏāt Ḥ[ ] "

ʿYN

subst. *ʿynm* Q 183/5

SIGHT [Sab *ʿyn* "eye," Ar *ʿayn*, Eth *ʿayn*, Heb *ʿayin*, Akk *ēnu* id.]

Q 183/5: *ʿynm nʿm*

"may (his) sight be pleasant"

ʿKR

verb *ʿkr* Q 40/17

TO RESIST, CONTRADICT, OPPOSE [Sab *ʿkr* "to contest, contradict," Ar *ʿakara* "to begin the attack again after having appeared to have fled"]

Q 40/17: *ʾyhnmw ʿkr*

"(let these decrees and directives be made known) wherever there may be opposition"

(where-[or what-]soever it-is-opposed)

ʿLW/ʿLY

verb *ʿly* Q 899/2; *ʿlym* Q 694/11

TO RAISE HIGH, ELEVATE [Sab *yʿly* "to bring up, raise," Ar *ʾʿalā* (y) "to raise high, hoist, elevate," Heb *heʿĕlāh* "to bring up, cause to rise"]

Q 899/2: *bnyw wʿly ws¹ḥdṯ qbrhmw*

"[ʾWS¹ʾL and the Minaeans] built and raised and newly constructed their burial-place"

t-infix *ʿtlyw* Q 40/23

TO SUPERVISE, PAY ATTENTION TO [RÉS, VI, 222, compares Ar *iṭṭalaʿa* "to supervise," but compare also *iʿtalā* "to take care for, pay heed to"]

Q 40/23: *wʿtlyw ʾs^{1}dm ʿlmw bḏn ftḥn ʾs^{1}m ʾs^{1}m bhṯ ḏmrs^{1}*

"those who have signed this decree have each seen to the promulgation of its correct reading"

(and-they-supervised who signed in-this decree man man the-announcement [of] its-correct-reading)

subst. *ʿlym* Q 40/17

HIGHLAND, HEIGHT [Cf. Sab *ʿly* "highland, high ground, plateau"]

Q 40/17: *bʿlym ws^{1}flm*

"in highland and lowland"

prep. *ʿly* Q 186A/23, 25; *ʿls^{1}ww* Q 83/8; *ʿlw* Q 695/7, 8; *ʿl* Q 687/8

ON, UPON, AGAINST [Sab *ʿly* on, upon, against," Ar *ʿalā*, Heb *ʿal* id.]

Q 186A/24-25: *wzʾ ʾns^{1}m ʿly ʾḫs^{1} bḫ[t]fr[m*

"someone has consistently cheated his fellow-trader"

(he-continued someone against his fellow-trader in-cheating)

prep. + prep. *bʿl*

See entry under B.

prep. + prep. *bʿlw*

See entry under B.

prep. + prep. *bʿly*

See entry under B.

prep. + prep. *bnʿlw*

See entry under BN I.

adv. *llʿl*

See entry under L I.

prep. + prep. *lʿlw*

See entry under L I.

ʿLM

verb *ʿlmw* Q 40/23

TO SIGN [Cf. Ar *ʾaʿlama* "to make a mark, sign a document"]

Q 40/23: *wʿtlyw ʾs^{1}dm ʿlmw bḏn ftḥn ʾs^{1}m ʾs^{1}m bhṯ ḏmrs^{1}*

"those who have signed this decree have each seen to the promulgation of its correct reading"

(and-they-supervised who signed in-this decree man man the-announcement [of] its-correct-reading)

t-prfx *tʿlm* Q 40/23, *tʿlmʾy* Q 66/12, 67/11, 68/10, 69/7, 70/5, 72/10, 78/13, Q 79/7, Q 202/6

TO SIGN

(ʿLM)

Q 67/11: *tʿlmʾy yd s²hr*

"signed by S²HR"

(signed the-hand [of] S²HR)

t-infix *ʿtlm* Q 40/22

TO SIGN

Q 40/21-22: *wl ys¹kn mnkṯs¹ hg ẓrʾs¹ ʾs¹mʿm ḏm ʿtlm bfthn*

"and let the witnesses who have signed this order punish its violation according to his proclamation"

(and-let punish its-violation according-to his-proclamation the-witnesses who signed this-order)

subst. *tʿlmn* Q 695/3-4 *tʿlms¹m* Q 40/17

WRITTEN DOCUMENT; DOCUMENTATION [Cf. Sab *ʿlm* "document"]

Q 695/3-4: *wʾḫḏ tbdd ʾrḍn wqwr tʿlmn*

"payment for the land has been received and the document has been engraved"

(and-received the-payment [of] the-land and-engraved the document)

ʿM

prep. *ʿmn* Q 244/11-12, Q 246/11

BY, THROUGH, BY MEANS OF, BY THE AUTHORITY OF [For a discussion of *ʿm* (which in this case has a suffix *-n*) see Beeston, 1962b, 57, 59; cf. Sab *ʿm(n)* "from, authorized by", Heb *ʿim* "with"]

Q 244/10-12: *wʿm lyzʾ ṣdqs¹n bkl mngw byktrbwn ʿmn thrgs¹*

"as for ʿAmm, may he continue to give them their due by all the good fortune which will be granted by his order"

(and-ʿAmm may-he-continue granting-them-their-due through-all the-good-fortune [which] will-be-granted by his-order)

prep. + prep. *bʿm*.

See entry under B.

prep. + prep. *bn ʿm* .

See entry under BN I.

ʿMD

subst. *ʿmd* Q 690b/2

CHIEF [Jamme, 1971, 91, compares the Ar *ʿumda* "a man who is the mainstay, support, or chief cornerstone of a thing, chief," and suggests that this office was inferior to that of the *mqtwy*]

Q 690b/1-3: *zyd ʿmd mrṯdm ʿkl*

"ZYD, chief of MRṮDM of ʿKL"

ʿMR

subst. *mʿmr* Q 83/1, Q 89.28, .41, .123, Q 127/1 + *mʿmrm* Q 83/7; *mʿmrn* Q 9/2; *mʿmrs*^{1} Q 83/7, Q 201/2-3, Q 507/2

MEMORIAL MONUMENT [Sab *mʿmr* id. See Pirenne, in CIAS 1:135-38, Jamme, 1952a, 343 (who says that *mʿmr* sometimes must mean "votive offering"), J. Ryckmans, 1953, 343-69, and Garbini, 1980, 55-59, for a thorough discussion of the meaning and associations of this word.]

Q 83/5-8: *wʾl s*^{3}*n s*^{1}*wḥs*^{3}*s*^{1} *bn brṯs*^{1} *lmʿmrm bymẓʾ ʿls*^{1}*ww*

"it is not permitted to remove it from its place for a memorial that replaces it"

(and-not-permitted removing it from its-place for-a-memorial replaces it)

ʿNY

t-infix *yʿtny* Q 72/8

TO TAKE NOTICE; TO TAKE RESPONSIBILITY [Min *ʿtny* id.; cf. Heb *ʿānāh* "to be occupied, busied with," Ar *iʿtanā* (y) "to be concerned about (something)"]

Q 72/8-9: *whmw ys*^{1}*s*^{1}*lb kbrn bn lṣq wqrw ... fl yʿtny mlkn*

"if the *kabīr* refuses to prosecute and accuse ... then let the king take responsibility"

(and-if refuses the-*kabīr* from prosecuting and-accusing ... then-let take-responsibility the-king)

ʿṢB

subst. pl. *ʿṣwb* Q 40/18

REQUIREMENT, OBLIGATION [Cf. Ar *ʿaṣaba* "to bind, join"]

Q 40/18: *nl yḏʾwn wkwn s*^{1}*m ʾfthn ʾw [w]mḥrtn wmnkṯs*^{1}*m s*^{3}*ẖwl wʿṣwb wnfwq wẖlwʿ wlkwʿ*

"let these ordinances or directives and the penalty for their violation be published and be a duty, obligation, requirement, and an abrogation of previous laws and a confirmation of current statutes"

(let go-forth and-being these ordinances or directives and-their-violation duties and-obligations and-requirements and-abrogations and-confirmations)

ʿṢM

verb *ʿṣm* Q 71A, Q 79/1-2; *byʿṣm* Q 66/3

TO BIND, TIE, LINK [Cf. Ar *ʿaṣama* "to tie, defend"]

Q 66/2-3: *wl yṣḥf wḥrg ḏn ṣḥfn ʿṣmm byʿṣm ʿm ḏlbẖ ṭd ʾns*^{1}*m*

(ʿṢM)

"let this document be written and administered as a patronage-tie which binds ʿAmm Ḏū Labaḫ to each man"
(and-let be-written and-administering this document as-a-patronage-tie [which] binds ʿAmm Ḏū-Labaḫ [to] one man)

subst. *ʿṣm* Q 66/9, Q 67/5, Q 68/4, Q 69/3, Q 79/1, Q 202/1; *ʿṣmm* Q 66/3; *ʿṣmn* Q 66/6

TIE, PATRONAGE-TIE [See discussion of this word in Beeston, 1971b, 9.]

See entry above.

ʿḌ

subst. *ʿḍ* Q 80/6; *ʿḍm* Q 40/21; *ʿḍs¹* Q 769/2a

WOOD [Sab *ʿḍ* "*building material in* wood (?)," Ar *ʿiḍḍ* "small thorn bush," Heb *ʿēṣ* "tree, wood," Akk *iṣu* "tree, wood"]

Q 80/6: *ʾbnw wʿḍ wblq wmrt*

"[Ḏū BYN YHNʿM built in] stone and wood, marble, and limestone"

ʿḌD

subst. *ʿḍd* Q 694/5; *ʿḍds¹ww* Q 540/2

1) DEFLECTOR DAM (?); ENCLOSURE (?) [Sab *ʿḍd* "deflector dam (?)"; cf. Ar *ʿiḍādatā ʾl-bāb* "the two sides or wooden sideposts of a door"]

Q 540/2-3: *[y]s¹rn wʿḍds¹ww rymt wrḥbt bn s²rs¹m ʿd frʿm*

"[Y]S¹RN and its deflector dam RYMT and RḤBT from the bottom to the top"

2) BORDER [Ar *ʿḍd* "side, adjacent part, boundary"]

Q 694/5: *bn ʿḍd byḥn mmqtytm lms²r[q]*

"from the border of Bayḥān eastward"

ʿQB

s¹-prfx *s¹ʿqb* Q 695/1

TO TRANSFER, EXCHANGE [Sab *hʿqb* "to give in exchange for, barter," Ar *ʾaʿqaba* "to exchange something for, recompense, requite"]

Q 695/1: *ḏn qf ʾrḍm ʾs¹y wnḥl ws¹ʿqb wqyḍ hwfʿm yhnʿm*

"this marks land which HWFʿM YHNʿM [and YDʿʾB YGL] have granted, leased, transferred, and assigned"

t-infix *ʿtqb* Q 66/8

TO IMPLEMENT [Cf. Ar *iʿtaqaba* "to arrive at a goal"]

Q 66/8: *wkwmw lyṣḥf wḥrg wʿtqb wṯtwb ḏn ṣḥfn ʾrbym byrby ʿm ḏlbḫ* "and thus let (all) whom ᶜAmm Ḏū Labaḫ chooses as *ʾrby* write down, administer, implement, and adhere to this agreement"

(and-thus let-him-write-down and-administering and-implementing and-adhering [to] this agreement *ʾthe-rby* he-makes-*rby* ᶜAmm Ḏū-Labaḫ

subst. dl. *ᶜqby* Q 690a/2

DEPUTY, REPRESENTATIVE [Sab *ᶜqbm* "governor, deputy," Ar *ᶜāqib* "vicar, lieutenant, second in command in the empire"]

Q 690a/2-3: *ᶜqby kwkbn wys¹rn*

"[RṮDM ᶜQFRB and his brother MRTḎᶜLN ʾS²Wᶜ] the two deputies of KWKBN and YS¹RN"

ᶜQL

subst. *ᶜqls¹* Q 172/6

COMPENSATION MONEY [Cf. Ar *ᶜaql* "expiation of a homocide by the payment of blood money"]

Q 172/5-6: *fks³ʾ s¹bʾm lqrḥn wᶜqls¹ bms¹ʾls¹*

"he announced to S¹BʾM through his oracle concerning the wound and its compensation"

(so-he-announced [to] S¹BʾM concerning-the-wound and-its-compensation-money in-his-oracle)

ᶜRB I

verb *ᶜrb* Q 1/3; *yᶜrb* Q 186A/8; *byᶜrb* Q 186B/13-14

1) TO ENTER [Cf. Akk *erēbu* "to enter, go in," and see the discussion of this root in ESA in Lundin, 1987, 50-51]

Q 1/3-5: *wᶜrb bᶜm nbᶜ qlbn mwṯb mkntn*

"and he entered, along with NBᶜ QLBN the sanctum of the inner shrine

(and-he-entered, along-with NBᶜ QLBN the-sanctum [of] the-inner-shrine)

2) TO PAY [Cf. Sab *tᶜrb* "to give pledges," Ar *ᶜarraba, ʾaᶜraba* "to give a pledge" Heb *ᶜārab̲* "to pledge one's self," and see Beeston, 1959, 12]

Q 186B/9-14: *wmn lys¹ᶜrb bn qtbn wbn mᶜnm wbn ḥwr tmnᶜ byts¹ wmḫtns¹ ḫdrm byᶜrb tmnᶜ*

"any Qatabanian, Minaean, or resident of Timnaᶜ who uses his house or residence as a place of business shall pay (the) Timnaᶜ (market tax)"

(ˁRB I)

(and-he-who uses from-among the-Qatabanians and-from-among the-Minaeans and-from-among the-residents [of] Timnaᶜ his-house and-his-residence [as] a-place-of-business he-shall-pay)

s[1]-prfx *s[1]ˁrb* Q 40/15, Q 186B/10; *s[1]ˁrbw* Q 40/11, 17

1) TO USE [See Beeston, 1971b, 3, for a discussion of this word and the phrase in Q 186B/10-13]

See entry above.

2) TO ANNOUNCE, PROCLAIM [Cf. Ar *ʾaˁraba* "to proclaim; to speak clearly"]

Q 40/17: *ʾfṯḥm wmḥrtm bs[1]m ʾl s[1]ˁrbw bs[1]m mlkn*

"orders and directives which they have announced in the name of the king"

ˁRB II

subst. *mˁrbn* Q 839/6-7

WEST, THE WEST [Sab *mˁrb*, Ar *maġrib*, *maġrab*, Heb *maˁarāḇ* id.]

Q 839/6-7: *ˁbrn mˁrbn*

"toward the west"

ˁRM

subst. *ˁrm* Q 497/1, Q 917/1

1) WIDOW [Cf. Heb *ˁārōm* "naked, uncovered," Ar *ˁarama* "to strip (a bone of its meat, a branch of its leaves)," and see the discussion of Beeston, 1981, 59-60.]

Q 497/1: *ʾbṣdq ˁrm whbʾl ḏhrn wḏḏrʾn*

"ʾBṢDQ, widow of WHBʾL Ḏū HRN and Ḏū ḎRʾN"

2) HOSTAGE (?) [Conjectured by Ryckmans, 1987, 174-75]

Q 917/1: ...] *ˁrm s[2]h[r*

"...] hostage (?) of S[2]H[R]"

ˁRR

subst. *ˁrn* Q 37/3, Q 178/1

HILL FORTRESS, CITADEL [Sab *ˁr* "mountain; citadel; hill-town," ModYem *ˁurr* "hill fortress"; cf. Heb *ˁîr* "city, town," Ug *ˁr*, Ph. *ˁr* id.]

Q 37/2-3: *qyf ˁṯtr wˁm ws[2]ms[1] bˁrn ʾbltm*

"(he) set up a *mqf* to ˁAṯtar and ˁAmm and S[2]ams[1] in the citadel ʾBLTM"

ʿS^{1}Y

verb *ʿs^{1}y* Q 74/5, Q 265/1, Q 478/1, Q 491/1; *ʿs^{1}yw* Q 490A/2, B/2, Q 556/1, 874/2, Q 900/2, Q 903/3

TO ACQUIRE [Sab *ʿs^{1}y* id., Heb *ʿāśāh* "to make, obtain"]

Q 490A/2: *ʿs^{1}yw ẓrbw bnyw qbrs^{1}m*

"(they) acquired, dedicated, and built their tomb"

ʿS^{1}M

subst. *ʿs^{1}m* Q 695/9

A NUMBER OF, A CONSIDERABLE AMOUNT OF [Sab *ʿs^{1}m* id.; see Beeston, 1975b, 188-89]

Q 695/8-9: *wbn ʿlw s^{1}nhtm s^{1}nt brm ʿs^{1}m ḫrwf*

"[this document is based] upon a code which has been observed in BRM for a number of years"

ʿS^{1}N

subst. *ʿs^{1}ns^{1}m* Q 89. Pl. XIII, fig. 5

CISTERN, UNDERGOUND CHAMBER [Sab *ʿs^{1}nm* "foundation, lower courses," Akk *esēnu* "vault, cave"]

Q 89. Pl. XIII, fig. 5: *...] ʿs^{1}ns^{1}m wmṣ[...*

"...] their cistern and[..."

ʿS^{1}T

card. num. *ʿs^{1}tnm* Q 72/3

ONE [Cf. Heb *ʿaštê ʿāśār* "eleven," Akk ***eštū, eštān***, f. ***ešteat, eštātu*** "one." For a usage similar to Q 72/3, cf. Heb *yôm ʾeḥāḏ* "the first day"]

Q 72/3: *bʿs^{1}tnm ḏfrʿm ws^{1}ḏtm ḏfqḥw*

"on the first of Ḏū FRʿM and on the sixth of Ḏū FQḤW"

ʿS^{2}Q

s^1-prfx. *s^{1}ʿs^{2}q* Q 67/12, Q 174/2, Q 178/1, Q 803/2-3

1) TO CULTIVATE [Cf. Sab *hʿs^{2}q* "to dig *a well*; to cut *a road*." Irvine, 1962, 164-65, suggests a basic sense of "to mark out, divide up (foundations, land, etc.)"; cf. also Akk *esēqu, ešēqu* "to scratch, incise"]

Q 174/2: *s^{1}ʿs^{2}q wṣrs^{1}m*

"[ʾLS^{1}ʿD ḎʾB...] cultivated their land allotment"

2) TO CARRY OUT, COMPLETE [Sense from context; see Beeston, 1971b, 11, who renders *s^{1}ʿs^{2}q* at Q 67/12 "execution."]

Q 67/12: *wtqdm ws^{1}ʿs^{2}q ʾs^{1}ṭr ḏn brṯn nbṭʿm*

"NBṬʿM directed and completed the inscriptions of this place"

subst.[1] *ʿs^{2}q* Q 38/2, Q 39/2, Q 72/5, 7, Q 112/2, Q 131/2, Q 167/3, Q 176/10, Q 803/3, Q 856/2

(ʿS²Q)

EXCAVATION, DIGGING UP; TILLING

Q 38/2-3: *tqdm wḥrg ws¹hlk kl ʿs²q wmb[n]y mḥfdn*

"[S²RḤʿṮT] supervised, directed, and carried out the whole excavation and construc[tio]n of the tower"

(he-supervised and-directing and-carrying-out the-excavation and-construc[tio]n [of] the-tower]

subst.² *ʿs²qts²* Q 838/3

ANNEX [Ar *ʿašiqa* "to cling *to something*"]

Q 838/1-3: *hwfʿm bwʿ wrbbm ʾb tqdmw bytn lwbn ykwḥ wkl mqḥs¹ wʿs²qts¹*

"HWFʿM BWʿ and RBBM ʾB supervised (the construction of) the house LWBN YKWḤ and all its courts and annexes"

subst.³ *mʿs²q* Q 80/6

CULTIVATION [Cf. Sab *ʿs²qn* "terracing"]

Q 80/6-7: *wʿwt mʿs²q ms²mn bʾmr ʿm ḏdwnm*

"[Ḏū BYN YHNʿM] carried out the cultivation of the field at the behest of ʿAmm Ḏū DWNM"

(and-he-carried-out the-cultivation [of] the-field at-the-command [of] ʿAmm Ḏū-DWNM)

ʿS²R

card. num. *ʿs²r* Q 72/6(2x), Q 74/10, 11

TEN [Sab *ʿs²r*, *ʿs²rt* "ten," Ar *ʿašr*, *ʿašara*, Eth *ʿašrū*, *ʿašartū*, Heb *ʿeśer*, *ʿăśārāh*, Akk *ešru*, *ešertu* id.]

Q 74/11: *ws¹dṯt ʿs²r ʾnḫlm bbḍʿ ḫdṣm*

"sixteen palmgroves in the area of ḪDṢM"

(and-six ten palmgroves in-the-area [of] ḪDṢM)

card. num. *ʿs²ry* Q 695/5

TWENTY [Sab *ʿs²ry* "twenty," Ar *ʿišrūna*, Eth *ešrā*, Heb *ʿeśrīm*, Akk *ešrā* id.]

Q 695/5: *ws¹bʿt wʿs²ry ʾqblm*

"twenty-seven *qbl*"

subst. *ʿs²r* Q 66/5

TENTH (fraction) [Sab *ʿs²r* "tenth," Ar *ʿušr* id.]

Q 66/5: *ʿs²r kl hnʾm wmwblm*

"a tenth of all crops watered by irrigation and by rain"

(a-tenth [of] every irrigated-crop and-rain-watered-crop)

ʿS³B

subst. *ʿsb* Q 167/2

CROPS, PRODUCE [Sab *ʿs³bt* "pastureland," Akk *ešēbu* "to be green," Heb *ʿēśeḇ* "plants, herbage," Ar *ʿušb* id.]

Q 167/2: *rdʾt ḏt ṣntm ʿs³b*

"[( )S²M] dedicated crops to Ḏāt ṢNTM"

Ǵ

ǴBR

subst. *ǵbrs¹m* Q 79/3

COMMON PEOPLE, PROLETARIANS [Ar *banū ǵabrāʾa* "people of a low condition, estate"]

Q 79/3: *wʾmtys¹m wʾdwms¹m wǵbrs¹m wwmys¹m*

"and their maidservants, vassals, common people, and dependents"

(and-their-female-servants and-their-subjects and-their-common-people and-their-dependents)

ǴYR

prt. of neg. *ǵyr* Q 78/6

WITHOUT, UN-, IM- [Sab *ǵyr* id., Ar *ǵayr* "not, no, un-"]

Q 78/6: *wmʿbrm ǵyr brṯm*

"an unpublished penal regulation"

(penal-regulation without publication)

F

F

prt. *f-* Q 40/3, Q 66/6, Q 72/9, Q 78/11, Q 172/5

AND; THEN [Sab *f*, Ar *fa* id.]

particle introducing apodosis in a conditional sentence:

Q 72/8-9: *whmw ys¹s¹lb kbrn bn lṣq wqrw ... fl yʿtny mlkn*

"if the *kabīr* refuses to prosecute and accuse ... then let the king take responsibility"

(and-if refuses the-*kabīr* from prosecuting and-accusing ... then-let take-responsibility the-king)

(F)

particle introducing the "comment" in a topic-comment construction (similar to Ar *fa* in *ammā ... fa* constructions):

Q 172/5: *ws^{1}w fks^{3}ʾ*

"and as for him ... he commanded"

FʾY

subst./partcp. *ms^{1}fʾym* Q 73/6, Q 201/3, Q 207/3, Q 254/6

ONE WHO INJURES, DESTROYS [Cf. Min *s^{1}fʾy* "to beat, destroy," Ar *faʾā* "to divide, split," Heb *hip̱ʾāh* "to cleave in pieces"]

Q 73/6: *bnkl ḫssm wḫblm wsnḥm wms^{1}fʾym wms^{1}nkrm bn ʾbrṯs^{1}m*

"against any who would harm, damage, deface, destroy, or remove them from their places"

(from-every one-who-harms and-one-who-damages and-one-who-defaces and-one-who-destroys and-one-who-removes from their-places)

FʾL

subst./partcp. *ms^{1}fʾlm* Q 183/5-6

ONE WHO WISHES ILL, ILL-WISHER [Cf. Sab *fʾl* "to wish ill to *someone*"; Ar *faʾʾala* "to give a good omen"]

Q 183/5-6: *bn ms^{1}fʾlm wms^{1}nkṯ[m b]n brṯs^1*

"[ʾBRTʿ Ḏū ḤDN ʾLS^{2}R has placed his household and his property] against any ill-wisher or one who remove[s it fr]om its place"

FDFD

verb *fdfd* Q 700/2; *fdfds^1* Q 700/5

TO EXPAND, IMPROVE [Cf. Sab *fdfdm* "fruitful," Eth *fadfada* "to increase"]

Q 700/4-5: *wbny ʾqrḍs^1 wḥrts^{1}yw wfdfds^1 ws^{1}nbṭ ʾbʾrs^1*

"he built its dykes and aqueducts, and he improved it and dug its wells"

FWD

s^1-prfx. *bys^{1}fd* Q 66/3

TO BRING TO AN END [Cf. Akk *pādu* "to cease," Ar *ʾafāda* "to cause to die"]

Q 66/3-4: *bnkm bynfṯ ʿdkm bys^{1}fd ḫr[f]myw*

"since he was appointed until he completes two yea[r]s"

(since he-is-appointed until he-finishes two-yea[r]s)

FḪḎ

subst. *fḫḏs¹* Q 172/3

CLAN, FAMILY, SUB-TRIBE [Cf. Ar *faḫiḏ* "sub-tribe, smallest division of a tribe," Soq *faḥid* "people, Meh *fḫedet* "tribe"]

Q 172/3: *ḏs¹wld bn fḫḏs¹ mrʾm*

"(a child) whom he sired from his clan, a male"
(whom-he-begot from his-tribe a-male)

FḪR

t-infix *ftḫr* Q 186A/14-15

TO ENTER INTO PARTNERSHIP, ASSOCIATE WITH [Cf. Akk *paḫāru* "to gather together, muster," Dof *foḥra* "together," Soq *faḥere* "all, everything; together"]

Q 186A/13-16: *wmty yḫdr ḫdrm wʾḏw bys²tyṭ ʾw ftḫr bʿm kl ḫdrm wms²ṭm*

"when he sets up a trading-stall, he may then trade or enter into a partnership with any possessor of a trading-stall and merchandise"
(and-when he-sets-up a-trading-stall and-then he-may-trade or entering-into-partnership with any possessor-[of]-a-trading-stall and-merchandise)

FẒR

subst. *mfẓr* Q 695/4

EXTENT [Sense from context; see Beeston, 1976, 420-21]

Q 695/4-5: *wkwn tqbl kl ʾrḍn kwḥd mṯmn wmfẓr ws²lṯy bqlm ws¹bʿt wʿs²ry ʾqblm*

"the size of the whole land together in value and extent is thirty *bql* and twenty-seven *qbl*"
(and-is the-dimension [of] all the-land together value and-extent both-thirty *bql* and-seven and-twenty *qbl*)

FLṬ

verb *flṭ* Q 202/5

TO DELIVER, ENTRUST [Cf. Heb *pālaṭ* "to bring into security," Ar *ʾaflata* "to escape," Syr *pəlaṭ* "to flee, escape," Akk *balāṭu* "to recover, live"]

Q 202/5-6: *wbḏl wflṭ nfs¹s¹ wqnys¹ lydʿb*

"he entrusted and delivered himself and his possessions to YDʿB"

FLY

subst. pl. *flytnm* Q 695/7

DECREE, ORDINANCE [Cf. Sab *flyt* "ordinance, regulation (?)"]

Q 695/7-8: *wkwn ḏn s¹ṭrn bn ʿlw ʾfqdm wflytm kwn bn ʿm wʾnby*

"this document is based on directives and decrees which are from ʿAmm and ʾAnbay"

(and-is this document from on directives and-decrees [which] are from ʿAmm and-ʾAnbay)

FLʿ

flʿ Q 257B

TO CUT [Ar *falaʿa* "to cut, split, cleave"]

Q 257B: *grl flʿ ḥg s²ln*

"GRL cut (this stone) according to (the instructions) of S²LN"

FʿL

verb *fʿl* Q 694/11

TO MAKE, DO [Sab *fʿl*, Ar *faʿala*, Heb *pāʿal* id.]

Q 694/11-12: *lyḥrm bn ʿlym wfʿl wṣyr llʿl bqlm wṣyrm wḥrtm wʾwwd*

"it is forbidden to take water up or to do anything to keep it above: crops, water pits, aqueducts, or retaining walls"

(let-be-forbidden from elevating and-making and-embanking above plants and-a-water-pit and-an-aqueduct and-retaining-walls)

subst. *fʿln* Q 688/6; *fʿlk* Q 687/10

WORK, TASK

Q 688/6: *whẓl fʿln*

"and he completed the work"

FQD

subst. pl. *ʾfqdm* Q 695/7

DECREE, DIRECTIVE [Cf. Syr *pūqdānā* "order, directive"]

Q 695/7-8: *wkwn ḏn s¹ṭrn bn ʿlw ʾfqdm wflytm kwn bn ʿm wʾnby*

"this document is based on directives and decrees which are from ʿAmm and ʾAnbay"

(and-is this document from on directives and-decrees [which] are from ʿAmm and-ʾAnbay)

FQḌ

subst. *fqḍt* Q 40/2; *fqḍtn* Q 40/10, 13, 14, 15

FQḌ, a class in Qatabanian society [Sab *fqḍ* "*social class*"; see RÉS VI, 220, and Rhodokanakis, 1924, 37-38.]

Q 40/14: *wqtbn ms³wdn wfqḍtn wbtln*

"the Qatabanian lords and *fqḍt* and *btl*"

FRᶜ I

verb *frᶜ* Q 241/2; *frᶜs¹* Q 254/2, Q 906/2; *frᶜw* Q 551/9

TO OFFER, PAY AS TRIBUTE [Sab *frᶜ* "to offer firstfruits," Ar *faraᶜ* "firstling offered as a sacrifice," and see Lundin, 1979, 108-9, for a discussion of this verb in the ESA dialects]

Q 241/1-3: *rṯdʾl bn mtᶜm bn s²ḥz s¹qny wfrᶜ lᶜm ḏrbḥw wnᶜmyn s²mry mwgln*

"RṮDʾL the son of MTᶜM the son of S²ḤZ made an offering and paid as tribute to ᶜAmm Ḏū RBḤW and NᶜMYN this alabaster votive object (?)"

(RṮDʾL the-son [of] MTᶜM [of] the-clan S²ḤZ made-an-offering and-paying-as-tribute to-ᶜAmm Ḏū-RBḤW and-NᶜMYN votive-object [of] alabaster)

subst. *frᶜm* Q 254/2, Q 906/3

OFFERING

Q 254/2: *ṣlm ḏhbn frᶜm frᶜs¹ ḥg ḥrg ᶜṯtr wᶜm bms¹ʾls¹my*

[S²ᶜRM HRN dedicated] a statue of bronze as an offering that he made to him as ᶜAṯtar and ᶜAmm directed in their oracle"

(statue [of] bronze an-offering he-offered-to-him ᶜAṯtar and-ᶜAmm directed in-their[dl.]-oracle)

FRᶜ II

subst. *frᶜm* Q 38/4, Q 39/3, Q 102/3-4, Q 203/3, Q 265/4, Q 540/3, Q 696/3, Q 770/5, Q 874/4, Q 899/2

TOP, SUMMIT OF [Sab *frᶜ*, *tfrᶜ* "summit, super-structure of a building," Ar *farᶜ* "top," Ar *faraᶜa* "excel," Heb *peraᶜ* "hairs of the head"]

Q 38/3-4: *bn s²rs¹m ᶜd frᶜm*

"from the foundation to the summit"

FRS¹

subst. *ʾfrs¹n* Q 677/2

CAVALRY, HORSEMEN [Sab *ʾfrs¹* id., Ar *fāris* "horseman"]

Q 677/1-2: *mwhbʾln ʾḥs²r ḏḥrmn nḥl ʾfrs¹n*

"MWHBʾLN ʾḤS²R of the clan of ḤRMN, commander of the cavalry"

FTḤ

verb *fth̩* Q 40/5, 15, 16, 22; *fth̩w* Q 40/1, 11, 14; *byfth̩wn* Q 40/9

TO ORDER, DIRECT [Cf. Sab *fth̩* "to obtain a judicial order," Him *fataḥa* "to give judgment"]

A) Q 40/11: *wbkl ʾftḥm bs¹m ftḥw qtbnmw ms³wdn wqtbn ṭbnn*
"by all the orders on the basis of which the Qatabanian lords and landowners have given orders"
(and-by-all orders on-them have-ordered Qatabanians lords and-Qatabanians landowners)

B) Q 40/14-15: *kl ʾftḥm wmḫrtm wʾṯfṭm wḫwlltm ftḥw ws¹ḥr wṯfṭ ws¹ṯb ws¹ḫl qtbn ms³wdn wfqḍtn*
"all orders, directives, decisions, and regulations which the Qatabanian lords-in-council and the *fqḍ* ordered, directed, decided, determined, and regulated"
(all orders and-directives and-decisions and-regulations [which] they-ordered and-directing and-deciding and-determining and-regulating the-Qatabanians the-lords-in-council and-the-*fqḍ*)

subst. *ftḥ* Q 40/9; *ftḥn* Q 40/21, 22(2x), 23; *ʾftḥ* Q 40/5, *ʾftḥm* Q 40/11, 10, 14, 15, 17; *ʾftḥn* Q 40/16, 18

ORDER, DIRECTIVE

See entry above.

FTḪ

verb *ftḫ* Q 66/10, Q 67/8, Q 68/7, Q 69/5, Q 70/3; *yftḫ* Q 40/21, Q 72/9

TO INSCRIBE, ENGRAVE [Cf. Sab *ftḫ* "decorated stonework," Heb *pittūaḥ* "incision," Heb *pattāḥ* "engraver," Akk *patāḫu* "to bore," Ph *ptḥ* "engraving, engraved work"]

Q 40/21: *wl yftḫ ḏn ftḥn wmḫrtn bʿḍm ʾw ʾbnm knm byhrm mlkn*
"let this order and directive be inscribed in wood or stone as the king commands"
(and-let be-inscribed this order and-directive in-wood or stone as commands the-king)

Ṣ

ṢBḤ I

verb *yṣbḥ* Q 186C/10

TO DAWN [Cf. Sab *ṣbḥ* "to do in the morning," Ar *ʾaṣbaḥa* "to be morning," Eth *ṣabḥa* "to grow light, to dawn"]

Q 186C/6-10: *wklḏw bys²ṭ kl ms²ṭm bs²mr blyl ybnwn lyṣbḥ*
"and everyone who sells any merchandise in S²MR at night shall keep his distance until morning"
(and-all-who sell any merchandise in-S²MR at-night they-shall-keep-apart until-it-dawns)

s¹-prfx. *ms¹ṣbḥtm* Q 681/3

TO DRESS, PREPARE A LAMP [Cf. Sab *mṣbḥ* "votive object, lamp," Ar *miṣbāḥ* "lamp, lighted wick," Ar *ʾaṣbaḥa miṣbaḥan* "to dress a lamp"]

Q 681/2-3: *ydm ms¹ṣbḥtm*
"a lamp shaped as a hand"
(a-hand dressed-as-a-lamp)

ṢBḤ II

subst. *ṣbḥt* Q 173/3

TAXES [Sab *ḍbḥ* "taxes (?)"; Eth *ṣabbāḥt* "tribute, taxes," Eth *ṣabbeḥa* "to exact/collect taxes or tribute"]

Q 173/3: *wl yfrwn ṣbḥt ṣfn[ ]*
"may the taxes be abundant which have been gathered"
(and-let be-abundant the-taxes [which] have-been-gathered)

ṢDʾ

subst. *mṣdʾn* Q 4/1

LORD, PRINCE [Sab *mṣdʾ* "*a functionary*, treasurer (?)" See Pirenne, CIAS 1:231-32, who cites the Ar *ṣadiʾa* "to stand erect," and cites the Heb *nāśî* "chief, lord, derived from *nāśāʾ*, whose primary significance is "to raise."]

Q 4/1 *ʾlnʾd mṣdʾn*
"ʾLNʾD the lord"

ṢDQ

verb *ṣdq* Q 909/3; *ṣdqs¹n* Q 244/11

TO GRANT ONE HIS DUE [Cf. Ar *ṣadaqa* "to be true, sincere in one's words," Eth *ṣadqa* "to be just, righteous, true, faithful," Heb *ṣeḏeq* "the right, righteousness"]

Q 909/3: *[y]zʾn ṣdq ws¹ʾmn ʿqrbn bkl ʾʾrḫ tkrb*
"may [Wadd] [con]tinue to show favor and protection to ʿQRBN in all the affairs that he undertakes"
(may-[con]tinue favoring and-protecting ʿQRBN in-all affairs he-has-undertaken)

t-infix *ṣtdq* Q 68/9; *yṣtdqwn* Q 70/4, Q 186B/23

TO RECEIVE ONE'S DUE

(ṢDQ)

Q 68/9: *wl yhlkwn wṣtdq ʾrby ʿm ḏlbḫ ḥgḏt mḥrtn wṣrytn*

"and let the *ʾrby* of ʿAmm Ḏū Labaḫ comply and receive their due according to this directive and announcement"

(and-let comply and-receiving-just-rights the-*ʾrby* [of] ʿAmm Ḏū Labaḫ according-to-this directive and-announcement)

subst. *ṣdqs¹m* Q 66/10, Q 67/7, Q 68/6, Q 69/5, Q 70/3

GOODWILL, CONCURRENCE, FAVOR

Q 66/8-10: *wṣry s²hr ʾrby ʿm ḏlbḫ ʿṣm ḏlbḫ ... bṣdqs¹m*

"S²HR has promulgated to the *ʾrby* of ʿAmm Ḏū Labaḫ this patronage-tie to Ḏū Labaḫ ... with their goodwill"

(and-promulgated S²HR [to] the-*ʾrby* [of] ʿAmm Ḏū-Labaḫ this-patronage-tie [to] Ḏū-Labaḫ ... with-their-goodwill)

ṢDR

subst. *ṣdrs¹* Q 844/9

BEST PART [Cf. Ar *ṣadr* "the best part of a thing"]

Q 844/8-9: *yfʿ bṣdrs¹*

"he deducted the best part of it"

ṢWB

subst. *ṣwbts¹ww* Q 38/3

SUBSTRUCTURE [Cf. Sab *ṣwbt* "*feature associated with town walls*"; cf. Ar *ṣawb* "side," Ar *ṣūba* "place where things are stored"]

Q 38/2-3: *tqdm wḥrg ws¹hlk kl ʿs²q wmb[n]y mḥfdn ʿrkm wṣwbts¹ww*

"[S²RḤʿṮT] supervised, directed, and carried out the whole excavation and construc[tio]n of the tower ʿRKM and its substructures"

(he-supervised and-directing and-carrying-out the-excavation and-construc[tio]n [of] the-tower ʿRKM and-its-substructures)

ṢWR

subst. *ṣwr* Q 195/3; *ṣwr[ ]* Q 876

LIKENESS [Heb *ṣār* "fashion, delineate," Syr *ṣār* "fashion," Ar *ṣūra* "form, fashion, figure, shape," Meh *ṣawir* "form, shape"]

Q 195/3: *ṣwr rbʿt*

"likeness of RBʿT"

ṢḤF

verb *yṣḥf* Q 66/2, 6, 8

TO WRITE; TO REGISTER, ENTER in a document [Cf. Sab *ṣḥf* "to write," Eth *ṣaḥafa* id.]

Q 66/2-3: *wl yṣḥf wḥrg d̲n ṣḥfn ʿṣmm*

"let this document be written and administered as a patronage-tie"

(and-let be-written and-administering this document as-a-patronage-tie)

subst. *ṣḥf* Q 66/1, Q 67/11; *ṣḥfn* Q 66/3, 4-5, 7, 8; *ṣḥftn* Q 66/10, 695/14

DOCUMENT, AGREEMENT [Cf. Sab *ṣḥft* "document," Ar *ṣaḥīfa* "a writing, a thing written," Eth *maṣḥaf* "book, document, writing, inscription," Dat *muṣḥaf* "book, copybook"]

See entry above.

ṢYD

verb *ṣyd* Q 697/2

TO HUNT [Sab *ṣd* Ar *ṣāda* (y), Ug *ṣd*, Heb *ṣāḏ*, Syr *ṣād* id. On the question of the hunt (especially the sacred hunt) in ancient South Arabia, see Pirenne, in CIAS 1:165-67, J. Ryckmans, 1976, 259-308, and Beeston, 1948, 183-96.]

Q 697/1-2: *ydʿʾb d̲byn bn s²hr mkrb qtbn ṣyd ls²ms¹*

"YDʿʾB D̲ū BYN the son of S²HR, *mkrb* of Qataban has hunted (there) for S²MS¹"

ṢYR

verb *ṣyr* Q 73/1, Q 694/11, Q 700/4

TO WALL, EMBANK [Cf. Sab *ṣyr* id., Ar *ṣayyara* "to hold back," Meh *ṣâr* "to stand (up)," Sh *ṣor* id.]

Q 73/1: *ǵlbm [ ]yb bn dws¹m bn qs³mm ṣyr wbqr wgrb wbql ws¹qḥ kl ʾs¹rrs¹ wgrwbs¹*

"ǴLBM [ ]YB the son of DWS¹M of the clan of QS³MM embanked, plowed, terraced, and cultivated, and set all his valleys and terraces in order"

(ǴLBM [ ]YB the-son [of] DWS¹M [of] the-clan [of] QS³MM embanked and-plowing and-terracing and-cultivating and-setting-in-order all his-valleys and-his-terraces)

subst. *ṣyrm* Q 694/11

WATER PIT

Q 694/11-12: *lyḥrm bn ʿlym wfʿl wṣyr llʿ bqlm wṣyrm wḥrtm wʾwwd*

"it is forbidden to take water up or to do anything to keep it above: crops, water pits, aqueducts, or retaining walls"

(ṢYR)

(let-be-forbidden from elevating and-making and-embanking above plants and-a-water-pit and-an-aqueduct and-retaining-walls)

ṢLW

subst. *ṣlw* Q 89.193, Q 119/1, Q 250/1

GRAVE (DOCUMENT) [Sab *ṣlwt* "boundary stone"; see Höfner, 1953, 150, who associates this word with Min *ṣlwt* "document" from which she derives the meaning "grave document," i.e., the document showing the deceased to be rightful owner of the grave. See also Müller, 1974, 149-50.]

Q 119/1-3: *ṣlw ddʾl bn ḫrmm*

"grave (document) of DDʾL the son of ḪRMM"

ṢLL

verb *ṣll* Q 36/3, Q 856/2; *ṣllhw* Q 696/4

TO PAVE [Rhodokanakis, 1951, 295, n. 6, compares Ḥaḍ *ṣlal* "paving stone"]

Q 36/3: *mḫḍ wbrr wwzl wṣll mnqln mblqt*

"[YDᶜᵒB Ḏū BYN] hewed out, dug up, smoothed, and paved the mountain pass road MBLQT"

(he-hewed-out and-digging-up and-smoothing and-paving the-mountain-pass-road MBLQT)

subst. sing. *ṣll* Q 176/10; dl. *ṣllmyw* Q 696/4

1) PAVING

Q 176/9-11: *ʾws¹ᶜm bn yṣrᶜm bn mdhm tqdm wḥrg kl ᶜs²q wwzl wṣll mnqln ẓrm btḥrg mrʾs¹ ydᶜᵒb*

"ʾWS¹ᶜM the son of YṢRᶜM of the clan of MDHM directed and supervised all the digging up, smoothing, and paving of the mountain pass ẒRM under the direction of his lord YDᶜᵒB"

(ʾWS¹ᶜM the-son [of] YṢRᶜM [of] the-clan [of] MDHM directed and-supervising the-whole digging-up and-smoothing and-paving the-mountain-pass ẒRM under-the-direction [of] his-lord YDᶜᵒB)

2) PAVEMENT, LAYER OF PAVING STONE

Q 696/2-4: *bny mwdyn byḥn bn s²rs¹m ᶜd frᶜm wṣllhw ṯny ṣllmyw*

"he built the cistern of Bayḥān from the foundation to the top and paved it with two layers of paving stone"

(he-built the-cistern [of] Bayḥān from the foundation to the-top and-he-paved-it [with] two pavements)

ṢLM

subst. sing. *ṣlm* Q 89.86/3, .137/3-4, Q 244/5, Q 246/5, Q 254/2, 6, Q 496/2, Q 494/3; *ṣlmn* Q 244/14-15, Q 246/14, Q 483/2, Q 487/2; *ṣlmt* Q 269/2; *ṣlmts*^{1} Q 245/3, 497/3-4; dl. *ṣlmy* Q 806/2; *ṣlmnyhn* Q 261/2, 489/2; pl. *ʾṣlmm* Q 495/3; *ʾṣlms*^{1}*m* Q 495/5

STATUE [Sab *ṣlm* id., Heb *ṣelem* "image, likeness, statue," Akk *ṣalmu* "statue, relief," Syr *ṣalmā* "image, idol," BibAram *ṣlmʾ* "statue," Nab and palm *ṣlm* "statue"]

A) Q 494/2-4: *s*^{1}*qny ʾnby s*^{2}*ymn ṣlm ḏhbn*
"[RGNM] dedicated to ʾAnbay S^{2}YMN this bronze statue"

B) Q 487/1-2: *s*^{1}*qnyw ʾnby s*^{2}*ymn ʿd rṣfm ṣlmn*
"[YṢRʿM and GWṮʾL] dedicated this statue to ʾAnbay S^{2}YMN in RṢFM"

ṢʿQ

verb *ṣʿq* Q 40/4

TO ANNOUNCE [Cf. Heb *ṣāʿaq* "to cry, call out, call," Ar *ṣaʿiqa* "to bellow (said of a bull)," Ar *ṣāʿiqa* "thunderbolt"]

Q 40/3-4: *wʾy ṣʿq ws*^{1}*ṣʿq s*^{2}*ʿbn*
"whatever the tribe has announced or caused to announce"

s^1-prfx. *s*^{1}*ṣʿq* Q 40/4

TO HAVE ANNOUNCED, CAUSE TO ANNOUNCE
See entry above.

ṢFN

verb *ṣfn[ ]* Q 173/3

TO GATHER, STORE, AMASS [Cf. Heb *ṣāpan* "to hide, treasure up"]

Q 173/3: *wl yfrwn ṣbḥt ṣfn[ ]*
"may the taxes be abundant which have been gathered"
(and-let be-abundant the-taxes [which] have-been-gathered)

ṢRḤ

subst. *ṣrḥts*^{1} Q 74/7(2x), 8, 9; *ṣrḥts*^{1}*my* Q 74/6; *ṣrḥts*^{1}*m* Q 74/8, 8-9, Q 243/4, 6; *ṣrḥtyhw* Q 89.141/2, Q 265/3; *ṣrḥtys*^{1}*my* Q 74/6-7; *ṣrḥts*^{1}*ww* Q 82/3-4, Q 99/4, Q 100/3-4, Q 266/3, Q 268/2, Q 790/2, Q 860/3

UPPER STORY, UPPER CHAMBER [Eth *ṣerḥ* "upper story of a building," Ar *ṣarḥ* "lofty structure," ModYem *ṣarḥa* "vestibule of a house"]

Q 74/7: *wrbʿ byt bnw ynzr wṣrḥts*^{1}
"and a fourth of the house of the Banū YNZR with its upper story"

ṢRY

verb *ṣry* Q 66/8, Q 67/1, 6, Q 68/1, 6, Q 69/4, Q 70/1, Q 78/5, 6; *ṣrys^{1}m* Q 70/2; *byṣrys^1* Q 78/13

TO DECREE, ANNOUNCE, PROMULGATE [Cf. Sab *ṣry* "deliver a favorable oracular response or decision," Ar *ṣarā baynahum* "to decide"]

A) Q 68/6: *wṣry s^{2}hr ʾdms^1 ʾrby ʿm ḏlbḫ wtʾnṯs^{1}m wbnys^{1}m bṣdqs^{1}m ḥg ḏt mḥrtn wṣrytn*

"S^{2}HR announced to his dependents the *ʾrby* of ʿAmm Ḏū Labaḫ and their female relatives and their sons with their goodwill according to this order and announcement"

(and-announced S^{2}HR [to] his-dependents *ʾrby* [of] ʿAmm Ḏū-Labaḫ and-their-female-kindred and-their-sons with-their-goodwill according-to this order and-announcement)

B) Q 78/5: *knm byṯfṭs^1 ws^{1}ḥr ws^{1}ʿbr wṣry mlkn*

"as the king decides, directs, orders, and announces"

subst.[1] *ṣyrtm* Q 68/9, Q 70/1, 2; *ṣrytn* Q 68/5-6, 6, 9, Q 69/4, 5; *ṣryts^{1}m* Q 70/2

ANNOUNCEMENT, DIRECTIVE

See entry (A) above.

subst.[2] *ṣryn* Q 1/2

PROTECTION [Cf. Sab *ṣry* "to protect," Ar *ṣarā* "to protect, rescue"]

Q 1/2: *s^{1}ṭd ṭly bṣryn ʿm wḥwkm*

"he sacrificed (?) a lamb because of the protection of ʿAmm and ḤWKM"

ṢRF

subst. *ṣrf[n]* Q 89.148/3

SILVER [Sab *ṣrf* id., Ar *ṣarīf*, Akk *ṣarpu* id., Heb *ṣārap̱* "to refine, smelt"]

Q 89.148/3: *[ṣl]mn ḏṣrf[n]*

"this statue of silver"

ṢRR

subst. *ṣrs^{1}m* Q 135/2

SLUICE GATE [Cf. Ar *ṣarra* "to bind, tie up," Heb *ṣārar* "to bind, tie up, be restricted," Syr *ṣār* "to bind"]

Q 135/2: *wṣrs^{1}m wqrws^{1}m*

"their sluice gate and their reservoir"

Ḍ

ḌBB

verb *ḍb* Q 665/3

TO STOP, STAY [Cf. Ar *ḍabba* "to be fixed in the ground"]

Q 665/1-3: *hwfʿm ḏyʿlf ḍb bʾḏn ʿm ws²ms¹m*

"HWFʿM Ḏū YʿLF stayed (here), by permission of ʿAmm and S²MS¹M"

ḌBR

subst. *ḍbr* Q 186A/6(2x)

CONTROLLER [Beeston, 1959, 5, compares Ar *ḍabara* "to bind firmly," Heb *ṣāḇar* "to heap up." Further, see Beeston, 1954, 319-22.]

Q 186A/6: *ḍbr tmnʿ wḍbr wld ʿm*

"controller of Timnaʿ and controller of the children of ʿAmm"

ḌYF

s¹t-prfx. *bys¹tḍf* Q 186A/17-18

TO ASK TO MAKE A TRADING JOURNEY [Cf. Ar *ḍiyāfat* "the guest-host relationship." According to Beeston, 1959, 7, "*ḍiyāfat* would be applicable to the behavior of a colporteur or traveling peddler who visited the village communities with his goods."]

Q 186A/16-18: *wmty lyks³ʾ ʿhr s²mr kḏm bys¹tḍf qtbn bʿm ʾs²ʿbm*

"and when the overseer of S²MR announces that he wishes the Qatabanians to make trading journeys among the tribes"

(and-when announces the-overseer [of] S²MR that wishes-that-trade the-Qatabanians among the-tribes)

ḌMR

verb *ḍmr* Q 694/9

TO JOIN, MAKE [Cf. Eth *ḍamara* "to join, unite"]

Q 694/9: *bn ḍmr ḍmrm ʾw ḥrṯ kl ʾwdm*

"[this land is to be free] of the making of water conduits or the terracing of any retaining wall"

(from the-joining [of] the-water-conduit and-cultivation [of] any retaining-wall)

subst. *ḍmrm* Q 694/9

WATER CONDUIT [Pirenne, 1971, 128, suggests this additional sense of "water conduit" which may have been made of hollowed-out tree trunks.]

(ḌMR)

See entry above.

ḌNW

ḍntm Q 695/12

EXTENT [Cf. Ar *ḍanā* (w) "to augment, increase." Jamme, 1972, 30, prefers the rendering "production."]

Q 695/11-12: *wʾṣlmw mlkm ʾw s²ʿbm bys³f ʾw byrbᶜ ḍnt ḏt ʾrḍn*

"the family of the king or tribe which enlarges or decreases the extent of this land"

(the-family of-the-king or tribe which increase or decrease the-extent [of] this land)

ḌFR

subst. pl. *ʾḍfrm* Q 35/6

STRUCTURES (?) [Cf. Ar *ḍafara* "to build with stones without cement"]

Q 35/6-7: *wbʿm ʾḍfrm qny hwrn*

"and along with the structures (?) in the house that HWRN acquired"

ḌRW

subst. *ḍrw* Q 89.50, Q 155, Q 161, Q 518, Q 530ter, Q 538

BALSAM, AROMATIC RESIN or FRUIT used as incense [Sab *ḍrw* id., Ar *ḍarw/ḍirw* "fruit of the gum tree (Pisticia lentiscus)," ModYem *ḍarw/ḍorw* "aromatic shrub"; cf. K. Nielsen, 1986, 18, 61-62, and Crone, 1987, 62-65]

Q 161: *rnd ḍrw lbny qs¹ṭ*

"nard (?), balsam, storax, costus"

ḌRR

subst. *ḍr* Q 183/3; *ḍrm* Q 74/3

WAR [Sab *ḍr* "war," Eth *ḍarara* " to be hostile," Ar *ḍarra* "to hurt, injure," Soq *ḍér(r)* "to strike"]

Q 74/3: *bḍrm*

"during the war"

Q

QBL I

verb *qbl* Q 641/2, Q 840/4

1) TO RECEIVE [Sab *qbl*, Ar *qabala*, Heb *qibbēl* id.]

Q 641/1-2: *lḥyʿm ḏmwbʾ qbl ʾrḍn*

"LḤYʿM of the clan of MWBʾ has received the land"

2) TO ENJOIN, IMPOSE [G. Ryckmans, 1949, 65, compares the Ar *qabala* "to eagerly pursue a thing">"to exact, impose"]

Q 840/4: *ʾʾrḫm qbl ʿlys*^{1}*m*

"(in fulfillment of) orders which he had enjoined upon them"

(the-commands he-enjoined on-them)

prep. *qbl* Q 40/9

BEFORE, PRIOR TO [Sab *qbl*, Ar *qabla* id.]

Q 40/9: *qbl ḏn wrḫn*

"before this (current) month"

QBL II

subst.^{1} *ʾqblm* Q 695/5

QBL, UNIT OF MEASURE [See Beeston, 1976, 420-21, who views this as a unit of measure, possibly of area.]

Q 695/4-5: *wkwn tqbl kl ʾrḍn kwḥd mṯmn wmfẓr ws*^{2}*lṯy bqlm ws*^{1}*bʿt wʿs*^{2}*ry ʾqblm*

"the size of the whole land together in value and extent is thirty *bql* and twenty-seven *qbl*"

(and-is the-dimension [of] all the-land together value and-extent both-thirty *bql* and-seven and-twenty *qbl*)

subst.^{2} *tqbl* Q 695/4; *tqbln* Q 695/6

SIZE, EXTENT, DIMENSION [See Beeston, 1976, 420, who sees this as a denominative of *ʾqbl*.]

See entry above.

QBR

s^1-prfx. *s*^{1}*qbrbs*^{1} Q 902

TO BURY [Cf. Ar *ʾaqbara* "to make a tomb for someone; to cause to be buried"]

Q 902: *s*^{1}*lzmkm ʾbʿl qbrn s*^{2}*ymn bn s*^{1}*qbrbs*^{1} *kl ms*^{2}*kmym*

"the owners of the grave S^{2}YMN have enjoined you not to bury anyone of base birth in it"

(QBR)

(have-enjoined-you the-owners [of] the-grave S^{2}YMN from burying-in-it any base-born)

subst.^{1} *qbrn* Q 490A/2, B/3, Q 899/5, Q 902; *qbrs^1* Q 218/1, Q 478/1; *qbrhw* Q 491/1-2; *qbrs^{1}my* Q 3/2, Q 900/2; *qbrs^{1}m* Q 490 A/2, B/2, Q 903/3; *qbrhmw* Q 874/3, Q 899/2

BURIAL-PLACE, GRAVE, TOMB [Sab *qbr*, Ar *qabr*, Heb *qeḇer*, Syr *qaḇrā*]

Q 478/1-2: *ṣbḥkrb ḏnʿmn ʿs^{1}y ẓrb qbrs^1 gwr*

"ṢBḤKRB Ḏū NʿMN acquired and dedicated his tomb GWR"

subst.^{2} *mqbrm* Q 98/3

BURIAL SITE [Sab *mqbr* id.]

Q 98/3: *mqbrm ẓrbm ls^{1}m*

"(as) a secure grave site for themselves"

(a-grave-site a-secure-location for-themselves)

QDM

verb *qdm* Q 76/1

TO DIRECT, SUPERVISE, OVERSEE [Cf. Sab *qdm* "to undertake a military expedition"]

Q 76/1-2: *rbḥm bn ʾbln qdm mbny rydn mnẖy ḥdnm*

"RBḤM the son of ʾBLN has directed the construction of RYDN in the direction of ḤDNM"

(RBḤM the-son [of] ʾBLN he-has-directed the-building [of] RYDN in-the-direction [of] ḤDNM)

t-prefx. *tqdm* Q 38/2, Q 39/2, Q 66/14, Q 67/12, Q 112/1, Q 176/9, Q 180/2, Q 677/4, Q 688/3, Q 855/1, Q 856/2; *tqdmw* Q 677/4, Q 690a/3, Q 803/2, Q 838/2, Q 899/5

TO DIRECT, OVERSEE [Sab *tqdm* "to be in charge of"]

Q 66/13-14: *wnbṭʿm bn ʾls^{1}mʿ bn hybr tqdm ḏtn ʾs^{1}trn*

"NBṬʿM the son of ʾLS^{1}Mʿ of the clan of HYBR directed these inscriptions"

t-infix *qtdmm* Q 186B/7

TO BE IN EXCESS; TO GO IN ADVANCE [Sab *qdm* "to act as vanguard; confront, do battle with," Ar *iqtadama* "to be at the head"]

Q 186B/5-8: *wʾwlw hmd ʿhr s^{2}mr s^{2}tyṭm n w qtdmm qtbn*

"those whom the overseer of S^{2}MR has assessed a market tax of *n* gold pieces in excess of what the Qatabanians pay"

(those-who assessed-a-tax the-overseer [of] S^{2}MR [on] trading *n* pieces-of-gold being-in-excess-of the Qatabanians)

subst. *mqdm* Q 73/4, Q 478/2

DIRECTION, COMMAND

Q 73/4: *bʾmr wmqdm ʿṯtr*

"[ǴLBM ( )YB did all this] at the command and direction of ʿAṯtar"

adj. *qdmn* Q 40/23, Q 66/12(2x), Q 67/10, Q 72/10, Q 79/7, Q 694/14

FIRST, FORMER [Beeston, 1962, 43, notes that this adjective is generally constructed with *ʾḫrn* "second, latter." Cf. also Sab *qdm* "former, preceding," Ar *qadama* "precede," Ar *qadīm* "old, ancient"]

Q 67/9-10: *ḫrf ʿmʿly ḏgrbm qdmn*

"the first eponymate of ʿMʿLY Ḏū GRBM"

prep. + prep. *bqdmw*

See entry under B.

QHL

subst. *qhlm* Q 40/13

ASSEMBLY [Sab *qhlm* id., Heb *qāhāl* "congregation"; cf. Syr *qəhal* "to assemble, gather," Akk *quʾulu* id.]

Q 40/13: *wys¹ṯb s²hr wqtbn ms³wdn gw qhlm wfqḍtn wbtln*

"(and which) S²HR and the Qatabanian lords-in-council as an assembled body and the *fqḍ* and *btl* will decree"

(and-will-decree S²HR and-the-Qatabanians the-lords-in-council [as] body [of] assembly and-the-*fqḍ* and-the-*btl*)

QWḤ

s¹(h)-prfx. *s¹qḥ* Q 72/2, Q 73/1, Q 179/1; *hqḥ* Q 98/2, Q 611/1, Q 679/6; *s¹qḥm* Q 72/5, 7; *hqḥw* Q 690a/7

TO PREPARE, SET IN ORDER a field or a house which is being constructed [Sab *hqḥ* id. Müller, 1962, 93, compares the Ar *qāḥa* (w) "sweep, scour, sweep clean"]

Q 73/1: *ǵlbm [ ]yb bn dws¹m bn qs³mm ṣyr wbqr wgrb wbql ws¹qḥ kl ʾs¹rrs¹ wgrwbs¹*

"ǴLBM [ ]YB the son of DWS¹M of the clan QS³M M embanked, plowed, terraced, cultivated, and set all his valleys and terraces in order"

(ǴLBM [ ]YB the-son [of] DWS¹M [of] the-clan [of] QS³MM embanked and-plowing and-terracing and-cultivating and-setting-in-order all his-valleys and-terraces)

subst. *mqḥ* Q 690a/7; *mqḥn* Q 687/8; *mqḥs¹* Q 838/2

COURT, AREA, SPACE [Ar *qāḥa* id.]

Q 690a/7: *bmqḥ hqḥw*

"in the court that they have set in order"

QWL

subst. pl. *ʾqwl* Q 679/5

TRIBAL CHIEF: GOVERNOR [Sab *ql, qwl* "member of the leading clan in the *s²ʿb*"; cf. Ar *qayl*, pl. *ʾaqyāl, ʾaqwāl* "title of South Arabian prince," and see Müller, 1962, 94, and under QYL below]

Q 679/5-6: *ʾqwl wmḥrgw ʾs²ʿbn mdḥym wdtnt ws¹frm*

"the governors and administrators of the tribes MDḤYM and Datinat and S¹FRM"

QWM

verb *qwm* Q 40/7; *qwmw* Q 40/3

TO ASSEMBLE, GATHER TOGETHER [RÉS VI, 220, compares the sense implied in Q 40/3 with the Ar *maqāma* "session."]

Q 40/3: *qwmw wʾtm wʾttm*

"they assembled and agreed and adhered to the agreement"

h(s¹)-prfx. *hqmhw* Q 876/2

TO SET UP [Cf. Ar *ʾaqāma* "to erect"]

Q 876/2: *hqmhw wtrʾ[l]*

"WTRʾ[L] set it up"

subst.[1] *mqms¹* Q 183/4, Q 254/5, Q 269/4, Q 681/5, Q 844/10, Q 905/5, Q 906/6, Q 910/6; *mqm[š]* Q 905/3-4; *mqmhw* Q 40/12; *mqmhs¹m* Q 40/20; pl. *mqmhys¹my* Q 256/7

PROPERTY, GOODS [Sab *mqm* "material resources"; cf. also Botterweck, 1950, 442, for *mqm* in this sense.]

Q 844/9-11: *rṯds¹ nfs¹s¹ wmqms¹ bn kl s²yntm*

"[HWFʾL] has entrusted to his protection himself and his property from every dishonor"

(he-entrusted-to-him himself and-his-property from-every dishonor)

subst.[2] dl. *mqmnyhn* Q 40/10, 13

ASSEMBLY, MEETING

Q 40/10: *bkl ʾʾrḥm wʾftḥm wḥrtm wʾṯftm wʾtmtm kwn bs¹myt mqmnyhn*

by all the orders, directives, decisions, judgments, and agreements which were in these two meetings"

(by-all the-orders and-the-directives and-the-decisions and-the-judgments and-the-agreements [which] were in-these-two meetings)

QWR

verb *qwr* Q 694/13, Q 695/3

1) TO DIG [Cf. Ar *qāra* and *qawwara* "to cut holes in something"]

Q 694/13: *ḥrmw bn qwr bs¹m kl b'rm*
"it is forbidden to dig any well in them"
(they-have-forbidden from the-digging in-them any well)

2) TO ENGRAVE
Q 695/3-4: *w'ḫd tbdd 'rḍn wqwr tʿlmn*
"payment for the land has been received, and the document has been engraved"
(and-received the-payment [of] the-land and-engraved the-document)

QṬN
subst.[1] pl. *'qṭnt* Q 695/13-14
DETAILS [Cf. Sab *qṭn* "small (?)," Heb *qaṭōn*, Eth *qaṭin* id.]
Q 695/13-14: *lwz' 'w nky b'qṭnt 's¹tr ḏt ṣḥftn*
"to add to or diminish the details of the text of this document"

subst.[2] *mqṭn* Q 218/2
GATHERING PLACE OF THE PEOPLE [RÉS VII, 461, compares *mqṭn* with *qṭn* "common people " in R 3563B/3.]
Q 218/2: *mqṭn w'lhw ws¹r […]*
"gathering place of the people and the gods of WS¹R [..."

QẒR
verb *qẓr* Q 72/2, 241/4
1) TO WORK HARD, LABOR [Cf. Syr *qəṭar* "to bind" Eth *qʷaṣara* "to enclose or fortify with a wall"]
Q 72/2: *kḏm byfrwn w'gw w'hw wḥrṯ wqẓr*
"in order that they till, struggle, toil, plow, and labor"
(in-order-that they-till and-struggling and-toiling and-plowing and-laboring)

2) TO BE IN CHARGE OF THE OFFERING [see under subst. *qẓr* below]
Q 241/1-4: *rṯd'l bn mtʿm bn s²ḥz s¹qny wfrʿ lʿm ḏrbḥw wnʿmyn s²mry mwgln ywm qẓr*
"RṮD'L the son of MTʿM of the clan S²ḤZ made an offering and paid as tribute to ʿAmm Ḏū RBḤW and NʿMYN this alabaster votive object (?) on the occasion when he was placed in charge of the offering"
(RṮD'L the-son [of] MTʿM [of] the-clan S²ḤZ made-an-offering and-paying-tribute to-ʿAmm Ḏū-RBḤW and-NʿMYN votive-object [of] alabaster when he-was-placed-in-charge-of-the-offering)

(QẒR)

s[1]-prfx. *s¹qẓr* Q 551/4

TO MAKE AN ADMINISTRATOR of money offerings

Q 551/4-5: *ws¹qẓr wdʾl bnyhw ʿs³bm wklybm*

"WDʾL made his two sons ʿS³BM and KLYBM administrators (of the money offerings)"

subst.[1] *qẓr* Q 35/3, Q 80/3, Q 240/2, Q 769/1b; pl. *qẓrw* Q 551/3-4, 5

ADMINISTRATOR (of money offerings) [See Pirenne, in CIAS 1:128, and cf. Tig *qʷaṣāri* "accountant," *taqʷaṣāri* "tax collector"]

Q 35/3-4: *qẓr qyn rs²w ʿmm_tntm*

"administrator of the money offerings, attendant, and *rs²w* for the second year"

subst.[2] *qẓrt* Q 269/4

FEMALE ADMINISTRATOR (of money offerings)

Q 269/4-5: *qẓrt ʿm ḏrbḥw*

"the administrator of money offerings for ʿAmm Ḏū RBḤW"

QYL

subst. *qyln* Q 688/2

TRIBAL LEADER [Cf. Sab *qyl*, *ql* "tribal leader, chief of a subject tribe" and see under QWL above]

Q 688/2: *ʾlht qyln*

"those of the tribal leader"

QYN

subst. *qyn* Q 35/3, Q 80/3, Q 240/2, Q 769/1b

ADMINISTRATOR, ATTENDANT, OFFICIATOR [Sab *qyn* "administrator"]

Q 35/3-4: *qẓr qyn rs²w ʿmm_tntm*

"administrator of the money offerings, attendant, and *rs²w* for the second year"

QYF

verb *qyf* Q 37/2, Q 89.120; *qf* Q 695/1

1) TO SET UP A *MQF* [Denominative verb. See the etymology under *mqf*]

Q 37/2: *qyf ʿm*

"(he) set up a *mqf* to ʿAmm"

2) TO MARK

Q 695/1: *ḏn qf ʾrḍm ʾs¹y wnḥl ws¹ʿqb wqyḍ hwfʿm yhnʿm*

"this marks land which HWFᶜM YHNᶜM [and YDᶜᵓB YGL] have granted, leased, transferred, and assigned"

subst.[1] *mqf* Q 89.94, 158, Q 114, Q 509/1, Q 510, Q 511/1, Q 513A, Q 777

VOTIVE OBJECT or CULT STONE or ALTAR [Sab *mqf* "stela, boundary." There is some discussion on the precise meaning of this word. Jamme, 1952, 206, and 1972, 47-48, who understands it as a "votive object." Müller, 1962, 95-96, prefers "stela, cult stone" and gives as a cognate ModYem *mugwaf* "stones standing upright to support vines."]

Q 89.94: *mqf lḥyᶜm ᶜbd mlkn*

"votive object of LḤYᶜM, servant of the king"

subst.[2] *qf* Q 694/12; *qyf* Q 89.120

STELA, MONUMENT

Q 694/12: *bn qf ẓrn*

"from the stela of ẒRN"

QYḌ

verb *qyḍ* Q 695/1

ASSIGN [Thus Beeston, 1976, 422; cf. Sab *qyḍ* "barter, exchange," Ar *qāḍa* and *qāyaḍa* id.]

Q 695/1: *ḏn qf ᵓrḍm ᵓs¹y wnḥl ws¹ᶜqb wqyḍ hwfᶜm yhnᶜm*

"this marks land which HWFᶜM YHNᶜM [and YDᶜᵓB YGL] have granted, leased, transferred, and assigned"

QLM

subst. *qlm* Q 155

(AROMATIC) CALAMUS [Sab *qlm*, Gk *kalamos* id.; cf. Crone, 1987, 61-62, 264-66]

Q 155: *qlm ḍrw rnd ḥḏk*

"(aromatic) calamus, balsam, nard (?), (pungent) incense (?)"

QNY

verb *qny* Q 35/7, Q 51/2, Q 74/5, Q 80/5, Q 82/2, Q 99/2, Q 265/1, Q 903/3; *qnyw* Q 77/2, Q 183/5, Q 254/6, Q 840/9, Q 906/4; *yqny* Q 66/4

TO ACQUIRE [Sab *qny*, Ar *qanā* (y), Eth *qanaya*, Heb *qānāh* id.]

Q 74/5-6: *wḏn ᵓbyt wᵓrḍtm qny wᶜs¹y ws²ᵓm yḏmrmlk*

"and these are the houses and lands which YḎMRMLK acquired, obtained, and purchased"

(and-these the-houses and-lands he-acquired and-obtaining and-purchasing YḎMRMLK)

(QNY)

s^1(h)-prfx. *s^{1}qny* Q 35/7, Q 41, Q 48, Q 66/1, Q 89.86/2, Q 90/2-3 +; *s^{1}qnyt* Q 252, Q 269/1-2, Q 493/2, Q 497/2, Q 558/3; *s^{1}qnyn* Q 244/3, Q 246/3; *s^{1}qnyw* Q 89.147, Q 256/2, Q 487/1, Q 551/8, Q 806/1, Q 840/1-2; *hqny* Q 477/2

TO DEDICATE [Sab *hqny* id. Perhaps there is a semantic development "to cause to possess">"to dedicate."]

Q 89.86/1-3: *ʾl̠drʾ bn yṣrʾl ... s^{1}qny d̠t ṣntm ṣlm d̠hbn*

"ʾL̠DRʾ the son of YṢRʾL ... dedicated a statue of bronze to D̠āt ṢNTM"

subst.^{1} *qnym* Q 186A/11, Q 243/4; *qnyn* Q 840/9; *qnys^1* Q 7/3, Q 186B/15, Q 202/5, Q 296/4, Q 911/3; *qnyhw* Q 35/8, Q 74/14; *qnys^{1}my* Q 840/8; pl. *ʾqny* Q 40/12, Q 74/5; *ʾqnys^{1}my* Q 806/4; *ʾqnys^{1}m* Q 40/20, Q 247/3 Q 496/4

POSSESSIONS, PROPERTY, ACQUISITIONS, GOODS; CHATTEL, SLAVES

Q 74/14: *d̠n [s^1]ṭrn wʾrḍhw wqnyhw*

[YD̠MRMLK placed] this [in]scription and his land and his possessions [under the protection of ʿAmm]"

subst.^{2} *s^{1}qnyt* Q 840/3, Q 844/4; *s^{1}qnytm* Q 66/7 Q 681/3, Q 905/2; *s^{1}qnyts^1* Q 681/5; *s^{1}qnyts^{1}m* Q 906/6

DEDICATION, OFFERING

Q 840/3: *s^{1}qnyt d̠hbn*

"[S^{2}RḤʾL and ZYDʾL made] an offering of bronze"

subst.^{3} *tqntm* Q 66/5

ACQUISITION

Q 66/5: *ʿs^{2}r kl hnʾm wmwblm wtqntm wtrṯm*

"a tenth of all crops watered by irrigation and by rain and acquisitions and inheritances"

(a-tenth [of] every irrigated-crop and-rain-watered-crop and-acquisitions and-inheritance)

QRW

verb *qrw* Q 72/8, 9

TO ACCUSE, PROSECUTE [Cf. Sab *yqrtn* "to be punished," Ar *qarā* "to pursue " Ar *iqtarā* "to pursue, prosecute"]

Q 72/7-8: *wl ylṣq wqrw ws^{1}ʿḏb*

"let [the lord of Timnaʿ] prosecute, accuse, and punish"

subst. *qrws^{1}m* Q 135/2

WATER RESERVOIR [Cf. Sab *qrw* "channel opening out into a basin (?)," Ar *qarw* "channel opening out into basin"]

Q 135/2: *wṣrs¹m wqrws¹m*
"and their sluice gate and their reservoir"

QRḤ

verb *qrḥ* Q 183/2
TO WOUND [Sab *qrḥ*, Ar *qaraḥa* id.]
Q 183/2: *l'[q]rḥm qrḥ*
"concerning the w[ou]nds he received"

subst. *qrḥn* Q 172/6
WOUND, INJURY [Sab *qrḥ* "wound," Ar *qarḥ* "injury, wound"]
Q 172/5-6: *fks³' s¹b'm lqrḥn wʿqls¹ bms¹'ls¹*
"he announced to S¹B'M through his oracle concerning the wound and its compensation"
(and-he-announced [to] S¹B'M concerning-the-wound and-its-compensation-money in-his-oracle)

QRḌ

subst. sing. *qrḍn* Q 700/2, 5; pl. *'qrḍm* Q 694/8-9; *'qrḍs¹* Q 700/4
DAM [Jamme, 1972, 32, compares Ar *qaraḍa* "to pinch with the fingers; cut, sever" and suggests that this meaning developed from the idea of cutting off the flow of water.]
Q 700/2: *bny qrḍn ylb' wʿglmts¹ wr's¹s¹*
"[S²HR YGL] built the dam YLB' and its conduit and its spout"

QS¹Ṭ

subst. *qs¹ṭ* Q 161, Q 538
COSTUS, a kind of incense [Sab *qs¹ṭ* , Grk *kostos* Lat *costus* id.; cf. Crone, 1987, 73-74]
Q 161: *rnd ḍrw lbny qs¹ṭ*
"nard (?), balsam, storax, costus"

QS²B

s¹(h)-prfx. *s¹qs²b* Q 914/2; *hqs²b* Q 98/2; *hqs²bw* Q 679/8; *hqs²bn* Q 677/4, Q 690a/3
TO BUILD; TO REFURBISH, RENOVATE [Sab *hqs²b* "to build, construct, make"; see discussion of the verb in Jamme, 1971, 83]
Q 98/1-2: *klybm wklbn lḥy wṣbʿ [ ]t hs²qw whqs²b whqḥ*
"KLYBM and KLBN LḤY and ṢBʿ [ ]T have dug up, built, and completed [the whole grave]"
(KLYBM and-KLBN LḤY and-ṢBʿ [ ]T they-have-dug-up and-building and-completing)

QTW

subst. *mqtwy* Q 690c/1-2; pl. *mqtwtn* Q 689/8-9

STEWARD [Sab *mqtwn*, *mqtwy* id, Ar *maqtawī* "servant, domestic," Ar *qatā* (w) "to perform well as a servant or domestic," Eth *ʾaqtawa* "to impose (tribute), bind, oblige"]

Q 690c/1-3: *zyd mqtwy mrṯdm ḏʿkl*

"ZYD, steward of MRṮDM, of the clan of ʿKL"

QTL

verb *qtl* Q 621

TO KILL, SLAY [Sab *qtl*, Ar *qatala*, Heb *qāṭal*, Syr *qəṭal* id.]

Q 621: *qbḍm qtl qrwm*

"QBḌM killed QRWM"

R

RʾB

verb *rʾb* Q 73/3

TO HARVEST [Cf. Ar *raʾaba* "to bind, collect a thing together, and to bind it gently." Beeston, 1976, 417, prefers "to set in good order"]

Q 73/2-4: *wgrb wbql wrʾb bs¹rs¹ ḏrbḍt wmlgʾs¹ nḥql ṯmnt ʾʾlfm bqlm ls¹ wl wlds¹ wḏʿdrs¹*

"and he constructed terraces and planted and harvested in his valley Ḏū RBḌT, and in its tenant farmland in particular, eight thousand plots for himself and his children and dependents" (and-he-constructed-terraces and-planting and-harvesting in-his-valley Ḏū-RBḌT and-its-tenant-farmland in-particular eight thousand plots for-himself and-for his-children and-his-dependents)

RʾS¹

subst. *rʾs¹s¹* Q 700/2

SPOUT [Cf. Ar *raʾs* "head; end of a thing," here in the sense of the spout at the end of the conduit]

Q 700/2: *bny qrḍn ylbʾ wʿglmts¹ wrʾs¹s¹*

"[S²HR YGL] built the dam YLBʾ and its conduit and its spout"

RBY

verb *byrby* Q 66/8, Q 203/5

TO CHOOSE, ADOPT AS *RBY* [This sense is clearly derived from the noun *rby*. See under *rby* for the etymology.]

Q 66/8: *wkwmw lyṣḥf wḥrg wʿqb wṯtwb ḏn ṣḥfn ʾrbym byrby ʿm ḏlbḫ*

"and thus let (all) whom ʿAmm Ḏū Labaḫ chooses as *ʾrby* write down, administer, implement, and adhere to this agreement"

(and-thus let-him-write-down and-administering and-implementing and-adhering [to] this agreement the-*ʾrby* he-makes-*ʾrby* ʿAmm Ḏū-Labaḫ)

subst. sing. *rby* Q 35/4, Q 80/4; pl. *ʾrbyw* Q 551/6; *ʾrby* Q 66/9, 10, Q 67/4, 6, 7, 8, 10, Q 68/3, 5, 6, 7, 9, Q 69/2, 3, 4, 5, Q 70/3(2x); *ʾrbym* Q 66/8; *ʾrbys¹* Q 66/1, 7, Q 67/13

RBY, priest or class of persons attached to the temple [Müller, 1962, 54, posits Akk *rabū* "to grow, become large," Ug *rb* "great," Heb *rāḇāh* "to grow large," Ar *rabbā* "to nourish," and cites Rhodokanakis, 1922, 72, who understands *rby* in the sense of "one nourished (by a god)." Further, see CIAS 2:138, RÉS VI, 199, Rhodokanakis, 1919, 16-20, 65-70, and Jamme, 1955f, 511, who understands the word as "an administrator of the estates belonging to a temple and not necessarily a 'priest administrator.'"]

A) Q 35/4: *sḥr wrby ʿm ryʿn*

"[S²HR HLL] priest and *rby* of ʿAmm RYʿN"

B) Q 69/4-5: *wṣry s²hr ʾdms¹ ʾrby ʿm ḏlbḫ wtʾnṯs¹m wbnys¹m*

"and S²HR directed his subjects, the *ʾrby* of ʿAmm Ḏū Labaḫ, their female relatives, and their sons"

(and-instructed S²HR his-subjects the-*ʾrby* [of] ʿAmm Ḏū-Labaḫ and-their-female-relatives and-their-sons)

subst. *rbytm* Q 203/5

FEMALE *RBY*

Q 203/4-5: *wl yḥr ḏn bytn byḥn wḫtbs¹ [r]bym wrbytm byrby ʿṯtr nwfn*

"may the *[r]by* and *rbyt* whom ʿAṯtar Nawfan has chosen occupy this house Bayḥān and its lower story"

(and-let occupy this house Bayḥān and-its-lower-story the-male-*[r]by* and-the-female-*rby* chooses-as-*rby* ʿAṯtar Nawfan)

RBʿ

verb *byrbʿ* Q 695/11-12

TO DECREASE [Cf. Ar *rabaʿa* "to cut (a rope) into four pieces"]

(RBᶜ)

Q 695/11-12: *wʾṣlmw mlkm ʾw s²ᶜbm bys³f ʾw byrbᶜ ḍnt ḏt ʾrḍn*
"the family of the king or tribe which enlarges or decreases the extent of this land"
(the-family of-the-king or tribe which increase or decrease the-extent [of] this land)

card. num.[1] *ʾrbᶜ* Q 78/12; *ʾrbᶜt* Q 11/2, Q 74/11
FOUR [Sab *ʾrbᶜ*, *ʾrbᶜt* "four," Ar *ʾarbaᶜ*, *ʾarbaᶜa*, Heb *ʾarbaᶜ*, *ʾarbāᶜāh* id.]
Q 74/11: *wʾrbᶜt ʾnḫlm bbḍᶜ hgrn*
"and four palmgroves in the vicinity of the town"

card. num.[2] *ʾrbᶜy* Q 690a/10
FORTY [Ar *ʾarbaᶜūn* "forty," Heb *ʾarbaᶜîm*, Syr *ʾarbəᶜīn* id.]
Q 690a/9-12: *wrḫhw ḏᶜddn ḏlḫms¹t wʾrbᶜy wṯlṯ mʾtm ḫrftm*
"in the month of Ḏū ᶜDDN of the of the year 345"

subst. *rbᶜ* Q 74/6(2x), 7(3x), 8(2x), 9 (3x), 12(3x); *rbᶜm* 903/3, 4(3x)
FOURTH (fraction) [Sab *rbᶜ* "fourth," Ar *rubᶜ*, Heb *rōḇaᶜ* id.
Q 74/9: *wrbᶜ byt bnw ḥlkm wṣrḥts¹ bhgrn ᶜrmn*
"and one fourth of the house of the Banū ḤLKM with its upper story in the town of ᶜRMN"

RBQ

subst. *rbq* Q 694/1
ADMINISTRATOR [Cf. Ar *rabaqa* "to tie, to bind fast"; Beeston, 1981a, 64, prefers Ar *raqaba* "to exercise surveillance," and thinks, ibid., 63-64, that "the *rbq* both in Maᶜin and Qataban was responsible for the control of water supplies"]
Q 694/1-2: *kn wqh ʾnby wrbq brm bs¹ʾl s¹ʾl ydᶜʾb ygl mlk qtbn*
"in response to the inquiry which YDᶜʾB YGL the king of Qataban has made, ʾAnbay and the administrator of BRM have decreed thus"
(thus decreed ʾAnbay and-the-administrator [of] BRM at-the-request [which] requested YDᶜʾB YGL king [of] Qataban)

RDʾ

verb *rdʾ* Q 8/3, Q 203/3; *rdʾt* Q 167/2; *rdʾw* Q 899/6; *yrdʾs¹* Q 90/4; *yrdʾwn* 254/3; *trdʾ* Q 256/4

1) VOW, DEDICATE [sense from context]
Q 167/2: *rdʾt ḏt ṣntm ᶜs³b*
"[(..)S²M] dedicated the crops to Ḏāt ṢNTM"

2) TO AID, HELP, FAVOR [Cf. Sab *hrdʾ* id., Ar *radaʾa* "to support," Eth *ʾardeʾa* "to give help"]

Q 899/6: *ʾnby wnkrḥm rdʾw*

"may ʾAnbay and NKRḤM give their aid"

subst.[1] *rdʾ* Q 73/4(2x), Q 102/6, Q 177/4, Q 611/4, Q 688/4, Q 914/4

AID, HELP

Q 177/4-5: *wb rdʾ wtḥrg mrʾs¹m wrwʾl ǵyln yhnʿm*

"and with the help and direction of their lord WRWʾL ǴYLN YHNʿM

subst.[2] pl. *ʾrdʾhw* Q 688/4

WORKER, HELPER [Cf. verb *rdʾ* "to aid, help"]

Q 688/3-4: *wtqdm ʾrdʾhw bḏn mʾgln bnʾ*

"and he directed his workers in (the construction of) this cistern BNʾ"

RDY

subst. *rdn* Q 186B/14-15

PROFIT [Beeston, 1971b, 3, compares Eth *redē* "interest"]

Q 186B/14-15: *bḏl rdn qnys¹ wmrṯds¹*

"in what is included in his profits on his possessions and goods"

[in-that-which-to the-profit his-possessions and-his-goods]

RWY

subst. *mrwhw* Q 611/2-3

IRRIGATION SYSTEM [Sab *mrw*, *mryt* "irrigation"; cf. Ar *marwī* "well watered," Ar *riyy*, *rayy* "irrigation"]

Q 611/1-3: *hwfʿm ḏʿrgn hqḥ wbql wynhw ḏʾln bbḏʿ hgrn hkr wmrwhw*

"HWFʿM Ḏū ʿRGN set in order and cultivated his vineyard ḎʾLN in the direction of the town HKR and its irrigation system"

RḤB

subst. *mrḥbm* Q 694/8; *mrḥbmʾy* Q 694/9

1) LAND OPEN TO IRRIGATION [See the discussion of this root by Pirenne, 1971, 127, who compares the Heb *rāḥaḇ* "to expand," and Ar *raḥuba* "to be wide, vast," and suggests the specific sense in Qatabanian of being open to the flow of water or irrigation.]

Q 694/8-9: *mrḥbm bn nḫlm wḥrṯ ʾwd wbqlm bqlm wbny ḥrtm wʾqr[w]m wbn ḍmr ḍmrm ʾw ḥrṯ kl ʾwdm wmrḥbmʾy*

(RḤB)

"this land shall be open to irrigation and free from palmgroves, the terracing of (the area held by) a retaining wall, the cultivation of plants, the construction of aqueducts and canals, and from the making of water conduits or the terracing of any retaining wall and any irrigation equipment"
(land-open-for-irrigation from palm-gardens and the-terracing [of] a-retaining-wall and-cultivating [of] plants and-the-building [of] aqueducts and-canals and-from the-joining [of] the-water-conduit and-terracing [of] any retaining-wall and-irrigation-equipment)

2) IRRIGATION EQUIPMENT, IRRIGATION TECHNIQUE
See entry above.

RND

subst. *rnd* Q 155, Q 161, Q 530ter, Q 538
AN AROMATIC PLANT used for incense = NARD (?) [Sab *rnd* id.; cf. perhaps Heb *nērd* "nard," Gk *nardos* "artemisia pontica or abyssinica," and see K. Nielsen, 1986, 18, 64, and Crone, 1987, 72-73]
Q 161: *rnd ḍrw lbny qs¹ṭ*
"nard (?), balsam, storax, costus"

RFD

subst. pl. *rfdhys¹m* Q 265/3
FOUNDATION [Sab *rfd* "supporting wall, buttress of house"; cf. Ar *rafada* "to support, prop up"]
Q 265/3: *ms²rqytm bnḏn bytn wṣrḥtyw wnfs¹hys¹m wrfdhys¹m*
"east from this house and its upper story and their roof terraces and foundations"

RS²W

verb *rs²w* Q 915/2; *rs²ww* Q 898/7
1) TO GIVE FEES, DUES [Sab *rs²w* "to make a grant of something." Ghul, 1959, 7, compares Ar *rišwa* "fees or gratuity due to a priest or diviner" and the verb *rašā* (w) "to give *rišwa*"]
Q 898/7-9: *wʾmrʾs¹ rs²ww ywm drf wntṣf bmrs²wmyw ʾrb[ʿ]t wḫms¹y ḫrwf s¹tlwt*
"and his lords were paid their dues when he selected and paid out, according to their due, fifty-f[ou]r sheep for their bearing responsibility for (his) safety"

(and-his-lords they-were-paid when he-selected and-he-paid according-to-the-due f[ou]r and-fifty sheep bearing-responsibility-for-safety)

2) TO SERVE AS *RS²W* [Sab *rs²w* id.]

Q 915/1-2: *bny ws¹ḥdṯ tḥmy gnn s³dw lʿm ḏdwnm bʿl s³dw ywm rs²w ʿmm s²lṯtm*

"[S²HR HLL YHNʿM] built and newly constructed the wall of the garden of S³DW for ʿAmm Ḏū DWNM, lord of S³DW, when he served as *rs²w* for the third year"

(he-built and-newly-constructing the-wall [of] the-garden [of] S³DW for-ʿAmm Ḏū-DWNM lord [of] S³DW when he-served-as-*rs²w* [for] the-year third)

subst.[1] *rs²w* Q 1/1, Q 35/3, Q 80/3(2x), Q 240/2, Q 551/7, Q 769/1b

RS²W, holder of a religious office [Sab *rs²w* "title of holder of a religious function." Pirenne, who has dealt with this word in a series of studies—CIAS 1:113; 1976a, 177-218; 1976b, 137-43—rejects the traditional sacerdotal interpretation of the word, noting that many of those individuals who served as *rs²w* also had other nonpriestly functions.]

Q 769/1b: *qẓr qyn rs²w ʿmm*

"administrator of money offerings, attendant, and *rs²w* for the year"

subst.[2] *rs²wt* Q 269/5

RS²WT, female holder of a religious office

Q 269/4-5: *qẓrt ʿm ḏrbḥw rs²wt ʿm ḏdymt*

"administrator of the money offerings for ʿAmm, Ḏū RBḤW, *rs²wt* for ʿAmm Ḏū DYMT"

subst.[3] *mrs²wmyw* Q 898/8

DUE

See entry under the verb *rs²w* above.

RS³ᶜ

subst. *mrs³ʿt* Q 179/1, Q 914/2

UPPER STORY; CONSTRUCTION [Cf. perhaps Sab *rs³ᶜ* "to construct"; Ar *rassaʿa* "to build, construct"]

Q 179/1: *lḥyʿt bn ṣwbn yʿb brʾ ws¹wṯr ws¹qḥ mrs³ʿt wmwṯr byt[s¹]*

"LḤYʿT the son of ṢWBN YʿB constructed, laid the foundation, and set in order the upper story and foundation of [his] house"

(LḤYʿT the-son [of] ṢWBN YʿB he-constructed and-laying-the-foundation and-setting-in-order the-upper-story and-the-foundation [of] [his]-house)

RṮD

verb *rṯd* Q 11/6, Q 73/5, Q 74/13, Q 89.129/2, Q 183/4, Q 247/2, Q 494/5, Q 496/3, Q 681/4, Q 840/9, Q 858/3, Q 898/9, Q 904/4 Q 905/4, Q 906/5, Q 916/3-4; *rṯds*^{1} Q 540/3, Q 844/9; *rṯdhw* Q 178/2; *rṯdt* Q 201/2, Q 497/3, Q 911/1; *rṯdw* Q 244/14, Q 246/13, Q 487/3, Q 495/5, Q 551/9, Q 806/2, Q 840/6-7

TO ENTRUST, COMMIT TO THE PROTECTION of a deity [Sab *rṯd* id.]

A) Q 73/5-6: *wrṯd ǵlbm ḏtn ʾs*^{1}*ṭrn ʿṯtr s*^{2}*rqn*
"ǴLBM entrusted these inscriptions to ʿAṯtar S^{2}RQN"
(and-entrusted ǴLBM these inscriptions [to] ʿAṯtar S^{2}RQN)

B) Q 844/9-11: *rṯds*^{1} *nfs*^{1}*s*^{1} *wmqms*^{1} *bn kl s*^{2}*yntm*
"[HWFʾL] has entrusted to his protection himself and his property from every dishonor"
(he-entrusted-to-him himself and-his-property from-every dishonor)

subst. *mrṯdn* Q 186B/17; *mrṯds*^{1} Q 186B/15

GOODS

Q 186B/14-15: *bḏl rdn qnys*^{1} *wmrṯds*^{1}
"in what is included in his profits on his possessions and goods"
[in-that-which-to the-profit his-possessions and-his-goods]

S^1

S^{1}ʾL

verb *s*^{1}*ʾl* Q 694/2

ASK, SEEK, INQUIRE [Sab *s*^{1}*ʾl*, Ar *saʾala*, Heb *šāʾal*, Akk *šaʾālu* id.]

Q 694/1-2: *kn wqh ʾnby wrbq brm bs*^{1}*ʾl s*^{1}*ʾl ydʿʾb ygl mlk qtbn*
"in response to the inquiry which YDʿʾB YGL the king of Qataban has made, ʾAnbay and the administrator of BRM have decreed thus"
(thus decreed ʾAnbay and-the-administrator [of] BRM at-the-request [which] requested YDʿʾB YGL king [of] Qataban)

subst.[1] *s*^{1}*ʾl* Q 40/2, Q 694/1

INQUIRY, REQUEST

See entry above.

subst.[2] /partcp. *s*^{1}*ʾlm* Q 40/2, Q 694/1

ONE WHO INQUIRES

Q 40/2: *wʾmmm bs^{1}ʾlm s^{1}ʾl*
"as instruction for one inquiring"
(and-instruction for-the-one-who-inquires an-inquiry

subst.[2] *ms^{1}ʾls^1* Q 89.137.5, Q 172/6, Q 901/3, Q 908/5; *ms^{1}ʾlhw* Q 83/10; *ms^{1}ʾls^{1}m* Q 37/3
ORACLE [Sab *ms^{1}ʾl* id.]
Q 89.137/5: *ḥg wqh ʾbs^1 wdm bms^{1}ʾls^1*
"as his father WDM commanded in his oracle"
(according-as commanded his-father WDM in-his-oracle)

S^{1}Bʾ

verb *s^{1}bʾ* Q 244/9, Q 910/4
TO SET OUT, GO [Sab *s^{1}bʾ* "to set out on a journey, undertake a project"; cf. Ar *subʾa* "long journey"]
Q 244/7-10: *lwfy mrʾs^1[n nb]ṭm yhnʿm mlk qtbn bywm bs^1 s^{1}bʾ ʿd rḥbtn*
"(they made the dedication which they had promised) for the safety of the[ir] lord [NB]ṬM YHNʿM the king of Qataban on the day on which he set out for RḤBTN"
(for-the-safety [of] the[ir]-lord [NB]ṬM YHNʿM the-king [of] Qataban on-the-day on-it he-set-out for RḤBTN)

subst.[1] *s^{1}bʾt* Q 910/4
JOURNEY, UNDERTAKING, EXPEDITION
Q 910/4: *[b]kl s^{1}bʾt ḍrn bʿm mrʾhmy y[hqm]*
"on every journey in which ḌRN set out with their lord Y[HQM]
([on]-every journey [in which] ḌRN with their-lord Y[HQM])

subst.[2] *ms^{1}bʾ* Q 176/5
MOUNTAIN ROAD, HIGH ROAD [Ar *masbaʾ* "road in a mountain, road"]
Q 176/5-6: *nqz wwzl wbrr ms^{1}bʾ wmnql ẓrm*
"they laid out, paved, and dug up the mountain road and the pass ẒRM"

S^{1}Bʿ

card. num. *s^{1}bʿt* Q 74/10(2x), Q 695/5
SEVEN [Sab *s^{1}bʿ*, *s^{1}bʿt* "seven," Arab *sabʿ*, *sabʿa*, Heb *šeḇaʿ*, *šiḇʿāh*, Akk *sibi*, *sibitti* id.]
Q 74/10: *ws^{1}bʿt ʾnḫlm bs^{1}rn nʿmn ws^{1}bʿt ʾnḫlm bʿrm ḏgylm*
"seven palmgroves in the valley NʿMN and seven palmgroves in ʿRM Ḏū GYLM"

S^{1}GF

h(s^1)-prfx. *hs^{1}gf* Q 687/4

TO BUILD A ROOF OVER a structure [W. Müller, in von Wissmann, 1968, 81, calls this form "certainly the same" as Sab *hs^{1}gf* "to build a roof," with the *g* and *q* interchanged just as occurs in the modern dialects of South Arabia; Jamme, 1971, 87, compares Ar *sajf* "veil, curtain, cover"]

Q 687/4: *wnqb hs^{1}gf bmṯbr ṯwyfm*

"he bored a hole (for runoff water) and built a roof over the ruin ṮWYFM"

S^{1}DṮ

card. num. *s^{1}dṯt* Q 74/11

SIX [Sab *s^{1}dṯ*, *s^{1}dṯt* "six," Ar *sitt*, *sitta*, Heb *šēš*, *šiššāh*, Akk *šišši*, *šiššit* id.]

Q 74/11: *ws^{1}dṯt ʿs^{2}r ʾnḫlm*

"sixteen palmgroves"

(six ten palmgroves)

ord. num. *s^{1}dṯm* Q 72/3

SIXTH

Q 72/3: *ws^{1}dṯm dfqḥw*

"[on] the sixth of Ḏū FQḤW "

S^{1}HM

subst. *s^{1}hmm* Q 243/4

DOMESTICS, MAN- AND MAIDSERVANTS [Thus Höfner, 1987, 43, who compares Ar *sahm* "Anteil," in the sense of "those who (that which) takes part in the same undertaking." Pirenne, in CIAS 1:143-44, who understands the word as "*le butin (de prisonniers)*," compares the Ar *sahama* and its various derived forms, which have to do with playing a game of chance, as well as Ar *sahm*, a substantive denoting a type of arrow used in the game of chance known as *maysir*, and suggests that *s^{1}hmm* denotes something which is acquired by lot, such as captives to be used as slaves (here contrasted with *qnym*, which are slaves acquired by purchase).]

Q 2435: *wkl s^{1}hmm wqnym*

"all the domestics and slaves"

S^{1}W

dem. pro. masc. sing. nom. *s^{1}w* Q 78/4, 7, Q 172/5, Q 695/14; masc. sing. non-nom. *s^{1}wt* Q 40/6, Q 901/4; fem. sing. non-nom. *s^{1}yt* Q 72/6;

masc. dl. non-nom. *s¹myt* Q 40/10, 13; masc. pl. nom. *s¹m* Q 40/5, 18; masc. pl. non-nom. *s¹mt* Q 40/16, 20

THIS, THAT; THESE, THOSE [Cf. Sab *h'*, *hw'*, *hwt* "this"; Sab dl. *hmyt*, masc. pl. *hmw*, fem. pl. *hn* "these"; cf. also Ar *hum* "they," Heb *hēm* id. See Beeston, 1962b, 47-48, and 1984, 66, for his discussion of these forms of "demonstratives of remoter deixis" in Qat]

Q 78/4: *wl yḥrm s¹w 'ns¹n hrgn*

"let this murderer be punished"

S¹WY

verb *s¹wy* Q 642/2

TO DO, MAKE [Jamme, 1972, 15, compares Ar *sawiya* "to make, form, fashion something in a suitable manner"]

Q 642/2: *ys²'m ḏys²bm s¹wy b'ḏn 'm*

"YS²'M ḎYS²BM has done this, by authority of 'Amm"

S¹WR

verb *s¹wr* Q 687/2

TO BUILD A WALL AROUND [Cf. Sab *hs¹r* "to build *a wall*" Ar *sawwara* "to enclose, wall in," ModYem *swār* "wall of a reservoir"]

Q 687/2: *s¹wr bn' m'gl ms¹qt gḏ*

"[the dignitaries of S¹'DM YHS¹KR] built a wall around BN', the irrigation cistern of GḎ"

(built-a-wall-around BN' the-cistern [of] irrigation [of] GḎ)

S¹ṬR

verb *s¹ṭr* Q 66/11, Q 67/8, Q 68/7, 9, Q 69/5, Q 70/3, Q 243/9, Q 570/2; *s¹ṭrw* Q 40/16 *bys¹ṭrwn* Q 40/16

TO WRITE, WRITE DOWN, ENGRAVE [Sab *s¹ṭr* id., Akk *saṭāru* "to write," Heb *šōṭēr* "officer, official" (originally "scribe, secretary"?), Ar *saṭara* "to rule a book, write," Aram *šəṭārā'* "document," Nab and Palm *šṭr* id.]

Q 66/10-11: *wṯfṭ s²hr 'rby 'm ḏlbḫ lfṯḥ ws¹ṭr ḏtn 's¹ṭrn*

"S²HR directed the *'rby* of 'Amm Ḏū Labaḫ to inscribe and engrave these inscriptions"

(and-directed S²HR the-*'rby* [of] 'Amm Ḏū-Labaḫ to-inscribe and-engraving these inscriptions)

subst. sing. *s¹ṭrn* Q 695/7; pl. *'s¹ṭr* Q 67/12, Q 694/6, 12, Q 695/10, 14; *'s¹ṭrn* Q 66/11, 14, Q 67/7, 8, Q 68/7, Q 69/5, Q 70/4, Q 73/5, 694/12-13; *'s¹ṭrs¹* Q 66/10, Q 68/7, Q 69/5

1) ENGRAVING, INSCRIPTION

Q 73/5-6: *wrṯd ǵlbm ḏtn 's¹ṭrn 'ṯtr s²rqn*

(S^{1}ṬR)

"and ǴLBM entrusted these inscriptions to ᶜAṯtar S^{2}RQN"

(and-entrusted ǴLBM these inscriptions [to] ᶜAṯtar S^{2}RQN)

2) TEXT

Q 695/13-14: *lwzʾ ʾw nky bʾqṭnt ʾs^{1}ṭr ḏt ṣḥftn*

"to add to or diminish the details of the text of this document"

S^{1}KT

subst. *s^{1}kt* Q 67/4, Q 68/4, Q 69/3

CEASING, FALLING INTO ABEYANCE [Cf. Ar *sakata* "fall silent, become mute," Heb *hiskîṯ* "to keep silence"]

Q 67/4-5: *bn s^{1}nṣfm ws^{1}kt wʾhḏ wgddm*

"without any falling short, ceasing, detraction, or termination"

S^{1}LB

s^1-prfx. *ys^{1}s^{1}lb* Q 72/8

TO REFUSE [Cf. Ar *salb,* used in logic and grammar to indicate privation and negation in a general sense.]

Q 72/8-9: *whmw ys^{1}s^{1}lb kbrn bn lṣq wqrw*

"if the *kabīr* refuses to prosecute and accuse"

(and-if refuses the-*kabīr* from prosecuting and-accusing)

S^{1}M

susbt. *s^{1}m* Q 40/11 (3x)

NAME [Sab *s^{1}m*, Ar *ism*, Heb *šēm*, Akk *šumu* id.]

Q 40/11: *ʾl s^{1}rbw bs^{1}m mlkn*

"(laws) which they have proclaimed in the name of the king"

S^{1}MY

verb *ys^{1}myn* Q 172/3-4, Q 839/3-4, 6

TO NAME, CALL [Cf. Sab *ys^{1}myn* "to name, call; to be named, called," Ar *sammā* "to name, call"]

Q 839/5-6: *bn ʾrḍ nḫln mqẓm ḏys^{1}myn mwhrtn nḫl[n s^{2}ᶜb]n yqhmlk wbn brṣm*

"from the land of the palmgrove MQẒM which the [trib]e of YQHMLK and BN BRṢM call MWHRTN NḪL[N]"

(from the-land [of] the-palmgrove MQẒM which-they-name MWHRTN NḪL[N] the-[trib]e [of] YQHMLK and-BN BRṢM)

S^{1}Mᶜ

subst. pl. *ʾs^{1}mᶜm* Q 40/22, Q 78/8

WITNESSES [Sab *s^{1}mᶜm*, Ar *sāmiᶜ* id.]

Q 78/8: *mwt ʾw mʿbr bnfs¹ ms¹tʿdwn ʾs¹mʿm*
"(whoever kills the culprit need not fear) death or compensation for the life of that wrongdoer. Witnesses: ..."

S¹NN

verb *s¹nt* Q 695/8

TO OBSERVE a regulation or ordinance [Cf. Ar *sanna* "observe such and such a rule or ordinance." For a discussion of this and the following word see Beeston, 1976, 421.]

Q 695/8-9: *wbn ʿlw s¹nhtm s¹nt brm ʿs¹m ḫrwf*
"[this document is based] upon a code which has been observed in BRM for a number of years"

subst. (coll.) pl. *s¹nhtm* Q 695/8

CODE OF OBSERVANCES

See entry above.

S¹FḤ

verb *s¹fḥ* Q 67/1, Q 68/1

TO DECREE, ANNOUNCE [Sab *s¹fḥ* "to order, decree; to summon, call out *someone*"; see J. Ryckmans, 1973, 83-85, for a discussion of this word]

Q 68/1: *s²hr hll yhnʿm bn ydʿʾb mlk qtbn ṣry ws¹fḥ bn mḥrm ʿm*
"S²HR HLL YHNʿM son of YDʿʾB king of Qataban, announced and decreed"

t-infix *ys¹tfḥwn* Q 67/5, Q 68/5, Q 69/3

TO HOLD ONESELF BOUND [Perhaps the semantic development here is parallel to that for Sab *s¹fḥ* "to order, decree" posited by J. Ryckmans, 1972, 385; cf. Eth *safḥa* "to spread">"to publish">"to decree, order." Here there is the development "to decree for oneself">"to hold oneself bound."]

Q 67/5-6: *nl ys¹tfḥwn ʾrby ʿm ḏlbḫ wtʾnṯs¹m bʿlw ḏt mḥrtn*
"so let the ʾ*rby* of ʿAmm Ḏū Labaḫ and their female kindred hold themselves bound in accordance with this directive"
(so-let hold-themselves-bound ʾ*rby* [of] ʿAmm Ḏū-Labaḫ and-their-female-kindred according-to this directive)

S¹FL

subst. *s¹flm* Q 40/17

LOWLAND [Sab *s¹fl* "low-lying land, lower part of a tract of land," Ar ʾ*asāfil* "lower or lowest parts of valleys," Heb *šəp̱ēlāh* "lowland"; see also the discussion under S³FL]

(S^{1}FL)

Q 40/17: *bʿlym ws^{1}flm*
"in highland and lowland"

S^{1}QB

subst. *s^{1}qbs^{1}ww* Q 99/9-10

ATTENDANT [Sense from context; see Jamme, 1972, 75, who compares Min Fakhry 14/15]

Q 99/8-10: *wbmrʾs^1 ydʿʾb ynf yhnʿm mlk qtbn ws^{1}qbs^{1}ww ʿmkrb yhwḍʿ*

"by his lord YDʿʾB YNF YHNʿM, king of Qatabar, and his attendant ʿMKRB YHWḌʿ"

S^{1}QY

t-infix *ys^{1}tq* Q 687/7

TO BE GIVEN WATER TO DRINK; TO SLAKE ONE'S THIRST [Sab *ys^{1}tqyn*, Ar *istaqā* id.]

Q 687/7: *lys^{1}tq btʾẖr dnẖk zm ʾs^{1}rb wʾṯwr*

"after a delay let this charge, the herd of sheep and cattle, be given water to drink"

(let-be-given-water-to-drink after-a-delay this-charge the-herd [of] sheep and-cattle)

subst. *ms^{1}qt* Q 687/2

IRRIGATION; IRRIGATION SYSTEM [Sab *ms^{1}qt, ms^{1}qyt* "canals, canalized irrigation schemes; irrigation (in general)" Ar *saqy* "watering, irrigation," ModḤaḍ *saqiya* "canal"]

Q 687/2: *s^{1}wr bnʾ mʾgl ms^{1}qt gḏ*

"[the dignitaries of S^{1}ʿDM YHS^{1}KR] built a wall around BNʾ, the irrigation cistern of GḎ"

(built-a-wall-around BNʾ the-cistern [of] irrigation [of] GḎ)

S^{1}QM

subst. *s^{1}qmtm* Q 203/2

IRRIGATION [Cf. S^{1}QY above and see RÉS VII, 434, which compares the occurrence of *s^{1}qm* at RÉS 4053/2]

Q 203/2: *s^{2}hr ǵyln ʾbs^{2}bm mlk qtbn bny ws^{1}ḥd[ṯ …] ʾlhw s^{1}qmtm*

"S^{2}HR ǴYLN ʾBS^{2}BM, king of Qataban, built and newly construct[ed …] the irrigation gods"

S^{1}QF

subst.[1] *s^{1}qfm* Q 914/3

VESTIBULE, (ARCADED) ENTRANCE GALLERY, PORTICO [Cf. Ar *saqafa* "to roof, vault over," Ar *saqf* "arched, vaulted roof, Ar *musaqqaf* "roofed over," ModYem *sagīf* "open vestibule, entrance hall on the ground floor of a Yemeni house (without windows)"]

Q 914/1-3: *s²ᶜbn ḏmrytm ḥwr hgrn ẓfr br'w ws¹qs²b mrsᶜt yrdᶜ ws¹qfm ṣrbt*

"the tribe Ḏū MRYTM, residents of the town of ẒFR, have contructed and built the structure YRDᶜ and the vestibule ṢRBT"

(the-tribe Ḏū-MRYTM residents [of] the-town ẒFR have-constructed and-building the-structure YRDᶜ and-the-vestibule ṢRBT)

subst.² *ms¹qfts¹* Q 266/3; *ms¹qfthw* Q 265/2-3

VESTIBULE, (ARCADED) ENTRANCE GALLERY [Sab *ms¹qf* "roofed hall, roofed structure"]

Q 266/2-3: *byts¹ yfs² wkl 'ḫ̣tbs wṣrḥts¹ww wmfs¹hs¹ww wms¹qfts¹*

"[ṮWYBM purchased] his house YFS² and all its lower stories and its upper rooms and roof terraces and vestibule"

(his-house YFS² and-all its-workshops and-its-upper-rooms and-its-terraces and-its-vestibule)

S¹RB

subst. pl. *'s¹rb* Q 687/7

SHEEP; SMALL CATTLE [Cf. Ar *sarība* "sheep"]

Q 687/7: *lys¹tq bt'ḫr dnḫk zm 's¹rb w'ṯwr*

"after a delay let this charge, the herd of sheep and cattle, be given water to drink"

(let-be-given-water-to-drink after-a-delay this-charge the-herd [of] sheep and-cattle)

S¹RR

subst. sing. *s¹rn* Q 67/8, Q 68/7, Q 69/6, Q 74/10; *s¹rs¹* Q 73/3; *s¹rhmw* Q 679/7, 8; dl. *s¹rnyhn* Q 695/3; pl. *'s¹rrn* Q 40/3; *'s¹rrs¹* Q 73/1

VALLEY, SIDE of a valley open to cultivation [Sab *s¹rn* "slope, valley; side of a valley on either side of a wadi (subject to cultivation)," Ar *sirr* "good land," Ar *asirra* "good land in the middle of a wadi," ModYem *sirr* "better part of the wadi"]

Q 73/3: *bs¹rs¹ ḏrbḍt wmlg's¹*

"in his valley Ḏū RBḌT and in its tenant farmland"

S²

S²ʾM I

verb *s²ʾm* Q 74/5, Q 99/2, Q 265/1, Q 266/2; *s²ʾmw* Q 790/1

TO PURCHASE, BUY [Sab *s²ʾm* "to buy", Akk *šāmu* "to buy," Meh *sêm* "to sell," Soq *śiom* "to sell," Ar *sāma* "to place on sale"]

A) Q 99/2-3: *brm s²ʾm wqny wbrʾ wẓrb byts¹*
"[… (son of) FLS¹ʾB] purchased, acquired, constructed, and took possession of his house"

B) Q 74/5-6: *wḏn ʾbyt wʾrḍtm qny wʿs¹y ws²ʾm yḏmrmlk*
"and these are the houses and lands which YḎMRMLK acquired, obtained, and purchased"
(and-these the-houses and-lands he-acquired and-obtaining and-purchasing YḎMRMLK)

s¹(h)-prfx. *s¹s²ʾm* Q 186A/12; *hs²ʾmn* Q 839/5

TO SELL

Q 186A/11-12: *byḫdr wʾrm ws¹s²ʾm bs²mr*
"[he] shall have a trading-stall and conduct business and sell in S²MR"

t-infix *s²tʾm* Q 186B/5

TO PURCHASE

Q 186B/4-5: *bʿlw ms²ṭm bys²tytwn ws²tʾm qtbn*
"on merchandise which the Qatabanians may trade and buy"

S²ʾM II

subst. pl. *ʾs²ʾmn* Q 176/5

THOSE OF THE NORTH, NORTHERNER [Cf. Sab *s²ʾmt* "north, northern region"]

Q176/4-5: *ʾymnn wʾs²ʾmn*
"those of the south and those of the north"

S²Bʿ

adv. *s²bʿm* Q 174/3

ABUNDANTLY, TO SATIETY [Sab *s²bʿm* "in abundance"; cf. Ar *šabiʿa* "to be sated," Heb *śaḇēʿa* "to be sated, satisfied," Akk *šēbu* id.]

Q 174/3: *ḏt s²bʿm wb n[…]*
"abundantly and […]

S²HD

comp. prep. *bs²hd*

See entry under B.

S^{2}HR

subst. *s²hr* Q 66/6

NEW MOON, FIRST DAY of the month [Sab *s²hrm* "beginning of the month," Ar *šahr* id.]

Q 66/6: *wl yṣḥf wḥrg ʿṣmn bn s²hr wrḫn ḏtmnʿ*

"let this patronage-tie be written and administered from the new moon of the month Ḏū-Timnaʿ"

(and-let be-written and-administering this-patronage-tie from the-new-moon [of] the-month Ḏū-Timnaʿ)

S^{2}ḪB

verb *s²ḫb* Q 769/2a

TO PROVIDE WITH; TO PROVIDE WITH ABUNDANTLY [Cf. Ar *šaḫaba* "to flow"]

Q 769/2a: *ws²ḫb ʾbns¹ wblqs¹ wʿḍs¹ wmrt[s¹]*

"he provided its stone, its marble, its wood, and [its] limestone"

S^{2}YṬ

verb *bys²ṭ* Q 186A/18-19

TO SELL, TRADE [Eth *šēṭa* "to sell," Eth *tašāyaṭa* "to buy," ModYem *štāṭ* "to buy"; cf. perhaps Eg *šdj* "to trade," Cop *šōt* "to trade."]

Q 186A/18-20: *bys²ṭ tmnʿ wḫdr ms²ṭs¹ bs²mr*

"while he [the overseer of S²MR] trades in Timnaʿ and sets up a trading-stall for his merchandise in S²MR"

t-infix *ys²tyṭwn* Q 186A/20, B/4-5; *bys²tyṭ* Q 186A/14, B/18; *bys²tyṭwn* Q 186B/26-27

TO TRADE

A) Q 186A/13-16: *wmty yḫdr ḫdrm wʾḏw bys²tyṭ ʾw ftḫr bʿm kl ḏḫdrm wms²ṭm*

"when he sets up a trading-stall, he may then trade or enter into a partnership with any possessor of a trading-stall and merchandise"

(and-when he-sets-up a-trading-stall and-then he-may-trade or entering-into-partnership with any possessor-[of]-a-trading-stall and-merchandise)

B) Q 186B/4-5: *bʿlw ms²ṭm bys²tyṭwn ws²tʾm qtbn*

"on merchandise which the Qatabanians may trade and buy"

(S^{2}YṬ)

subst.[1] *s^{2}yṭm* Q 186A/8, B/19, 26

1) MERCHANDISE

Q 186A/7-8: *mn ms^{2}yṭ tmnᶜ wbrm s^{2}yṭm*

"whoever is a trader of Timnaᶜ and BRM in merchandise"

2) TRADING ACTIVITY

Q 186B/25-28: *wl ykn s^{2}yṭm bys^{2}tyṭwn qtbn … bᶜhr q[…]*

"let the trading activity that the Qatabanians carry on … be through the overseer of Q[…]"

subst.[2] *ms^{2}ṭ* Q 186B/8; *ms^{2}ṭs^1* Q 186A/19; *ms^{2}ṭm* Q 186A/10, 15-16, 23, B/4, C/2, 8

1) MERCHANDISE

A) Q 186A/9-10: *wʾṯrm qtbn bms^{2}ṭm*

"one who goes to Qataban with merchandise"

(and-the-one-who-goes [to] Qataban with-merchandise)

B) Q 186A/19-20: *wḫdr ms^{2}ṭs^1 bs^{2}mr*

"and a trading-stall for his merchandise in S^{2}MR"

2) MARKET, MARKET PLACE

Q 186B/8: *bms^{2}ṭ s^{2}mr*

"in the market of S^{2}MR"

subst.[3] *ms^{2}yṭ* Q 186A/7

TRADER

Q 186A/7-8: *mn ms^{2}yṭ tmnᶜ wbrm s^{2}yṭm*

"whoever is a trader of Timnaᶜ and BRM in merchandise"

S^{2}YM I

verb *s^{2}ym* Q 562, Q 563 d, j, k, Q 638/3; *s^{2}ymw* Q 267; *ys^{2}mn* Q 495/4

1) TO SECURE, PROTECT [Semantic development "establish" >"secure, protect"; cf. Sab *s^{2}ym* "to confirm, protect," and in the broader sense of "to set up, establish"; cf. Eth *šēma* "to put," Heb *śīm* "to put, set; to establish (a law); to appoint (a person)"]

Q 495/4-5: *wʾnby lys^{2}mn wfys^{1}m*

"and may ʾAnbay secure their saftey"

2) TO DECORATE, FURNISH (?) [Conjectural. Jamme, 1958a, 189, also conjectures "to inaugurate."]

Q 267: *ṯwybm wᶜqrbm ḏwy mhṣnᶜm s^{2}ymw yfs^2*

ṮWYBM and ᶜQRBM of the clan of MHṢNᶜM furnished (?) the house of YFS^2"

subst. *s^{2}ymn* Q 11/5, Q 66/9, Q 67/2, Q 68/2, Q 69/1, Q 173/2, Q 239/4, Q 244/17, Q 246/18, Q 247/1, 2, Q 261/2, Q 484/3, Q 487/2, Q 494/3, Q 495/2, Q 496/2, Q 497/2-3, Q 498/2, Q 700/8, Q 771/2, Q 806/2 +

PATRON (DEITY) [Sab *s^{2}ym* id.]

Q 247/2: *r*ṯ*d* ᵓ*nby s²ymn nfs¹s¹*
"he placed himself under the protection of ᵓAnbay, the patron (deity)"

S²YM II

subst. *ms²mn* Q 80/7

(ARABLE) FIELD [Sab *ms²m* "cultivated field," Ar *šayām* "plain"]

Q 80/6-7: *w*ᶜ*wt m*ᶜ*s²q ms²mn b*ᵓ*mr* ᶜ*m* ḏ*dwnm*
"[Dū BYN YHNᶜM] carried out the cultivation of the field at the behest of ᶜAmm Ḏū DWNM"
(and-he-carried-out the-cultivation [of] the-field at-the-command [of] ᶜAmm Ḏū-DWNM)

S²YN

subst. *s²yntm* Q 844/11

DISHONOR [Ar *šāna* "to dishonor," *šayn* "dishonor"; cf. Sab *s²yn* "to suffer *physical injury, incapacity, disfigurement*"]

Q 844/9-11: *r*ṯ*ds¹ nfs¹s¹ wmqms¹ bn kl s²yntm*
"[HWFᵓL] has entrusted to his protection himself and his property from every dishonor"

S²Yᶜ

s¹t-prfx. *s¹ts²*ᶜ*m* Q 202/3

TO PROCLAIM [Cf. Ar *šā*ᶜ*a* "to spread out; become known"]

Q 202/3: *bn*ḏ*w s¹ts²*ᶜ*m ws¹ts³mkm bn qtbn*
"from this proclamation and guarantee on the part of the Qatabanians"

S²KM

subst. *ms²kmym* Q 902

ONE OF LOW BIRTH, BASE-BORN [Cf. Soq *miškim* "salaried men," Soq *škom* "to repay," Ar *šakama* "to repay, compensate"]

Q 902: *s¹lzmkm* ᵓ*b*ᶜ*l qbrn s²ymn bn s¹qbrbs¹ kl ms²kmym*
"the owners of the grave S²YMN have enjoined you not to bury anyone of base birth in it"
(have-enjoined-you the-owners [of] the-grave S²YMN from burying-in-it any base-born)

S²LṮ

card. num.[1] *s²l*ṯ*t* Q 74/8 (2x), Q 490A/4, B/4; *s²l*ṯ Q 52

THREE [Sab *s²l*ṯ, *s²l*ṯ*t*, "three," Ar ṯ*alā*ṯ, ṯ*alā*ṯ*a*, Heb *šālōš*, *šəlōšāh*, Akk *šalāši*, *šalāšti* id.]

THREE [Sab *s²l̠t*, *s²l̠tt*, "three," Ar *t̠alāt̠*, *t̠alāt̠a*, Heb *šālōš*, *šəlōšāh*, Akk *šalāši*, *šalāšti* id.]

(S²LT̠)

Q 74/8: *rbᶜ s²l̠tt ᵓbyt*

"a fourth of three houses"

card. num.² *s²l̠ty* Q 695/4-5

THIRTY [Ar *t̠alāt̠ūn* "thirty," Heb *šəlōšîm*, Syr *təlāt̠īn* id.]

Q 695/4-5: *s²l̠ty bqlm*

"thirty *bql*"

ord. num. *s²l̠tm* Q 694/14; *s²l̠ttm* Q 915/2

THIRD

Q 694/14: *ywmyt s²l̠tm d̠fqḥw d̠bs²mm*

"the date of the third of D̠ū FQḤW of the month D̠ū BS²MM"

S²MR

subst.¹ *s²mr* Q 35/2-3, Q 80/3, Q 240/2, Q 769/1b

POWER [Cf. Ar *šamara* "to exert oneself with power or ability"]

Q 769/1b: *wḥwkm d̠ᵓmr ws²mr*

"ḤWKM of the oracle and of power"

subst.² dl. *s²mry* Q 241/3, Q 265/3

VOTIVE OBJECT (?) [Thus Lundin, 1979, 107, 112-14, who discusses *s²mry* in detail and concludes that it must be understood as "*objet dédié*." According to Pirenne, CIAS 1:126, 128, *s²mr* means "*l'efficient, bienfaiteur*," with which she compares Heb *šōmēr* "guard"]

Q 241/1-3: *rt̠dᵓl bn mtᶜm bn s²ḥz s¹qny wfrᶜ lᶜm d̠rbḥw wnᶜmyn s²mry mwgln*

"RT̠Dᵓ L the son of MTᶜM the son of S²ḤZ made an offering and paid as tribute to ᶜAmm D̠ū RBḤW and NᶜMYN the this alabaster votive object (?)"

(RT̠DᵓL the-son [of] MTᶜM [of] the-clan S²ḤZ made-an-offering and-paying-as-tribute to-ᶜAmm D̠ū-RBḤW and-NᶜMYN votive-object [of] alabaster)

S²MS¹

subst. *s²ms¹* Q 89.142; *s²ms¹s¹* Q 73/4; *s²ms¹hw* Q 611/4; *s²ms¹hmw* Q 89.120

SUN (DEITY) [Sab *s²ms¹* "tutelary deity of clan or dynasty," Ar *šams*, Heb *šemeš*, Akk *šamšu* id.]

Q 89.120: *qyf s²ms¹hmw*

"the stela of their sun (deity)"

ENEMY [Sab *s²n'm* "enemy," Heb *śōnē'*, Moab *šn'* id.; cf. Ar *šana'a* "to hate," BibAram *śənā'*, Syr *sənā'* id.]

Q 840/8-9: *wḏs¹mwy lys¹ṯb kl s²n's¹my ws²n' ḏn qnyw wbqnyn*

"as for Ḏū S¹amāwī, may he deliver over every enemy of theirs and enemy of that which they have acquired and will acquire" (and-Ḏū-S¹amāwī may-he-deliver-over every their[dl.]-enemy and-enemy [of] that-which they-have-acquired and-will-acquire)

S²NṢ

subst. *s²nṣm* Q 11/3

CARE [Jamme, 1971, 57, compares Ar *šanaṣa* "to apply oneself with care to something"]

Q 11/3: *[…] s²nṣm nfs¹s¹ w w'[…]*

"[…] carefully himself and […]"

S²ʿB I

verb *s²ʿb* Q 248/3

TO MOVE, RECONSTITUTE [Pirenne, in CIAS 1:243, sees the opposing senses of the word in Ar *šaʿaba* "to scatter, separate; to gather, collect" as both relevant in the context of beekeeping, where bees are removed from one apiary and gathered at another]

Q 248/1-3: *'l'z bn ḍb'm bn mrn s¹ḥḏṯ l'ṯrt ws²ms¹ ywm s²ʿb mnḥlm*

"'L'Z son of ḌB'M of the clan MR when he moved the bee shed"

susbt. *s²ʿbm* Q 72/3(2x), Q 186A/24, B/21; *s²ʿbn* Q 40/3, 4, 5, 6, 8, Q 66/2 (2x), Q 72/1, Q 73/5, Q 74/1, 14, Q 79/2 Q 177/2, Q 695/2, Q 839/2, 4, 5, Q 914/1; *s²ʿbs¹m* Q 899/6; *s²ʿbhmw* Q 74/4; pl. *'s²ʿb* Q 74/11 *'s²ʿbm* Q 74/3, Q 78/3, Q 186A/13, 18, 21; *'s²ʿbn* Q 40/3, Q 679/6; *'s¹ʿbs¹m* Q 695/13; *s²ʿwb* Q 74/13

TRIBE, TRIBAL GROUP [Sab *s²ʿb* id.; cf. Ar *šaʿb* "people, nation, tribe." Beeston, 1972, 258, discusses the term as it applies to ancient South Arabian society, and notes that it refers to confederation or affiliation rather than kinship.]

A) Q 72/1: *s²hr hll … mlk qtbn s²ʿbn qtbn wḏʿls³n*

"S²HR HLL … king of Qataban, the tribe of Qataban, and Ḏū ʿLS³N

B) Q 74/14: *s²ʿbn ḏbḥn*

"the tribe ḎBḤN

S²ˁB II

subst. pl. *s²ˁwb* Q 74/13

CANAL [Cf. Ar *šiˁb* "watercourse, place in which water flows," Soq *śaˁab* "valley, wadi, gulf"]

Q 74/13: *wkl s²ˁwb ˁzˁz[…]*

"and all the canals of ˁZˁZ[…]'

S²FT

verb *s²fts¹* Q 483/3, Q 495/3; *s²ftns¹* Q 244/7, Q 246/6

TO PROMISE [Sab *s²ft* id.; see also Beeston, 1958, 216-17 for a further discussion of this word]

Q 495/2-4: *s¹qny ˀnby s²ymn brṣfm ṯlṯt ˀṣlmm ḏhbm hg s²fts¹ lˀlwds¹*

"[he] dedicated to ˀAnbay the patron in RṢFM three statues of bronze for his children as he promised him"

subst.¹ *s²ftm* Q 67/5, Q 68/4, Q 69/3, Q 70/2

PROTECTION [Cf. Sab *s²ft* "promise; vow; order." Perhaps there is a semantic development "promise, oracular decree">"protection"]

Q 67/5: *lˁṣm wdm wbntm ws²ftm lˁm wˀṯrt*

"[S²HR YGL has promulgated the formation of] a patronage-tie of friendship, affiliation, and protection to ˁAmm and ˀAṯirat"

subst.² *ts²fts¹* Q 681/3-4

PROMISE

Q 681/3-4: *hg ts²fts¹ ws¹ˀmnts¹*

"according to his promise and pledge"

S²QṢ

subst. (pl.?) *ms²qṣs¹m* Q 99/5

ROOM, SECTION, PART [Cf. Ar *šaqqaṣa* "to divide into parts or pieces, Ar *šiqṣ* "part or piece (of a thing)"]

Q 99/2-5: *brm s²ˀm wqny wbrˀ wẓrb byts¹ mrdˁm wˀḫṭbs¹ wṣrḥts¹ww wˀmtˁs¹m wnfs¹hys¹m wms²qṣs¹m*

"[… (son of) FLS¹ˀB] purchased, acquired, built, and dedicated his house MRDˁM and its lower stories and upper story and their guest chambers, roof terraces, and rooms"

(he-purchased and-acquiring and-building and-taking-possession-of his-house MRDˁM and-its-lower-stories and-its-upper-story and-their-guest-chambers and-their-roof terraces and-their-rooms)

S²QQ

h(s¹)-prfx. *hs²qw* Q 98/2

DIG UP [Cf. Ar *šaqqa* "to plow, till, break up"]

Q 98/1-2: *klybm wklbn lḥy wṣbᶜ [ ]t hs²qw whqs²b whqḥ kl q[br*

"KLYBM and KLBN LḤY and ṢBᶜ [ ]T have dug up, built, and completed the whole gr[ave]"

(KLYBM and-KLBN LHY and-ṢBᶜ [ ]T they-have-dug-up and-building and-completing the-whole gr[ave])

S²QR I

s¹-prfx. *s¹s²qr* Q Q 177/2, Q 181/2, Q 239/2, Q 240/4, Q 857/1

TO ERECT, CONSTRUCT a building [Sab *s²qr* id; cf. Akk *šaqāru*, *zaqāru* "to erect a wall," ModYem *mušgurī* "flower wreath worn on the head." Perhaps there is a semantic development "to build to the top">"to complete (a building);" *s¹s²qr* refers to the last state of building, constrasted with *s¹wṯr* "to lay the foundation"]

Q 177/1-2: *brʾw ws¹wṯr ws¹s²qr ḏn mḥfdn yḥḍr*

"[the tribe Ḏu HRBT] constructed, laid the foundation, and completed this tower YḤḌR"

(they-constructed and-laying-the-foundation and-completing this-tower YḤḌR

S²QR II

subst. *s²qr* Q 38/6, Q 39/4, Q 176/6, Q 700/7

BRIGHTNESS [Cf. Beeston, 1951b, 130-31, who suggests the basic meaning "to be bright" for this root in the Semitic languages, as well as for its metathesized form *s²rq*.]

Q 38/6: *wbᶜm ḏs²qr*

"by ᶜAmm the bright"

(and-by-ᶜAmm he-of-brightness)

S²RḤ

subst. *s²rḥm* Q 243/1

SAFETY; PROSPERITY [Cf. Sab *s²rḥtm* "safety; deliverance"; cf. Eth *šarḥa* "to cause to succeed," ModYem *šaraḥ* "to protect, guard")

Q 243/1-3: *s²rḥm w[w]fym ᶜs¹n wrwʾl wʾmlk qtbn lʾdms¹m wḏrᶜm wʾḥdb ws¹ᶜdm wlbns¹m*

"WRWʾL and the kings of Qataban have established prosperity and [se]curity for their subjects WḎRᶜM and ʾḤDB and S¹ᶜDM and for their children"

(S²RḤ)

(prosperity and-[se]curity have-established WRWʾL and-the-kings [of] Qataban for-their-subjects WḎRʿM and-ʾḤDB and-SʿDM and-for-their-children)

S²Rʿ

subst. *s²rʿs¹* Q 551/8, Q 916/3

JUST DUE, RIGHTS [Sab *s²rʿ* "rights, dues" Eth *šerʿat* id., Ar *šarʿ* "divine law; equal"]

Q 551/8: *s¹qnyw ʿm ryʿn ms³ndn wkl s²rʿs¹*

"[WDʾL, YSRM, and ṢBḤM] have dedicated to ʿAmm RYʿN this votive inscription and all his due"

(they-have-dedicated [to] ʿAmm RYʿN this-votive-inscription and-all his-due)

S²RQ

subst. *ms²rq* Q 694/12

EAST, EASTERN PART [Sab *ms²rq*, Ar *mašriq* id.]

Q 694/12: *lms²rq wllʿl*

"eastward and upward"

subst. *ms²rqytm* Q 265/3; *ms²rqytn* Q 73/5

1) EAST, EAST PART

Q 265/3: *ms²rqytm bnḏn bytn*

"east from this house"

2) DIRECTION OF THE RISING SUN

Q 73/5: *kl s²ʿbn ḏmḥrḏw wms²rqytn*

"every tribe of 'the lawgiver' and 'the rising sun'"

S²RS¹

subst. *s²rs¹m* Q 38/3-4, Q 102/3, Q 203/3, Q 265/4, Q 540/3, Q 696/3, Q 720/1, Q 770/5, Q 874/3-4, Q 899/2

FOUNDATION, BOTTOM [Sab *s²rs¹* "foundation," Min *ʾs²rs¹* "foundation (of a building)"; cf. Ar *širš* "root," Heb *šōreš*, Ug *šrš*, Ph *šrš*, Akk *šuršu* id.]

Q 540/2-3: *[y]s¹rn wʿḏds¹ ww rymt wrḥbt bn s²rs¹m ʿd frʿm*

"[Y]S¹RN and its deflector dam RYMT and RḤBT from the bottom to the top"

S^3

S^{3}WD I

subst. *ms^{3}wds^1* Q 3/2, Q 490A/2, 4, B/2, 3, Q 491/2, Q 556/3, Q 874/3, Q 903/3; *ms^{3}wdhw* Q 265/1; *ms^{3}wds^{1}m* Q 243/4, 5

1) RECEPTION ROOM, GUEST HALL of a house [Sab *ms^{3}wd* "hall; audience chamber, reception hall." The Qatabanian word has been variously translated as "fire altar," "incense-altar sanctuary," and "sacrificial altar," cf. Jamme 1958a, 185. Beeston, 1978, 195-97, questions the cultic associations with this word and prefers the rendering "guest hall, reception room," comparing the Heb *sôḏ* "council" and Eth *soda* "to burn."]

Q 265/2-3: *bythw yfs^2 wʾẖṭbhw wms^{3}wdhw wms^{1}qfth*

"[HWFʿM bought … and newly constructed] his house YFS^2 and its lower stories and its reception room and its arcades"

(his-house YFS^2 and-its-lower-stories and-its-reception-room and-its-arcades)

2) OUTER CHAMBER, GUEST CHAMBER of a tomb [Beeston, 1978, 196, notes that some South Arabian tombs have a central chamber, while "Nabataean tombs normally have an entrance chamber with installations designed for the holding of commemorative feasts by the relatives of the deceased"]

Q 490A/3-4: *wkwn lʾs^{2}hrm bn ḏt qbrn wms^{3}wds^1 wnfs^{1}hs^{1}yw s^{2}lṯt ʾẖms^{1}m wl s^{2}krm ws^{2}ʿbm ṯnw ẖms^{1}myw*

"three-fifths of this tomb and its outer chamber and inner chambers belong to ʾS^{2}HRM and two-fifths to S^{2}KRM and S^{2}ʿBM"

(and-was to-ʾS^{2}HRM from this tomb and-its-outer-chamber and-its-inner-chambers three fifths and-to S^{2}KRM and-S^{2}ʿBM two fifths)

S^{3}WD II

subst. *ms^{3}wdn* Q 40/1, 2, 5, 6, 8, 10, 11, 12, 13, 14, 15, 19; *ms^{3}wds^1* Q 203/2

LORDS, LORDS IN COUNCIL, COUNCIL OF LORDS [Sab *ms^{3}wd* "landlords (?)," cf. Ar *sāda* (w) "to be lord," Ar *sayyid* "lord," ModḤaḍ *musawwad* "lord." Beeston, 1951, 18, compares Heb *sôḏ* "council." However, see also Jamme, 1958a, 185.]

Q 40/8: *qtbn ms^{3}wdn wṭbnn*

"the Qatabanian lords and the landowners"

S^{3}WR

subst. pl. *ms^{3}wrs^{1}my* Q 174/4

SPOUTS [Cf. Eth *masāwer* "spouts," and see Beeston, 1951b, 129-30.]

Q 174/4: *...]s^{1}my wmswrs^{1}my w[...*

"and their[dl.] spouts"

S^{3}ḤR

s^1-prfx. *s^{1}s^{3}ḥr* Q 551/2, 3

TO MAKE A PRIEST [Denominative verb. For the etym. see the subst. below.]

Q 551/2-3: *ws^{1}s^{3}ḥr ys^{2}rm bnyhw ṣbḥm wṣdqm wʾbnm*

"YS^{2}RM made his sons ṢBḤM and ṢDQM and ʾBNM priests"

subst. *s^{3}ḥr* Q 35/4; *s^{3}ḥrw* Q 551/1

PRIEST [Cf. Sab *s^{3}ḥr* "talismanic stone," Ar *saḥr* "incantation," Ar *sāḥir* "enchanter, wizard"]

Q 35/3-4: *s^{3}ḥr wrby ʿm ryʿn*

"[S^{2}HR HLL] priest and *rby* of ʿAmm RYʿN"

S^{3}H̠L

subst. *sẖwl* Q 40/18

DUTY, OBLIGATION [Sab *s^{3}ẖl* "to be bound, bind oneself"]

Q 40/18: *nl ydʾwn wkwn s^{1}m ʾftḥn ʾw [w]mḥrtn wmnkṯs^{1}m s^{3}ẖwl wʿṣwb wnfwq wẖlwʿ wlkwʿ*

"let these ordinances or directives and the penalty for their violation be published and be a duty, obligation, requirement, and an abrogation of previous laws and a confirmation of current statutes"

(let go-forth and-being these ordinances or directives and-their-violation duties and obligations and-requirements and-abrogations and-confirmations)

S^{3}Lʾ

verb *s^{3}lʾt* Q 556bis/2, Q 557/1

TO OFFER AS A GIFT, DEDICATE [Sab *s^{3}lʾ* "to make over, hand over," Ar *salaʾa* "to pay"]

Q 556bis/2: *s^{3}lʾt bntyʾl ʿd ʾmr*

"[LBʾ] dedicated [a gift] to the (two) daughters of ʾL in ʾMR"

S^{3}MD

subst. pl. *s^{3}md* 687/9; *s^{3}mdt* Q 687/1

DIGNITARIES [Cf. perhaps Ar *samada* "to be lofty, elevated"]

Q 687/1: *s^{3}mdt s^{1}ʿdm yhs^{1}kr bn ḥṣbḥ*
"the dignitaries of S^{1}ʿDM YHS^{1}KR of the clan HṢBḤ"

S^{3}MK

verb *ys^{3}mk* Q 202/2

TO UNDERTAKE [Cf. Sab *s^{3}mk* "to raise, sustain," Eth *asmaka* "to prop up, support," Ar *samaka* "to raise, lift up (an edifice)" Heb *sāmaḵ* "to lean, support," Syr *səmaḵ* "to support, sustain, uphold"]

Q 202/2: *wḏtw ṭhrgn ʾs^{1}dm ys^{3}mk bn t[…*
"and (according to) this directive a man will undertake from T[…"

s^{1}t-prfx. *s^{1}ts^{3}mkm* Q 202/3

TO GUARANTEE [Sense according to context]

Q 202/3: *bnḏw s^{1}ts^{2}ʿm ws^{1}ts^{3}mkm bn qtbn*
"from this proclamation and guarantee on the part of the Qatabanians"

S^{3}ND

subst. *ms^{3}ndn* Q 551/8, Q 858/3

INSCRIPTION; VOTIVE PLAQUE, VOTIVE TABLET bearing an inscription [Sab *ms^{3}ndn* id., Ar *musnad* "Old South Arabian script"]

Q 551/8: *s^{1}qnyw ʿm ryʿn ms^{3}ndn wkl s^{2}rʿs^{1}*
"[WDʾL, YS^{2}RM, and ṢBḤM] have dedicated to ʿAmm RYʿN this votive inscription and all his due"
(they-have-dedicated [to] ʿAmm RYʿN this-votive inscription and-all his-due)

S^{3}NḤ I

subst./partcp. *s^{3}nḥm* Q 73/6; *s^{3}nḥn* Q 40/6, 9

ONE WHO INJURES, CAUSES MISFORTUNE [Cf. Ar *sanaḥa* "to render wretched, miserable"]

Q 73/6: *bnkl ẖs^{3}s^{3}m wẖblm ws^{3}nḥm wms^{1}fʾym wms^{1}nkrm bn ʾbrṯs^{1}m*
"against any who would harm, damage, deface, destroy, or remove them from their places"
(from-every one-who-harms and-one-who-damages and-one-who-defaces and-one-who-destroys and-one-who-removes from their-places)

S^{3}NḤ II

subst. *s^{3}nḥm* Q 40/4

SHOWING GOODWILL [Cf. Ar *sunḥ* "prosperity, good fortune, good luck"]

Q 40/4: *ḫlṣmʾy ws^{3}nḥm*

"in sincerity and with goodwill"

S^{3}NN

verb *s^{3}n* Q 83/6

TO BE LAWFUL, PERMITTED [Sab *s^{3}n* id., cf. Ar *sanna* "to enact a law or custom," Ar *sunna* "customary procedure or action"; J. Ryckmans, 1953, 343-57, discusses this passage and others in which the phrase *wʾl sn* is used.]

Q 83/5-7: *wʾl s^{3}n s^{1}wḥs^{3}s^1 bn brṯs^1*

"and it is not permitted to remove it from its place"

(and-not permitted its-removal from its-place)

S^{3}FL

subst. *s^{3}fln* Q 186B/22-23

PLATEAU, TABLELAND [See Beeston, 1971b, 5, who compares this with Heb *sēpel* "bowl, dish, platter." Against Höfner and others, he does not consider this word to be related to *s^{1}flm* "lowland," in Q 40/17 and Sab *s^{1}flthmy* id., in R 3966/10, since he does not think "at this early date we could already encounter confusion" between *s^1* and *s^3* (however, cf. *s^{3}n* "to be lawful, permitted," in Q 83/6 with *s^{1}nt* "to observe a regulation or ordinance," in Q 695/8, both of which appear to be cognate with Ar *sanna* "to enact a law or custom; to observe such and such a rule or ordinance.")]

Q 186B/21-23: *[b]n ʿm nkr s^{2}ʿbm nb bʿm qtbn wb ʿm s^{3}fln*

"with another tribe instead of with Qataban and the tableland"

T

TBʿ

s^1-prfx. *s^{1}tbʿ* Q 102/3, Q 240/4, Q 860/2

TO COMPLETE [Cf. Sab (R 4069/8) *tbʿt* "completion, extension," Ar *tābaʿa* "to make work sound or free from defect"]

Q 102/2-3: *brʾw ws^{1}wṯr ws^{1}tbʿ [byts^1]m*

"they built, laid the foundation, and completed th[eir house]"

TḤT

prep. *tḥthw* Q 677/7, Q 678/3, Q 679/7

UNDER, BENEATH [Sab *tḥt*, Ar *taḥta*, Heb *taḥat* id.]

Q 679/6-7: *brʾw whqḥ mʾglyhmw ylgb wḏtḥthw yhlgb*

"they built and set in order their two cisterns, YLGB and the one which is beneath it, YHLGB"

prep. + prep. *bn tḥt.*

See entry under BN I.

TLW

s¹-prfx. *s¹tlwt* Q 898/9

TO BEAR RESPONSIBILITY FOR someone's SAFETY [Ghul, 1959, 6, compares the Ar *ʾatlāʾhu ḏimma* "he gave him a bond or an obligation whereby he became responsible for his safety."]

Q 898/7-9: *wʾmrʾs¹ rs²ww ywm drf wntṣf … ʾrb[ʿ]t wḫms¹y ḫrwf s¹tlwt*

"and his lords were paid their dues when he selected and paid out … fifty-fo[ur] sheep for their bearing responsibility for (his) safety"

(and-his-lords they-were-paid when he-selected and-he-paid … fo[ur] and-fifty sheep bearing-responsibility-for-safety)

TLF

subst. *tlf* Q 40/20; *tlf[ ]m* Q 165/5

DAMAGE, LOSS [Sab *tlft* "ruin, perishing," Sab *tlftm* "loss, loss of life," Ar *talafa* "to perish, pass away," Ar *talaf* "loss, ruin"]

Q 166/5: *kl bʾs¹tm wtlf[ ]m*

"every damage and loss"

TS¹ʿ

card. num. *ts¹ʿn* Q 8/3-4, Q 40/22

NINE [Sab *ts¹ʿ*, Ar *tisʿ* id.]

Q 8/1, 3-4: *rdʾ lʾṯrt ts¹ʿn bḥtn*

[(ʿ)BDʾL MʿDN) vowed to ʾAṯirat nine votive objects

Ṯ

ṮBR

subst. *mṯbr* Q 687/4

RUIN [Sab *mṯbr* "damage; rupture; rout"]

Q 687/4: *wnqb hs¹gf bmṯbr ṯwyfm*

"he bored a hole (for runoff water) and built a roof over the ruin ṮWYFM"

ṮWB

verb *ṯwb* Q 66/4; Q 857/2; *ṯwbw* Q 177/3, Q 914/3

1) TO SUCCEED [Cf. Ar *ṯāba* (w) "to return"]

Q 66/4: *wṯwb ʾḫs¹ lḏn tḥrgn*

"[when he completes two years] and another succeeds to this administration"

2) TO OFFER

Q 177/3: *bn mṯbm ṯwbw lʾls¹m ʿm*

"from the offering which they made to their god ʿAmm"

s¹(h)-prfx. *s¹ṯb* Q 40/1, 15, 16; *s¹ṯbw* Q 840/6; *ys¹ṯb* Q 40/13, Q 840/8; *hṯb* Q 74/1

1) TO DECREE [Cf. Ar *ṯawwaba* "to call, summon to prayer and to other things"]

Q 40/1: *[ḥgkm] ftḥw ws¹ṯb ws¹ḫr s²hr ygl yhrgb bn hwfʿm mlk qtbn wqtbn ms³wdn gw*

"[thus] S²HR YGL YHRGB the son of HWFʿM, king of Qataban, and the Qatabanian lords assembled, have initiated, decreed, and directed"

2) TO DELIVER, TURN OVER

Q 840/8-9: *wḏs¹mwy lys¹ṯb kl s²nʾs¹my ws²nʾ ḏn qnyw wbqnyn*

"as for Ḏū S¹amāwī, may he deliver over every enemy of theirs and enemy of that which they have acquired and will acquire" (and-Ḏū-S¹amāwī may-he-deliver-over every their[dl.]-enemy and-enemy [of] that-which they-have-acquired and-will-acquire)

t-infix *ṯtwb* Q 66/8

TO ADHERE

Q 66/8: *wkwmw lyṣḥf wḥrg wʿtqb wṯtwb ḏn ṣḥfn ʾrbym byrby ʿm ḏlbḫ*

"and thus let (all) whom ʿAmm Ḏū Labaḫ chooses as *ʾrby* write down, administer, implement, and adhere to this agreement"
(and-thus let-him-write-down and-administering and-implementing and-adhering [to] this agreement the-*ʾrby* he-makes-*ʾrby* ʿAmm Ḏū-Labaḫ)

subst.[1] *ṯwbk* Q 687/6
ABODE [Cf. Ar *maṯāba* "place of assembly"]
Q 687/6: *ṯwbk ʾrḥb bmḥrr ṯwyʿn*
"this abode ʾRḤB in the (stony) land ṮWYʿN"

subst.[2] *mṯbm* Q 177/3, 4, Q 914/3
OFFERING, GIFT
Q 177/3: *bn mṯbm ṯwbw lʾls¹m ʿm*
"from the offering which they made to their god ʿAmm"

ṮWR
subst. sing. *ṯwr[m]* Q 173/4; pl. *ʾṯwr* Q 687/7
STEER, BULL [Sab *ṯwr, ṯr,* Ar *ṯawr,* Heb *šôr,* Akk *šūru* id.]
Q 173/4: *wẓlʿ ḏʾyd ẓlʿ ṯwr[m]*
"Ḏū ʾYD paid the penalty of a steer"

ṮLṮ
card. num. *ṯlṯt* Q 495/2, Q 690a/11
THREE [Sab *ṯlṯ, ṯlṯt* "three"; cf. also *s²lṯ*]
Q 495/2-3: *ṯlṯt ʾṣlmm ḏhbm*
"three statues of bronze"

ṮMN I
card. num. *ṯmnt* Q 73/3
EIGHT [Sab *ṯmny, ṯmnyt* "eight," *ṯmn, ṯmnt,* Ar *ṯamanin, ṯamaniya,* Heb *šəmôneh, šəmônāh,* Akk *samānū, samāntū* id.]
Q 73/3: *ṯmnt ʾʾlfm bqlm*
"eight thousand plots of land"

ṮMN II
subst. *mṯmn* Q 695/4
EXTENT; VALUE [Cf. Ar *ṯaman* "price value"]
Q 695/4-5: *wkwn tqbl kl ʾrḍn kwḥd mṯmn wmfẓr ws²lṯy bqlm ws¹bʿt wʿs²ry ʾqblm*
"the size of the whole land together in value and extent is thirty *bql* and twenty-seven *qbl*"

(ṮMN II)

(and-is the-dimension [of] all the-land together value and-extent both-thirty *bql* and-seven and-twenty *qbl*)

ṮMR

subst. *ṯmr* Q 67/11

FRUIT, CROPS(S) [Sab *ṯmr* "crops," Ar *ṯamar* "fruit, yield," ModYem *ʾaṯmar* "cereal crops." Beeston, 1971b, 11, translates *ṯmr* at Q 67/11 "arable land"]

Q 67/11: *ws²wb wṯmr ʿm*

"produce and crops of ʿAmm"

ṮN(W/Y)

card. num. *ṯny* Q 696/4; *ṯty* Q 679/8

TWO [Sab *ṯny*, *ṯnty*, *ṯty* "two," Ar *iṯnāni*, *iṯnatāni*, Heb *šənayim*, *šətayim*, Akk *šinā*, *šittēn* id.]

Q 696/4: *ṣllhw ṯny ṣllmyw*

"he paved it with two layers of paving stone"

ord. num. *ṯntm* Q 35/3-4

SECOND [Sab masc. *ṯny*, fem. *ṯnty* id., and see Bron, 1987, 24-25, for a discussion of this form]

Q 35/3-4: *qẓr qyn rs²w ʿmm ṯntm*

"administrator of the money offerings, attendant, and *rs²w* for the second year"

subst. *ṯnw* Q 74/10, Q 490A/4, B/4

HALF (fraction)

Q 74/10: *wṯnw nḫlmyw*

"half of a palmgrove"

adv. *ṯnym* Q 40/7

SECOND TIME [Sab *ṯnytm* id.]

Q 40/7: *ṯnym mqmm*

"a second time in (their) meeting"

ṮʿD

verb *ṯʿd* Q 66/4

TO USE AS AN ALLOTMENT [See Lundin, 1987, 53-55, for a discussion of the occurrences and meanings of this root in the ESA dialects]

Q 66/4-5: *wl yqny wṯʿd ḏm byḥrg ḏn ṣḥfn … ʿs²r kl hnʾm wmwblm*

"let the one who administers this agreement acquire and use as his allotment ... a tenth of all crops watered by irrigation and by rain"
(and-let acquire and-using he-who administers this agreement ... a-tenth [of] every irrigated-crop and-rain-watered-crop)

ṮFṬ

verb *ṯfṭ* Q 40/15, Q 66/10, Q 67/8, Q 68/7, Q 69/5, Q 70/3 Q 243/8; *byṯfṭ* Q 202/4; *byṯfṭs*^{1} Q 78/5

TO DECIDE, DIRECT [Cf. Sab *ṯfṭ* "judgment, decision," Heb *šāp̱aṭ* "to judge, determine, settle a dispute," Ug *ṯfṭ* "to judge, decide," Akk *šapāṭu* "to decide"]

Q 66/10-11: *wṯfṭ s*^{2}*hr ʾrby ʿm ḏlbẖ lftẖ ws*^{1}*ṭr ḏtn ʾs*^{1}*ṭrn*

"S^{2}HR directed the *ʾrby* of ʿAmm Ḏū Labaẖ to inscribe and engrave these inscriptions"
(and-directed S^{2}HR the-*ʾrby* [of] ʿAmm Ḏū-Labaẖ to-inscribe and-engraving these inscriptions)

subst. *ṯfṭm* Q 66/5; pl. *ʾṯfṭ* Q 40/5; *ʾṯfṭm* Q 40/10, 14; *ʾṯfṭn* Q 40/16

DECISION, JUDGMENT

Q 40/4-5: *wʾy ftḥ ws*^{1}*ḥr ʾftḥ wmḥrtm wʾṯfṭ wẖwlltm ws*^{1}*ṭ s*^{1}*wt mqmn*

"whatever directives, orders, judgments, and decisions which [the Qatabanian lords and landowners] have directed and ordered in that meeting"
(and-whatever order and-directing directives and-orders and-judgments and-decisions in that meeting)

ṮQL

subst. pl. *ṯqwls*^{1}*m* Q 73/2

ACCOUTREMENTS, HANGING PARAPHERNALIA [Cf. Eth *saqala* "to hang, be suspended"]

Q 73/2: *wkl ʾbʾrs*^{1}*m wṯqwls*^{1}*m wmʾtws*^{1}*m wbnys*^{1}*m*

"and all their wells and their accoutrements, channels, and buildings"
(and-all their-wells and-their-hanging-paraphernalia and-their-channels and-their buildings)

APPENDIX A

GENERAL ABBREVIATIONS

abbrv.	abbreviation
adj.	adjective
adv.	adverb
card.	cardinal
cf.	compare
coll.	collective
comp.	compound
conj.	conjunction
D	verb stem with doubled second radical (cf. Ar *faʿʿala*)
def.	definite
dem.	demonstrative
dl.	dual
encl.	enclitic
esp.	especially
etym.	etymology
fem.	feminine
fig.	figure(s)
G	simple verb stem (Qat *fʿl*; cf. Ar *faʿala*)
h-stem	morphological equivalent of s^1-prfx.
id.	the same meaning
indef.	indefinite
inf.	infinitive
impf.	imperfect
L	verb stem with long vowel in first syllable (cf. Ar *faʿala*)
masc.	masculine
N	verb stem with n-prfx. (cf. Ar *infaʿala*, Heb *nipʿal*)
neg.	negative, negation
nom.	nominative
non-nom.	non-nominative
num.	numeral
ord.	ordinal
p.	page(s)
partcp.	participle
perf.	perfect
pl.	plural; plate
prep.	preposition

prfx.	prefix
pro.	pronoun
prt.	particle
pt.	part
q.v.	which see
rel.	relative
sing.	singular
subst.	substantive
suf.	suffix
s.v.	under the word
s^1-prfx.	verb stem with s^1-prfx. (cf. Ar *ʾafʿala*, Heb *hipʿîl*)
s^1t-prfx.	verb stem with s^1t-prfx. (cf. Ar *istafʿala*)
t-infix	verb stem with t-infix (cf. Ar *iftaʿala*)
t-prfx.	verb stem with t-prfx. (cf. Ar *tafaʿʿala, tāfaʿala*)
var.	variation
vol.	volume

APPENDIX B

ABBREVIATIONS OF LANGUAGES AND DIALECTS

Akk	Akkadian
Amh	Amharic
Ar	Classical Arabic
Aram	Aramaic
BibAram	Biblical Aramaic
CollAr	Colloquial Arabic
Cop	Coptic
ComSem	Common Semitic
Daṯ	Daṯina
Dof	Dofari (MSA dialect)
Eg	Egyptian
Eng	English
ESA	Epigraphic South Arabian
Eth	Classical Ethiopic (Geʿez)
Gk	Greek
Gur	Gurage
Ḥaḍ	Ḥaḍrami (ESA dialect)
Ḥar	Ḥarsūsi (MSA dialect)
Heb	Biblical Hebrew
Him	Himyarite
ImpAram	Imperial Aramaic
JewAram	Jewish Aramaic
Lat	Latin
Liḥ	Liḥyanite
Mand	Mandaic
Meh	Mehri (MSA dialect)
Min	Minaean (ESA dialect)
MishHeb	Mishnaic Hebrew
Moab	Moabite
ModḤaḍ	Modern Ḥaḍrami (MSA dialect)
ModYem	Modern Yemeni (MSA dialect)
MSA	Modern South Arabian
Nab	Nabataean
OAram	Old Aramaic
Om	Omani (MSA dialect)

Palm	Palmyrene
Ph	Phoenician
Qat	Qatabanian
Sab	Sabaean (ESA dialect)
Saf	Safaitic
Śḥ	Śḥeri (MSA dialect)
Soq	Soqotri (MSA dialect)
Syr	Syriac
Tham	Thamudic
Tig	Tigre
Tña	Tigriña
Ug	Ugaritic

APPENDIX C

LIST OF ABBREVIATIONS APPEARING IN APPENDIX D

In this list of abbreviations I have generally adopted the relevant abbreviations found in Harding, 1971, ix-xxxiii.

AM	Aden Museum registration numbers. Numbers preceded by 60 were formerly in the Muncherjee Collection
AP	Aden Protectorates, texts copied by C. H. Inge
Ash	Ashmolean Museum, Oxford, registration numbers
ASS	M. Höfner, "Altsüdarabische Stelen und Statuetten," in *Festschrift für den Frankfurter Ethnologen Ad. E. Jensen*, Eike Haberland, Meinhard Schuster, and Helmut Straube, eds. (Munich: K. Renner, 1964), p. 217-32
B	Berlin Museum registration numbers
BAD	Bowen, Richard L. Jr., and Frank P. Albright, *Archaeological Dicoveries in South Arabia* (Baltimore: Johns Hopkins University Press, 1958)
Bal	Inscription acquired by F. Balsan
Bard	Texts collected by P. Bardey for the Musée du Louvre
BBSIS	W. L. Brown and A. F. L. Beeston, "Sculptures and Inscriptions from Shabwa," *JRAS* (1954): 43-62
BEAG	A. F. L. Beeston, "Epigraphic and Archaeological Gleanings from South Arabia," *OrAnt* 1(1962): 41-52
BEQ	François Bron, "A propos de l'éponymie qatabanite," in *Ṣayhadica*, Christian Robin and Muḥammad Bāfaqīh, eds. (Paris: Paul Geuthner, 1987), p. 21-27
Besse	A. Besse collection
BH	Bellerby-Habban collection
BHI	J. Bird, "Himyaric Inscriptions from Aden and Saba," *Journal of the Bombay Branch of the Royal Asiatic Society* 8(1844): 30-40
BM	British Museum registration numbers
BMus	Bayḥān Museum registration numbers
BNL	A. F. L. Beeston, "Notes on Old South Arabian Lexicography," I-XII, in *Mus* 63-94
Bom	Bombay Museum registration numbers
BSM	Baroda State Museum
BQ	A. F. L. Beeston, *Qahtan: Studies in Old South Arabian Epigraphy* I: 1959; II: 1971 (London: Luzac and Co.)

CIAS *Corpus des inscriptions et antiquités sud-arabes* (Louvain: Editions Peeters, 1977-86). Vol. 1 in 3 parts; vol. 2

ClASAN R. L. Cleveland, *An Ancient South Arabian Necropolis, Objects from the Second Campaign (1951) in the Timnaʿ Cemetery.* (Baltimore: Johns Hopkins University Press, 1965)

Cohen M. Cohen, *Documents sudarabiques* (Paris: Adrien-Maisonneuve, 1934)

CRC C. Conti Rossini, *Chrestomathia arabica meridionalis epigraphica, edita et glossario instructa* (Rome: Istituto per l'Oriente, 1931)

CRE ---, *Storia d'Etiopia* (Milan: Officina d'arte grafica, 1928)

CRI ---,"Iscrizioni sabee," *Rendiconti della Accademia dei Lincei. Classe di scienze morali, storiche e filologiche.* Ser. 6, Vol. 1(1925): 169-93

CRR ---, "Dalle rovine di Ausan," *Dedalo* 7(1927): 727-54

CUM Cambridge University Museum registration numbers

Denny A. R. Denny collection

DoCA D. B. Doe, "The Site of ʾAmʿadiya near Mukeiras, on the Audhali Plateau, South West Arabia," *Aden* 2(1963): 1-12

DoF Six sheets of D. B. Doe's facsimiles of South-Arabian rock inscriptions

DoSA D. B. Doe, *Southern Arabia* (London: Thames and Hudson, 1971)

DoWS ---, "The Wadi Shirjan," *Bulletin Nr. 4, Department of Antiquities Report, 1961-1963* (Aden, 1964)

Ferris R. E. Ferris collection

Folkard Folkard collection

Foster Giraud V. Foster collection

GA A. Grohmann, *Arabien* (Munich: C. H. Beck, 1963)

GB Texts collected by N. Groom in Wadi Bayḥān

GG A. Grohmann, *Göttersymbole und Symboltiere aus südarabischen Denkmälern. DSAWW* 58:1(1914)

GKH ---, "Ḳatabanische Herrscherreihen," *AAWW* 53(1916): 41-49

Gl Eduard Glaser collection

GlN E. Glaser, *Altjemenische Nachrichten* (Munich: G. Franz, 1906)

GlS E. Glaser, *Skizze der Geschichte und Geographie Arabiens* II (Berlin: Weidmannsche Buchhandlung, 1890)

GlSt ---, *Altjemenische Studien. MVÄG* 28:2(1923)

Graf S. U. Graf collection

GUB	H. Grimme, "Aus unedierten südarabischen Inschriften des Berliner Staatsmuseums," *Mus* 45(1932): 91-116
H	Second expedition at Hajar bin Ḥumeid
HAA	D. Nielsen, *Handbuch der altarabischen Altertumskunde* (Copenhagen: Arnold Busck, 1927)
HAF	M. Hartman, *Die arabische Frage.* Vol. II in *Der islamische Orient* (Leipzig: R. Haupt, 1909)
HalES	J. Halévy, "Études sabéenes," *JA* 7e sér. 1(1873): 434-521; 2(1873): 305-65, 388-93; 4(1874): 497-505
HalS	---, "Six inscriptions sabéenes inédites," *Revue Sémitique* 16(1908):293-97
Ham	R. A. B. Hamilton collection
HAuf	F. Hommel, *Aufsätze und Abhandlungen arabistisch-semitologischen Inhalts* I-III (Munich: G. Franz, 1892-1901)
HBH	*Hajar bin Ḥumeid. Investigations at a Pre-Islamic Site in South Arabia* (Baltimore: Johns Hopkins University Press, 1969)
HChr	---, *Südarabische Chrestomathie* (Munich: G. Franz, 1893)
HEA	A. M. Honeyman, "Epigraphic South Arabian Antiquities," *JNES* 21(1962): 38-43
HI	First expedition at Hajar bin Ḥumeid
HK	Hagr Koḥlan
HMus	Hamburg Museum registration numbers
HN	Maria Höfner, "Neuinterpretation zweier altsüdarabischer Inschriften," in *Ṣayhadica,* Christian Robin and Muḥammad Bāfaqīh, eds. (Paris: Paul Geuthner, 1987), 37-46, pl. 4, 5
Höf	—, "Eine qatabanische Weihinschrift aus Timna^{c}," *Mus* 74(1961): 453-59
Hole	D. H. Müller, "Mitteilung von einem sabäischen Steine mit figuralen Darstellungen im Besitze des Zivilgouverneurs von Rhodesia, Sir Marshall Hole, B. A. in Bulawayo," *AAWW* 40(1903): 20-23.
HomEth	F. Hommel, *Ethnologie und Geographie des Alten Orients* (Munich: C. H. Beck, 1926)
HomLan	F. Hommel, editor of squeezes of inscriptions taken by the Comte de Landberg in HAuf II
HRh	M. Höfner and N. Rhodokanakis, "Zur Interpretation altsüdarabischer Inschriften III," *WZKM* 43(1936): 211-34
HS	M. Hartmann, "Südarabisches," I-IX, in *OLZ* 10(1907), 11(1908)
HSG	M. Höfner, *Die Sammlung Eduard Glasser. SBAWW* 222(1944): 5. Abhandlung

HSH ---,"Eine südarabische Handelsinschrift," *Forschungen und Fortschritte* 10(1934): 274-75

HW ---, "Die ḳatabanischen und sabäischen Inschriften der südarabischen Expedition im Kunsthistorischen Museum in Wien," *WZKM* 42(1935): 31-36.

IB Texts copied by C. H. Inge in Wadi Bayḥān

Ist Istanbul Museum registration numbers

J Texts edited by A. Jamme

JAden A. Jaussen, "Inscriptions copiées à Aden," *RB* 23(1915): 569-73

JAF A. Jamme, "Antiquités funéraires épigraphiques qatabanites," *Cahiers de Byrsa* 7 (1957): 189-95

JaIRM A. Jamme, "Les inscriptions rupestres de la région de Mukérâs," *Bulletin de l'Acdémie Royale de Belgique. Classe des Lettres et des Sciences morales et politiques.* 5e ser. 37(1951): 307-20

JaMAR ---, *Miscellanées d'ancient* (sic) *arabe* II (Washington, 1971); III (Washington, 1972)

James T. James collection

JASI A. Jamme, "An Archaic South-Arabian Inscription in Vertical Columns," *BASOR* 137 (1955): 32-38

JaTAQ ---, "Trois antiquités qatabanites en bronze Ja 886-888," *OrAnt* 2(1963): 133-35

JaYE *Yemen Expedition. Carnegie Museum 1974-75* (Pittsburgh: Carnegie Museum of Natural History, 1976)

JDA ---,"Deux autels à encens de l'Université de Harvard," *BiOr* 10(1953): 94-95

JDS ---, "Documentation sud-arabe, I et II," *RSO* 38 (1963): 303-22

JIH A. Jaussen, "Inscriptions himyarites," *RB* 35(1926): 548-82

JIR A. Jamme, "Inscription rupestre et graffites qatabanites photographiés par le Major M. D. van Lessen," *RSO* 37 (1962): 231-41

JP J. Pirenne collection

JPE A. Jamme, *Pièces épigraphiques de Ḥeid bin ʿAqil, la nécropole de Timnaʿ (Hagr Koḥlan)* (Louvain: Publications universitaires, 1952)

JPEQ ---, "Les pierres épigraphiques qatabanites Lyon 818 bis et ter," *Cahiers de Byrsa* 7 (1957): 205-17

JPIM —, "Pre-Islamic Arabian Miscellanea," in *Al-Hudhud: Festschrift Maria Höfner zum 80. Geburtstag*, Roswitha G. Stiegner, ed. (Graz: Karl-Franzens-Universität, 1981)

JPQ	---, "Pièces qatabanites et sabéenes d'Aden," *Anadolu Araştırmaları* 1 (1955): 117-26
JQB	—, "A Qatabanian Votive Lamp Offering," *BiOr* 27(1970): 178-79
JQDI	---, "A Qatabanian Dedicatory Inscription," *JAOS* 75(1955): 97-99
JQI	---, *Quatre inscriptions sud-arabes.* Washington, mimeographed publication, 1957
JR WBrashear	Jacques Ryckmans-William Brashear inscription numbers
JSA	---, "South-Arabian Antiquities in the U.S.A.," *BiOr* 12 (1955): 152-54
JSAC	---, "The South-Arabian Collection of the University Museum (Cambridge, England), Documentation sud-arabe, IV," *RSO* 40 (1965): 43-55
JSI	---, "South Arabian Inscriptions," in J. B. Pritchard, ed., *Ancient Near Eastern Texts,* 3rd ed. (Princeton: Princeton University Press, 1974)
JSQI	---, "Some Qatabanian Inscriptions Dedicating 'Daughters of God,'" *BASOR* 138 (1955): 39-47
Kalli	Ioannes Kallisperis collection
Lake	Texts in the Lake Library, Aden
Land	C. Landberg collection
LB	Mayer Lambert, "Les inscriptions yémenites du Musée de Bombay," *RAA* 20(1923): 72-78
LE	M. Lidzbarski, *Ephemeris für semitische Epigraphik* I-III (Giessen: J. Ricker, 1901-1915)
Leg	L. Legrain, "Au pays de la reine de Saba," *Gazette des Beaux-Arts* 6e per., T. XI 76e année (1934): 65-85
LIQ	A. G. Lundin, "L'inscription qatabanite du Louvre AO 21.124," *Raydān* 2(1979): 107-19
Lo	Musée du Louvre registration numbers
Louvain	See G. Ryckmans in "Un sceau avec inscription sud-arabe," *Mus* 34(1921): 115
LQS	L. Legrain, "In the Land of the Queen of Sheba," *American Journal of Archaeology* 38(1934): 329-37
Lyon	Muséum d'histoire naturelle, Lyon, registration numbers
M	D. H. Müller, "Anzeigernotiz über ein neuentdecktes sabäisches Bas-Relief mit Inschrift," *AAWW* 40(1903): 113-15
MAG	M. A. Ghul, "New Qatabani Inscriptions," *BSOAS* 22(1959): 1-22; 419-38

Marg	D. S. Margoliouth, "Two South Arabian Inscriptions Edited from Rubbings in the Possession of Major-General Sir Neill Malcolm," *Proceedings of the British Academy* (1924-25): 177-85
MATG	"Die angeblichen 'Töchter Gottes' im Licht einer neuen qatabanischen Inschrift," *NESE* 2(1974): 145-48.
MM	J. H. Mordtmann and E. Mittwoch, *Sabäische Inschriften* (Hamburg: Friedrichsen, De Gruyter, 1931)
MMA	J. H. Mordtmann and E. Mittwoch, "Altsüdarabische Inschriften," *Or* 1(1932): 24-33, 116-28, 257-73; 2(1932): 50-60; "Bemerkungen zu altsüdarabischen Inschriften," *Or* 3(1934):42-62
MMH	J. H. Mordtman and E. Mittwoch, *Himjarische Inschriften in den staatlichen Museen zu Berlin. MVÄG* 37:1(1932)
Mont	J. A. Montgomery, "An Enactment of Fundamental Constitutional Law in Old South Arabic," *Proceedings of the American Philosophical Society* 67(1928): 207-13
MSO	E. Mittwoch and H. Schlobies, "Altsüdarabische Inschriften im Hamburgischen Museum für Völkerkunde," *Or* 5(1936): 1-34, 278-93, 349-57; 6(1937): 83-100, 222-23, 305-16; 7(1938): 95-99, 233-38, 343-54
Muk	Mukerâs
MWQ	"Weitere qatabanische und hadramitische Stuecke der Sammlung Graf," *NESE* 2(1974): 149-53.
Mun	Squeezes sent by Glaser to Munich
NAM	New Aden Museum registration numbers
NEnv	J. and H. Derenbourg, Nouveaux envois du Yemen," *Revue Archéologique* (1903): 407-12
NKI	D. Nielsen, *Neue ḳatabanische Inschriften und der Vokalbuchstabe h im Minäischen. MVÄG* 11:4(1906)
NS	---, *Studier over Oldarabiske Inskrifter* (Copenhagen: Det Schonbergske Forlag, 1906)
NTY	H. Derenbourg, "Nouveaux textes yémenites inédits, publiés et traduits," *RAA* 5(1903): 117-28
NYU	New York University registration number
Os	E. Osiander, "Zur himjarischen Altertumskunde, aus seinem Nachlasze herausgeg. von Prof. Dr. M. A. Levy," *ZDMG* 19(1865): 159-293; 20(1866): 205-87
P	S. Perowne collection
PCE	J. Pirenne, "Contribution a l'épigraphie sudarabique," *Semitica* 16(1966): 73-99
Penn	Pennsylvania Museum registration numbers

Per	S. Perowne, comments at the end of F. Stark, "Some Pre-Islamic Inscriptions on the Frankincense Route in Southern Arabia," *JRAS* (1939): 480-98
PLH	J. Pirenne, "Une législation hydrologique en Arabie due Sud antique," in *Hommages à André Dupont-Sommer* (Paris: Adrien-Maisonneuve, 1971)
PN	F. B. Prideaux, "Himyaric Inscriptions Lately Discovered near Sanʿa in Arabia," *Transactions of the Society of Biblical Archaeology* 4(1876): 196-202; "Notes on the Himyaritic Inscriptions Contained in the Museum of the Bombay Branch of the Royal Asiat. Society," *Transactions of the Society of Biblical Archaeology* 6(1879): 305-15
PNA	J. Pirenne, "Notes d'archéologie sud-arabe," *Syria* 37(1960): 326-47; 39(1962): 257-62
PPS	---, *Paléographie des inscriptions sud-arabes. Contribution à la chronologie et à l'histoire de l'Arabie du Sud antique* (Brussels: Palais der Academien, 1956)
PQS	W. Phillips, *Qataban and Sheba* (New York: Harcourt Brace, 1955)
PR	J. Pirenne, "RShW, RShWT, FDY, FDYT and the Priesthood in Ancient South Arabia," *PSAS* 6(1976): 137-44
PRAP	---, "La religion des Arabes préislamiques d'après trois sites rupestres et leurs inscriptions," *Al Bāḥiṯ: Festschrift Joseph Henninger* (St. Augustin bei Bonn: Verlag des Anthropos-Instituts, 1976), 177-217
PRS	---, *Le Royaume Sud-arabe de Qataban et sa datation d'après l'archéologie et les sources classiques jusqu'au Périple de la Mer Érythrée* (Louvain: Publications universitaires, 1961)
PSG	F. B. Prideaux, "A Sketch of Sabaean Grammar with Examples of Translation," *Transactions of the Society of Biblical Archaeology* 5(1876): 177-224; 5(1877): 384-425
R	*Répertoire d'épigraphie sémitique*, Vols. I-VIII
RRA	C. Robin and J. Ryckmans, "L'attribtuion d'un bassin à une divinté en Arabie du Sud antique," *Raydān* 1(1978) 39-64
RhAST	N. Rhodokanakis, *Altsabäische Texte* I. *SBAWW* 206:2 (1927); II in *WZKM* 39(1932): 173-226
RhGr	---, *Der Grundsatz der Öffentlichkeit in den südarabischen Urkunden. SBAWW* 177:2(1915)
RhKBU	---,"Die ḳatabanische Bodenverfassungsurkunde," *WZKM* 31(1924): 22-52
RhKo	---, *Die Inschriften an der Mauer von Koḥlan. SBAWW* 200:2 (1924)

RhKT	---, *Ḳatabanische Text zur Bodenwirtschaft. SBAWW* 194:2 (1919); (Zweite Folge) *SBAWW* 198:2(1922)
RhSt	---, *Studien zur Lexikographie und Grammatik des Altsüdarabischen* I: *SBAWW* 178:2(1915); II: *SBAWW* 185: 3(1917); III *SBAWW* 213:3(1931)
RIS	J. Ryckmans, "Inscriptions sud-arabes d'une collections privée londonienne," in *Ṣayhadica*, Christian Robin and Muḥammad Bāfaqīh, eds. (Paris: Paul Geuthner, 1987), 165-80
RNE	G. Ryckmans, "Notes Épigraphiques," I: *Mus* 43(1930): 389-407; II: 50(1937): 323-44; 54(1941): 139-59; IV *Mus* 60(1947): 149-70; V: 71(1958): 125-39; VI: *Mus* 75(1962): 459-68
Ry	---, edited in the series "Inscriptions sud-arabes" in *Mus* 40(1927)-78(1965)
RyAP	---, "À propos des inscriptions himyarites," *RB* 36(1927): 377-90
RyGQ	---, "Graffites qatabanites au Muséum d'histoire naturelle de Lyon," *RB* 48(1939): 549-53
RyRAP	---, *Les religions arabes préislamiques* (Louvain: Publications Universitaires, 1951)
RyTIQ	---, "Trois inscriptions qatabanites," *RB* 37(1928): 116-18
SAden	Collection of J. E. Scott
SE	Südarabische Expedition (South Arabian Expedition of the Viennese Academy of Sciences)
Seyrig	Inscription belonging to H. Seyrig
SIM	A. Jamme, *Sabaean Inscriptions from Maḥram Bilqîs (Mârib)* (Baltimore: John Hopkins University Press, 1962)
SND	H. Schlobies, "Neue Dokumente zur altsüdarabischen Epigraphik," *Or* 5(1936): 57-63
Stubbs	T. W. Stubbs collection
TC	Timna[c] Cemetery
Thom	Collection of D. B. Thompson at Port Sudan
TO	Timna[c] Obelisk
TS	Timna[c] South (Gate)
TTI	Timna[c] Temple I
UT	A. Jamme, *The al-ʿUqla Texts* (Washington: Catholic University of America, 1963)
Va	Vienna Museum registration numbers
VB	G. W. Van Beek, "The Rise and Fall of Arabia Felix," *Scientific American* 221(December 1969): 36-46
VL	van Lessen collection
VL C	van Lessen copy

WB	Wadi Bayḥān
WBar	J. Walker, "A South Arabian Inscription in the Baroda State Museum," *Mus* 59(1946): 159-62
WHB	H. von Wissmann and M. Höfner, *Beiträge zur historischen Geographie des vorislamischen Südarabien. Akademie der Wissenschaften und der Literatur zu Mainz* (1952): 4. Abhandlung
WiZAG	H. von Wissmann. *Zur Archäologie und antiken Geographie von Südarabien* (Istanbul: Nederlands Historisch-Archaeologisch Instituut in het Nabije Oosten, 1968)
WŠ	Wadi Širjan
WSt	O. Weber, *Studien zur südarabischen Alterthumskunde* I-III. *MVÄG* 1901, 1907
WVQ	J. Walker, "Un vase avec inscription qatabanite," *Mus* 46(1933):273-75
ZIA	"Zur Interpretation altsüdarabischer Inschriften" I. N. Rhodokanakis, in *WZKM* 43(1936): 21-76 II. M Höfner, in *WZKM* 43(1936): 77-108 III. M. Höfner and N. Rhodokanakis, in *WZKM* 43(1936): 211-34

APPENDIX D

CONCORDANCE OF QATABANIAN INSCRIPTIONS

I have been greatly aided in the preparation of this concordance of Qatabanian inscriptions by G. Lankester Harding's *An Index and Concordance of Pre-Islamic Arabian Names and Inscriptions.* "=" in this concordance indicates that the work cited contains material relating to the respective inscription, in whole or in part. I have not included anepigraphic pieces of Qatabanian provenance in this concordance, nor have I attempted to include here all Qatabanian inscriptions that contain only proper names.

Q 1	= R 311 = CRC 88 = Gl 1405 = GlSt p. 1-2 = HS II col. 189-90 = HS V col. 428 (= Lo 4543 + 4544) = LE II p. 105-6 = NTY II = PR p. 37-38= PRAP p. 179-80 = PRS pl. IXb = RhKo p. 33-37 = R 3539 = SE 94 = WSt III p. 37-38
Q 2	= R 312 = R 3540 = SE 85. Cited as Q 35 (= R 3540)
Q 3	= R 313 = AM 60.1306 = JaMAR II p. 136 = LE II p. 108 = NTY IV = R 3541 = RhSt III p. 30-32 = SE 126 = WSt III p. 44
Q 4	= R 454 = Bard 4 = CIAS 96.51/o1/R71 = CRC 93 = GlSt p. 31 = LE II p. 382 = Lo 4098 = M p. 113-14 = NEnv I = R 3543A
Q 5	= R 456 = Bard 6 = HW II p. 42 = Land 1 = LE II p. 387 = Lo 4100 = NEnv III = R 3543B = R 4331 = SE 102 = WSt III p. 25, n. 1
Q 6	= R 461 = CRC 96 = GlSt p. 29-30 = Hole 2 = LE II p. 384 = R 3542
Q 7	= R 853 = BM 102483 = HalS 2 p. 297 = JaMAR II p. 55 = Land 2 = Lo 7 = R 3567bisA = Ry 32 = WSt III p. 25
Q 8	= R 856 = BM 102484 = HalS 5 p. 299-300 = JaMAR II p. 55 = R 3902.160
Q 9	= R 2646 = BNL V p. 111-12 = Bom F 127 = BHI 5 = HChr p. 67 = JaMAR II p. 32 = MMA p. 32-33 = PN III p. 307 = PNA I, 1 = ZIA III p. 223
Q 10	= R 2692 = BM 125051 = HalES 35 = JaMAR II p. 55-56 = Os 28 = PSG XXXV
Q 11	= R 2701 = BM 125348 = HalES 34 = JaMAR II p. 57 = Os 37 = PSG XXXIV
Q 12	= R 3506 = Kalli. Cited as Q 73 (= R 3856)
Q 13	= R 3507 = GKH p. 47. Cited as Q 177 (= R 4329)
Q 14	= R 3516 = HAuf II p. 151 n. I = HomLan I

Q 15	= R 3517 = HAuf II p. 151 n. II = HomLan II
Q 16	= R 3518 = HAuf II p. 151 n. III = HomLan III
Q 17	= R 3519 = HAuf II p. 151 n. IV = HomLan IV = J 881A = Lyon 818bis = R 5028 = RyGQ 15. Cited as Q 565A (= J 881A)
Q 18	= R 3520 = HAuf II p. 151 n. V = HomLan V
Q 19	= R 3521 = HAuf II p. 152 n. VI = HomLan VI
Q 20	= R 3522 = HAuf II p. 152 n. VII = HomLan VII
Q 21	= R 3523 = HAuf II p. 152 n. VIII = HomLan VIII
Q 22	= R 3524 = HAuf II p. 152 n. IX = HomLan IX
Q 23	= R 3525 = HAuf II p. 152 n. X = HomLan X
Q 24	= R 3526 = HAuf II p. 152 n. XI = HomLan XI
Q 25	= R 3527 = HAuf II p. 153 n XII = HomLan XII
Q 26	= R 3528 = HAuf II p. 153 n. XIII = HomLan XIII
Q 27	= R 3529 = HAuf II p. 153 n. XIV = HomLan XIV
Q 28	= R 3530 = HAuf II p. 153 n. XV = HomLan XV
Q 29	= R 3531 = HAuf II p. 153 n. XVI = HomLan XVI
Q 30	= R 3532 = HAuf II p. 153 = HomLan XVII
Q 31	= R 3533 = HAuf II p. 153 = SE 33
Q 32	= R 3534 = GB 12b = GKH p. 45 = Gl 1599 = HAuf II p. 206-8 = HSG p. 35 = JaMAR III p. 56 = RhKo p. 35 = Ry 390 = VL 47a = WB 3-52. Cited as Q 856 (= Ry 390)
Q 33	= R 3534bis = Cohen p. 11, 26-27, pl. XII, n. 8 = Gl 1621 = HAuf II p. 207 = Lo 4732 = Ry p. 169-70. Cited as Q 168 (= R 4274)
Q 34	= R 3537 = GKH p. 47 = Gl 1406 = RhSt II p. 98-99 = WSt II p. 27
Q 35	= R 3540 = CIAS 47.10/r3/c82 = CRC 85 = HAF p. 165 = JSI p. 667-68 = LE II p. 107 = MMA 1:27 = NTY III = RhKo p. 37-45 = SE 85 (= R 312) + SE 60 (= Va 715) = WSt III p. 39
Q 36	= R 3550 = CRC 84 = GB 12a = Gl 1600 = HomEth p. 660 = JaMAR III p. 56-58 = NKI p. 3-16 = NS p. 127-44 = Ry 389 = VL 47b = VL C 23 = WB 3-51 = WSt III p. 9-22
Q 37	= R 3551 = Gl 1402 = GlN p. 60-66 = JaMAR III p. 73 = NKI p. 17-27 = NS p. 145-59 = SE 122 = GKH p. 47 = WB 3-49
Q 38	= R 3552 = BNL III p. 130-31 = CRC 86 = Gl 1119 = NKI p. 28-34 = NS p. 160-67 = WSt III p. 5-6
Q 39	= R 3553 = BNL III p. 130 = CRC 87 = Gl 1581 = NKI p. 35-42 = NS p. 168-77
Q 40	= R 3566 = BNL II p. 265-66= CRC 92 = Gl 1394, 1400-1401, 1605-6 = GlN p. 162-90 = JaMAR III p. 58-59 = Mont p. 207-13 = NKI p. 43-48 = NS p. 178-79 = RhGr p. 33-49 = RhKBU

p. 23-52 = Ry 498 = SE 78-79 =TS d(=IB 53) + TS e(= IB 54) = VL 58

Q 41 = R 3641 = GG p. 39b, fig. 93 = Gl 1111

Q 42 = R 3642 = GG p. 66b, fig. 172 = GKH p. 43 = RhAST I p. 44 n. 1. Cited as Q 176 (= R 4328)

Q 43 = R 3643 = GB 15 = GG p. 41a = Gl 1426 = JaMAR III p. 59-60 = Ry 392-93 = VL 19 = VL C 56 = WB 3-59

Q 44 = R 3644 = GG p. 41a = Gl 1424

Q 45 = R 3645 = GG p. 41a = Gl 1425

Q 46 = R 3646 = GG p. 70b = Gl 1427

Q 47 = R 3647 = GG p. 23a fig. 47, 28a = Gl 1434

Q 48 = R 3654 = GG p. 39-40 = Gl 1747-48 = Mun 93-94

Q 49 = R 3659 = GG p. 64ab

Q 50 = R 3665 = JAden p. 571 n. 4

Q 51 = R 3666 = JAden 6 = RyTIQ p. 116-17

Q 52 = R 3666bis = GUB p. 100 = JAden 7

Q 53 = R 3667 = GKH p. 43 = Gl 1347

Q 54 = R 3668 = GKH p. 44 = Gl 1117

Q 55 = R 3669 = GKH p. 44 = Gl 1333

Q 56 = R 3670 = GKH p. 44 = Gl 1339

Q 57 = R 3671 = GKH p. 44 = Gl 1343

Q 58 = R 3672 = GKH p. 44 = Gl 1344

Q 59 = R 3673 = GKH p. 44 = Gl 1345

Q 60 = R 3674 = GKH p. 44 = Gl 1346

Q 61 = R 3675 = GKH p. 44 = Gl 1587 = Gl 1121

Q 62 = R 3677 = GKH p. 45 = Gl 1336

Q 63 = R 3680 = GKH p. 46 = Gl 1115

Q 64 = R 3681 = GKH p. 46 = Gl 1348 = R 4162

Q 65 = R 3683 = GKH p. 47 = Gl 1420

Q 66 = R 3688 = BQ II p. 12-15 = GB 45 = Gl 1601 = JaMAR III p. 60 = RhKT I p. 7-56; II p. 95-99 = Ry 490 = VL 26 = VL C 43 = WB 3-39

Q 67 = R 3689 = BNL II p. 267-68 = BQ II p. 10-12 = GB 46 = Gl 1602 JaMAR II p. 73-74; III p. 60-61 = RhKT I p. 57-115; II p. 99-101 = Ry 491 = VL 27 = VL C 44 = WB 3-40

Q 68 = R 3691 = BNL II p. 267-68 = CRC 90 = Gl 1395 = Gl 1604[a + b = 1421] = JaMAR III p. 61-62 = JSI p. 668-69 = RhKT I p. 121-30; II p. 103 = SE 84 = TS i = VL 59a

Q 69 = R 3692 = Gl 1612[= Gl 1412 + 1417] = JaMAR III p. 61, 62 = RhKT I p. 130-32 = SE 81 = TS f = VL 59b

Q 70 = R 3693 = Gl 1613[= Gl 1413 + 1418] = JaMAR III p. 61, 62 = RhKT I p. 132-43; II p. 103-4 = SE 82 = TS g = VL 59c

Q 71 = R 3694 = RhKT I p. 44 note 2
Q 72 = R 3854 = CRC 91 = Gl 1396 = Gl 1610 = JaMAR III p. 61, 62 = RhKT II p. 5-28, 104-5 = SE 83 = TS h = VL 59d
Q 73 = R 3856 = BNL II p. 267 = CRC 89 = JaMAR III p. 62-63 = RhKT II p. 28-41 = SE 48 = VL 32 = VL C 2
Q 74 = R 3858 = Gl 1693 = Mun 37-39 = RhKT II p. 41-95 = RNE V p. 127
Q 75 = R 3870 = Bom 36 = Cohen p. 62-63, pl. VII, fig. 3 = JaMAR II p. 33-34 = LB p. 78 n. V
Q 76 = R 3871 = Bom 36 + 123 = CRC 50 = JaMAR II p. 34 = LB p. 83-84 n XIV
Q 77 = R 3872 = Bom 49 = JaMAR II p. 34 = LB p. 86 n. XVIII
Q 78 = R 3878 = BNL X p. 416-17 = Gl 1397a ; 1399; 1416; 1608b; Gl 1907 = J 105 (= AM 60.1311A = JIH 140 + 144A = R 3902.140, 144A) = JaMAR III p. 73-74 = RhKo p. 14-25 = RyTIQ p. 117 = SE 80
Q 79 = R 3879 = RhKo p. 25-32 = SE 80a [= Gl 1398;1609]
Q 80 = R 3880 = Gl 1410 = Gl 1618 = RhKo p. 45-47
Q 81 = R 3881 = Gl 1404 = Gl 1614 = IB 49 = J 2436 = RhKo p. 48-49 = Ry 494 = SE 77 = TS c. Cited as Q 769 (= J 2436)
Q 82 = R 3882 = RhKo p. 49-50 = SE 86
Q 83 = R 3884bis = AM 60.1228 = BNL XII p. 66-69 = CIAS 49.10/p2/n1 = CRC 95 = JIH 22 = Marg p. 6 n. II = MMA p. 35-36 = NAM 601 = RhAST I p. 97-98 = RyAP p. 379-80 = ZIA III p. 228-34
Q 84 = R 3885 = AM 60.1228 = CRR p. 728 = HAA p. 165 fig. 5b = JIH 4 = Marg p. 6 n. I = PNA II pl. XIII, b
Q 85 = R 3886 = AM 60.1231 = CRR p. 732 = JIH 3 = Marg p. 6 n. 2
Q 86 = R 3887 = AM 60.1229 = CRR p. 730-31 = JIH 2 = Marg p. 7 n. 3 = PNA II pl. XIII, c
Q 87 = R 3888 = AM 60.1232 = CRE pl. XIX n. 66 = CRR p. 734, 735 = JIH 1 = Marg p. 7 n. 4 = PNA II p. XV, a, b
Q 88 = R 3896 = CRI 11-16
Q 89 = R 3902. See Harding, 1971, p. 878-80
Q 90 = R 3914 = BM 115657 = JaMAR II p. 67 = MM p. 209 = Ry 8
Q 91 = R 3928 = BM 117813 = JaMAR II p. 69, pl. 2 = Ry 23
Q 92 = R 3937 = CRR p. 739
Q 93 = R 3938 = AM 60.520 = CRR p. 751 = MMA p. 31 n. 31
Q 94 = R 3939 = AM 60.419 = CRE p. 751 = MMA 29-30 n. 27
Q 95 = R 3940 = AM 60.417 = CRE pl. XIX, n. 69 = CRR p. 751 = MMA p. 28 n. 22 = PPS pl. XVIII, c

Q 96 = R3941 = AM 60.416 = CRR p. 751 = MMA p. 28-29 n. 23 = PPS pl. XVIII, b
Q 97 = R 3942 = AM 60.424 = CRR p. 751 = MMA p. 29 n. 26 = PPS pl. XVIII, d
Q 98 = R 3961 = RhSt III p. 27-30 = SE 46
Q 99 = R 3962 = JaMAR III p. 74-75 = RhSt III p. 33-39 = SE 93 = WB 3-41
Q 100 = R 3963 = Gl 1622 = RhSt III p. 39-40 = SE 97
Q 101 = R 3964 = IB 50 = JaMAR III p. 63 = RhSt III p. 40 = Ry 495 = SE 98 = VL C 50
Q 102 = R 3965 = CIAS 47.11/b5 = Gl 1415 = JaMAR III p. 75 = RhSt III p. 41-42 = PCE VII = SE 95 = WB 3-37
Q 103 = R 4070 = Ry 64; pl. VI = SAden 1
Q 104 = R 4071 = ASS pl. 3, 4 = PNA I fig. 2 = Ry 65, pl. VI = SAden 2
Q 105 = R 4072 = ASS pl. 3 = Ry 66 = SAden 3
Q 106 = R 4073 = Ry 67 = Thom 1
Q 107 = R 4074 = Ry 68 = Thom 2
Q 108 = R 4075 = Ry 69 = Thom 3
Q 109 = R 4076 = Ry 71 = Thom 5
Q 110 = R 4077 = Ry 72 = Thom 6
Q 111 = R 4078 = Ry 73 = Thom 7
Q 112 = R 4094 = AM 60.1282 = J 116 = MMA 1 = ZIA III p. 211
Q 113 = R 4095 = AM 60.1302 = MMA 3
Q 114 = R 4096 = MMA 4 = ZIA III p. 212
Q 115 = R 4097 = AM 60.1324 = MMA 5
Q 116 = R 4098 = AM 60.1300 = MMA 6
Q 117 = R 4099 = AM 60.1329 = MMA 7
Q 118 = R 4102 = AM 60.707 = CIAS 49.10/o1/n1 = NAM 2159 = MMA 10
Q 119 = R 4103 = AM 60.736 = MMA 12
Q 120 = R 4104 = AM 60.727 = MMA 13
Q 121 = R 4112 = AM 60.415 = MMA 21
Q 122 = R 4113 = AM 60.423 = MMA 24
Q 123 = R 4114 = AM 60.418 = MMA 25
Q 124 = R 4115 = MMA 28
Q 125 = R 4116 = MMA 29
Q 126 = R 4117 = AM 60.521 = MMA 30
Q 127 = R 4118 = Lake 1 = MMA B1 = ZIA III p. 222
Q 128 = R 4119 = Lake 2 = MMA B2
Q 129 = R 4120 = Lake 3 = MMA B3
Q 130 = R 4161 = B 7808 = MMH p. 57 n. 48

Q 131	= R 4162 (cf. R 3681) = B 5336 + 7819 = MMH p. 57-58 n. 50 = PCE VII
Q 132	= R 4163 = B 7771 = MMH 51 = ZIA I p. 54
Q 133	= R 4164 = B 7811 = MMH p. 59 n. 53
Q 134	= R 4165 = B 7816 = MMH p. 59 n. 54, pl. XVIII
Q 135	= R 4195bis = HW I p. 20 = PCE IV = SE 63
Q 136	= R 4218 = MMA B19 = Ry 683
Q 137	= R 4219 = MMA B20 = Ry 684
Q 138	= R 4225 = WVQ p. 273-75
Q 139	= R 4232 = Leg p. 65, 72, fig. 1 = Penn 30.47.34 = Ry 116, pl. I
Q 140	= R 4234 = Leg p. 67, 78-79, fig. 5 = Penn 30.47.9 = Ry 125, pl. II
Q 141	= R 4235 = Leg p. 67, 78, fig. 6 = Penn 30.47.8 = Ry 126, pl. II
Q 142	= R 4236 = Leg p. 68, 80, fig. 10 = Penn 30.47.3 = Ry 120, pl. II
Q 143	= R 4237 = Leg p. 68, fig. 11 = LQS p. 331, fig.1a = Penn 30.47.2 = Ry 119, pl. II
Q 144	= R 4238 = Leg p. 69, 81, fig. 12 = Penn 30.47.5 = Ry 117
Q 145	= R 4239 = Leg p. 69, 80-81, fig. 14 = Penn 30.47.4 = Ry 121
Q 146	= R 4240 = Leg p. 70, 80, fig. 15 = LQS p. 331, fig. 1b = Penn 30.47.1 = Ry 118
Q 147	= R 4241 = Leg p. 72, 82, fig. 17 = LQS fig. 2a = Penn 30.47.23 = PPS pl. IX, i = Ry 131
Q 148	= R 4242 = Leg p. 81, fig. 16 = Penn 30.47.17b = Ry 127
Q 149	= R 4243 = Leg p. 82, fig. 18 = Penn 30.47.24 = PPS pl. IX, h = Ry 132, pl. III
Q 150	= R 4244 = Leg p. 73, fig. 19, 21 = Penn 30.47.13
Q 151	= R 4245 = Leg p. 73, fig. 20 = LQS fig. 3a = Penn 30.47.11 = Ry 123, pl. II
Q 152	= R 4246 = Leg p. 74, fig. 22 = LQS fig. 2b = Penn 30.47.25 = Ry 133, pl. II
Q 153	= R 4247 = Leg p. 74, fig. 23 = LQS fig. 4. = Penn 30.47.26 = Ry 135, pl. II
Q 154	= R 4248 = Leg p. 74, fig. 24 = Penn 30.47.27 = Ry 134, pl. II
Q 155	= R 4249 = Leg p. 76, fig. 29 = Penn 30.47.31 = Ry 136, pl. IV
Q 156	= R 4250 = Leg p. 79, fig. 36 = Penn. 30.47.60 = Ry 140, pl. III
Q 157	= R 4251 = Leg p. 79, fig. 40 = LQS fig. 8a = Penn 30.47.69 = Ry 141, pl. IV
Q 158	= R 4252 = Leg p. 79, fig. 41 = Penn 30.47.48 = Ry 145, pl. IV
Q 159	= R 4253 = Leg p. 79, fig. 42 = Penn 30.47.51 = Ry 144, pl. IV
Q 160	= R 4254 = Leg p. 83-84 = Penn 30.47.45 = Ry 143, pl. III
Q 161	= R 4255 = LQS p. 336, fig. 6 = Penn 30.47.32 = Ry 137, pl. III
Q 162	= R 4256 = LQS p. 336, fig. 7a = Penn 30.47.49 = Ry 147, pl. IV

Q 163 = R 4257 = LQS p. 336, fig. 7b = Penn 30.47.50 = Ry 146, pl. IV
Q 164 = R 4258 = LQS p. 336, fig. 8b = Penn 30.47.68 = Ry 142, pl. IV
Q 165 = R 4269 = Cohen p. 10 = Lo 4095
Q 166 = R 4272 = Cohen p. 11, 24-25, pl. XII, n. 6 = Lo 4729
Q 167 = R 4273 = Cohen p. 11, 25-26, pl. XI, n. 7 = Lo 4731 = SND p. 61-62
Q 168 = R 4274 = Cohen p. 26-27, pl. XII, n. 8 = Lo 4732 = Ry p. 169-70
Q 169 = R 4277 = Cohen p. 11, 28, pl. XI, n. 11 = Lo 4741
Q 170 = R 4279 = Cohen p. 13-14, pl. IV, fig. e
Q 171 = R 4315 = Cohen p. 75 = SND p. 63
Q 172 = R 4324 = HW II p. 31-33 = RhKo p. 47 = SE 58
Q 173 = R 4325 = HW II p. 33 = SE 61
Q 174 = R 4326 = BNL III p. 129 = HW II p. 34 = PCE IV = RhKo p. 47 = SE 62
Q 175 = R 4327 = HW II p. 34-35 = SE 74
Q 176 = R 4328 = GB 47 = GG p. 66b = GKH p. 43 = Gl 1422 = Gl 1620 = HW II p. 35-37 = JaMAR III p. 63-64 = JSI p. 668 = R 3642 = Ry 492 = SE 90-91 = VL 18 = VL C 33 = WHB p. 43
Q 177 = R 4329 = GB 16 = GKH p. 43 = Gl 1392 = HW II p. 40-41 JaMAR III p. 64-65 = R 3507 = Ry 460bis = SE 96 = VL 17 = VL C 40, 49 = WB 3-62
Q 178 = R 4330 = GB 11c = HSG p. 92 = HW II p. 41 = JaMAR III p. 78 = JSI p. 668 = RhKT II p. 80 = Ry 388 = SE 99 = WB 3-55
Q 179 = R 4332 = HM pl. I = HW II p. 42 = J 1096 = Muk 117 = SE 106 = VL 34 = WiZAG p. 71
Q 180 = R 4333 = GB 11a = HSG p. 92 = HW II p. 42 = Ry 386 = SE 119 = WB 3-53 = JaMAR III p. 78
Q 181 = R 4334 = HW II p. 42-43 = SE 121
Q 182 = R 4335 = HW II p. 43 = SE 123
Q 183 = R 4336 = HW II p. 43-47 = SE 101 = SIM p. 324
Q 184 = R 4336bis = HW II p. 65 = SE 72
Q 185 = R 4336ter = ASS p. 13, 3a = HW II p. 65 = PPS pl. IX,b = SE 108
Q 186A = R 4337A = BNL VI p. 319 = BQ I p. 3-4, 5-6; II p. 2-3 = Gl 1407a-d=Gl 1615a-c = HSH = HW II p. 47-61 = SE 87 = TO D = VL 56
Q 186B = R 4337B = BQ I p. 4, 8-9; II p. 3-4 = Gl 1393a + 1617 (= Gl 1409) + Gl 1411 = Gl 1393 + Gl 1603 = HSH = HW II p. 47 = JaMAR III p. 65-66 = SE 89

Q 186C = R 4337C = BQ I p. 4, 10-11 = Gl 1616ab = 1408 = HSH = HW II p. 47 = JaMAR III p. 66-67 = SE 88
Q 187 = R 4567 = Penn 30.47.10 = PPS pl. IXg = Ry 122, pl. II
Q 188 = R 4568 = Penn 30.47.12 = Ry 124, pl. II
Q 189 = R 4569 = JSI p. 669 = Penn 30.47.28 = Ry 128, pl. IV
Q 190 = R 4570 = Penn 30.47.29 = Ry 129, pl. IV
Q 191 = R 4571 = JSI p. 669 = Penn 30.47.30 = Ry 130, pl. IV
Q 192 = R 4572 = Penn 30.47.33 = Ry 138, pl. IV
Q 193 = R 4573 = Penn 30.47.59 = Ry 139, pl. IV
Q 194 = R 4574 = BM 125340 = JaMAR II p. 69 = Ry 148
Q 195 = R 4575 = BM 125341 = JaMAR II p. 69 = Ry 149 = RNE V p. 128
Q 196 = R 4637 = R 3902.119 = HRh p. 225, n.1 = JIH
Q 197 = R 4643 = HMus 1626 = MSO p. 13-14, n. 6
Q 198 = R 4686 = Ry 156
Q 199 = R 4687 = Ry 157-58
Q 200 = R 4688 = BM 125349 = JaMAR II p. 70 = Ry 159, pl. IV
Q 201 = R 4704 = Louvain 4 = Ry 175
Q 202 = R 4931 = IB 48 = P 1 = Per p. 497 = Ry 215, pl. IV, 493, pl. III
Q 203 = R 4932 = IB 51 = P 2 = Per p. 497 = Ry 216, pl. III, 496, pl.
Q 204 = R 4933 = P 3 = Per p. 497 = Ry 217
Q 205 = R 4934 = AM 150 = P 5 = Ry 219, pl. III = RyRAP p. 323
Q 206 = R 4936 = AM 204 = Ry 221, pl. IV
Q 207 = R 4937 = Ry 222
Q 208 = R 4953 = AM 152 = Ry 247, pl. III
Q 209 = R 4954 = AM 153 = Ry 248, pl. VI
Q 210 = R 4955 = AM 161 = Ry 249, pl. VI
Q 211 = R 4956 = AM 158 = Ry 250, pl. VI
Q 212 = R 4957 = AM 159 = Ry 251, pl. VI
Q 213 = R 4958 = AM 160 = Ry 252, pl. VI
Q 214 = R 4959 = AM 162 = Ry 253, pl. VI
Q 215 = R 4960 = AM 163 = Ry 254, pl. VI
Q 216 = R 4961 = AM 164 = Ry 255, pl. VI
Q 217 = R 4968 = AM 171A = J 867 = Ry 263, pl. VI
Q 218 = R 4971 = CIAS 49.12/f1/n1 = NAM 191 (AM 174) + NAM 2380 = Ry 266, pl. VI
Q 219 = R 4973 = AM 176 = Ry 268, pl. VI
Q 220 = R 4974 = AM 179 = Ry 269, pl. VI
Q 221 = R 4975 = Ry 270, pl. III
Q 222 = R 4976 = ASS p. 3,1 = Ry 270bis, pl. III
Q 223 = R 4977 = Ry 270ter, pl. III

Q 224 = R 5014 = J 882M = Lyon 1 = RyGQ p. 550-51, n. 1. Cited as Q 566M (= J 882M)
Q 225 = R 5015 = J 882N = Lyon 2 = RyGQ p. 551, n. 2. Cited as Q 566N (= J 882N)
Q 226 = R 5016 = J 882O = Lyon 3 = Ry GQ p. 551, n 3. Cited as Q 566O (= J 882O)
Q 227 = R 5017 = J 882S = Lyon 4 = RyGQ p. 551, n. 4. Cited as Q 566S (= J 882S)
Q 228 = R 5018 = J 882L = Lyon 5 = RyGQ p. 551, n. 5. Cited as Q 566L (= J 882L)
Q 229 = R 5019 = J 882J, K = Lyon 6 = RyGQ p. 551, n. 6. Cited as Q 566J, K (= J 882J, K)
Q 230 = R 5020 = J 882E = Lyon 7 = RyGQ p. 551, n. 7. Cited as Q 566E (= J 882E)
Q 231 = R 5021 = J 882A = Lyon 8 = RyGQ p. 552, n. 8. Cited as Q 566A (= J 882A)
Q 232 = R 5022 = J 882B = Lyon 9 = RyGQ p. 552, n. 9. Cited as Q 566B (= J 882B)
Q 233 = R 5023 = J 881L; cf. J 881K/2 = Lyon 10 = RyGQ p. 552, n. 10. Cited as Q 565K, L (= J 881 K, L)
Q 234 = R 5024 = J 881I, J = Lyon 11 = RyGQ p. 552, n. 11. Cited as Q 565I, J (= J 881I, J)
Q 235 = R 5025 = J 881F/1, E/2 = Lyon 12 = RyGQ p. 552-53, n. 12. Cited as Q 565F/1, E/2 (= J 881F/1, E/2)
Q 236 = R 5026 = J 881E/1, F/2 = Lyon 13 = RyGQ p. 553, n. 13. Cited as Q 565E/1, F/2 (= J 881E/1, F/2)
Q 237 = R 5027 = J 881D = Lyon 14 = RyGQ p. 553, n. 14. Cited as Q 565D (= J 881D)
Q 238 = R 5029 = J 881B = Lyon 16 = RyGQ p. 553, n. 16. Cited as Q 565B (= J 881B)
Q 239 = BEAG 7, p. 47-49 = HBH p. 338-41
Q 240 = BEAG 9, p. 50-51
Q 241 = CIAS 47.11/o1 = JP 4 = LIQ p. 107-19 = Lo 21.124
Q 242 = CIAS 47.12/p2/S21
Q 243 = CIAS 47.82/jl = Folkard 1 = HN p. 39-45
Q 244 = CIAS 47.82/o2 = AM 757 = JP 2
Q 245 = CIAS 95.11/o1 n.1 = AM 140
Q 246 = CIAS 95.11/o2 = AM 177 + 208
Q 247 = CIAS 95.11/o9 = AM 136
Q 248 = CIAS 98.Ve/b6
Q 249 = Graf 6 = MATG p. 146-48
Q 250 = Graf 7 = MWQ p. 149-50

Q 251 = Graf 8 = MWQ p. 151
Q 252 = Graf 9 = MWQ p. 151
Q 253 = Graf 10 = MWQ p. 151
Q 254 = Höf p. 453-54, pl. 1 = AM 736 = JaMAR II p. 136 = MAG II p. 438 = VL 31
Q 255 = Stubbs 3 = HEA p. 38-39
Q 256 = Stubbs 5 = HEA p. 40-42 = JaMAR III p. 10 = PCE p. 73-80 = VL C 45 = VL C 48
Q 257 = HI 2 A-B = HBH p. 337
Q 258 = HI 3 = HBH p. 341-42
Q 259 = HI 18 = HBH p. 342-43
Q 260 = HI 19 = HBH p. 343
Q 261 = HI 22 = HBH p. 343
Q 262 = HI 30 = HBH p. 344
Q 263 = HI 53+54 = HBH p. 345
Q 264 = HI 61 = HBH p. 345
Q 265 = J 118 = BAD p. 186-87 = RNE V p. 136-37 = TS m
Q 266 = J 119 = BAD p. 187-89 = PQS 100-1 = RNE V p. 137 = TS n
Q 266bis = J 119bis = BAD p. 189 = TS 780
Q 267 = J 120 = BAD p. 189-90
Q 268 = J 121 = BAD p. 190-91 = TS 795
Q 269 = J 122 = BAD p. 191-93 = CIAS 47.11/o1/F72 = TS 1120
Q 270 = J 123 = JPE p. 16 = TC 2168
Q 271 = J 124 = JPE p. 17 = TC 1039
Q 272 = J 125 = JPE p. 17-18 = TC 631
Q 273 = J 126 = JPE p. 18 = TC 1757
Q 274 = J 127 = JPE p. 32-33 = TC 1836
Q 275 = J 128 = JPE p. 33 = TC 1599
Q 276 = J 129 = JPE p. 33-34 = TC 16
Q 277 = J 130 = JPE p. 34 = TC 1860
Q 278 = J 131 = JPE p. 35 = TC 928
Q 279 = J 132 = JPE p. 35-36 = TC 1902
Q 280 = J 133 = JPE p. 36-37 = TC 2116
Q 281 = J 134 = JPE p. 37-38 = TC 20
Q 282 = J 135 = JPE p. 38-39 = WB 3-4
Q 283 = J 136 = JPE p. 39 = TC 1359
Q 284 = J 137 = JPE p. 39-40 = TC 964
Q 285 = J 138 = JPE p. 40-41 = TC 1666
Q 286 = J 139 = JPE p. 41-42 = TC 1927
Q 287 = J 140 = JPE p. 42 = TC 1820
Q 288 = J 141 = JPE p. 42-43 = TC 1742
Q 289 = J 142 = JPE p. 43 = TC 1505

Q 290 = J 143 = JPE p. 43-44 = TC 1711
Q 291 = J 144 = JPE p. 44-45 = TC 2052
Q 292 = J 145 = JPE p. 45 = TC 1716
Q 293 = J 146 = JPE p. 46 = TC 1727
Q 294 = J 147 = JPE p. 46-47 = TC 1618
Q 295 = J 148 = JPE p. 47 = TC 2089
Q 296 = J 149 = JPE p. 47-48 = TC 1615
Q 297 = J 150 = JPE p. 48-49 = TC 1887
Q 298 = J 151 = JPE p. 49-50 = TC 1789
Q 299 = J 152 = JPE p. 50 = TC 1136
Q 300 = J 153 = JPE p. 50-51 = TC 2044
Q 301 = J 154 = JPE p. 51-52 = TC 1621
Q 302 = J 155 = JPE p. 52-53 = TC 1725
Q 303 = J 156 = JPE p. 53 = TC 1237
Q 304 = J 157 = JPE p. 53-54 = TC 1702
Q 305 = J 158 = JPE p. 54 = TC 1678
Q 306 = J 159 = JPE p. 54-56 = TC 818
Q 307 = J 160 = JPE p. 56-57 = TC 1700
Q 308 = J 161 = JPE p. 57-58 = TC 827
Q 309 = J 162 = JPE p. 58 = TC 1767
Q 310 = J 163 = JPE p. 59 = TC 1364
Q 311 = J 164 = JPE p. 59-60= TC 2211
Q 312 = J 165 = JPE p. 60 = TC 990
Q 313 = J 166 = JPE p. 60-61 = TC 1537
Q 314 = J 167 = JPE p. 61-62 = TC 1726
Q 315 = J 168 = JPE p. 62-63 = TC 1503
Q 316 = J 169 = JPE p. 63-64 = TC 1853
Q 317 = J 170 = JPE p. 64 = TC 1901
Q 318 = J 171 = JPE p. 65 = TC 8
Q 319 = J 172 = JPE p. 65-66 = TC 1736
Q 320 = J 173 = JPE p. 66 = TC 1191
Q 321 = J 174 = JPE p. 67-68 = TC 1611
Q 322 = J 175 = JPE p. 68 = TC 1928
Q 323 = J 176 = JPE p. 68-69 = TC 1831
Q 324 = J 177 = JPE p. 69 = TC 2085
Q 325 = J 178 = JPE p. 70 = TC 1869
Q 326 = J 179 = JPE p. 70-71 = TC 1845
Q 327 = J 180 = JPE p. 71 = TC 1652
Q 328 = J 181 = JPE p. 71-72 = TC 1926
Q 329 = J 182 = JPE p. 72-73 = TC 1925
Q 330 = J 183 = JPE p. 73-74 = TC 1650
Q 331 = J 184 = JPE p. 74-75 = TC 2163

Q 332 = J 185 = JPE p. 75 = TC 1760
Q 333 = J 186 = JPE p. 75-76 = TC 1766
Q 334 = J 187 = JPE p. 76-77 = TC 1186
Q 335 = J 188 = JPE p. 77 = TC 1
Q 336 = J 189 = JPE p. 77-78 = TC 1665
Q 337 = J 190 = JPE p. 78-79 = TC 1609
Q 338 = J 191 = JPE p. 79-80 = TC 727
Q 339 = J 192 = JPE p. 80 = TC 1859
Q 340 = J 193 = JPE p. 80-81 = TC 2278
Q 341 = J 194 = JPE p. 81-82 = TC 1752
Q 342 = J 195 = JPE p. 82 = TC 1737
Q 343 = J 196 = JPE p. 82-83 = TC 2009
Q 344 = J 197 = JPE p. 83-84 = TC 1917
Q 345 = J 198 = JPE p. 84 = TC 1523
Q 346 = J 199 = JPE p. 84-85 = TC 2040
Q 347 = J 200 = JPE p. 85-86 = TC 2242
Q 348 = J 201 = JPE p. 86 = TC 1749
Q 349 = J 202 = JPE p. 87 = TC 1539
Q 350 = J 203 = JPE p. 87-88 = TC 1821
Q 351 = J 204 = JPE p. 88 = TC 1842
Q 352 = J 205 = JPE p. 88-89 = TC 1878
Q 353 = J 206 = JPE p. 89 = TC 2183
Q 354 = J 207 = JPE p. 89-90 = TC 1783
Q 355 = J 208 = JPE p. 90-91 = TC 1624
Q 356 = J 209 = JPE p. 91= TC 1876
Q 357 = J 210 = JPE p. 92 = TC 1135
Q 358 = J 211 = JPE p. 92 = TC 1668
Q 359 = J 212 = JPE p. 92-93 = TC 1950
Q 360 = J 213 = JPE p. 93-94 = TC 1782
Q 361 = J 214 = JPE p. 94 = TC 1787
Q 362 = J 215 = JPE p. 94-95 = TC 1750
Q 363 = J 216 = JPE p. 95-96 = TC 2274
Q 364 = J 217 = JPE p. 96 = TC 1997
Q 365 = J 218 = JPE p. 96-97 = TC 1534
Q 366 = J 219 = JPE p. 97-98 = TC 1569
Q 367 = J 220 = JPE p. 98-99 = TC 1521A
Q 368 = J 221 = JPE p. 99 = TC 2170
Q 369 = J 222 = JPE p. 99-100 = TC 1211
Q 370 = J 223 = JPE p. 100 = TC 27
Q 371 = J 224 = JPE p. 100-1 = TC 674
Q 372 = J 225 = JPE p. 101-2 = TC 2047
Q 373 = J 226 = JPE p. 102-3 = TC 2161

Q 374 = J 227 = JPE p. 103 = TC 1502
Q 375 = J 228 = JPE p. 103-4 = TC 1533
Q 376 = J 229 = JPE p. 104 = TC 1994
Q 377 = J 230 = JPE p. 104-5 = TC 2212
Q 378 = J 231 = JPE p. 105 = TC 1528
Q 379 = J 232 = JPE p. 105-6 = TC 1571
Q 380 = J 233 = JPE p. 106 = TC 2051
Q 381 = J 234 = JPE p. 106-7 = TC 1903
Q 382 = J 235 = JPE p. 107 = TC 2079
Q 383 = J 236 = JPE p. 108 = TC 1341
Q 384 = J 237 = JPE p. 108-9 = TC 1377
Q 385 = J 238 = JPE p. 109-10 = TC 2014
Q 386 = J 239 = JPE p. 110 = TC 1723
Q 387 = J 240 = JPE p. 110-11 = TC 2048
Q 388 = J 241 = JPE p. 111 = TC 1573
Q 389 = J 242 = JPE p. 112 = TC 1919
Q 390 = J 243 = JPE p. 113 = TC 1779
Q 391 = J 244 = JPE p. 113 = TC 1527
Q 392 = J 245 = JPE p. 114 = TC 2078
Q 393 = J 246 = JPE p. 114-15 = TC 2046
Q 394 = J 247 = JPE p. 115 = TC 1538
Q 395 = J 248 = JPE p. 115-16 = TC 2
Q 396 = J 249 = JPE p. 116-17 = TC 1888
Q 397 = J 250 = JPE p. 117 = TC 857
Q 398 = J 251 = JPE p. 117-18 = TC 1877
Q 399 = J 252 = JPE p. 118-19 = TC 893
Q 400 = J 253 = JPE p. 119-20 = TC 1572
Q 401 = J 254 = JPE p. 120 = TC 1522
Q 402 = J 225 = JPE p. 120-21 = TC 2167
Q 403 = J 256 = JPE p. 121 = TC 1305
Q 404 = J 257 = JPE p. 121-22 = TC 22
Q 405 = J 258 = JPE p. 122-23 = TC 4
Q 406 = J 259 = JPE p. 123 = TC 28
Q 407 = J 260 = JPE p. 124 = TC 2109
Q 408 = J 261 = JPE p. 124-25 = TC 18
Q 409 = J 262 = JPE p. 125 = TC 1590
Q 410 = J 263 = JPE p. 125-26 = TC 2090
Q 411 = J 264 = JPE p. 126 = TC 1616
Q 412 = J 265 = JPE p. 127 = TC 724
Q 413 = J 266 = JPE p. 127-28 = WB 1-1
Q 414 = J 267 = JPE p. 128 = TC 927
Q 415 = J 268 = JPE p. 129 = HK 6

Q 416	= J 269 = JPE p. 130 = TC 26
Q 417	= J 270 = JPE p. 131 = HK 5
Q 418	= J 271 = JPE p. 131-32 = TC 788
Q 419	= J 272 = JPE p. 132 = TC 15
Q 420	= J 273 = JPE p. 132-33 = TC 1790
Q 421	= J 274 = JPE p. 133 = TC 2171
Q 422	= J 275 = JPE p. 133-34 = TC 7
Q 423	= J 276 = JPE p. 134 = TC 1354
Q 424	= J 277 = JPE p. 135 = TC 2088
Q 425	= J 278 = JPE p. 135-36 = TC 1213
Q 426	= J 279 = JPE p. 136-38 = TC 766
Q 427	= J 280 = JPE p. 138-39 = TC 1337
Q 428	= J 281 = JPE p. 139 = TC 1478
Q 429	= J 282 = JPE p. 140 = TC 5
Q 430	= J 283 = JPE p. 140-41 = TC 2537
Q 431	= J 284 = JPE p. 141 = TC 701
Q 432	= J 285 = JPE p. 141-43 = TC 556
Q 433	= J 286 = JPE p. 143 = TC 1610
Q 434	= J 287 = JPE p. 143-44 = TC 1107
Q 435	= J 288 = JPE p. 144 = TC 540
Q 436	= J 289 = JPE p. 144-45 = TC 1446
Q 437	= J 290 = JPE p. 145 = TC 2084
Q 438	= J 291 = JPE p. 145-46 = TC 685
Q 439	= J 292 = JPE p. 146 = TC 24
Q 440	= J 293 = JPE p. 147 = TC 1995
Q 441	= J 294 = JPE p. 147-48 = TC 653
Q 442	= J 295 = JPE p. 148 = TC 1612
Q 443	= J 296 = JPE p. 149 = TC 1415
Q 444	= J 297 = JPE p. 149-50 = TC 697
Q 445	= J 298 = JPE p. 150-51 = TC 1765
Q 446	= J 299 = JPE p. 151 = TC 1376
Q 447	= J 300 = JPE p. 151-52 = TC 784
Q 448	= J 301 = JPE p. 152 = TC 3
Q 449	= J 302 = JPE p. 152-53 = TC 741
Q 450	= J 303 = JPE p. 153-54 = TC 1333
Q 451	= J 304 = JPE p. 154 = TC 1641
Q 452	= J 305 = JPE p. 154-55 = TC 786
Q 453	= J 306 = JPE p. 155-56 = TC 1843
Q 454	= J 307 = JPE p. 156-57 = TC 2240
Q 455	= J 308 = JPE p. 157 = TC 2536
Q 456	= J 309 = JPE p. 157-58 = TC 23
Q 457	= J 310 = JPE p. 158 = TC 21

Q 458 = J 311 = JPE p. 158-59 = TC 765
Q 459 = J 312 = JPE p. 159 = TC 1622
Q 460 = J 313 = JPE p. 160 = TC 1759
Q 461 = J 314 = JPE p. 160-61 = TC 17
Q 462 = J 315 = JPE p. 161 = TC 1414
Q 463 = J 316 = JPE p. 161-62 = TC 1536
Q 464 = J 317 = JPE p. 162 = TC 6
Q 465 = J 318 = JPE p. 163 = TC 1651A-B
Q 466 = J 319 = JPE p. 163 = TC 1879
Q 467 = J 320 = JPE p. 163-64 = TC 714
Q 468 = J 321 = JPE p. 164 = TC 1691
Q 469 = J 322 = JPE p. 164-65 = TC 19
Q 470 = J 323 = JPE p. 165 = TC 1300
Q 471 = J 324 = JPE p. 166 = TC 1184
Q 472 = J 325 = JPE p. 166-67 = TC 1378
Q 473 = J 326 = JPE p. 167 = TC 1654
Q 474 = J 327 = JPE p. 167-68 = TC 29
Q 475 = J 328 = JPE p. 168-69 = TC 1137
Q 476 = J 329 = JPE p. 169 = TC 30
Q 477 = J 330 = JPE p. 170-71 = TC B
Q 478 = J 331 = JPE p. 171-72 = TC F
Q 479 = J 332 = JPE p. 172-73 = TC 647
Q 480 = J 333 = JPE p. 173-74 = TC 654
Q 481 = J 334 = JPE p. 174-75 = TC 755
Q 482 = J 335 = JPE p. 175-77 = TC 791 + 704 + 1046
Q 483 = J 336 = JPE p. 177-78 = TC 898
Q 484 = J 337 = JPE p. 178-79 = TC 913
Q 485 = J 338 = JPE p. 179-80 = TC 921
Q 486 = J 339 = JPE p. 180-81 = TC 1166
Q 487 = J 340 = JPE p. 181-83 = TC 1171
Q 488 = J 341 = JPE p. 183-84 = TC 1174
Q 489 = J 342 = JPE p. 184-85 = TC 1175
Q 490 = J 343 = JPE p. 185-89 = RNE V p. 135-36 = TC 1778
Q 491 = J 344 = JPE p. 189-90 = RNE V p. 130 = TC 2114
Q 492 = J 345 = JPE p. 190 = TC 1824
Q 493 = J 346 = JPE p. 190-91 = TC 1825
Q 494 = J 347 = JPE p. 191-92 = TC 1976
Q 495 = J 348 = JPE p. 192-94 = TC 2115
Q 496 = J 349 = JPE p. 194 = TC 2502
Q 497 = J 350 = JPE p. 195-99 = JSI p. 669 = TC 969
Q 498 = J 351 = JPE p. 199-200 = TC 1173
Q 499 = J 352 = JPE p. 200 = TC 673

Q 500 = J 353 = JPE p. 200-201 = TC 699
Q 501 = J 354 = JPE p. 201-2 = TC 1016 + 1024 + 1023
Q 502 = J 355 = JPE p. 202 = TC 1072
Q 503 = J 356 = JPE p. 202-3 = TC 1152
Q 504 = J 357 = JPE p. 203 = TC 1170
Q 505 = J 358 = JPE p. 203-4 = TC 1172
Q 506 = J 359 = JPE p. 204 = TC 1236
Q 507 = J 360 = JPE p. 204-5 = TC 1334
Q 508 = J 361 = JPE p. 205 = TC 2080
Q 509 = J 362 = JPE p. 206 = TC 1506
Q 510 = J 363 = JPE p. 206-7 = TC 1532
Q 511 = J 364 = JPE p. 207 = TC 1667
Q 512 = J 365 = JPE p. 207-8 = TC 1844
Q 513 = J 366 = JPE p. 208-9 = TC 1881
Q 514 = J 367 = JPE p. 209-10 = TC 698
Q 515 = J 368 = JPE p. 210 = TC 1520
Q 516 = J 369 = JPE p. 211 = TC 1519
Q 517 = J 370 = JPE p. 211-12 = TC 536
Q 518 = J 371 = JPE p. 212 = TC 1867
Q 519 = J 372 = JPE p. 213 = TC 1109
Q 520 = J 373 = JPE p. 213 = TC 1110
Q 521 = J 374 = JPE p. 214 = TC 1501
Q 522 = J 375 = JPE p. 214-15 = TC 1530
Q 523 = J 376 = JPE p. 215-16 = TC 1747
Q 524 = J 377 = JPE p. 216 = TC 1785
Q 525 = J 378 = JPE p. 216-17 = TC 570
Q 526 = J 379 = JPE p. 217 = TC 1045
Q 527 = J 380 = JPE p. 218 = TC 1168
Q 528 = J 381 = JPE p. 218 = TC 1247
Q 529 = J 382 = JPE p. 219 = TC 1613
Q 530 = J 383 = JPE p. 219 = TC 2511
Q 530bis = J 384 = JDA p. 94-95
Q 530ter = J 385 = JDA p. 95
Q 531 = J 386 = Besse 1 = BM 130900 = JPQ p. 118
Q 532 = J 387 = Besse 2 = BM 130899 = JPQ p. 119
Q 533 = J 388 = Besse 3 = BM 130898 = JPQ p. 119
Q 534 = J 389 = Besse 4 = BM 130897 = JPQ p. 119-20
Q 535 = J 390 = Besse 5 = BM 130882 = JPQ p. 120-21
Q 536 = J 391 = Besse 6 = BM 130885 = JPQ p. 121-22
Q 537 = J 392 = Ferris 1 = JPQ p. 122
Q 538 = J 397 = James 1 = JPQ p. 124-25
Q 539 = J 398 = Denny 1 = JPQ p. 125

Q 540	= J 405 = BAD p. 143-45, 147 = WB 1-8
Q 541	= J 406 = BAD p. 145, 147 = WB 1-7
Q 543	= J 408 = AM 754 = JDS p. 317-22 = VL 15
Q 544	= J 409 = BH 3i = Ry 434i = UT p. 62
Q 545	= J 483 = JAF p. 189-90
Q 546	= J 484 = JAF p. 190-91
Q 547	= J 485 = JAF p. 191
Q 548	= J 486 = JAF p. 191-92
Q 549	= J 487 = JAF p. 192-93
Q 550	= J 488 = JAF p. 193-94
Q 551	= J 852 = JQDI p. 97-99
Q 552	= J 860 = JSA p. 154 = LQS p. 333, fig. 3B = Penn 30.47.14
Q 553	= J 861 = JSA p.154 = Leg p. 81, fig. 44 = Penn 30.47.90
Q 554	= J 862 = JSA p. 154 = Leg p. 83, fig. 49 = Penn 30.47.97
Q 555	= J 863 = JASI p. 32-38
Q 555bis	= J 864 = JQI p. 1-2 = PQS p. 277
Q 556	= J 867 = AM 171A (= R 4968) + B = JQI p. 6-7
Q 556bis	= J 868 = JSQI p. 39, 41 = TTI 35
Q 557	= J 869 = JSQI p. 41 = TTI 138
Q 558	= J 870 = JSQI p. 41-42 = TTI 363
Q 559	= J 871 = JSQI p. 42 = TTI 747
Q 560	= J 872 = JSQI p. 42, 44 = TTI 863
Q 561	= J 873 = JaMAR III p. 95 = JSQI p. 46 = TTI B
Q 562	= J 874 = JSQI p. 46-47 = TTI A
Q 563	= J 875 = JSQI p. 47 = TTI 15 + 83 + 212 + 214 + 334 + 335 + 367 + 491 + 492 + 571 + 738
Q 564	= J 880 = BM 122016 = JaMAR II pl. 2 = UT p. 63
Q 565	= J 881 = JPEQ p. 208-1 = Lyon 818bis = R 5023-29
Q 566	= J 882 = JPEQ p. 211-17 = Lyon 818ter = R 5014-22
Q 567	= J 883 = Ash 1954-753 = JAF p. 194
Q 568	= J 884 = Ash 1954-752 = JAF p. 194-95
Q 569	= J 888 = JaTAQ p. 134-35, pl. 24 = VL 11
Q 570	= J 889 = JIR p. 231-33 = VL 12 = VL C 47
Q 571	= J 890 = JIR p. 233-39 = VL 13 = UT p. 37
Q 572	= J 891 = JIR p. 239-40 = VL 14
Q 573	= J 893 = JDS p. 304-6 = Va 1158
Q 574	= J 894 = JDS p. 307, 305 = Va 1159 + 1165
Q 575	= J 895 = JDS p. 307, 305 = Va 1160
Q 576	= J 896 = JDS p. 307, 305 = Va 1161
Q 577	= J 897 = JDS p. 307-8, 305 = Va 1162
Q 578	= J 898 = JDS p. 308-9, 305 = Va 1163
Q 579	= J 899 = JDS p. 309-10, 305 = Va 1164

Q 580 = J 900 = JDS p. 310, 305 = Va 1166
Q 581 = J 901 = JDS p. 310-11, 305 = Va 1167
Q 582 = J 902 = JDS p. 311-14, 305 = Va 1168
Q 583 = J 903 = JDS p. 314-15, 305 = Va 1169
Q 584 = J 904 = JDS p. 315, 319 = Va 1170
Q 585 = J 905 = JDS p. 315, 319 = Va 1171
Q 586 = J 906 = JDS p. 315-16, 319 = Va 1172
Q 587 = J 907 = JDS p. 316, 319 = Va 1173
Q 588 = J 908 = JDS p. 316-17, 319 = Va 1174
Q 589 = J 909 = JDS p. 317, 319 = Va 1175
Q 590 = J 1063 = CUM 48.1956 = JSAC p. 43-44, pl. I, 1
Q 591 = J 1064 = CUM 48.1958 = JSAC p. 44, pl. I, 2
Q 592 = J 1065 = CUM 49.1957 = JSAC p. 44, pl. II, 3
Q 593 = J 1066 = CUM 49.627 = JSAC p. 44-45, p. II, 4
Q 594 = J 1067 = CUM 49.632 = GB 38 = JSAC p. 45-46, pl. II, 5 = Ry 483
Q 595 = J 1068 = CUM 49.635 = IB 25 = JSAC p. 46, pl. II, 6 = Ry 467
Q 596 = J 1069 = CUM 49.636 = IB 22 = JSAC p. 46, pl. III, 7 = Ry 469
Q 597 = J 1070 = CUM 49.637 = IB 24 = JSAC p. 46, pl. III, 8 = Ry 470
Q 598 = J 1071 = CUM 49.638 = IB 29 = JSAC p. 47, pl. III, 9 = Ry 474
Q 599 = J 1072 = CUM 49.639 = IB 31 = JSAC p. 47, pl. III, 10 = Ry 476
Q 600 = J 1073 = CUM 49.640 = IB 20 = JSAC p. 47-48, pl. IV, 11 = Ry 465
Q 601 = J 1074 = CUM 49.641 = JSAC p. 48, pl. IV, 12
Q 602 = J 1075 = CUM 49.642 = GB 41 = Ry 486 = JSAC p. 48, pl. V, 13
Q 603 = J 1076 = CUM 49.643 = GB 7=37 = JSAC p. 48-49, pl. V, 14 = Ry 482
Q 604 = J 1077 = CUM 49.644 = IB 23 = JSAC p. 49, pl. VI, 15 = Ry 468
Q 605 = J 1078 = CUM 49.645 = GB 40 = JSAC p. 49-50, pl. VI, 16 = Ry 485
Q 606 = J 1079 = CUM 49.646 = IB 21 = JSAC p. 50, pl. VI, 17 = Ry 466
Q 607 = J 1080 = CUM 49.647 = IB 30 = JSAC p. 50, pl. VII, 18 = Ry 475
Q 608 = J 1081 = CUM 49.648 = JSAC p. 50-51, pl. VII, 19
Q 609 = J 1082 = CUM 49.649 = JSAC p. 51, pl. VIII, 20

Q 611 = J 1093 = BEAG p. 51-52 = HN p. 37-39 = JaIRM p. 308, 310 = JaMAR II p. 91-92, pl. 7 = Muk 342 = VL 5
Q 612 = J 1105 = DoF 12 = JaMAR III p. 11, pl. 1 = Muk 35 = VL 35a
Q 613 = J 1106 = DoF 13 = JaMAR III p. 11, pl. 1 = Muk 36 = VL 35b
Q 614 = J 1107 = DoF 14 = JaMAR III p. 11, pl. 1 = Muk 37 = VL 35c
Q 615 = J 1108 = DoF 15 = JaMAR III p. 11, pl. 1 = Muk 38 = VL 35d
Q 616 = J 1109 = DoF 16 = JaMAR III p. 11, pl. 1 = Muk 39 = VL 35e
Q 617 = J 1110 = DoF 18 = JaMAR III p. 11-12, pl. 1 = Muk 40 = VL 35f
Q 618 = J 1111 = DoF 17 = JaMAR III p. 12, pl. 1 = Muk 41 = VL 35g, h
Q 619 = J 1112 = DoF 19 = JaMAR III p. 12, pl. 1 = Muk 42 = VL 35i
Q 620 = J 1115 = DoF 3 = JaMAR III p. 12, pl. 1 = Muk 45 = VL 35j
Q 621 = J 1116 = DoF 4 = JaMAR III p. 12, pl. 1 = Muk 46 = VL 35k
Q 622 = J 1116bis = JaMAR III p. 12, pl. 1 = Muk 47 = VL 35l
Q 623 = J 1117 = DoF 5a = JaMAR III p. 12, pl. 1 = Muk 47 = VL 35m
Q 624 = J 1118 = DoF 5b = JaMAR III p. 12-13, pl. 1 = Muk 47a = VL 35n
Q 625 = J 1119 = DoF 7 = JaMAR III p. 13, pl. 1 = Muk 47b = VL 35o
Q 626 = J 1120 = JaMAR III p. 13, pl. 1 = Muk 48 = VL 35p
Q 627 = J 1121 = DoF 6 = JaMAR III p. 13, pl. 1 = Muk 49 = VL 35q
Q 628 = J 1122 = DoF 7 = JaMAR III p. 13 = Muk 50 = VL 35r
Q 629 = J 1122bis = JaMAR III p. 13, pl. 2 = Muk 50a = VL 36a
Q 630 = J 1123 = DoF 8 = JaMAR III p. 13, pl. 2 = Muk 51 = VL 36b
Q 631 = J 1124 = DoF 10 = JaMAR III p. 14, pl. 2 = Muk 52 = VL 36c
Q 632 = J 1125 = DoF 9 = JaMAR III p. 14, pl. 2 = Muk 53 = VL 36d
Q 633 = J 1126 = JaMAR III p. 14, pl. 2 = Muk 54 = VL 36e
Q 634 = J 1127 = DoF 11 = JaMAR III p. 14, pl. 2 = Muk 55 = Vl 36f
Q 635 = J 1130 = DoF 1 = JaMAR III p. 115, pl. 20 = Muk 59
Q 637 = J 1132 = DoF 2b = JaMAR III p. 115, pl. 20 = Muk 59b
Q 638 = J 1140 = DoF 21 = JaMAR III p. 115-16, pl. 20 = Muk 67
Q 639 = J 1142 = DoF 20= JaMAR III p. 116, pl. 20 = Muk 69
Q 640 = J 1147 = DoF 22 = JaMAR III p. 116, pl. 20 = Muk 74
Q 641 = J 1268 = JaMAR III p. 14, pl. 2 = Muk 368 = VL 37
Q 642 = J 1301 = JaMAR III p. 14-15, pl. 2 = Muk 400 = VL C 64
Q 643 = J 1478 = JaMAR III p. 15, pl. 2 = Muk 784 = VL C 78
Q 644 = J 1481 = JaMAR III p. 15, pl. 2 = Muk 787 = VL C 76a
Q 645 = J 1482 = JaMAR III p. 15, pl. 2 = Muk 788 = VL C 76b
Q 646 = J 1483 = JaMAR III p. 15, pl. 2 = Muk 789 = VL C 76c
Q 647 = J 1484 = JaMAR III p. 16, pl. 2 = Muk 790 = VL C 76d
Q 648 = J 1492 = JaMAR III p. 16, pl. 2 = Muk 798 = VL C 73
Q 649 = J 1504 = JaMAR III p. 16, pl. 2 = Muk 810 = VL C 74

Q 650 = J 1507 = JaMAR III p. 16, pl. 2 = Muk 813 = VL C 69a
Q 651 = J 1508 = JaMAR III p. 16, pl. 2 = Muk 814 = VL C 69b
Q 652 = J 1520 = JaMAR III p. 16, pl. 2 = Muk 826 = VL C 67
Q 653 = J 1522 = JaMAR III p. 16, pl. 2 = Muk 828 = VL C 68
Q 654 = J 1523 = JaMAR III p. 16-17, pl. 2 = Muk 829 = VL C 70a
Q 655 = J 1524 = JaMAR III p. 17, pl. 2 = Muk 830 = VL C 70b
Q 656 = J 1526 = JaMAR III p. 17, pl. 2 = Muk 832 = VL C 70c
Q 657 = J 1527 = JaMAR III p. 17, pl. 2 = Muk 833 = VL C 70d
Q 658 = J 1529 = JaMAR III p. 17, pl. 2 = Muk 835 = VL C 77a
Q 659 = J 1530 = JaMAR III p. 17, pl. 2 = Muk 836 = VL C 77b
Q 660 = J 1531 = JaMAR III p. 18, pl. 2 = Muk 837 = VL C 66a
Q 661 = J 1532 = JaMAR III p. 18, pl. 2 = Muk 838 = VL C 66b
Q 662 = J 1533 = JaMAR III p. 18, pl. 2 = Muk 839 = VL C 71
Q 663 = J 1594 = JaMAR III p. 18, pl. 3 = Muk 656 = VL 40a
Q 664 = J 1595 = JaMAR III p. 18, pl. 3 = Muk 657 = VL 40b
Q 665 = J 1596 = JaMAR III p. 18, pl. 3 = Muk 658 = VL 40c
Q 666 = J 1597 = JaMAR III p. 18-19, pl. 3 = Muk 659 = VL 40d
Q 667 = J 1598 = JaMAR III p. 19, pl. 3 = Muk 660 = VL 40e
Q 668 = J 1599 = JaMAR III p. 19, pl. 3 = Muk 660bis = VL 40f
Q 669 = J 1600 = JaMAR III p. 19, pl. 3 = Muk 661 = VL 40g
Q 670 = J 1601 = Muk 662 = VL 40h, i = JaMAR III p. 19-20, pl. 3
Q 671 = J 1602 = JaMAR III p. 20, pl. 3 = Muk 663 = VL 40j
Q 672 = J 1603 = JaMAR III p. 20, pl. 3 = Muk 664 = VL 40k
Q 673 = J 1656 = JaMAR III p. 20, pl. 4 = Muk 718 = VL 42a
Q 674 = J 1657 = JaMAR III p. 20, pl. 4 = Muk 719 = VL 42b
Q 675 = J 1657bis = JaMAR III p. 20-21, pl. 4 = VL 42bis
Q 676 = J 1816 = DoWS p. 1-3, 8, pl. 16-17 = JaIRM p. 308 = JaMAR II p.78-79, 82 = MAG II p. 429 = Muk 104 = VL 22 = WiZAG p. 79, 87 = WS 21
Q 677 = J 1817 = JaIRM p. 308 = JaMAR II p. 82-83, pl. 6 = Muk 105
Q 678 = J 1818 = DoWS p. 1-3, 8, pl. 14 = JaIRM p. 308 = JaMAR II p. 83-84 = MAG II p. 427, 429 = Muk 106 = VL 21 = WiZAG p. 79 = WS 20
Q 679 = J 1819 = DoWS p. 1, 3, 7-8, pl. 13 = JaIRM p. 308 = JaMAR II p. 78-79, 84-85, pl. 5 = MAG II p. 427, 429 = Muk 107 = VL 23 = WiZAG p. 79-80 = WS 19
Q 680 = J 2098a-e = DoCA 11-12 = JaMAR III p. 21, pl. 4 = VL 43a-e
Q 681 = J 2195 = VB p. 44 = JQB p. 178-79
Q 682 = J 2213a-b = BM 117816-17 = JaMAR II p. 53, pl. 2
Q 683 = J 2218a-c = BM 122012-14 = JaMAR II p. 54, pl. 3
Q 684 = J 2219 = BM 122019 = JaMAR II p. 54, pl. 3
Q 685 = J 2221 = BM 125338 = JaMAR II p. 55, pl. 3

Q 686 = J 2224 = JaMAR II p. 76, pl. 4 = VL 3
Q 687 = J 2353 = DoWS p. 2-3, 6-7 = JaMAR II p. 78-82, 86-88, pl. 6 = MAG II p. 427-29 = VL 24 = WiZAG p. 80-82 = WS 14
Q 688 = J 2354 = DoWS p. 3-4, pl. 4 = JaMAR II p. 78-79, 88 = MAG II p. 425-29 = VL 25 = WiZAG p. 82 = WS 1
Q 689 = J 2355 = DoWS p. 2-3, 5, pl. 5 = JaMAR II p. 89 = WiZAG p. 82 = WS 2
Q 690 = J 2356a = DoWS p. 3, 5, pl. 6, 7 = JaMAR II p. 89-91, pl. 7 = MAG II p. 429 = VL 29a = WiZAG p. 82 = WS 3 + 4
= J 2356b = VL 29b = JaMAR II p. 91, pl. 7
= J 2356c = DoWS p. 3, 6 = JaMAR II p. 91, pl. 7 = VL 29c = WS 9
Q 691 = J 2357 = JaMAR II p. 92 = VL C 21 = WiZAG p. 68. Cited as Q 909 (= NAM 1646 = CIAS 49.81/r9/n1)
Q 692 = J 2358 = GA p. 223 = JaMAR III p. 21-22, pl. 4 = VL 2
Q 693 = J 2359 = AM 256b = JaMAR III p. 22, pl. 4 = VL 4
Q 694 = J 2360 = GB 33 = JaMAR III p. 22-26, pl. 5 = MAG I p. 5 = PLH p. 117-35 = VL 6 = WB 1-10
Q 695 = J 2361 = BNL X p. 420-23, XII p. 56-57 = GB 34 = JaMAR III p. 26-30, pl. 6 = MAG I p. 5 = VL 7 = RRA p. 54 = WB 3-64
Q 696 = J 2362 = JaMAR III p. 31, pl. 4 = VL 8
Q 697 = J 2363 = CIAS 47.91/r3 = JaMAR III p. 31, pl. 4 = JP 5 = WB 2-40
Q 698 = J 2364 = JaMAR III p. 31, pl. 7 = VL 16 = VL C 57
Q 699 = J 2365 = JaMAR III p. 31-32 = VL 20
Q 700 = J 2366 = VL 30 = VL C 32 = WB 3-56
Q 701 = J 2367 = JaMAR III p. 33, pl. 7 = VL 38a
Q 702 = J 2368 = JaMAR III p. 33, pl. 7 = VL 38b
Q 703 = J 2369 = JaMAR III p. 33-34, pl. 7 = VL 38c
Q 704 = J 2370 = JaMAR III p. 34, pl. 8 = VL 39a
Q 705 = J 2371 = JaMAR III p. 34, pl. 8 = VL 39b
Q 706 = J 2372 = JaMAR III p. 34, pl. 8 = VL 39c
Q 707 = J 2373 = JaMAR III p. 34, pl. 8 = VL 39d
Q 708 = J 2374 = JaMAR III p. 34-35, pl. 8 = VL 39e
Q 709 = J 2375 = JaMAR III p. 35, pl. 8 = VL 39f
Q 710 = J 2376 = JaMAR III p. 35, pl. 8 = VL 39g
Q 711 = J 2377 = JaMAR III p. 35, pl. 8 = VL 39h
Q 712 = J 2378 = JaMAR III p. 35, pl. 8 = VL 41a
Q 713 = J 2379 = JaMAR III p. 35, pl. 8 = VL 41b
Q 714 = J 2380 = JaMAR III p. 35, pl. 8 = VL 41c
Q 715 = J 2381 = JaMAR III p. 35, pl. 8 = VL 41d
Q 716 = J 2382 = JaMAR III p. 35, pl. 8 = VL 41e

Q 717 = J 2383 = JaMAR III p. 35-36, pl. 8 = VL 41f
Q 718 = J 2384 = JaMAR III p. 36, pl. 8 = VL 41g
Q 719 = J 2385 = JaMAR III p. 36, pl. 8 = VL 41h
Q 720 = J 2386 = JaMAR III p. 36, pl. 8 = VL C 22 = VL 44
Q 721 = J 2387 = JaMAR III p. 37, pl. 9 = VL 45a
Q 722 = J 2388 = JaMAR III p. 37, pl. 9 = VL 45b
Q 723 = J 2389 = JaMAR III p. 37, pl. 9 = VL 45c
Q 724 = J 2390 = JaMAR III p. 37, pl. 9 = VL 45d
Q 725 = J 2391 = JaMAR III p. 37, pl. 9 = VL 45e
Q 726 = J 2392 = JaMAR III p. 37, pl. 9 = VL 45f
Q 727 = J 2393 = JaMAR III p. 37, pl. 9 = VL 45g
Q 728 = J 2394 = JaMAR III p. 37, pl. 9 = VL 45h
Q 729 = J 2395 = JaMAR III p. 37, pl. 9 = VL 45i
Q 730 = J 2396 = JaMAR III p. 37, pl. 9 = VL 45j
Q 731 = J 2397 = JaMAR III p. 37, pl. 9 = VL 45k
Q 732 = J 2398 = JaMAR III p. 37-38, pl. 9 = VL 45l
Q 733 = J 2399 = JaMAR III p. 38, pl. 9 = VL 45m
Q 734 = J 2400 = JaMAR III p. 38, pl. 9 = VL 45n
Q 735 = J 2401 = JaMAR III p. 38, pl. 10 = VL 46a
Q 736 = J 2402 = JaMAR III p. 38, pl. 10 = VL 46b
Q 737 = J 2403 = JaMAR III p. 38, pl. 10 = VL 46c
Q 738 = J 2404 = JaMAR III p. 38, pl. 10 = VL 46d
Q 739 = J 2405 = JaMAR III p. 38, pl. 10 = VL 46e
Q 740 = J 2406 = JaMAR III p. 38-39, pl. 10 = VL 48a
Q 741 = J 2407 = JaMAR III p. 39, pl. 10 = VL 48b
Q 742 = J 2408-9 = JaMAR III p. 39, pl. 10 = VL 48c, d
Q 743 = J 2410 = JaMAR III p. 39, pl. 10 = VL 48e
Q 744 = J 2411 = JaMAR III p. 39 = VL 48f
Q 745 = J 2412 = JaMAR III p. 39, pl. 10 = VL 48g = VL C 24
Q 746 = J 2413 = JaMAR III p. 39, pl. 10 = VL 49a = VL C 14a
Q 747 = J 2414 = JaMAR III p. 39-40, pl. 10 = VL 49b = VL C 14b
Q 748 = J 2415 = JaMAR III p. 40, pl. 10 = VL 49c = VL C 15
Q 749 = J 2416 = JaMAR III p. 40, pl. 10 = VL 50a
Q 750 = J 2417 = JaMAR III p. 40, pl. 10 = VL 50b
Q 751 = J 2418 = JaMAR III p. 40, pl. 10 = VL 50c
Q 752 = J 2419 = JaMAR III p. 40, pl. 10 = VL 51 = VL C 17
Q 753 = J 2420 = JaMAR III p. 41, pl. 10 = VL 52a
Q 754 = J 2421 = JaMAR III p. 41, pl. 10 = VL 52b
Q 755 = J 2422 = JaMAR III p. 41, pl. 11 = VL 53a = VL C 16a
Q 756 = J 2423 = JaMAR III p. 41, pl. 11 = VL 53b = VL C 16b
Q 757 = J 2424 = JaMAR III p. 41, pl. 11 = VL 53c = VL C 16c
Q 758 = J 2425 = JaMAR III p. 41, pl. 11 = VL 53d = VL C 16d

Q 759 = J 2426 = JaMAR III p. 41, pl. 11 = VL 53e = VL C 16e
Q 760 = J 2427 = JaMAR III p. 41, pl. 11 = VL 54a
Q 761 = J 2428 = JaMAR III p. 42, pl. 11 = VL 54b
Q 762 = J 2429 = JaMAR III p. 42, pl. 11 = VL 54c
Q 763 = J 2430 = JaMAR III p. 42, pl. 12 = VL 55a = VL C 37
Q 764 = J 2431 = JaMAR III p. 42, pl. 12 = VL 55b, c = VL C 38a, b
Q 765 = J 2432 = JaMAR III p. 42, pl. 12 = VL 55d = VL C 39a
Q 766 = J 2433 = JaMAR III p. 42, pl. 12 = VL 55e
Q 767 = J 2434 = JaMAR III p. 42, pl. 12 = VL 55f = VL C 39b
Q 768 = J 2435 = JaMAR III p. 42, pl. 12 = VL 55g
Q 769 = J 2436 = CIAS 47.11/b2 = JaMAR III p. 42-44, pl. 12 = TS b (= VL 57) + TS c (= R 3881 = Gl 1404[1614] = IB 49 = SE 77 = Ry 494)
Q 770 = J 2437 = JaMAR III p. 44-45, pl. 12 = TS k
Q 771 = J 2438 = JaMAR III p. 45, pl. 12 = VL 60 = VL C 59
Q 772 = J 2439 = JaMAR III p. 45-46, pl. 12 = VL 61
Q 773 = J 2440 = AM 243d = JaMAR III p. 46, pl. 13= VL 62 = VL C 30
Q 744 = J 2441 = AM 243a = JaMAR III p. 46, pl. 13 = VL 63 = VL C 28 = VL 63 = VL C 28
Q 775 = J 2442 = AM 243f = JaMAR III p. 46, pl. 13 = VL 64 = VL C 26
Q 776 = J 2443 = JaMAR III p. 46, pl. 13 = VL 65
Q 776bis = J 2443bis = JaMAR III p. 47 = VL 65bis
Q 777 = J 2444 = JaMAR III p. 47-48, pl. 13 = VL 66
Q 778 = J 2445 = JaMAR III p. 48, pl. 13 = VL 67
Q 779 = J 2446 = AM 243b, c = JaMAR III p. 48, pl. 13 = VL 68 = VL C 25
Q 780 = J 2447 = JaMAR III p. 48, pl. 13 = VL 69
Q 781 = J 2448 = JaMAR III p. 49, pl. 13 = VL 70 = VL C 60
Q 782 = J 2449 = JaMAR III p. 49, pl. 13 = VL 71
Q 783 = J 2450 = JaMAR III p. 49, pl. 13 = VL 72
Q 784 = J 2451 = JaMAR III p. 49, pl. 13 = VL 73
Q 785 = J 2452a-f = JaMAR III p. 49-50, pl. 14 = VL 74a-f
Q 786 = J 2453 = JaMAR III p. 50, pl. 14 = VL 75
Q 787 = J 2454 = JaMAR III p. 50-51, pl. 14 = VL 76a-e = WB 2-104c, 2-105a-d
Q 788 = J 2455 = JaMAR III p. 51, pl. 14 = VL 77
Q 790 = J 2457 = JaMAR III p. 51-52, pl. 14 = VL C 1
Q 791 = J 2458 = JaMAR III p. 52, pl. 15 = VL C 5
Q 792 = J 2459 = JaMAR III p. 53, pl. 15 = VL C 6
Q 793 = J 2460 = JaMAR III p. 53, pl. 15 = VL C 8

Q 794 = J 2461 = JaMAR III p. 53, pl. 15 = VL C 11
Q 795 = J 2462 = JaMAR III p. 53, pl. 15 = VL C 13
Q 796 = J 2463 = JaMAR III p. 53, pl. 15 = VL C 18
Q 797 = J 2464 = JaMAR III p. 53, pl. 15 = VL C 19
Q 798 = J 2465 = JaMAR III p. 53, pl. 15 = VL C 27
Q 799 = J 2466 = JaMAR III p. 53-54, pl. 15 = VL C 29
Q 800 = J 2467 = JaMAR III p. 54, pl. 15 = VL C 31
Q 801 = J 2468 = JaMAR III p. 54, pl. 15 = VL C 34
Q 802 = J 2469 = JaMAR III p. 54, pl. 15 = VL C 42
Q 803 = J 2470 = JaMAR III p. 54-55, pl. 15 = VL C 46
Q 804 = J 2471 = JaMAR III p. 55, pl. 15 = VL C 51
Q 805 = J 2472 = JaMAR III p. 55, pl. 15 = VL C 55 = WB 3-61
Q 806 = J 2473 = J 341 + VL C 61 = JaMAR III p. 55-56, pl. 16
Q 807 = J 2474 = JaMAR III p. 56, pl. 16 = VL C 62
Q 808 = J 2475 = JaMAR III p. 80, pl. 17 = NYU 1
Q 809 = J 2489 = DoSA pl. 69 = JaMAR III p. 96
Q 810 = J 2490 a-l = DoSA pl. 76 = JaMAR III p. 96-97
Q 811 = J 2497 = ClASAN pl. 73 = JaMAR III p. 104 = TC 1871
Q 812 = J 2498 = ClASAN pl. 78 = JaMAR III p. 104 = TC 927
Q 813 = J 2499 = ClASAN pl. 73 = JaMAR III p. 104 = TC 2009
Q 814 = J 2500 = ClASAN pl. 81 = JaMAR III p. 104 = TC 1950
Q 815 = J 2501 = ClASAN pl. 78 = JaMAR III p. 104-5 = TC 788
Q 816 = J 2502 = ClASAN pl. 81 = JaMAR III p. 105 = TC 1900
Q 817 = J 2503 = ClASAN pl. 77 = JaMAR III p. 105 = TC 1917
Q 818 = J 2504 = ClASAN pl. 78 = JaMAR III p. 105 = TC 857
Q 819 = J 2505 = ClASAN pl. 79 = JaMAR III p. 105 = TC 1446
Q 820 = J 2506 = ClASAN pl. 81 = JaMAR III p. 105 = TC 1759
Q 821 = J 2507 = ClASAN pl. 78 = JaMAR III p. 105 = TC 893
Q 822 = J 2508 = JaMAR III p. 105-6
Q 823 = J 2509 = JaMAR III p. 106
Q 824 = J 2510 = JaMAR III p. 106
Q 825 = J 2511 = ClASAN pl. 37 = JaMAR III p. 106 = TC 1822
Q 826 = J 2512 = ClASAN pl. 81 = JaMAR III p. 106 = TC 1817
Q 827 = J 2513 = ClASAN pl. 79 = JaMAR III p. 106 = TC 1341
Q 828 = J 2514 = JaMAR III p. 106-7
Q 829 = J 2515 = ClASAN pl. 39 = JaMAR III p. 107 = TC 1604
Q 830 = J 2516 = ClASAN pl. 81 = JaMAR III p. 107 = TC 1853
Q 831 = J 2517 = ClASAN pl. 83 = JaMAR III p. 107 = TC 1860
Q 832 = J 2518 = ClASAN pl. 79 = JaMAR III p. 107 = TC 1237
Q 833 = J 2519 = ClASAN pl. 81 = JaMAR III p. 107 = TC 1743
Q 834 = J 2520 = JaMAR III p. 107
Q 835 = J 2521 = ClASAN pl. 82 = JaMAR III p. 107 = TC 2085

Q 836 = J 2522 = JaMAR III p. 107
Q 837 = J 2523 = JaMAR III p. 107-8
Q 838 = J 2863 = JaYE p. 113-14
Q 839 = Ry 366 = AM 206
Q 840 = Ry 367 = AM 335 = CIAS 47.11/p8/n1 = NAM 483
Q 841 = Ry 368 = AM 355
Q 842 = Ry 369 = AM 356
Q 843 = Ry 370 = AM 359
Q 844 = Ry 371 = AM 360 = J 865 = JQI p. 2-5
Q 845 = Ry 376 = GB 1
Q 846 = Ry 377 = GB 2
Q 847 = Ry 378 = GB 3
Q 848 = Ry 379 = GB 4
Q 849 = Ry 380 = GB 5
Q 850 = Ry 381 = GB 6
Q 851 = Ry 382 = GB 7
Q 852 = Ry 383 = GB 8
Q 853 = Ry 384 = GB 9
Q 854 = Ry 385 = GB 10
Q 855 = Ry 387 = GB 11b = JaMAR III p. 72, 78 = WB 3-54
Q 856 = Ry 390 = HSG p. 35, 36 = R 3534
Q 857 = Ry 391 = GB 13 = IB 52 = Ry 497
Q 858 = Ry 461 = GB 17 = JaMAR III p. 72 = WB 3-68
Q 859 = Ry 462 = GB 18
Q 860 = Ry 463 = GB 19a
Q 861 = Ry 464 = GB 19b
Q 862 = Ry 471 = IB 26
Q 863 = Ry 472 = IB 27
Q 864 = Ry 473 = IB 28
Q 865 = Ry 477 = IB 32
Q 866 = Ry 478 = GB 33
Q 867 = Ry 479 = GB 34
Q 868 = Ry 480a-b = GB 35a-b
Q 869 = Ry 481 = GB 36
Q 870 = Ry 484 = GB 39
Q 871 = Ry 487 = GB 42
Q 872 = Ry 488 = GB 43 = VL C 52 = WB 3-61bis
Q 873 = Ry 489 = GB 44 = VL C 53
Q 874 = Ry 521 = BM 103059
Q 875 = Ry 525 = Va 713
Q 876 = Ry 526 = Va 714
Q 877 = Ry 530 = Va 797

Q 878 = Ry 531 = Va 798
Q 879 = Ry 552 = Ist 7678
Q 880 = Ry 555 = Bal 1 = Louvain 9
Q 881 = Ry 557 = BM 132169
Q 882 = Ry 558 = BM 132171
Q 883 = Ry 559 = BM 132172
Q 884 = Ry 560 = BM 132173
Q 885 = Ry 561 = BM 132174
Q 886 = Ry 562 = BM 132175
Q 887 = Ry 563 = BM 132176
Q 888 = Ry 564 = BM 132177
Q 889 = Ry 565 = BM 132178
Q 890 = Ry 566 = BM 132179
Q 891 = Ry 567 = BM 132180
Q 892 = Ry 568 = BM 132182
Q 893 = Ry 569 = BM 132183
Q 894 = Ry 570 = BM 132184
Q 895 = Ry 571
Q 896 = Ry 573 = Seyrig 1
Q 897 = Ry 581 = Bom 56
Q 898 = VL 1 = BM 132529 = JaMAR II p. 44-45, III p. 7 = MAG I p. 1-22 = VL C 58
Q 899 = VL 9 = JaMAR III p. 67 = MAG II p. 419-23, pl. 1
Q 900 = VL 10 = JaMAR III p. 67 = MAG II p. 423-25, pl. 2
Q 901 = Ham 7 = Ash 1952.515 = BBSIS p. 54-55
Q 902 = WBar p. 159-63
Q 903 = AM 60.1284 = JaMAR II p. 132-33
Q 904 = AM 60.1332 = CIAS 95.11/r8/n1 = JaMAR II p. 133-34 = NAM 2374
Q 905 = AM 60.1477 = CIAS 95.11/p8/n1 = JaMAR II p. 134-35 = NAM 2694
Q 906 = AM 60.1478 = JaMAR II p. 135-36
Q 907 = AM 737 = CIAS 47.10/p2/n1 = NAM 346
Q 908 = AM 223 = CIAS 49.10/o1/n3 = NAM 232
Q 909 = NAM 1646 = CIAS 49.81/r9/n1
Q 910 = AM 200 = CIAS 95.11/o2/n2 = NAM 213
Q 911 = NAM 2770 = CIAS 95.11/o9/n3
Q 912 = NAM 2340 = CIAS 95.11/p9/n1
Q 913 = NAM 224 = CIAS 95.11/w5/n1
Q 914 = J 2898 = JPIM p. 98-100
Q 915 = BMus 8 = BEQ p. 21-27, pl. 2
Q 916 = JR WBrashear 1 = RIS p. 165-73

Q 917 = JR WBrashear 2 = RIS p. 173-75
Q 918 = JR WBrashear 3 = RIS p. 175-76
Q 919 = JR WBrashear 4 = RIS p. 176-77
Q 920 = JR WBrashear 5 = RIS p. 177-78

BIBLIOGRAPHY

A. Periodical Abbreviations in the Lexicon, Appendixes, and Bibliography

AAWW	*Anzeiger der (kaiserlichen) Akademie der Wissenschaften in Wien. Philosophisch-historische Klasse.*
BASOR	*Bulletin of the American School of Oriental Research*
BiOr	*Bibliotheca Orientalis*
BSOAS	*Bulletin of the School of Oriental and African Studies*
CIAS	*Corpus des inscriptions et antiquités sud-arabes*
CIH	*Corpus Inscriptionum Himyariticarum*
DSAWW	*Denkschriften der (kaiserlichen) Akademie der Wissenschaften in Wien. Philosophisch-historische Klasse.*
JA	*Journal Asiatique*
JAOS	*Journal of the American Oriental Society*
JNES	*Journal of Near Eastern Studies*
JRAS	*Journal of the Royal Asiatic Society of Great Britain and Ireland*
JSS	*Journal of Semitic Studies*
Mus	*Le Muséon*
MVÄG	*Mitteilungen der Vorderasiatisch-Aegyptischen Gesellschaft*
NESE	*Neue Ephemeris für Semitische Epigraphik*
OLZ	*Orientalische Literaturzeitung*
Or	*Orientalia*
OrAnt	*Oriens Antiquus*
PSAS	*Proceedings of the Seminar for Arabian Studies*
RAA	*Revue d'Assyriologie et d'Archéologie Orientale*
RB	*Revue Biblique*
RÉS	*Répertoire d'épigraphie sémitique*
RSO	*Rivista degli Studi Orientali*
SBAWW	*Sitzungsberichte der (kaiserlichen) Akademie der Wissenschaften in Wien. Philologisch-historische Klasse.*
WZKM	*Wiener Zeitschrift für die Kunde des Morgenlandes*
ZDMG	*Zeitschrift der Deutschen Morgenländischen Gesellschaft*

B. Books, Monographs, Articles referred to

Académie des Inscriptions et Belles Lettres
1977-86 *Corpus des inscriptions et antiquités sud-arabes.* Louvain: Editions Peeters. 3 vols.

Avanzini, Alessandra
1977 *Glossaire des inscriptions de l'Arabie du sud, I.* Florence: Università di Firenze
1980 *Glossaire des inscriptions de l'Arabie du sud, II.* Florence: Università di Firenze
1987 "For a Study on the Formulary of Construction Inscriptions," in *Ṣayhadica*, Christian Robin and Muḥammad Bāfaqīh, eds. Paris: Paul Geuthner, p. 11-20

Bargès
1849 "Termes himyariques rapportés par un écrivain arabe," *JA* 4e Ser. 14: 327

Beeston, A. F. L.
1937 "Sabaean Inscriptions." Unpublished doctoral dissertation, Oxford
1948 "The Ritual Hunt: A Study in Old South Arabian Religious Practice," *Mus* 61: 183-96
1950a "Notes on Old South Arabian Lexicography I," *Mus* 63: 53-57
1950b "Notes on Old South Arabian Lexicography II," *Mus* 63: 261-68
1951a "Angels in Deuteronomy 33," *Journal of Theological Studies*, N. S. 2: 30-31
1951b "Notes on Old South Arabian Lexicography III," *Mus* 64: 127-32
1951c "Phonology of the Epigraphic South Arabian Unvoiced Sibilants," *Transactions of the Philological Society* 1-26
1952 "Notes on Old South Arabian Lexicography IV," *Mus* 65: 139-47
1953 "Notes on Old South Arabian Lexicography V," *Mus* 66: 109-22
1954 "Notes on Old South Arabian Lexicography VI," *Mus* 67: 311-22
1956 *Epigraphic South Arabian Calendars and Dating.* London: Luzac

1958 "The Syntax of the Adjective in Old South Arabian: Remarks on Jamme's Theory," *JSS* 3: 142-45

1959 *Qahtan: Studies in Old South Arabian Epigraphy. Fasicule I: The Mercantile Code of Qataban.* London: Luzac

1962a "Arabian Sibilants," *JSS* 7: 222-33

1962b *A Descriptive Grammar of Epigraphic South Arabian.* London: Luzac

1962c "Epigraphic and Archaeological Gleanings from South Arabia," *OrAnt* 1: 41-52

1971a "Functional Significance of the Old South Arabian 'Town.'" *PSAS* 1: 26-28

1971b *Qahtan: Studies in Old South Arabian Epigraphy. Fasicule 2: The Labakh Texts.* London: Luzac

1972a "Kingship in Ancient South Arabia," *Journal of the Economic and Social History of the Orient* 15: 256-68

1972b "Notes on Old South Arabian Lexicography VII," *Mus* 85: 535-44

1973 "Notes on Old South Arabian Lexicography VIII," *Mus* 86: 443-53

1975a "Epigraphic South Arabian Auxiliaries," *JSS* 20: 191-92

1975b "Notes on Old South Arabian Lexicography IX," *Mus* 88: 187-98

1976 "Notes on Old South Arabian Lexicography X," *Mus* 89: 407-23

1977 "On the Correspondence of Hebrew s to ESA s²," *JSS* 22: 50-57

1978a "Epigraphic South Arabian Nomenclature," *Raydan, Journal of Ancient Yemeni Antiquities and Epigraphy* 1: 13-21

1978b "Notes on Old South Arabian Lexicography XI," *Mus* 91: 195-209

1978c "Ḳatabān," in E. van Donzel, Bernard Lewis, and Charles Pellat, eds., *Encyclopedia of Islām*, new edition. Leiden: Brill. 4: 746-48

1981a "Notes on Old South Arabian Lexicography XII," *Mus* 94: 55-73

1981b "Two Epigraphic South Arabian Roots: HYᶜ and KRB," in *Al-Hudhud: Festschrift Maria Höfner zum 80. Geburtstag*, Roswitha G. Stiegner, ed. Graz: Karl-Franzens-Universität, p. 21-30

1984 *Sabaic Grammar.* Manchester: Manchester University Press

1986 "The Qatabanic Text VL 1," *PSAS* 16: 7-11

Beeston, A. F. L., M. A. Ghul, W. W. Müller, and J. Ryckmans

1982 *Sabaic Dictionary (English-French-Arabic).* Louvain: Peeters, 1982

Biberstein-Kazimirski, A. de

1860 *Dictionnaire arabe-français.* Paris: Maisonneuve. 2 vols

Biella, Joan C.

1982 *A Dictionary of Old South Arabic, Sabaean Dialect.* Chico, CA: Scholars Press

Bird, J.

1844 "Himyaric Inscriptions from Aden and Saba," *Journal of the Bombay Branch of the Royal Asiatic Society* 8: 30-40

Brittner, Maximilian

1917 *Studien zur Šh̲auri-Sprache in den Bergen von Ḍofar am persischen Meerbusen.* Index (Šh̲auri-deutsches Glossar). *SBAWW* 183: 5. Abhandlung

Botterweck, G. J.

1950 "Altsüdarabische Glaser-Inschriften," *Or* N. S. 19: 435-44

Bowen, Richard L. Jr., and Frank P. Albright

1958 *Archaeological Dicoveries in South Arabia.* Baltimore: Johns Hopkins University Press

Brockelmann, Carl

1928 *Lexicon syriacum.* Zweite Auflage. Halle: Max Niemeyer

Bron, François

1987 "A propos de l'éponymie qatabanite," in *Ṣayhadica*, Christian Robin and Muḥammad Bāfaqīh, eds. Paris: Paul Geuthner, p. 21-27

Brown, W. L., and A. F. L. Beeston

1954 "Sculptures and Inscriptions from Shabwa," *JRAS* p. 43-62

Cleveland, R. L.

1965 *An Ancient South Arabian Necropolis, Objects from the Second Campaign (1951) in Timnaᶜ Cemetery.* Baltimore: Johns Hopkins University Press

Cohen, David

1970 *Dictionnaire des racines sémitiques ou attestées dans les langues sémitiques.* Paris: Mouton. Vol. I

1976 *Dictionnaire des racines sémitiques ou attestées dans les langues sémitiques.* Paris: Mouton. Vol. II

Cohen, Marcel

1934 *Documents sudarabiques.* Paris: Adrien-Maisonneuve

Conti Rossini, C.

1925 "Iscrizioni sabee," *Rendiconti della Accademia dei Lincei. Classe di scienze morali, storiche e filologiche.* Ser. 6, Vol. 1: 169-93

1927 "Dalle rovine di Ausan," *Dedalo* 7: 727-54

1928 *Storia d'Etiopia.* Milan: Officina d'arte grafica

1931 *Chrestomathia arabica meridionalis epigraphica, edita et glossario instructa.* Rome: Istituto per l'Oriente

Crone, Patricia

1987 *Meccan Trade and the Rise of Islam.* Princeton: Princeton University Press.

Derenbourg, H.

1903a Nouveaux envois du Yémen," *Revue Archéologique* 4ᵉ. sér. 1: 407-12

1903b "Nouveaux textes yéménites inédits, publiés, traduits," *RAA* 5: 117-28

Dillmann, August
1865 *Lexicon Linguae Aethiopicae*. Leipzig: Weigel. Reprint New York: Frederick Ungar, 1955

Doe, D. B.
1963 "The Site of ʾAmʿadiya near Mukeiras, on the Audhali Plateau, South West Arabia," *Aden* 2: 1-12
1964 "The Wadi Shirjan," *Bulletin Nr. 4, Department of Antiquities Report, 1961-1963* (Aden)
1971 *Southern Arabia*. London: Thames and Hudson

Drewes, A. J.
1979 "A Note on ESA ʾSY," *Raydān* 2: 101-4

Garbini, G.
1980 "Encore quelques mots sur le *MʿMR*," *Raydān* 3: 55-59

Ghul, M. A.
1959 "New Qatabāni Inscriptions," *BSOAS* 22: 1-22, 419-38

Glaser, Eduard
1889 *Skizze der Geschichte Arabiens von den ältesten Zeiten bis zum Propheten Muḥammad* I. Munich: F. Straub
1890 *Skizze der Geschichte und Geographie Arabiens* II. Berlin: Weidmannsche Buchhandlung
1923 *Altjemenische Studien. MVÄG* 28:2

Gordon, Cyrus
1965 *Ugaritic Textbook*. Rome: Pontificium Institutum Biblicum

Grimme, H.
1932 "Aus unedierten südarabischen Inschriften des Berliner Staatsmuseums," *Mus* 45: 91-116

Grohmann, A.
1916 "Ḳatabanische Herrscherreihen," *AAWW* 53: 41-49
1963 *Arabien*. Munich: C. H. Beck
1914 *Göttersymbole und Symboltiere aus südarabischen Denkmälern. DSAWW* 58: 1. Abhandlung

Halévy, J.

1873 "Études sabéennes," *JA* 7e Ser. 1: 434-521; 2: 305-65, 388-93

1874 "Études sabéennes," *JA* 7e Ser. 4: 497-505

1908 "Six inscriptions sabéennes inédites," *Revue Sémitique* 16: 293-97

al-Hamdānī, al-Ḥasan ibn Aḥmad

1884-91 *Ṣifat al-Jazīra.* See under D. H. Müller, 1884-1891

Harding, G. Lankester

1971 *An Index and Concordance of Pre-Islamic Arabian Names and Inscriptions.* Toronto: University of Toronto Press

Hartman, M.

1907 "Südarabisches," I-IX, in *OLZ* 10

1908 "Südarabisches," I-IX, in *OLZ* 11

1909 *Die arabische Frage.* Vol. II in *Der islamische Orient* Leipzig: R. Haupt

Höfner, M.

1934 "Eine südarabische Handelsinschrift," *Forschungen und Fortschritte* 10: 274-75

1935 "Die ḳatabanischen und sabäischen Inschriften der südarabischen Expedition im Kunsthistorischen Museum in Wien," *WZKM* 42: 31-66

1936 "Zur Interpretation altsüdarabischer Inschriften II," *WZKM* 43: 77-108

1943 *Altsüdarabische Grammatik.* Leipzig: Otto Harrassowitz.

1944 Die Sammling Eduard Glaser. *SBAWW* 222: 5. Abhandlung

1955 "Über einige Termini in qatabanischen Kaufurkunden," *ZDMG* 105: 74-80

1961 "Eine qatabanische Weihinschrift aus Timnaᶜ," *Mus* 74: 453-59

1964 "Altsüdarabische Stelen und Statuetten," in *Festschrift für den Frankfurter Ethnologen Ad. E. Jensen,* Eike Haberland, Meinhard Schuster, and Helmut Straube, eds. Munich: K. Renner, p. 217-32

1987 "Neuinterpretation zweier alsüdarabischer Inschriften," in *Ṣayhadica,* Christian Robin and Muḥammad Bāfaqīh, eds. Paris: Paul Geuthner, p. 37-46.

Höfner, M., and N. Rhodokanakis

1936 "Zur Interpretation altsüdarabischer Inschriften III," *WZKM* 43:211-34

Hommel, F.

1893 *Südarabische Chrestomathie.* Munich: G. Franz

1899 "Eine ḳatabanische Inschrift," *ZDMG* 52: 98-101

1892-1901 *Aufsätze und Abhandlungen arabistisch-semitologischen Inhalts* I-III. Munich: G. Franz

1926 *Ethnologie und Geographie des Alten Orients.* Munich: C. H. Beck

Honeyman, A. M.

1962 "Epigraphic South Arabian Antiquities," *JNES* 21: 38-43

Irvine, A.

1962 "A Survey of Old South Arabian Lexical Materials Connected with Irrigation Techniques." Unpublished doctoral dissertation, Oxford

1964 "Some Notes on Old South Arabian Monetary Terminology," *JRAS*, p. 18-36

1967 "Homicide in Pre-Islamic Arabia," *BSOAS* 30: 277-91

Jamme, A.

1951a "Les inscriptions rupestres de la région de Mukérâs," *Bulletin de l'Académie Royale de Belgique. Classe des Lettres et des Sciences morales et politiques.* 5e Ser. 37: 307-20

1951b "Pièces anépigraphiques sud-arabes d'Aden," *Mus* 64: 157-76

1952a *Pièces épigraphiques de Ḥeid bin ʿAqil, la nécropole de Timnaʿ (Hagr Koḥlan).* Louvain: Publications universitaires

1952b "Pièces épigraphiques sud-arabes de la collection K. Muncherjee, I," *Mus* 65: 95-137

1953 "Deux autels à encens de l'Université de Harvard," *BiOr* 10: 94-95

1955a "An Archaic South-Arabian Inscription in Vertical Columns," *BASOR* 137: 32-38

1955b "Pièces qatabanites et sabéenes d'Aden," *Anadolu Araştırmaları* 1: 117-26

1955c "A Qatabanian Dedicatory Inscription," *JAOS* 75: 97-99

1955d "Some Qatabanian Inscriptions Dedicating 'Daughters of God,'" *BASOR* 138: 39-47

1955e "South-Arabian Antiquities in the U.S.A.," *BiOr* 12: 152-54

1955f "South Arabian Inscriptions," in J. B. Pritchard, *Ancient Near Eastern Texts.* Princeton: Princeton University Press

1957a "Antiquités funéraires épigraphiques qatabanites," *Cahiers de Byrsa* 7: 189-95

1957b "Les pierres épigraphiques qatabanites Lyon 818 bis et ter," *Cahiers de Byrsa* 7: 205-17

1957c *Quatre inscriptions sud-arabes.* Washington, mimeographed publication

1958a "Inscriptions Related to the House Yafash in Timnaᶜ," in *Archaeological Discoveries in South Arabia*, R. L. Bowen, Jr., and F. P. Albright, eds. Baltimore: Johns Hopkins University Press, p. 183-98

1958b "The Sheᶜb edh-Dhaqab Inscriptions," in *Archaeological Discoveries in South Arabia*, R. L. Bowen, Jr., and F. P. Albright, eds. Baltimore: Johns Hopkins University Press, p. 143-47

1959 "La jarre épigraphique qatabanite de Hağr bin Ḥumeid et son étude par Paulo Boneschi," *RSO* 34: 127-36

1962a "Inscription rupestre et graffites qatabanites photographiés par le Major M. D. van Lessen," *RSO* 37: 231-41

1962b *Sabaean Inscriptions from Maḥram Bilqîs (Mârib).* Baltimore: John Hopkins University Press

1963a "Documentation sud-arabe, I et II," *RSO* 38: 303-22

1963b "Trois antiquites qatabanites en bronze Ja 886-888," *OrAnt* 2: 133-35

1963c *The al-ᶜUqla Texts* (Documentation sud-arabe III). Washington: Catholic University of America

1965 "The South-Arabian Collection of the University Museum (Cambridge, England), Documentation sud-arabe, IV," *RSO* 40: 43-55

1970 "A Qatabanian Votive Lamp Offering," *BiOr* 27: 178-79

1971 *Miscellanées d'ancient* (sic) *arabe* II. Washington, mimeographed publication

1972 *Miscellanées d'ancient* (sic) *arabe* III. Washington, mimeographed publication

1976 *Yemen Expedition. Carnegie Museum 1974-75.* Pittsburgh: Carnegie Museum of Natural History.
1981 "Pre-Islamic Arabian Miscellanea," in *Al-Hudhud: Festschrift Maria Höfner zum 80. Geburtstag,* Roswitha G. Stiegner, ed. Graz: Karl-Franzens-Universität, 95-100

Jaussen, A.
1915 "Inscriptions copiées à Aden," *RB* 23: 569-73
1926 "Inscriptions himyarites," *RB* 35: 548-82

Jean, Ch.-F., and J. Hoftijzer
1965 *Dictionnaire des inscriptions sémitiques de l'ouest.* Leiden: Brill

Johnstone, T. M.
1977 *Ḥarsusi Lexicon and English-Ḥarsusi Word-List.* London: Oxford University Press

Klein, Ernest
1987 *A Comprehensive Etymological Dictionary of the Hebrew Language for Readers of English.* Jerusalem: Carta/Haifa: The University of Haifa

Koehler, Ludwig, and Walter Baumgartner
1958 *Lexicon in Veteris Testament libros.* Leiden: Brill

Lambert, Mayer
1923 "Les inscriptions yéménites du Musée de Bombay," *RAA* 20: 72-88

Lambdin, T. O.
1953 "Egyptian Loan Words in the Old Testament," *JAOS* 73: 145-55

Landberg, Carl de
1920-42 *Glossaire daṯinois.* Leiden: Brill. 3 vols.

Lane, Edward W.
1863-93 *Arabic-English Lexicon.* London: Williams and Norgate. 8 parts

Legrain, L.

1934 "Au pays de la reine de Saba," *Gazette des Beaux-Arts* 6e per., T. XI 76e année: 65-85

1934 "In the Land of the Queen of Sheba," *American Journal of Archaeology* 38: 329-37

Leslau, Wolf

1938 *Lexique soqotri (sudarabique moderne).* Paris: Klincksieck

Lidzbarski, M.

1901-15 *Ephemeris für semitische Epigraphik* I-III. Giessen: J. Ricker

Lundin, A. G.

1979 "L'inscription qatabanite du Louvre AO 21.124," *Raydān* 2: 107-19

1987 "Sabaean Dictionary: Some Lexical Notes," in *Ṣayhadica*, Christian Robin and Muḥammad Bāfaqīh, eds. Paris: Paul Geuthner, p. 49-56

Margoliouth, D. S.

1924-25 "Two South Arabian Inscriptions Edited from Rubbings in the Possession of Major-General Sir Neill Malcolm," *Proceedings of the British Academy*, p. 177-85

Mittwoch, E., and H. Schlobies

1936 "Altsüdarabische Inschriften im Hamburgischen Museum für Völkerkunde," *Or* 5: 1-34, 278-93, 349-57

1937 "Altsüdarabische Inschriften im Hamburgischen Museum für Völkerkunde," *Or* 6: 83-100, 222-23, 305-16

1938 "Altsüdarabische Inschriften im Hamburgischen Museum für Völkerkunde," *Or* 7: 95-99, 233-38, 343-54

Montgomery, J. A.

1928 "An Enactment of Fundamental Constitutional Law in Old South Arabic," *Proceedings of the American Philosophical Society* 67: 207-13

Mordtmann, J. H., and E. Mittwoch

1931 *Sabäische Inschriften*. Hamburg: Friedrichsen, De Gruyter

1932a "Altsüdarabische Inschriften," *Or* 1: 24-33, 116-28, 257-73; 2: 50-60

1932b *Himjarische Inschriften in den staatlichen Museen zu Berlin. MVÄG* 37:1

1934 "Bemerkungen zu altsüdarabischen Inschriften," *Or* N.S. 3: 42-62

Müller, D. H.

1884-91 *Al-Hamdani's Geographie der Arabischen Halbinsel.* Leiden: Brill, 2 vols.

1903a "Anzeigernotiz über ein neuentdecktes sabäisches Bas-Relief mit Inschrift," *AAWW* 40: 113-15.

1903b "Mitteilung von einem sabäischen Steine mit figuralen Darstellungen im Besitze des Zivilgouverneurs von Rhodesia, Sir Marshall Hole, B. A. in Bulawayo," *AAWW* 40: 20-23.

Müller, W. W.

1962 *Die Wurzeln Mediae und Tertiae Y/W im Altsüdarabischen.* Tübingen, doctoral dissertation.

1974a "Die angeblichen 'Töchter Gottes' im Licht einer neuen qatabanischen Inschrift," *NESE* 2: 145-48.

1974b "Weitere qatabanische und hadramitische Stuecke der Sammlung Graf," *NESE* 2: 149-53.

1974c "Zur Herkunft von *líbanos* und *libanōtós*" *Glotta* 52: 53-59.

1976 "Notes on the Use of Frankincense in South Arabia," *PSAS* 6: 124-36.

1980 "Altsüdarabische Miszellen," *Raydān* 3: 63-73.

Nielsen, D.

1906a *Neue ḳatabanische Inschriften und der Vokalbuchstabe h im Minäischen. MVÄG* 11:4. Abhandlung.

1906b *Studier over Oldarabiske Inskrifter* Copenhagen: Det Schonbergske Forlag.

1927 *Handbuch der altarabischen Altertumskunde.* Copenhagen: Arnold Busck.

Nielsen, Kjeld.

1986 *Incense in Ancient Israel.* Leiden: Brill.

Osiander, E.

1865 "Zur himjarischen Altertumskunde, aus seinem Nachlasze herausgeg. von Prof. Dr. M. A. Levy," *ZDMG* 19: 159-293.

1866 "Zur himjarischen Altertumskunde, aus seinem Nachlasze herausgeg. von Prof. Dr. M. A. Levy," *ZDMG* 20: 205-87.

Philips, W.

1955 *Qataban and Sheba*. New York: Harcourt Brace.

Pirenne, J.

1956 *Paléographie des inscriptions sud-arabes. Contribution à la chronologie et à l'histoire de l'Arabie du Sud antique.* Brussels: Paleis der Academiën.

1960 "Notes d'archéologie sud-arabe," *Syria* 37: 326-47

1961 *Le royaume sud-arabe de Qataban et sa datation d'après l'archéologie et les sources classiques jusqu'au Périple de la Mer Érythrée.* Louvain: Publications universitaires

1962 "Notes d'archéologie sud-arabe," *Syria* 39: 257-62

1966 "Contribution a l'epigraphie sudarabique," *Semitica* 16: 73-99

1968 (ed.) ***Répertoire d'épigraphie sémitique.*** Vol 8. Paris: Imprimerie nationale

1971 "Une législation hydrologique en Arabie du Sud antique," in *Hommages à André Dupont-Sommer*. Paris: Adrien-Maisonneuve

1976a "La religion des Arabes préislamiques d'après trois sites rupestres et leurs inscriptions," *Festschrift Joseph Henninger*. St. Augustin bei Bonn: Verlag des Anthropos-Instituts

1976b "RShW, RShWT, FDY, FDYT and the Priesthood in Ancient South Arabia," *PSAS* 6: 137-44

Prideaux, F. B.

1876a "Himyaric Inscriptions Lately Discovered near Sanᶜa in Arabia," *Transactions of the Society of Biblical Archaeology* 4: 196-202

1876b "A Sketch of Sabaean Grammar with Examples of Translation," *Transactions of the Society of Biblical Archaeology* 5: 177-224

1877 "A Sketch of Sabaean Grammar with Examples of Translation," *Transactions of the Society of Biblical Archaeology* 5: 384-425

1879 "Notes on the Himyaritic Inscriptions Contained in the Museum of the Bombay Branch of the Royal Asiatic Society," *Transactions of the Society of Biblical Archaeology* 6: 305-15

Pritchard, J. B.

1974 (ed.) *Ancient Near Eastern Texts,* 3rd ed. Princeton: Princeton University Press

Rabin, C.

1983 "Etimologiyyot qatabaniyot," in *Meḥqərē Lāšon Muggashīm liZēḇ Ben-Ḥayyīm bəHaggīʿô ləŠēḇāh,* Moshe Bar Asher and Aharon Dothan, eds. Jerusalem: J. Magnes Press, p. 483-96

Rhodokanakis, N.

1915a *Der Grundsatz der Öffentlichkeit in den südarabischen Urkunden. SBAWW* 177:2. Abhandlung

1915b *Studien zur Lexikographie und Grammatik des Altsüdarabischen. SBAWW* 178: 4. Abhandlung

1917 *Studien zur Lexikographie und Grammatik des Altsüdarabischen. SBAWW* 185: 3. Abhandlung

1919 *Ḳatabanische Texte zur Bodenwirtschaft. SBAWW* 194: 2. Abhandlung

1922 *Ḳatabanische Texte zur Bodenwirtschaft. (Zweite Folge). SBAWW* 198: 2. Abhandlung

1924a *Die Inschriften an der Mauer von Koḥlan. SBAWW* 200: 2. Abhandlung

1924b "Die ḳatabanische Bodenverfassungsurkunde S.E. 78, 79 = Gl. 1394, 1400, 1406, 1606, 1401, 1605 (Fundort Koḥlan)," *WZKM* 31: 22-52

1927 *Altsabäische Texte* I. *SBAWW* 206:2

1931 *Studien zur Lexikographie und Grammatik des Altsüdarabischen. III. Heft. SBAWW* 213: 3. Abhandlung

1932 "Altsabäische Texte II," in *WZKM* 39: 173-226

1936 "Zur Interpretation altsüdarabischer Inschriften," *WZKM* 43: 21-76

Robin, C.
1979 "Qataban," in *Dictionnaire de la Bible*, Supplément, L. Pirot, A. Robert, H. Cazelles, and A. Feuillet, eds. Paris: Letouzey & Ané, 9: 598-601

Robin, C. and Muḥammad Bāfaqīh
1987 (eds.) *Ṣayhadica: Recherches sur les inscriptions de l'Arabie préislamique offertes par ses collégues au Professeur A. F. L. Beeston.* Paris: Paul Geuthner

Robin, C. and J. Ryckmans
1978 "L'attribution d'un bassin à une divinité en Arabie du Sud antique," *Raydān* 1: 39-64

Rossi, E.
1939 *L'Arabo parlato a Ṣanʿāʾ*. Rome: Instituto per l'Oriente.
1940 "Vocaboli sud-arabici nelle odierne parlate arabe del Yemen," *RSO* 18: 299-314

Ryckmans, Gonzague
1921 "Un sceau avec inscription sud-arabe," *Mus* 34: 115
1927a "À propos des inscriptions himyarites," *RB* 36: 377-90
1927b "Inscriptions sud-arabes," *Mus* 40: 161-200
1928 "Trois inscriptions qatabanites," *RB* 37: 116-18
1929 (ed.) *Répertoire d'épigraphie sémitique*, Vol 5. Paris: Imprimerie nationale
1930 "Notes épigraphiques," I, *Mus* 43: 389-407
1932 "Inscriptions sud-arabes," *Mus* 45: 285-313
1935 (ed.) *Répertoire d'épigraphie sémitique*, Vol 6. Paris: Imprimerie nationale
1937a "Incriptions sud-arabes, 4e ser.," *Mus* 50: 51-112
1937b "Notes épigraphiques," II, *Mus* 50: 323-44
1939a "Graffites qatabanites au Muséum d'histoire naturelle de Lyon," *RB* 48: 549-53
1939b "Inscriptions sud-arabes, 5e ser.," *Mus* 52: 51-112
1939c "Inscriptions sud-arabes, 6e ser.," *Mus* 52: 297-319
1941 "Notes épigraphiques," III, *Mus* 54: 139-59
1942 "Inscriptions sud-arabes, 7e ser.," *Mus* 55: 125-30
1947 "Notes épigraphiques," IV, *Mus* 60: 149-70
1949 "Inscriptions sud-arabes, 8e ser.," *Mus* 62: 55-124
1950 (ed.) *Répertoire d'épigraphie sémitique*, Vol. 7. Paris: Imprimerie nationale

1951a "Inscriptions sud-arabes, 9e ser.," *Mus* 64: 93-125

1951b *Les religions arabes préislamiques.* Louvain: Publications universitaires

1954 "Inscriptions sud-arabes, 11e ser.," *Mus* 67: 99-126

1957 "Inscriptions sud-arabes, 15e ser.," *Mus* 70: 97-126

1958a "Inscriptions sud-arabes, 16e ser.," *Mus* 71: 105-19

1958b "Notes épigraphiques," V, *Mus* 71: 125-39

1962 "Notes épigraphiques," VI, *Mus* 75: 459-68

Ryckmans, Jacques

1953 "À propos du *mʿmr* sud-arabe: RES 3884 bis," *Mus* 66: 343-69

1967 "Études d'épigraphie sud-arabe en russe," *BiOr* 24: 271- 73

1973 "Un rite d'istisqâʾ au temple sabéen de Mârib," *Université Libre de Bruxelles. Annuaire de l'Institut de Philologie et d'Histoire Orientales et Slaves* 20: 379-88

1974 "Formal Inertia in the South Arabian Inscriptions (Maʿin and Saba)" *PSAS* 4: 131-39

1976 "La chasse rituelle dans l'Arabie du Sud ancienne," in *Al-Baḥīṯ: Festschrift Joseph Henninger.* St. Augustin bei Bonn: Verlag des Anthropos-Instituts, p. 259-308

1987 "Inscritions sud-arabes d'une collection privée londonienne," in *Ṣayhadica*, Christian Robin and Muḥammad Bāfaqīh, eds. Paris: Paul Geuthner, .p. 165-80

Schlobies, H.

1936 "Neue Dokumente zur altsüdarabischen Epigraphik," *Or* 5: 57-63

Stark, Freya

1939 "Some Pre-Islamic Inscriptions on the Frankincense Route in Southern Arabia," *JRAS*, p. 480-98

Tomback, Richard S.

1978 *A Comparative Semitic Lexicon of the Phoenician and Punic Languages.* Missoula: Scholars Press

Van Beek, G. W.

1969a "The Rise and Fall of Arabia Felix," *Scientific American* 221(December): 36-46

1969b *Hajar bin Ḥumeid. Investigations at a Pre-Islamic Site in South Arabia.* Baltimore: Johns Hopkins University Press

Walker, J.
1933 "Un vase aveç inscription qatabanite," *Mus* 46: 273-75
1946 "A South Arabian Inscription in the Baroda State Museum," *Mus* 59: 159-62

Weber, O.
1907 *Studien zur südarabischen Altertumskunde. MVÄG* 12:2

Wissmann, H. von
1968 *Zur Archäologie und antiken Geographie von Südarabien.* Istanbul: Nederlands Historisch-Archaeologisch Instituut in het Nabije Oosten

Wissmann, H. von, and M. Höfner
1952 *Beiträge zur historischen Geographie des vorislamischen Südarabien. Akademie der Wissenschaften und der Literatur zu Mainz.* 4. Abhandlung

TIPOGRAFIA POLIGLOTTA DELLA PONTIFICIA UNIVERSITÀ GREGORIANA
PIAZZA DELLA PILOTTA, 4 - ROMA